WAMPUM BELTS
&
PEACE TREES

George Morgan, Native Americans, and Revolutionary Diplomacy

Gregory Schaaf

Fulcrum Publishing
Golden, Colorado

Book Design by Jody Chapel, Cover to Cover Design

Credits: Cover painting—"Mohawk Chief" by John Kahionhes Fadden, courtesy
of owner, Sally Benedict. Morgan journal and letters facsimiles courtesy of
Sotheby's, with the permission of Richard Dietrich. Map—"The Indian Frontier
in Revolutionary America," created by and used courtesy of Susan Kuramiya.

Library of Congress Cataloging-in-Publication Data

Schaaf, Gregory, 1953–
    Wampum belts and peace trees : George Morgan, native Americans,
and revolutionary diplomacy / Gregory Schaaf.
        p.   cm.
    Includes bibliographical references (p.
    Includes index.
    ISBN 1-55591-064-5
    1. Morgan, George, 1743–1810. 2. Indian agents–United States-
-Biography. 3. Indians of North America–Government relations–To 1789.
I. Title.
E93.M83S33   1990
973.3'2–dc20   90–3973
                                                                              CIP

Printed in the United States of America

0 9 8 7 6 5 4 3 2 1

Fulcrum Publishing
350 Indiana Street, Suite 350
Golden, Colorado

Dedicated to Peace

May the dream of the peacemaker—
A World Without War—
one day come true

CONTENTS

Acknowledgments   ix

Introduction: "The Discovery"   xv

Chapter One
Liberty and Justice for All: The Dream vs. Reality   1

Chapter Two
Menachk-sink: The Establishment of the First U.S. Indian Agency at Fort Pitt   25

Chapter Three
Dark Clouds over the Revolutionary Frontier
      British, American, and Indian Intrigues   47

Chapter Four
Black Robes in the Pasture of Light: The Christian Indian Mission   71

Chapter Five
Balance of Power
      The Courtship of Indian Nations Early in the Revolution   87

Chapter Six
Brother Tamanend's Mission to the Lenni Lenape   111

Chapter Seven
The White Deer's Mission to the Shawnee   127

Chapter Eight
The Council House and the Mingo Nation   143

Chapter Nine
The 1776 U.S.–Indian Peace Treaty   161

Chapter Ten
"The Right to Life, Liberty and the Pursuit of Happiness"   197

Notes   211

Appendix: The Morgan Papers: Inventory and Background   255
Bibliographical Essay   261

Index   273

ACKNOWLEDGMENTS

I THANK THE many people who helped enhance *Wampum Belts and Peace Trees*. My learning process has been founded on principles of cooperation instilled by my parents, Curtis and Luella Schaaf. They passed on to me and my sisters, Charlotte and Kimberly, the teachings of our grandparents, William and Flara Schaaf and Cecil and Anna Crockett. Their philosophy of life—based on close family relationships and respect for the sacred nature of our land and life—fundamentally influenced my world view.

The opportunity to study the Morgan Papers would never have come about without the trust of Mrs. Susannah "Nan" Morgan, whose late husband was a direct descendant of George Morgan. Nan placed a formidable responsibility upon my shoulders to research her family's papers and often said a "little prayer" to give me inspiration.

The principal scholarly inspiration came from Dr. Wilbur R. Jacobs, my doctoral advisor and mentor. His standards for academic excellence and his ethnohistoric approach served as helpful models. Best of all, he treated me as a friend and helped to guide me through the long learning process. Furthermore, he arranged for the Morgan Papers to be examined by professional scholars at the Huntington Library in San Marino, California: Dr. Mary Robertson, Curator of Manuscripts; Virginia Rust, Associate Curator of Western American History; Ronald Tank, Specialist in Manuscript Conservation; and Virginia Renner, Head of Reader Services. Confirmation of our initial findings was made by Doris Harris, a member of the Antiquarian Booksellers Association of America, who examined and authenticated the original documents in the Morgan Papers. Dr. Jacobs also introduced me to Dr. Francis Jennings from the Newberry Library in Chicago and numerous other fine scholars.

I recall Dr. Jacobs's graduate seminars as a creative environment where young historians received constructive criticism. Our circle included many talented people who freely offered their advice, including Johnny Flynn, Rose Ann Barker, Rick Sturtevant, Steve Ireton, John Alley, Tomas Salinas, Eri Okubo, Chris Miller, and others who have commenced successful careers.

Dr. Alexander DeConde also created a similar atmosphere in his graduate seminars. A specialist in international diplomacy, Dr. DeConde offered a worldly perspective on the traditions of historic peacemakers. He introduced me to many of the classics in American history and made numerous editorial suggestions.

I also wish to thank Dr. Abraham Friesen, who introduced me to the development of European history, philosophy, and theology. He also recommended to me Dr. Horst M. Lorscheider from Santa Barbara, a linguist fluent in old German. Since some key Moravian Indian journals never had been translated or published, I am greatly indebted to Dr. Lorscheider, who graciously translated materials from old German into English.

The final member of my doctoral committee, Dr. Burr Wallen, expanded my appreciation for art and history. He also provided an opportunity for me to coauthor a publication for the Santa Barbara Museum of Art. The experience of completing the publication process was appreciated sincerely.

My colleagues at the University of California at Davis, who provided me with my first opportunity to teach Indian history and culture, were helpful and supportive. Dave and Barbara Risling kindly opened up their home and personal library on Indian material. George Longfish, Sarah Hutchinson, Jack Forbes, and others introduced me to many experiences within the Native American community. My students continue to inspire me to convey the teachings of the elders.

The chiefs and clan mothers of the Iroquois Six Nations, the elders of the Lenni Lenape, and numerous other Indian people such as Chief Leon Shenandoah, Chief Jake Swamp, Chief Tom Porter, and Clan Mother Alice Papineau have taught me the values of spiritual humbleness. I especially appreciate the opportunity to serve the traditional Hopi elders who sometimes call me Pah-ang-one-hoya, "Always Helpful," and forever will remember the teachings of the late Lenape elder, Winnie Poolaw, who taught me the secret of survival: "The harder times got; the harder we laughed. As long as you never lose your sense of humor, you will always survive." Her children, Linda, Corky, and Bryce, carry on the tradition.

I also thank the Hopi for introducing me to Dr. Robert Muller, then the Assistant Secretary General of the United Nations. He and his gracious wife, Margarita, invited me to deliver a presentation on the Morgan Papers and "The History of the American Indian Peace Movement" before the Pacem in Terris Society at the United Nations. Dr. Muller's books and teachings serve as a spring of knowledge for people dedicated to working for peace.

I hope the many people from America's libraries, historical societies, and private collections will forgive me for not mentioning all their names. First, I would like to recognize James Rhoads, former Archivist of the United States. His guidance at the National Archives led to the completion of John P. Butler's *Index: The Papers of the Continental Congress, 1774–1789,* one of the most helpful research tools for this study. Roger Sullivan and Jennifer Magnus at the Library of Congress expressed particular interest in the Morgan Papers and informed me of related papers in their collection. Archivist Elaine Mills at the National Anthropological Archives, Linguist Ives Goddard, and Historian Wilcomb Washburn, Head of American Studies, introduced me to the holdings of the Smithsonian Institution. Dorothy Twohig from the University of Virginia, who is involved in editing a new edition of the *Papers of George Washington,* informed me that the Washington letter in the Morgan Papers was previously unpublished and provided copies of related documents. Senior Curator William Stiles of the Museum of the American Indian, Heye Foundation, in New York provided access to the museum's holdings, especially the fine slide collection of American Indian artifacts. The staff of the New York Public Library also was helpful in locating several frontier journals and obscure articles. The Pennsylvania Historical and Museum Commission provided a wealth of material organized in fine catalogs as part of its microfilming project. Special credit is due James Stevenson, Chairman; Donald Kent, Director of Archives and History; and William Hunter, Chief of the Division of Research and Publications. The Western Pennsylvania Historical Society also has preserved substantial holdings on the history of Pittsburgh, Morgan's headquarters, and the collection has been well organized by William Smith, Director, and Rush Salisbury, Assistant Director and Librarian. The staff of the Andrew Carnegie Library at the University of Pittsburgh were especially helpful in providing access to the manuscript vault where part of Morgan's journal is preserved. The staff of the Fort Pitt Museum also provided a series of detailed studies which were useful for reconstructing life in a frontier fort. The Ohio Historical Society furnished additional material on the original Indian villages and frontier settlements Morgan visited during his tour of Indian territory. Special recognition is due David Larson, Division Chief; Andrea Lentz, Head Librarian; and Gerald Newborg, State Archivist.

Many scholars deserve acknowledgment for sharing research materials and interpretations of history. Dr. Duane Hale from the American Indian Institute was especially helpful. Dr. Paul Stevens, a specialist in British Indian affairs, and I carried on a long correspondence. We drew up lists of hundreds of questions and developed various theories of frontier historical development. Dr. Jay Miller, a Delaware Indian scholar from the University of Washington, shared the fruits of his research. Dr. George Clever, a Delaware Indian man, and Anne Medicine, an Iroquois woman at Stanford University, provided personal accounts from oral history tradition. Dr. C. A. Weslager provided access to his personal library and contributed a wealth of information through his extensive research on Delaware history. Dr. Stewart Rafert, Miami Indian scholar, also shared his vast knowledge of Indian history. Wes Stoltz provided Indian documents from the Canadian Archives and other sources.

I wish to express my condolences to the loved ones of two exceptional scholars who greatly helped me: Dr. Ralph Cooley, former professor at the University of Oklahoma, Norman, who started the Delaware Indian oral history project; and Dr. James Howard, former professor at Oklahoma State University, Stillwater, whose studies of the Shawnee and Delaware Indians are valued contributions.

Senator Daniel Inouye, the respected Chairman of the U.S. Senate Select Committee for Indian Affairs, invited me to testify on Indian influences on the Constitution. Legal and political questions on national Indian affairs were answered by Staff Director Alan Parker, attorneys Patricia Zell and Pete Taylor, computer networker Irene Herder, and former staff member Patty Marks. Michael Nephew, former editor of the *American Indian Law Journal* at the Institute for the Development of Indian Law, provided access to the institute's holdings. Ford Foundation scholar Gary Fife, former editor for the American Indian Planners Association and present head of Meji Communications, explained principles of U.S. relationships with American Indians. Michael Cox and Guy Fringer provided access to the Department of Interior Library and located original Indian papers from its holdings.

A special expression of appreciation is conveyed to University Librarian Joseph Boisse and the staff of the University of California at Santa Barbara Library. Chris Brun, Head of Special Collections, has been helpful for the past eight years, since the beginning of this project. His knowledge of rare manuscripts is exceptional, and his counsel is valued highly. Countless sources were located with the assistance of Head Reference Librarian Don Fitch and his staff: Carolbeth Gibbens, Alex Gonzales, Linda Broderick, Robert Crittenden, Patricia Gebhard, Gene Graziano, David Guttman, Barbara Silver, Sally Weymer, and Barbara Wellman.

The security of the original documents of the Morgan Papers was maintained by members of the Colonel George Morgan Document Preservation and Marketing Company: Dr. Harry S. Brown, Dr. Berton Kolp, Attorney James Marino, Sam Cannata, Edward Rebard, Thomas Hirashima, Karen Hansen, Jack Pannell, Genevieve Nowlin, and Isaac and Carol Abergel. Additional management assistance was provided by Aaron Spechler of Richard A. Berti and Company.

This book on the Morgan Papers grew out of a doctoral dissertation, and has been rewritten to broaden the scope and to refine the style. Although many people contributed to my learning process, I accept solely the responsibility of my interpretations. I would like to express my appreciation to Bob Baron and the professional staff at Fulcrum, Inc. They are true artists in the field of book publishing. And finally, a heartfelt thank you to my literary agent, Al Zuckerman, President of Writer's House, who performed the ceremony that gave birth to this book.

Introduction

"THE DISCOVERY"

ONE AFTERNOON IN the spring of 1976, when I was visiting a friend in Santa Barbara, California, we were talking about antiques and old treasures of the past. The telephone rang. It was one of my friend's casual acquaintances, Mrs. Susannah Morgan, who mentioned during the conversation that she had some old family papers and would like to find a historian to look into them.

A meeting was arranged. In all honesty, I agreed to go only as a small courtesy to an elderly woman. I expected to see "Uncle John's" love letters to "Aunt Mary" or the like. Much to my surprise, what I discovered has since been acclaimed as the most important rare document discovery of the Bicentennial.

When I arrived to examine the papers, I was greeted warmly by Mrs. Morgan, an eighty-four-year-"young" lady with silver hair. We talked about my studies at the University of California, my current research, and our mutual love for history. The conversation eventually turned to her family, and Nan began her story. "My late husband, William Duane Morgan, was a wonderful man from a respectable Pennsylvania family. He inherited some old papers which were preserved by his family for generations and finally passed down to my late husband by his Uncle Tom Morgan. He inherited the family papers from his father, the elder William Duane Morgan, who inherited them from his father, Thomas Morgan, who in turn inherited them from his father, Colonel George Morgan, my late husband's great-great-grandfather. George Morgan was an Indian agent for the Continental Congress during the Revolutionary War. He negotiated the first peace treaty the United States ever made with the Indians two hundred years ago. He later got into some kind of scuffle with George Washington; he blew the whistle on Aaron Burr, and I don't know what else! Maybe you can find out the truth."

My curiosity was immediately aroused. As a historian, I was trained to be critical and to reserve judgment, but frankly I could hardly wait to read these old documents. We drove down to her bank and went to the safety deposit box vault. We opened her box, and I gently unfolded the first document, which appeared to be an original letter from George Washington to George Morgan, dated May 11, 1779.

I carefully laid the Washington letter to one side and picked up the second letter, which was addressed to George Morgan's daughter-in-law, Katherine Duane Morgan, by Thomas Jefferson, dated January 26, 1822. Katherine Morgan and a group of intelligent women of her generation had apparently written the elder statesman with opinions on how to run the government more effectively. This letter was Jefferson's reply, penned two years before his death.

The third document was written in exquisite calligraphy. From Benedict Arnold, dated July 1777, it appeared to be a secret plan to capture British seaports in the South. This letter had been written two months before Benedict Arnold became a hero in Burgoyne's defeat at Saratoga and two years before he became an infamous traitor.

Although the letters of Benedict Arnold, Thomas Jefferson, and George Washington were impressive, the fourth letter, written by John Hancock, president of the Continental Congress, to George Morgan, most aroused my curiosity. Dated April 19, 1776, the document contained instructions to Morgan in his role as agent under the commissioners for Indian affairs in the Middle Department.

I remember thinking at that point: "This seems too good to be true." I suddenly thought of my grandfather, the person who initially sparked my interest in history. I recalled his advice about the search for knowledge: "Every bit of information must be questioned, no matter how obvious it seems."

The next step was to analyze the handwriting. I presumed that copies of the four letters would be in the Papers of the Continental Congress and in collections of presidential papers. However, after scanning reels of microfilm, I discovered that this was not the case. At first I was disturbed by my inability to locate copies of these documents in the historical record, but I soon became excited by the possibility that the letters had never been recorded.

The key to the value of the documents rested upon their historical significance. The letters of George Washington, Benedict Arnold, and Thomas Jefferson fit neatly into the historical record. However, the John Hancock letter presented a more formidable challenge. For an inquiring mind, the letter posed a tantalizing mystery. What happened when Indian agent George Morgan crossed the Appalachians on his mission of peace with the Indian "Sachems and warriors of the western nations"?

Every day I searched for the answer to this question. Every week I reported my findings to Nan, but the full details of Morgan's mission remained a two-hundred-year secret. I found a biography, *George Morgan: Colony Builder*, written by a respected scholar, Dr. Max Savelle, in 1932, but this study provided only a brief chapter on Morgan's role as a peacemaker among the Indians during the American Revolution. Savelle did make a fine contribution in describing Morgan's background as a young, energetic Welshman from Philadelphia who had inherited a share in an international trading venture and married the boss's daughter. Morgan also developed a love of the classics and an interest in Indian affairs from his neighbor Benjamin Franklin. Savelle portrayed Morgan as a man of vision who was involved in many grand ventures, including an attempt to create a utopian society along the Mississippi River on a site that was destroyed in 1812 by perhaps the most powerful earthquake in American history. The series of quakes reportedly rang the Liberty Bell in Philadelphia, shook down a mission in Santa Barbara, California, and made the Mississippi River run backwards!

By tracing Savelle's original sources, I located 350 pages of Morgan's journal at the Andrew Carnegie Library in Pittsburgh, but a mysterious gap existed for the key period from April to November 1776. I continued working for months, searching through huge volumes of documents and seemingly endless reels of microfilm.

Then one day, when I was visiting Nan, out of the blue she mentioned that there was another bundle of documents that might answer my questions. The bundle was heavy, yellowed around the edges, and packed tightly. I suspected there were many documents inside. I found old Indian treaties, land grants for millions of acres, papers signed by Aaron Burr, as well as documents concerning Patrick Henry, Benjamin Franklin, and many others. Finally, at the bottom of the stack, I found them—the missing seventy-three pages from Morgan's two-hundred-year-old journal.

A little-known chapter of American history was being unveiled before my eyes. These missing documents were critical to understanding an aspect of the

In the Delaware Council at Cohocking Tuesday June 11th 1776.
    Present all their Chiefs & principal Men.
The usual Ceremonies having pass'd I address'd them as follows

Brothers,
            I thank you for your kind Reception of me into your
Towns, & Council House at this place; which from the Friendship
you have now shewn to me, I see appears fair & clear like that of
our Ancestors —— You have wiped my Eyes that I may see you
all as Brothers & find my way clear — You have cleansed my
Body after the fatigues of my Journey, & made me appear fair &
white to all people — You have removed all bad report from
my Heart & open'd my Ears to hear your good Words — I thank
you for this kindness — And I feel myself refresh'd & much at
ease — It pleases me to meet you thus as it is a sure Testimony
of your remembring the Friendship you made with your Brethren
of the United Colonies last year at Pittsburgh — That Friendship
I hope will last forever — To promote it is the business of
my present visit to you. — Therefore now clear your Ears &
remove all bad Reports from your Hearts that what I am going
to say from the Wise Council of the United Colonies may have due
Impression on your Minds.   A String 400 —

Brethren,
            Our Brother Capt. White Eyes was all the last Winter on
a Visit among us —— I make no doubt but he has told you how
desirous all our Wise Men are to promote your Happiness & to live
in fast Friendship with you forever — He assured the Wise
Council at Philadelphia that you intended to live in Peace with
us & to keep fast hold of the Covenant Chain of Friendship you &
we entered into last Fall —— This made their Hearts glad &
all your white Brethren of the United Colonies rejoice in the
hope of living with you on this great Island as true Friends
and Brothers for ever.

Brothers,
            Last Fall you were told to expect another Treaty at
Pittsburgh this year —— You have lately been desired to send
all

Page from George Morgan's Journal

all the Western Nations to hold themselves ready to meet us or send some of their Wise Men to Pittsburgh as they might soon expect to be called there to meet some of our wise Counsellors who are appointed to hold a Treaty there —— I was directed to consult you, when would be the most suitable time, & for that purpose I lately sent a Message to request I might see two or three of your Wise Men to advise with them on that matter, & on what was necessary to be done to make our Friendship lasting —— As I have since received Instructions from Congress to call all Nations to meet their Commissioners at Pittsburgh the 20th of next Month when they propose to hold the Treaty, or as soon as you & all the Nations could be assembled there.—— I was directed to consult you on this Business & to desire that you would join your Endeavours with ours to call the Chiefs of all the Western Nations, to this Treaty to be held so soon as you think the Lake Indians, & the Ouabache Confederacy can have notice & arrive there — for these reasons Brothers, I thought it best to come here to see you myself as I was not sure of my Message coming in time —— Beside I can now have the good Council of all your wise Men here on which I shall depend & thank you for it.

A Belt 13 Stripes 2350

Brothers,

When you fix the time you think will best suit to hold the Treaty, I desire you will join me in sending a Belt through the Western Nations informing them thereof & that you will request their Chiefs to meet us at the time appointed. ——

As I have been inform'd that some of the Chiefs of your Grand Children the Shawnes are about to depart for the Lakes & on a Visit to the Six Nations —— I have sent them word to wait at home a few days for me —— I am therefore desirous to make haste lest they may be tired waiting —— I must for this reason request you will appoint three of your wisest Young Men to follow me to the Shawnese Towns in two or three days in order that they may be joined by a number of your Grand Children to go with the Belt of Invitation to the different Nations —

In Council June 12th. 1776.

Page from George Morgan's Journal

American Revolution long kept secret. A new explanation was emerging of how the United States originally gained power. The pieces of an elaborate historical puzzle were falling into place.

Beginning with Morgan's thoughts on the significance of John Hancock's letter, the journal contained evidence that the action taken by the Continental Congress at this time marked a major turning point, one that signaled the inevitable break with England. Only seventy-six days before the signing of the Declaration of Independence, Congress ordered Morgan westward on an Indian peace mission, because Indian nations held the balance of power in their hands. A united force of Indian warriors could either support or crush the Revolution.

To "keep Congress informed," Morgan established an elaborate intelligence network from Canada in the north to the Gulf Coast in the south, and from the Mississippi River to the Atlantic seaboard. His friends and allies, both Indian and white, kept him up-to-date on the latest developments on the frontier. Morgan's journal not only preserved a detailed record of these reports but also gave vivid accounts of his personal activities.

The traditional Indian philosophy of natural law seemed timeless and universal to Morgan. He embraced the teachings based on ancient divine instructions reportedly delivered over a thousand years before by a Great Peacemaker. The Delaware or Lenape people called this way of life the "Path to the Trail of Spirits." The Haudenausaunee Confederacy of Iroquois Six Nations called their system the "Great Law of Peace." In 1988, Congress finally passed a resolution officially recognizing that the U.S. Constitution was directly influenced by American Indians and that the U.S. government was "explicitly modeled after the Iroquois Confederacy." In the center of the three-part Iroquoian government stood the sacred symbol of their society—the Tree of Peace.

After recognizing in Morgan the qualities of a man of the "good mind," the Iroquois addressed him as Shanashase, representing the New Council House of the Thirteen Fires or Congress of the thirteen states. The Shawnee called Morgan Weepemachukthe, the "White Deer" who travels through the forest in peace. The Lenni Lenape or Delaware Indians, "Grandfathers" of the Algonquian family of nations, bestowed the highest honor on Morgan by giving him the title Brother Tamanend, the "Affable One," after the greatest peacemaker in their history. Morgan's journal, chronicling his career as an Indian agent, explained how he risked his life and earned respect from powerful Indian nations.

Morgan took a stand to defend a vision of America's future that was diametrically opposed to slavery, colonialism, and imperialism. Morgan found

In Congress, April 19. 1776.
Instructions to George Morgan Esquire agent under the commissioners for Indian affairs in the middle department.

Sir, You are required to provide, that the great belt presented to the Indians last fall at Pittsburg, be forwarded with all convenient expedition to the Sachems and warriors of the western nations; and endeavour to the utmost of your power to convince them of the good wishes and good intentions of the Congress for and towards them; and to cultivate harmony and friendship between them and the white people and to give Congress the most early intelligence of any interruption thereof, or of any disturbance which shall arise and which you cannot quiet.

Acquaint the Indians that Congress have formed the best plan they could devise to import foreign goods for their use, and have neglected no probable means to procure them in time; and if they should not be supplied so soon as they may be wanted, the misfortune is to be ascribed to the

the common enemies of them and us, who by obstructing our trade as well as in numberless other instances are daily injuring and distressing both: but that we have well grounded hopes of speedy relief; In expectation of which and by greater advantages in prospect the present inconveniences are being more patiently.

All differences and disputes, that shall happen between the Indians and the white people, you will have adjusted and determined in the mode prescribed by a resolve of Congress, of which you have a copy. And you are directed in a particular manner to prevent as much as you are able any impositions upon the former, by those who deal with them.

Treat all those people, whom you may meet with kindly and hospitably; inspire them with sentiments of Justice and humanity, and dispose them to introduce the arts of civil and social life and to encourage the residence of husbandmen and handicrafts men among them.

Advise

Advise the Congress from time to time of all occurrences, that may, in your opinion, deserve their attention.

By order of Congress.
John Hancock President.

Letter written to Colonel George Morgan
by John Hancock, President of the Continental Congress, 1776

that many Indian elders shared his vision of a future in which people of all races, creeds, and colors could live together with respect for natural law. While some colonial officials refused to recognize Indian rights, Congress recognized Indian sovereignty—their right to determine their own futures—and made many promises in 1776 at the first U.S.–Indian Peace Treaty.

Two years later, Congress ratified a treaty by which the Delaware Indians were to become the fourteenth state in the Union, an Indian state to be represented by Indian congressmen. For his part, Morgan served as guardian for three Indian boys who won highest academic honors while studying at Princeton to become future Indian statesmen. However, the plan for direct Indian participation in the U.S. government was undermined by powerful political factions who advocated a different course to ensure a return on their investments in plantations and slaves.

The Morgan Papers shed new light on America's origins. From the beginning I felt humbled by the task of retracing decades of history involving hundreds of people, places, and complex cultures. Nan was most supportive and encouraged me every step of the way. After months of preliminary research, we decided to contact a few scholars to check our initial findings. As news of the Morgan Papers spread through the scholarly world, interest in the documents became more intense. Before the year was out, Nan asked me to help her write an article to publicly announce the discovery of the papers. A week later Nan's picture appeared on the front page of the local paper with an article headlined, "Bicentennial Bonanza: Historical Letters Located Here." A few weeks later, the Associated Press picked up the story and wired it around the world. Articles appeared in *The New York Times,* the *London Times,* and hundreds of other newspapers from Tokyo to Rome. Nan and I were interviewed for television and radio programs, including "NBC News." *People* magazine (January 24, 1977) also published a three-page story entitled, "Historian Gregory Schaaf Finds a Mother Lode of History Among a Neighbor's Keepsakes."

Even the U.S. Senate made contact. We had quite a scare when we received a demand to disclose all the Morgan Papers and were informed of the subpoena powers of Congress. With a little research I learned that the American Indian Policy Review Commission was engaged in a joint investigation for Congress, but that its authority would expire in a few months. We didn't want the entire contents of the Morgan Papers to become public knowledge at this time for two reasons: first, I wanted the freedom to complete my research and to write an independent interpretation; and second, we did not know how Congress would handle some undisclosed evidence related to sovereign Indian claims. George

Morgan had documented Indian land rights to over twenty-five million acres. Was this one of the reasons the Morgan Papers had been kept secret for over two hundred years? Nan and I decided to keep the material out of federal hands, if possible, until my research was completed. (I have since testified twice before the U.S. Senate Select Committee for Indian Affairs.)

My most immediate concern was to help Nan, who needed income to provide for her security. We developed a plan that satisfied our mutual objectives. We decided to create "The Colonel George Morgan Document Preservation and Marketing Company." We sold 50 percent interest in the collection, like shares of stock in a corporation. Nan received the profits, and her heirs retained a major interest. All fifty shares were sold to a group of private investors. (On April 25, 1989, after unsuccessful attempts had been made to find a philanthropist to acquire the papers and donate them to the Iroquois Confederacy, the documents were sold at Sotheby's in New York. Microfilm copies are available at the University of California, Santa Barbara; California State University, Chico; and the Grand Council, Iroquois Confederacy.)

I then settled down to the long task of completing my research. With encouragement from Dr. Wilbur Jacobs, a scholar in colonial Indian affairs, I returned to graduate school at the University of California. Jacobs became my advisor and guided me toward earning a doctorate in American history with special emphasis in Native American studies. I reviewed early travel journals for vivid descriptions of frontier settlements, Indian villages, and natural landscapes. To be able to describe a natural world of people who lived in harmony with the land, I learned about the plants, animals, birds, fish, and other forms of wildlife that changed from region to region. To begin to understand the traditional way of life for complex Indian cultures, I started files on almost five hundred topics ranging from tribal government, wampum diplomacy, and religion to astronomy, music, and fine arts. I traveled from coast to coast, searching for more information in the National Archives, Library of Congress, Smithsonian Institution, university libraries, and local historical societies, as well as seeking knowledge from people rich in human experience.

Perhaps the most fascinating aspect of my activities has been my experiences with traditional Indian elders. I value highly the friendships I have made among Indian nations—from the Iroquois in the East to the Chumash in the West, and from the Lakota in the North to the Hopi in the South, as well as the Lenni Lenape who now live in the center of the continent. Natural law and ancient traditions of peace still flourish among the family of Indian nations. While sitting within the circle of elders, just as George Morgan did two hundred years ago, I humbly began to realize the responsibility each human being has to help promote a more peaceful world. The elders say we are all related as one great family in diversity. When they pray, it is not for themselves, but for "all our relations." In every decision we make in life, the Great Law states that first we must consider how our actions may influence "seven generations to come."

With these thoughts in mind, let us now commence a journey back in time to the dawn of the American Revolution. The story you are about to read is true to the documentary evidence. Some scenes you may find shocking. However, by facing the realities of the birth of America, your world view may change in enlightening ways.

WAMPUM BELTS
AND PEACE TREES

The Indian Frontier
in Revolutionary America
1775–1776
Based on the Morgan Papers
and other original sources

Morgan's route ·········
Girty's route ------
Indian village
Frontier fort

Hidatsa: Gregory L. Schaaf, Ph.D.
Artist: Susan K...

0   25   50   100 miles

Maspeth-daam sea

Chapter One

LIBERTY AND JUSTICE FOR ALL
The Dream versus Reality

CHIEF WHITE EYES, the wily old Indian ambassador, used his considerable diplomatic skills in lobbying the Continental Congress during the winter and spring of 1776. While the revolutionary delegates were on the verge of preparing the Declaration of Independence, White Eyes sought liberty, justice, and equal rights for Native American people. The Delaware chief appealed to the general membership of the Continental Congress to bridge the chasm between their cultures and to maintain friendly diplomatic channels. The political stakes were high: the future survival of his nation, the Lenni Lenape, as well as the security of millions of other Indian people rested precariously in the balance of power between the British and the American colonies. Conversely, since the Indian nations had the military might necessary to affect the outcome of the American Revolution, the British and Americans were also competing to win the favor of influential Indian leaders.[1]

White Eyes assumed grave personal risks in traveling to Philadelphia. His life was in danger because British spies frequented the rebel capital, and anti-Indian sentiments prevailed among many Americans. Since the Indians had been forced out of Pennsylvania by fraud and violent conflict, fears of reprisals by Indians fueled some whites' desire for bloodshed. Ironically, the strict, repressive policies that had been directed at Indians of the previous generation were now being directed at the general American populace by the British. Colonial oppression had grown to be so intolerable that a violent revolutionary backlash was gaining momentum, generating an overall atmosphere of violence and suspicion. Any mission of peace undertaken by an Indian leader would be further complicated by deep-seated prejudice.[2]

George Morgan, an Indian trader, frontier explorer, and the old Lenape chief's closest friend in Philadelphia, was very knowledgeable about the historical and cultural background of the problem. A series of brutal murders of Indians, some unsolved but others brazenly acknowledged, had occurred in the colonies in recent years.[3] Throughout the colonies, the majority of white and Indian people wanted liberty and justice, but a minority of violent and destructive individuals continually disrupted society and distorted the popular image of different races.[4] This land had not always been rife with prejudice and intolerance. Almost a hundred years earlier, in 1682, Quaker pacifists and peace-loving Lenape had agreed to live in harmony, vowing to follow the Creator's "Original Divine Instructions," which they recognized as being universal and eternal. According to local legend, colony builder William Penn had joined hands in friendship beneath a great Tree of Peace with Lenape Chief Tamanend, "The Affable One."[5] This was said to be one of the only treaties that was never signed and never broken. Where the two cultures had united in the center of the Lenape capital, Philadelphia now sprawled over the site originally called Shackamaxon, "The Place Where Chiefs Are Made." Thus Pennsylvania was established on a spiritual foundation generally known as "The Holy Experiment."[6]

Later a repressive government and prejudice toward the original people prevailed. For almost a generation, old storytellers claimed, not one Indian had been killed maliciously by a white man, nor had one white man been murdered by an Indian. But with changes in the political power structure, violence and special interests reigned. Colonial–Indian treaties were abrogated; military might was employed by some opportunists in a scheme to control the land, trade, and commerce. In the wake of colonial conquest, fundamental rights of the Indian people were abused. As violent acts were met with reprisals, colonial soldiers and vigilantes invaded Indian territory and Indian families were driven from their homes. Whole villages were burned to the ground. "The Holy Experiment" went up in smoke.[7]

White Eyes's childhood was scarred by the era of the Lenape's violent dispossession. However, his spiritual leader, Grandfather Netawatwees, who was nearly a century old, had also witnessed the previous generation of peace. Netawatwees, the "Skilled Advisor," had lived through the era of cooperation that proved that it was possible for people of different races, creeds, and colors to live together in peace and harmony. As a spiritual and political leader of the

Lenape nation, Netawatwees inspired younger men such as White Eyes to live up to their philosophy of peace.

During the spring of 1776 White Eyes also was impressed by the democratic ideals of the American revolutionaries. The Lenape religion recognized the equality of all people as a fundamental principle. In fact, Lenape philosophy was an ancient form of democracy. Traditional Lenape recognized not only the rights of all men, but those of all women. They also believed human beings should respect life—animals, plants, and even tiny insects—because all had been made by the Creator for a purpose. According to the Lenape the mountains, the rivers, the Earth, and the heavens above were created in harmony for a divine purpose. They viewed the entire universe as alive with spiritual power. Traditional religious leaders sought to maintain the cosmic balance between human beings, the natural world, and the "Great Mystery." Among traditional native people, the right to liberty meant more than just political freedom for male landowners and the abolition of slavery for some races. Liberty encompassed the divine right of everyone and everything to exist in a natural state as the Creator had intended.[8]

Among the Lenape a chief could not grandly impose his will, like a king, but rather governed with a circle of elders through the wisdom of their counsel. The right to lead was confirmed by the common consent of the people. If a chief's advice was fair and reasonable, the people followed it. A chief often became one of the poorest members of his nation during hard times, because the position entailed a social and moral responsibility to help those less fortunate. If a chief stopped serving the best interests of the nation, the people could depose him. Therefore, from a Lenape perspective, the growing call among Americans to revolt against a tyrannical British king was both justifiable and in accordance with tribal law.[9]

While White Eyes observed the tumult in Philadelphia, the center of American revolutionary activity, he sought first and foremost to maintain a peaceful, neutral posture for his nation. But he also wanted to make clear that just because the Lenape advocated peace, this did not mean they would not stand up for their rights. White Eyes risked his life by going to Philadelphia because he sought an opportunity for speaking out for the sovereign rights of his nation. The chief's efforts to promote close diplomatic relations with the revolutionary leadership were critical. If a new political order were to be established in America, Indians needed to develop close friends among delegates of the Continental Congress. And if Indian groups were to survive as sovereign, independent nations, the Americans had to recognize their right to self-determination.[10]

Chief White Eyes and other Indian leaders appeared before the Continental Congress, as well as before British officials, to appeal for political recognition, trade agreements, and confirmation of land titles. For over five months, from December to April, White Eyes cultivated influential allies among Americans in Philadelphia. He was treated as a guest, housed in special quarters next to the State House, soon to be known around the world as Independence Hall. But if White Eyes was to succeed in establishing friendly relations between his nation and the thirteen United Colonies, much would depend on the placement of key diplomats in positions of power.

White Eyes's good friend George Morgan lived only a few blocks from the State House, but he held no title of political authority. However, Morgan was knowledgeable about both the current rampant violence against Indians and the historical background to the problem. By the year 1776, Morgan had acquired an intimate knowledge of the diverse native cultures from the Great Lakes to the Ohio River Valley and from the rugged Appalachians to the mighty Mississippi. For more than a decade Morgan had explored the interior frontier, crossing the mountains on horseback caravans and then floating down waterways in birchbark canoes and rough log rafts. As the junior partner of an international trading enterprise, Baynton, Wharton and Morgan, he led numerous expeditions westward to transport to Indian nations vital trade goods: woodworking and leather tools, farming implements, colorful calicos, needles and thread, gunpowder for hunting, and other supplies. Indians traded in exchange valuable furs, well-tanned leather, vegetable seeds, and medicines, which were exported throughout the Americas and around the world. Morgan had earned a reputation among the Indians as one of the few honest traders. Less scrupulous men sometimes disappeared mysteriously, never to be seen again.[11]

As a specialist in Indian affairs and a patriot loyal to the revolutionary cause, Morgan was being evaluated privately by congressional delegates for a most important mission of peace to the Indian nations. Before the Americans dared declare their rights to "life, liberty, and the pursuit of happiness," they wanted a peace treaty, one that went beyond the conditions covered in the 1775 Fort Pitt Treaty, with the more powerful Indian nations. If the Indians joined the British in a concerted attack from the frontier, the American Revolution could be crushed.[12]

On the morning of April 10, 1776, less than three months before the signing of the Declaration of Independence, Congress prepared to set into action bold steps that would lead to the ultimate break with England. The president of Congress, John Hancock, requested George Morgan's presence before the Continental Congress on a matter regarding the security of the country.

Widespread concern over the safety of the colonists' homeland had intensified since the first musket shots had been fired at Lexington and Concord. George Morgan's colleagues in the American Philosophical Society, notably Dr. Benjamin Franklin, began to voice their conviction that an ultimate solution was required: the creation of a new, democratic United States of America.[13]

However, loyalty to the British crown still prevailed in many communities, where revolutionaries were condemned as traitors. Bounties were placed on their heads, creating a dilemma for patriotic family men like George Morgan. He needed to consider the well-being of his wife, Mary, and their four children, John, Ann, Mary, and George, Jr., a newborn baby, as well as the future of the coming generation. So much was at stake, and men like Morgan were willing to risk their lives to ensure a better way of life for the country.

The temper of the times influenced many young patriots. Thomas Jefferson and George Morgan were only thirty-two years old, yet both possessed skills vital to a successful revolution. Well educated and widely traveled, they were dedicated to reforming society so that it would be based on justice and freedom for all its citizens. Although the best path for achieving these goals was hotly debated, Jefferson and Morgan were in agreement about the important role of American Indians in affecting the outcome of the war.

But Morgan's commitment to his family was equally strong. Even when he journeyed far off into the frontier, he managed to exchange letters with his wife through the services of friends. Mary Morgan was an intelligent and articulate woman, and with revolutionary fervor growing, she must have been aware that her husband's involvement could be dangerous. However, she apparently made no attempts to prevent him from getting involved in potentially dangerous patriotic actions.

When George Morgan left the family's residence on that Wednesday morning in April 1776, it was to see what role in the Revolution Congress wanted him to play.[14] The walk along cobblestone streets from his home on Third Street to the State House led young Morgan past several notable sights. Philadelphia was growing with ever-expanding diversity, and it was now the richest and largest seaport in the country, with more than forty thousand citizens. On Elm Street was the prominent mercantile establishment, which he owned in partnership with Mary's mother.[15] Since George had been an orphan apprentice at the age of thirteen, for almost twenty years he had refined his knowledge of the complex chain of commerce. Growing prosperity and the expansion of the economy had extended his company's activities from the Atlantic seaboard to Europe in the east, Canada in the north, Indian country in the west, and the Caribbean in the south.

British officials were altering the delicate balance of trade and commerce in order to finance their colonial adventure. For the past two years, the Intolerable Acts had placed severe strains on free enterprise through the imposition of high taxes and customs duties. Morgan and other merchants were outraged because their hard-earned money was going to support British domination. And while the American colonies were suffering under the thumb of the British Army, the Indians certainly were not strangers to foreign, that is to say, American, intervention.[16]

At the same time that the Continental Congress was attempting to attain freedom for the United Colonies, Indian councils also were debating how to preserve their liberty. The Indian struggle for freedom was not entirely different from that of white Americans. A man who was poignantly aware of the increasing pressures on the Americans and the Indians lived a few blocks from the State House: Benjamin Franklin. A senior ambassador of the Continental Congress, he was away on that April day. The serenity of the budding green gardens around Franklin's home stood in sharp contrast to the turmoil of the surrounding city.[17]

Morgan became affiliated with the elder statesman through their mutual activities in the Indiana Land Company, and an intellectual association also developed through verbal exchanges in the American Philosophical Society. The elder scholar originally organized the discussion group under the revolutionary title "Junto."[18] Young Morgan, an eager student and avid reader, used this opportunity to explore diverse fields, ranging from experimental agriculture to the classics, from international diplomacy to Indian affairs.[19]

An understanding of the different Indian nations beyond the borders and within the United Colonies required a multifaceted examination into over a hundred ancient cultures, religions, and tribal histories. East of the Mississippi were four main families of nations: Iroquoian, Muskogean, Siouan, and Algonquian.[20] White Eyes's nation, the Lenni Lenape, were the "Grandfathers" of the Grand Old Algonquian Family.[21] Morgan was especially well versed in their wampum diplomacy, the ritual of Indian peacemakers, and his previous ten years' experience made him a logical candidate to represent the Continental Congress before the Indian nations.[22] It seemed possible that this might be the reason for his summons by the Congress.

To advance Indian negotiations independent of the British, Congress had designed three regional Departments of Indian Affairs structured under the guidance of Indian commissioners. Benjamin Franklin, Patrick Henry, and James Wilson had assumed positions representing the Middle Department, centered in the Ohio River Valley, where White Eyes's people lived. Before assuming command of the Continental Army, General George Washington had served as a leader of the Virginian Indian commissioners. John Walker, the Virginian land speculator, who was one of the main speakers at the Fort Pitt treaty conference, was now head of the Southern Department, while General Philip Schuyler led the Northern Department from the field.[23] With the Revolutionary War on the horizon, Congress was prepared to act also on the matter of Indian affairs.

On April 10, 1776, George Morgan and Chief White Eyes entered the halls of Congress. Classical white columns lined the room, interspersed with coffered archways. In contrast with rustic Indian tribal council houses, the Assembly Room reflected colonial splendor—large white panels delineated by four tall windows and flanked with crimson red curtains. Within this stately setting— forty feet square and with twenty-foot ceilings—the future welfare of more than three million people was debated by delegates from thirteen colonies who crowded around green baize-covered tables.[24]

John Hancock, president of the Continental Congress and one of the richest men in the country, reportedly arrived at the Assembly Room with all the pageantry of an oriental prince. An elegant and expensive dresser, he habitually wore a brocade coat, ruffled shirt, silk stockings, and a laced three-cornered hat. Most Indians loved bright, colorful clothing made of fine cloth; they also admired men of vision, integrity, and courage. They believed Hancock represented both attributes and called him by the honored title Karanduawn, the "Great Tree of Liberty."[25]

To the Indians, as to members of other civilizations, the Great Tree was a symbol of life, peace, and freedom whose origins reached back to the earliest days of recorded history. It appears in ancient tribal tablets, hieroglyphic papyrus rolls found in the pyramids of Egypt, and cuneiform tablets from ancient Sumeria, as well as in the oldest writings of India, China, Africa, and Europe. The symbolism of the Great Tree continues to be represented by the maypole, the Christmas tree, and even the Cross, all of which represent rebirth, resurgence, or renewal, among other things. Traditions from cultures around the world prophesy the end of oppression and sacrilege to be followed by an age of peace and prosperity, when the world will be purified and balanced in a natural state of liberty.[26]

Hancock, Jefferson, and other leading members of Congress were inspired by these traditions, especially treatises on natural law by the Swiss–French philosopher and reformer Jean-Jacques Rousseau. To achieve their ideals of liberty, loyalty to the king and the yoke of colonial oppression would have to be cast off. Although some leaders still trembled at the thought of creating a new nation and hoped for a last-minute reconciliation with the mother country, many congressional delegates were prepared to take steps necessary to set the plan into motion.[27]

Morgan and White Eyes waited to see how Congress would act that morning. Considering the appointment of a properly qualified agent for Indian affairs to negotiate with the various tribes would be a vital step toward securing the frontier. Hancock was accompanied by Secretary of Congress Charles Thomson, who had developed close friendships with many Indians over the previous twenty years. During earlier negotiations, he had been adopted by the Lenape tribal council and given the name Wegh-we-law-mo-end, "The Man Who Tells the Truth."[28] Thomson now sat next to the speaker's table, where each morning he called the Assembly to order. According to parliamentary procedure, the leader signaled with a nod, the gavel came down, and the meeting started after the locks in the doors clicked, in order to ensure the privacy of the assembly. Before the debate on Indian affairs could commence, however, the most urgent messages were read aloud. Two dispatches had arrived from General George Washington, then stationed at Cambridge, Massachusetts. The first letter warned that the British high command was threatening to incite the Indians of Nova Scotia to go on the warpath along the northeast coast if the white populace did not submit to British military authority. Washington informed Congress of the dilemma facing the people:

> They are in a distressed situation, and . . . are exceedingly apprehensive that they will be reduced to the disagreeable alternative of taking up Arms and Joining our Enemies, or to flee their Country, unless they can be protected against . . . the Indians (of which there are a good many) from taking the side of [the British] Government.[29]

The strategy of using fear to influence public opinion and loyalties was proving effective. Although no one could be certain that the Indian nations would actually side with the British, the mere threat of their going on the warpath evoked a strong response.

Not even Washington felt confident that he knew the best retaliatory tactic; as he had confessed earlier: "I am a little embarrassed to know in what Manner to conduct myself with Respect to the . . . Indians. . . . I am sensible that if they do not desire to be idle, that they will be for or against us."[30]

This was not a unanimous view. But it was certain that the only way to determine the true sentiments of different Indian nations was to send agents directly to their territories. An extensive intelligence network must be developed to communicate with tribal councils throughout the frontier. If certain warriors were going to take up arms, Congress needed to know in advance.

By the same token, Congress would be wise to nurture close relationships with chiefs who were committed to keeping the peace. To understand the complex political structure among shifting alliances of Indian nations, there was a need for men especially knowledgeable about Indian affairs. Intelligence agents could also gather useful information on British troop movements and on any outbreaks of violence along the frontier.

The second letter from General George Washington reported that military events in the East were moving forward with increased velocity. The general had recently received an express from Governor Cooke of Rhode Island warning the rebels of the arrival in Newport Harbor of a British man-of-war, while a flotilla of twenty-seven other ships was tacking around Seconet Point.[31] Washington informed Congress of his response:

> In consequence of this important Intelligence I immediately dispatched an Express after General Sullivan who is on his March to Norwich with six Regiments.... General Greene was to have marched this Morning with five more Regiments by way of Providence. I have ordered him to hasten his March and hope to collect a force there sufficient to prevent the Enemy from effecting their purpose. . . . I shall exert myself to the utmost to frustrate the design of the Enemy.[32]

Morgan's reaction to this news may have been heightened by his fear for the well-being of his brother, Dr. John Morgan, who was at Washington's camp as chief physician and director-general of the Continental Medical Corps.[33] This mobile medical team was already fighting its own battle, against an outbreak of smallpox. The dreaded disease was spreading across the colonies. Native Americans were particularly vulnerable because their bodies were not very resistant to European diseases. British officers had earlier used a gruesome form of germ warfare by giving Indians blankets infected with smallpox.[34] Epidemics had then ravaged the countryside, killing Indians, colonists, and even, finally, British citizens.

Dr. John Morgan's makeshift hospital at Harvard College was being uprooted as the Continental Army moved to New York. Almost 3,000 of 18,528 soldiers were sick or wounded.[35] One evening, while the weakest soldiers were being carried to awaiting wagons, General Washington, perhaps reflecting on the wretchedness of his sick men, expressed his sentiments in a private letter to fellow patriot Joseph Reed:

> No man does, no man can, wish the restoration of peace more fervently than I do, but I hope, whenever made, it will be upon such terms, as will reflect honor upon the councils and wisdom of America. . . . My countrymen I know . . . will come reluctantly into the idea of independence. . . . I find [Thomas Paine's] "Common Sense" is working a powerful change . . . in the minds of many men.[36]

The strength of American desire for independence might triumph over the paralyzing effects of disease, but other clandestine forces threatened to undermine the Revolution.

A dangerous conspiracy, which would plague George Morgan and the Americans throughout the decade of the 1770s, was revealed in the third letter read by President Hancock. The British high command was offering a rich reward to Tories who schemed to subvert the Revolution. Dr. John Connolly recently had been arrested while organizing a plan to enlist Indians in an attack on American rebels. The frontier doctor had been found with a secret message from British General Thomas Gage to former Virginia Governor Lord Dunmore proposing a daring mission that would involve a mixed battalion of Indian warriors and British Redcoats in a major offensive. The combined forces were to congregate at Fort Detroit, swoop down to overwhelm the American garrison at Pittsburgh, then cut a swath eastward to the coast. If they could control a strip across the middle of America, vital lines of supply and communication between the northern and southern colonies would be severed.[37] The American Revolution might thus have been reduced to no more than a short-lived, radical uprising.

From his cell in the Philadelphia jail on Walnut Street, Dr. Connolly was resigned to appealing for mercy from the Continental Congress: ". . . in whatever light I may appear as an enemy . . . my difference in political opinion, and the causes instigating me to action, however criminal they may appear . . . arose from a sense of duty and gratitude [toward the British] too powerful to be combatted by any contrary arguments."[38]

An opportunistic individual, Dr. Connolly tried to take refuge behind his political obligations to justify acts of violence. And although the revolutionaries viewed Dr. Connolly as a traitor, British sympathizers probably considered him a hero and a political prisoner. In the same way that some men were prepared to die for the revolutionary cause, others were willing to risk their lives to undermine the Revolution. One of Dr. Connolly's fellow inmates, a man named Molloy, managed to smuggle Connolly's plans and additional orders out of the Philadelphia prison. The concealed papers were transmitted to British spies stationed around Pittsburgh, the American frontier post to which George Morgan soon would be sent.[39]

Several years earlier, while George Morgan was in Pittsburgh, he had been introduced to the doctor by his uncle, George Croghan, a prominent old frontiersman. As the former British Assistant Superintendent for Indian Affairs, Croghan must be suspected of being involved in the plot to incite the Indians. On the one hand, his influence among the Indian nations was formidable. During the previous thirty years, he had established a network of frontier posts to trade with Indians. But his motive for trying to thwart the Revolution might have been related to his rivalry with rebel Virginia over western lands. Many prominent men, including George Washington, Benjamin Franklin, and George Morgan, were involved in the scramble. If Virginia-dominated revolutionaries were victorious, Croghan's land claims, and those of his associates, would be worthless pieces of paper. But Croghan was associated with a syndicate of wealthy investors who shrewdly attempted to preserve a neutral political image. Croghan's half-brother and fellow investor, William Trent, reportedly had received forty thousand pounds British sterling from Lord North, Great Britain's prime minister, who was willing to pay dearly for support from powerful frontiersmen.[40]

Against this background, White Eyes was worried about protecting the rights of his people, and he hoped to express his concerns directly to Congress on that April day. The old Lenape ambassador had worked hard to create a united confederation of Indian nations, and he did not want to see their future endangered. His presence before Congress was a bold attempt to obtain diplomatic recognition from the American revolutionaries. To overcome the prejudice against Indians that was ingrained in some congressional delegates, White Eyes carefully projected a respectable image: "The Chief was dressed in a good Suit of Blue Cloth with a Laced Hat. . . . White Eyes shook all the Members heartily by the Hand, beginning with the President."[41]

John Hancock, the Great Tree of Liberty, clearly ranked as a favorite among the Indians. John Adams did not. An opinionated New Englander, he openly called Indians uncivilized savages. He expounded his political, legal, and social ideas from a front-row desk, which reportedly was piled with papers that he rustled out of a bulging green satchel:

. . . as I know little of them, I always leave the measures relating to them to gentlemen who know a great deal. It is said they are very expensive and troublesome confederates in war, besides the incivility and inhumanity of employing such savages, with their cruel, bloody dispositions, against any enemy whatever.[42]

Thus for quite different, and somewhat ironic reasons, John Adams and White Eyes agreed that Indians should not become directly involved in the Revolutionary War. Both men also were outraged by the British policy of enlisting Indians through threats, bribery, liquor, or promises of glory. On this point Adams proclaimed: "Nevertheless, such have been the extravagancies of *British* barbarity, in prosecuting the war against us, that I think we need not be so delicate as to refuse the assistance of *Indians*, provided we cannot keep them neutral. I should not hesitate a moment in this case."[43]

Adams's attitude toward the Indian people was apparently twisted by past negative experiences. He had grown up in Massachusetts, a colony that had a history of offering bounties for Indian scalps. One of his earliest childhood memories was of curiously watching, with his playmate, John Hancock—from a cautious distance—while a few local Indians fished in the river near Braintree. A sense of fear was ingrained in him from boyhood, because his great-grandfather's brother, Henry Adams, had been killed generations earlier by a criminal band of Indians who had torched the village of Medfield, Massachusetts.[44]

Adams's legal colleague, the young, redheaded Thomas Jefferson, who sat in the rear corner of the Assembly Room, had been favored with more pleasant childhood associations with Indians. Local Native Americans had often visited his family's farm in the Blue Ridge Mountains. Jefferson also possessed a special kinship with the Indians because his mother was partly of Indian ancestry. He advocated a political unification with Indian nations without specifying a military alliance. In his proposal for acceptance of Indian leaders into the American political arena, Jefferson recalled how Indians had often visited his family's farm: "They often used to stop at my father's house. . . . I have always been curious about them. They have great qualities. I hope they will unite with us, join in our councils and form one people with us. We shall all be Americans."[45] Although on first consideration Jefferson's philosophy appears truly laudable, one must consider the implications of his ideas. Jefferson believed that Indians would be—should be— assimilated into the mainstream of white society. This approach would require them to abandon their own culture, religion, and traditional way of life in exchange for white Christianity and a nontribal existence. At that time many

Indian leaders wanted to join the American councils, but only if they could retain independent nationhood, sovereignty over tribal lands, and the right to determine their own future. White Eyes and Morgan would later attempt a compromise, the creation of a fourteenth state, for Indians. This was an approach that would evoke the ire of Indian nationalists on one side and white land developers on the other.[46]

Ben Franklin, one of the commissioners of Indian affairs for the Continental Congress, shrewdly was not committing himself to any set policy regarding the future position of Indian nations in the revolutionary government. He was away on a special diplomatic mission to Canada to win support for Americans, a mission that was doomed to failure. However, his experience there would convince him that the Indian nations were indeed an awesome force that could tip the balance of power. He therefore advocated an Indian policy based on respect, peace, and neutrality. To acknowledge both the danger of a full-scale Indian offensive undertaken in concert with the British and the vulnerability of the American frontier outposts as a defense, Franklin published the following warning:

> . . . security, will not be obtained by such forts, unless they were connected by a wall like that of China, from one end of our settlements to the other. If the Indians when at war, march'd like the Europeans, with great armies, heavy cannon, baggage and carriages . . . such armies could penetrate our country.[47]

The combined Indian–British threat was an important factor in making the colonies unite in their call to arms. Franklin recognized that his reports would strike fear into the hearts of many colonists. Although he sometimes referred to violent Indians as "savages," he still tried to dispel prejudice against Indian people in general. He observed that many Indians were dedicated to efforts for peace and interracial harmony and wrote with firm conviction that people of all colors must overcome the desire for revenge. To illustrate that the great diversity of Indian tribes was not unlike the multiplicity of European nations, Franklin composed the following analogy:

> If an Indian injures me, does it follow that I may revenge that Injury on all Indians? It is well known that Indians are of different Tribes, Nations and Languages, as well as the White People. In Europe, if the French, who are White-People, should injure the Dutch, are they to revenge it on the English, because they too are White People?[48]

Franklin elevated the issue of prejudice to an international level in order to illustrate the narrowmindedness of bigotry. He boldly sought to purge from America the desire for revenge:

> This is done by no civilized Nation in Europe. Do we come to America to learn and practise the Manners of Barbarians? . . . These poor [Indian] People have been . . . our Friends. Their Fathers received ours, when Strangers here, with Kindness and Hospitality. Behold the Return we have made them![49]

Franklin's reference to "barbarians" and "civilized nations" reveals his sense of superiority. However, his knowledge of Indian history made it difficult for him to reconcile inhumane treatment of Indian people with the supposedly superior European moral system.

Franklin supported Jefferson's proposal to invite leading Indian chiefs to join their councils, but the elder statesman added a compromise: "I think they [the Indians] ought to be invited. After Congress has settled the question of independence."[50] If Congress had kept its word, and when framing the U.S. Constitution had invited the Indian nations to assume an important and respectable role in the U.S. government, the bloody U.S.–Indian wars might never have come to pass.

The fundamental idea for creating a federated government was also found in the institutions of Native Americans. For many centuries, both the Iroquoian and Algonquian families of nations had united in a form of political alliance. In fact, Benjamin Franklin and his fellow commissioner of Indian affairs, James Wilson, were studying Indian political systems as a model for the government of the United States. The young Scottish attorney from Pennsylvania concurred with Franklin: "Indians know the striking benefits of confederation. They have an example of it in the union of the [Iroquois] Six Nations, and the idea of a union of the colonies struck them forcibly."[51] Although a few Americans recognized the political, social, and philosophical contributions of Indian societies, most white people did not accept Indians as equals.

When White Eyes addressed the Continental Congress, several delegates who sat before him were slave owners. In fact, the issue of slavery threatened to rip apart the proposed union along northern and southern lines.[52] To convince both sides that Indians were civilized people and to further his larger plan for peaceful relations, White Eyes asked Congress to provide his nation with Anglican ministers. The most fervent prejudices against Indians centered around the issue of religion. Indians who were not Christians were labeled heathens, a term that was also applied to irreligious, rude, or uncultured people. If the general populace had studied the tenets of Indian religions, many might have been surprised to discover sophisticated theologies that followed a set of original divine instructions similar to Christianity. Indians prayed to the same Creator, and many considered Jesus Christ to be the same "white brother" who had delivered the message of peace and universal brotherhood to their ancestors. Many also were familiar with the Bible, but they often were shocked by the actions of professed Christians, especially slave owners, who failed to follow the Ten Commandments. These same men were frequently the first to condemn Indians as cruel savages.[53]

To help prepare his young people for dealing on equal terms with Americans, White Eyes requested a good schoolteacher. And to promote technical trades, particularly in the field of metal working, the Lenape chief asked Congress to send a blacksmith. Congress deliberated on his proposals. Finally, John Hancock announced its favorable decision:

> That the commissioners for Indian affairs . . . be desired to employ, for reasonable salaries, a minister of the gospel, to reside among the Delaware [Lenni Lenape] Indians, and instruct them in the Christian religion; a school master to teach their youth reading, writing, and arithmetic; and also, a blacksmith to do the work of the Indians.[54]

White Eyes apparently had won a diplomatic victory; an important step had been taken toward breaking down racial barriers. The old chief believed that education would be the surest method of elevating his people to a level of parity in the eyes of intellectual members of Congress. Channels of communication were now open, and the Lenni Lenape nation was officially recognized. In accordance with frontier diplomatic protocol, Congress resolved:

> That the commissioners for Indian affairs in the middle department, be desired, at the expence of the United Colonies, to provide for the entertainment of the sachems and warriors of the Indians . . . with the accustomed hospitality, when they come to Pittsburg, to treat, or give intelligence of public affairs.[55]

Fort Pitt, the military and government headquarters in the frontier town of Pittsburgh, was the closest meeting place between the Lenape and American revolutionaries. Cooshocking (presently Coshocton, Ohio), the Lenape capital, was two hundred miles west of Pittsburgh. Pittsburgh was also an important trade center, where furs and other natural items were exchanged for vital imported goods. The Indian agent would be required to meet with Lenape chiefs and keep them supplied with vital necessities—a responsibility that would prove awesome when supplies became more scarce as the war heated up.

Before Congress took the ultimate step of declaring the nation's independence, it needed to protect its flanks on the frontier. To balance often conflicting Indian and American interests was no small task. Indian politics were complex. The frontier was composed of what Europeans might call independent city-states numbering in the hundreds. Alliances between nations could change overnight, especially over a hot issue like the Revolutionary War. More than ever, Congress needed a man with profound influence to negotiate with western Indian nations and keep them at peace.

John Hancock asked each delegate to write on a slip of paper the name of the man who should be entrusted with the Indian peace mission. Ballots were collected and counted by Secretary Charles Thomson, who handed the final tally to the president. On April 10, 1776, members of the Continental Congress elected their new agent for Indian affairs for the Middle Department—George Morgan.[56]

Morgan's first assignment would be to escort White Eyes back home when his trip was finished and then to establish his headquarters at Fort Pitt. Congress next passed a resolution to pay the Lenape chief the sum of three hundred dollars for expenses incurred during his visit to Philadelphia. Morgan was also asked to acquire two fine horses and saddles for the trip west. White Eyes graciously accepted the gifts while requesting that Congress commit its promises to paper in the same manner in which white people conducted business. The old chief was becoming aware of the ways of the white man. Among the Indians, a man's word was held sacred, but colonial law required documentary evidence.[57]

The following morning a letter addressed to the entire Lenape nation was presented to Chief White Eyes. The promotion of peace between the Indians and the white Americans would be well received by leaders of the American Indian nations—those chiefs and clan mothers who were convinced that they had to protect their homeland from becoming a battleground for the Revolutionary War.

The congressional plan to send an Anglican minister was more controversial. Like white colonial communities, Indian societies were divided on matters of religion as well as politics, and this decision would disturb some traditionalists. It could also be expected to upset German Protestant missionaries of the

Moravian faith, who were already well established among the Lenape. Furthermore, Congress was apparently oblivious to the potential backlash.

Many Indian ceremonies commenced with a prayer to "All Our Relations." There is evidence to show that most elders believed that all people were related, as creations of one Great Spirit. Their prayers to "All Our Relations" were directed not only to their personal relatives, but also to all land and life, which were created for a divine purpose. Many traditional elders also acknowledged a special kinship with Americans, because they lived on the same continent and thus were born from the same Mother Earth.[58] This belief would help Morgan in his goal of keeping Indian tribes at peace.

Morgan and White Eyes were faced with an awesome task in keeping the western frontier peaceful. To make war, only one side needed firepower and willpower, but to make peace, both sides needed to be brought together in agreement. Congress asked the Lenape chief to strive toward uniting families of Indian nations with their white brothers and sisters in a peaceful relationship called a "Covenant Chain of Friendship." White Eyes reportedly gave his personal best wishes to the assembly, and once again shook the hand of each delegate before departing from the Continental Congress.

A week later Congress was still working on the plan that would guide Morgan's Indian policy. Owing to the urgency of their mission, Morgan and White Eyes were compelled to leave immediately. Congress would forward directives by special courier later. Morgan was well equipped to deal with the logistics of the journey, but it must have been difficult to prepare for the emotional sacrifice of leaving behind his wife and children, especially his newborn baby. The mission would be dangerous, and he would be gone for months, perhaps even for years. He might never see his wife and children again.

On the morning of Wednesday, April 17, 1776, Agent George Morgan and Chief White Eyes loaded their pack horses for the long journey to Fort Pitt. The way out of town was down a long avenue called Market Street, which led to the ferry for the crossing of the Schuylkill River.

When the Schuylkill, or the "Hidden" River was first seen by European explorers in the early seventeenth century, the ancestors of Chief White Eyes, as Franklin had mentioned, were there to welcome the strangers.[59] The site of Philadelphia had then been an important Lenape village called Shackamaxon, "The Place Where Chiefs Are Made."[60] Beneath the shade of an old tree called the Shackamaxon Elm, William Penn reportedly had promised Chief Tamanend that Indian people and white people would share this land "to continue in peace and Love, and be as one Heart and Soule."[61]

After Penn's death, the document that recorded his promises mysteriously disappeared from colonial archives. Thousands of acres in the rich Delaware Valley were forfeited under European law in 1732, when six Lenape men accepted a gift from William Penn's debt-ridden sons. The "gift" included twenty gallons of rum; fifty pounds in money; and an assortment of ribbons, mirrors, and other baubles. When the effects of the rum wore off, Lenape families who lived along the Schuylkill River were rudely informed that they were trespassers in the homeland of their ancient ancestors.[62]

The Old Conestoga Road led Morgan and Chief White Eyes along the historic trail on which hundreds of dispossessed Indian families had been forced west in a tragic exodus. A few miles outside Philadelphia, the two men waded across three brooks and passed the entrances of dozens of farms and estates. The natural landscape had changed dramatically during the past four decades: huge sections of the forest had been chopped down and burned so tobacco, wheat, and other cash crops could be grown. Where wild animals had once flourished, herds of cows and sheep grazed. Indian villages had been replaced with white mansions, red brick plantations, and log cabins. Rivers had been dammed up, and the environment was in the process of being transformed, perhaps forever.[63]

Each spring an ever-increasing influx of pioneer families went west in search of the Promised Land. Like the Indians, many European immigrants had also been dispossessed by a ruling class. But when they arrived on the shores of America, they found rich coastal lands already controlled by the wealthy gentry. Some newcomers soon realized that their best hope of fulfilling their dreams of owning their own homes and controlling their own lives was to carve out a place for themselves somewhere on the frontier. With the American Revolution threatening to erupt into a full-scale war, the number of people moving west was increasing. By the end of the century, the muddy trail called the Conestoga Road would be developed into America's first cobblestone turnpike, leading to what was then the gateway to the West, the city of Lancaster.[64]

At the end of the second day of their journey, Morgan and White Eyes entered Lancaster, then the largest inland city in Pennsylvania, with a population of 35,493.[65] Settled principally by German and Scotch–Irish merchants and farmers, the area boasted a reputation as the "bread basket" of the colony. Three decades earlier city fathers and colonial officials had hosted a series of major Indian conferences to gain control of the land, which culminated with the Grand Treaty of Lancaster in 1744.[66]

The town was also known also as a dangerous place for Indians. As White Eyes and Morgan rode down King's Street, they passed the city prison, a house of terror for Native Americans. In 1763, a group of beleaguered Conestoga Indians was huddled in protective custody inside the prison walls when the Paxton Boys, a group of white vigilantes with their faces painted black, broke into the jail. One eyewitness reported:

> These murderers were permitted to break open the doors . . . with rifles, tomahawks, and scalping knives, equipped for murder. I ran into the prison yard, and there, O what a horrid sight presented itself to my view!! Near the back door . . . lay an old Indian and his squaw (wife), . . . with two children, of about the age of three years, whose heads were split with the tomahawk, and their scalps all taken off. Towards the middle of the gaol yard . . . lay a stout Indian . . . shot in the breast, his legs were chopped with the tomahawk, his hands cut off, and finally a rifle ball discharged in his mouth; so that his head was blown to atoms, and the brains were splashed against, and yet hanging to the wall. . . . In this manner lay the whole of them, men, women and children, spread about the prison yard: shot—scalped—hacked—and cut to pieces.[67]

This mass murder and a long series of other acts on the colonial frontier caused an Indian uprising. The most violent and destructive members of society, both red and white, unleashed their vengeance. Bands of armed men roamed the countryside, plundering villages and waylaying unwary travelers. One of Morgan's earlier supply convoys of eighty packhorses had been ambushed by the Paxton Boys, this time dressed in Indian buckskins and with their faces covered with war paint. Afterwards they had tried to pin the blame on those "vicious, uncivilized red savages."[68]

After countless thousands had died during the generation of revenge killings that followed the Lancaster Massacre and Pontiac's War, the frontier was precariously at peace under the terms of the 1775 Peace Treaty negotiated at Fort Pitt. Men and women of peace had come together to help heal old wounds and to reestablish friendly relations, but bitter feelings still remained, and as representatives of their different cultures, White Eyes and Morgan faced a difficult task trying to preserve peace. In fact, by assuming roles as peacemakers, their lives would inevitably be in danger.

White Eyes and Morgan were surrounded by a myriad of rocks, trees, and houses behind which an assassin could hide. The murder of a prominent chief like White Eyes might destroy their work for peace and ignite the frontier once again. Morgan had to find a safe place for the old chief to rest during the night.

One sympathetic citizen in Lancaster, Jasper Yeates, was helpful. Yeates, an attorney who was chairman of the County Committee for Intelligence and a candidate to become a congressional Indian commissioner, invited them into his home, thus affording the two men a chance to sleep safely.[69]

Early the next morning White Eyes and Morgan pressed on, crossing two mountain passes and wading their horses through streams brimming from the spring runoff. They had traversed twenty-two miles when late in the afternoon they arrived at the cabin of a Mr. White and his family. Dreadful news greeted the weary travelers: An elderly trader and trusted Indian interpreter, Isaac Still, was burning up inside with smallpox. Whenever this disease broke out, it could be spread rapidly by travelers. White Eyes had once contracted smallpox and miraculously survived, but still was in danger of joining a death toll totaling thousands.

Now fighting for his life, Still could look back on an honorable career as an interpreter who had served at many treaty councils. Morgan had brought Still's last pay, fifty dollars from the Continental Congress, a somewhat meager compensation for his wife and son. Before Morgan pushed on to the Susquehanna, he assured Still and his family that the gates at Fort Pitt always would be open for their protection.[70]

White Eyes and Morgan camped that second night near Harrisburg, then crossed the Susquehanna at Harris's Ferry, where everything from covered wagons to crates of chickens was loaded onto flat boats and floated over to the other side. A score of Indian trails on the western bank radiated into the forest. Morgan and White Eyes followed the path to Carlisle, taking the same route Ben Franklin had when he trekked to that settlement twenty years earlier for an Indian council meeting.[71] When they arrived at the small congregation of log cabins, they rested for the Sabbath and attended services at an Episcopal log chapel. They spent the evening near Ephraim Blaine's trading post, where hunters brought wild game to be shipped to American troops. Blaine was an important merchant who would help Morgan keep Fort Pitt supplied during the coming years.[72]

Before the two travelers mounted their horses for the next leg of their journey, a special courier from the Continental Congress caught up with them. He presented Morgan with John Hancock's secret orders. Three days earlier Congress had finally ratified an official directive to guide Morgan in shaping the new Indian policy. The letter directed Morgan to take a great peace belt with thirteen diamonds and twenty-five-hundred wampum beads to the sachems and warriors of the western Indian nations:

In Congress   April 19, 1776

Instructions to George Morgan Esquire
Agent under the commissioners for Indian
Affairs in the middle department.

Sir,
    You are required to provide, that the great [13 diamond
peace] belt presented to the Indians last fall at Pittsburgh be forwarded with all convenient expedition to the Sachems and warriors of
the western [Indian] nations; and endeavour to the utmost of your
power to convince them of the good wishes and good intentions of the
Congress for and towards them, and to cultivate harmony and friendship between them and the white people and to give Congress the
most early intelligence of any interruption thereof or of any disturbance which shall arrise [sic] and which you cannot quiet.[73]

Morgan was empowered to persuade Indian leaders of the "good wishes and
good intentions" of Congress. Furthermore, he was given authority "to cultivate
harmony and friendship" between Indians and white people. If conflicts arose
that Morgan could not resolve, he was directed to contact Congress as soon as
possible.

    To keep the council fires of peace burning brightly required an extraordi-
nary effort, at a time when threatening clouds of war hung heavy on the horizon.
The peace and liberty of the Indian people were in danger of being disturbed
by conflicting outside forces. Beyond the threats of British officers, Tory
conspirators, violent frontiersmen, and greedy land speculators, Indian societies faced internal perils. Dependence on trade with whites for gunpowder and
metal products imperiled their economy and their national security. President
Hancock advised Morgan:

    Acquaint the Indians that Congress have formed the best plan they
    could devise to import foreign goods for their use, & have neglected
    no probable means to procure them in time; and if they should not be
    supplied so soon as they may be wanted, the misfortune is to be
    ascribed to the common enemies of them and us [the British], who by
    obstructing our trade as well as in numberless other instances are daily
    injuring and distressing both; but that we have well grounded hopes
    of speedy relief; In expectation of which and of greater advantages in
    prospect the present inconveniences are born more patiently.[74]

Hancock suggested ways to pacify the Indians and indicated what they might be told. In reference to Indian concerns over shortages of supplies, Hancock suggested that the Indians be informed of congressional plans "to import foreign goods for their use." If foreign trade was obstructed, Morgan was to blame their "common enemies." This phrase implied that the British were enemies of both the Americans and the Indians.

Despite President Hancock's talk of opening trade and commerce, the fact remained that he could barely keep General Washington and the Continental Army supplied. If the Indians could not obtain the goods they wanted from the Americans, they would have no choice but to trade with the British at Fort Detroit and Fort Niagara. And if the British supplied the Indians with gunpowder, tribesmen would be expected to hunt more than game animals. Morgan's experience in the Indian trade would be critical in handling the commercial needs of frontier communities. Congress was aware of these potential difficulties, for President Hancock specifically cautioned Morgan to implement equitable measures for conflict resolution:

> All differences and disputes, that shall happen between the Indians and the white people, you will have adjusted and determined in the mode prescribed by a resolve of Congress of which you have a copy. And you are directed in a particular manner to prevent as much as you are able any impositions upon the former, by those who deal with them.[75]

There were hundreds of traders, soldiers, missionaries, and settlers who interacted with the Indians. Morgan's task would be to mediate between them and the Indians to preserve peace. Hancock counseled the young Indian agent to treat the Indians fairly, and to try to get them to adopt the ways of colonial farmers and welcome farmers and craftsmen who wanted to settle among them:

> Treat all those people, who you may meet with kindly and hospitably; inspire them with sentiments of Justice and humanity, and dispose them to introduce the arts of civil and social life and to encourage the residence of husbandmen and handicrafts men among them.
>
> Advise the Congress from time to time of all occurences, that may, in your opinion, deserve their attention.

> By Order of Congress
> John Hancock President[76]

Thus Morgan was officially empowered to serve the cause of the American Revolution. The young man embraced the opportunity to play a key role in the creation of a new nation; he was willing to give up his lucrative business as a partner in one of Philadelphia's leading merchant houses and to assume the work of an Indian agent.

Before the special courier returned, Morgan wrote a brief reply to Hancock:

> President of Congress:
>
> Carlisle April 22, 1776
>
> Sir:
> I have just now had the honour to receive the instructions of Congress . . . which they may be assured I will strictly observe; and that my attention, as I have now no other business to the westward, shall be devoted to the publick [*sic*] service.
>
> Isaac Still, the Interpreter, being taken ill with the smallpox at a Mr. White's, twenty-two miles on this side of Lancaster, I have left some money, and necessary directions for the care of him and his family, until further orders from the Commissioners.
>
> I am, with the greatest respect,
> your most obedient and very humble servant,
>
> George Morgan[77]

Morgan's service in the Revolution demanded a commitment to his fellow patriots. The American unification for independence was considered radical and illegal by most British authorities. Revolutionaries ran the risk of being tried, convicted, and executed for acts of treason against the British mother country.

With his revolutionary orders in hand, Morgan set out to attempt his mission. He and White Eyes continued their trek westward, scaling five chains of mountain ranges called the Appalachians. The further they rode from white settlements, the more dense and verdant the forest grew. The top of the "Endless Mountains" unveiled a panoramic view of the frontier. Green valleys and fertile plains extended for hundreds of miles beyond misty white horizons. From a high vantage point, one might envision an ancient land on the brink of a new age.

Chapter Two

MENACHK-SINK
The Establishment of the
First U.S. Indian Agency at Fort Pitt

AFTER RIDING WEST from Philadelphia for thirteen days, traveling almost three hundred long, arduous miles across the Appalachians, White Eyes and George Morgan coaxed their horses through Stony Creek on the last leg of their journey to Menachk-sink.[1] The April breeze was refreshing as they crossed the Hills of Laurel, an ancient symbol of truce. They camped for the night in the forest and pressed on early the next morning for Indian territory.[2]

Young Morgan had learned much about war and peace in early colonial–Indian affairs from his neighbor and fellow member of the American Philosophical Society, Benjamin Franklin, and from the veteran trader George Croghan. Morgan knew a great deal about the era of nonviolence promoted by Quaker Governor William Penn and the Lenape Sachem Tamanend, who had dreamed of a world without war.[3] They had succeeded for almost a generation, until the "treaty that was never signed and never broken" was finally destroyed by those who lusted for power and land. In the course of westward expansion, Indian nations along the seaboard, including the Lenni Lenape, were dispossessed. As a young child, White Eyes had seen his people forced from their homelands in Pennsylvania and Delaware at gunpoint. The elders often recalled the beautiful seacoast where their grandparents had long prayed toward the "Land of the White Eastern Light." But then came the long walk, the humiliation and injustice of being driven like cattle from the land of their ancestors.

As White Eyes and Morgan rounded Chestnut Ridge, they neared Bushy

Run, the site where many Indians had taken their revenge against the British Army in the 1755 battle known as Braddock's Defeat. When the Moravian missionary John Heckewelder later rode across this battleground he noted in his diary: "We suddenly found ourselves on the field of Braddock's defeat. A dreadful sight was presented to our eyes. Skulls and bones . . . lay scattered all around; and the sound of our horses' hoofs continually striking against them, made dismal music."[4] The scene was a haunting reminder of the deadly toll of war. Morgan's mission, as defined by John Hancock, was to try to defuse the potentially explosive situation by negotiating peace and neutrality with the Indians through wampum diplomacy.

Following the muddy trail near the banks of the Monongahela, White Eyes and Morgan cleared the last rise; there became visible the spike-tipped palisade protecting the perimeter of Fort Pitt, Morgan's new headquarters.[5] For more than five thousand years, the native people had prized this wedge of land between the Forks of the Ohio; the ancient ones named it Menachk-sink, meaning "Place of the Fork."[6] The point remained a formidable strategic bastion flanked by the Monongahela and the Allegheny rivers.

George Washington had targeted this location two decades earlier as a place of absolute strategic importance. When he first gazed upon the Forks in 1753 as a twenty-one-year-old explorer, Washington recorded in his journal: "I spent some Time in viewing the Rivers, & the Land in the Fork, which I think extreamly well situated for a Fort; as it has the absolute Command of both Rivers."[7] Washington's interest in locating future sites for forts predated the period when he would send armies into the frontier for a military takeover. Washington's training in the British Army, coupled with his observation of hit-and-run frontier tactics during the French and Indian War, prepared him to become commander-in-chief of the Revolutionary Army. Now as he turned his military skills against the British Crown, Fort Pitt on the Forks of the Ohio represented the new gateway to the West. In the course of twenty-five years of westward expansion, control of the Forks had shifted from the Indians to the French, who fortified the point with the construction of Fort Duquesne. After the British stormed the point, they expanded the fort and renamed it in honor of William Pitt, first Earl of Chatham. Now Fort Pitt was in the hands of the Americans, and General Washington held ultimate command as the Revolutionary War was heating up.[8]

Beyond its military importance, Fort Pitt played a valuable role as a strategic economic center in the future development of western land interests. Washington possessed a financial stake in the future of the West because he had invested heavily in unsecured grants to lands long claimed by Indian nations. Over the years, he had amassed a portfolio of lands deeded by the British to fellow veterans of frontier wars. From the perspective of disgruntled veterans, the British Crown had passed out grants to Indian lands with clouded titles in exchange for their years of dangerous service. When Washington bought up the veterans' grants at discount rates, it appeared to be an act of generosity. However, Washington's transactions were more likely shrewd investments, since the value of these lands would soar during his lifetime. In the eyes of western real estate speculators—both British and American— rich western lands were like a treasure chest of uncut gems that would be awarded to the victor of the Revolution.[9]

Because of the Indians' concern for the future of their sovereign territories, White Eyes and the powerful leaders of the western Indian nations generally distrusted land speculators. Morgan was not an innocent bystander; he had inherited a share in a Pennsylvania land company with interests in West Virginia. This potential conflict of interest threatened to undermine his credibility among the Indians and competitive Virginians. During the Revolution a moratorium (wisely) was placed on conflicting land claims around Fort Pitt.[10]

During the previous decade, Morgan had developed a reputation as a good man who traded fairly with the Indians. He was only twenty-three the first time he led a pack train across the Allegheny Mountains to deliver supplies vital to the Indians. His future as an Indian agent—and perhaps his very life—depended on his reputation, associations, and friendships. Much of his time as an Indian trader had been spent next to the fort at his trading post in Pittsburgh, then a frontier village with a reputation as one of the "wildest towns in the West."[11]

As White Eyes and Morgan neared the fort, the gentle sounds of the forest gave way to the noisy rabble of trappers, traders, mountain men, and off-duty soldiers. The scents of roast venison and rum filled the air when Morgan and White Eyes arrived on the evening of April 29, 1776, shortly after sundown. They rode cautiously between the rows of log cabins, passing storefronts and riding through the throngs of half-drunken frontiersmen. Simpson's saloon and the whorehouses were the most popular hangouts. White Eyes, like other Indian leaders who tried to prevent their young people from indulging in these vices, disliked the bad influence of the town:

> Here they barter their skins, dried meat, and fresh game for strong drink. They put a barrel of it in their canoes. . . . Now all the men become filled with strong drink. They yell and sing like demented people . . . drunken fights, debauchery and crime [are] caused by goniga-nongi [strong drink].[12]

Pittsburgh epitomized life at the fringes of so-called civilization. It was a place where people of many backgrounds—English, Scotch–Irish, German, French, African, Spanish, and Indians from various nations—all crossed trails. Among these men and women were friends who would risk their lives for Morgan and the Revolution. However, also among the crowd were British spies who would plot to undermine his mission. Whom could he trust? Morgan's success would depend on his ability to identify his enemies. Each new face demanded scrutiny. But after such a long, hard journey, he and White Eyes were too exhausted to think of much more than a good night's sleep. Inside the fort they could rest at ease.

White Eyes and Morgan rode down a winding path to the gates of the star-shaped fortress. Fort Pitt was an awesome sight. The huge structure covered eighteen acres and was surrounded by a deep moat like a European castle. Here, on the site of an ancient Indian village, the British had constructed in 1761 the largest fortification in America. The dual stockade, coupled with a brick-covered stone wall seven and one-half feet thick and fifteen feet high, stood in defiance of any cavalry charge, Indian attack, or artillery bombardment. The soldiers inside could be starved out, but their defenses would never be blasted away. In this center of power Morgan would maintain his headquarters for the next three years.[13]

White Eyes and Morgan entered the fort by crossing the first drawbridge to a triangular island called a *ravelin*, then crossed a second drawbridge where an archway opened into a broad parade area. The master of the guard barked orders to the sentries, who had to walk nearly half a mile to complete a circuit atop the walls around Fort Pitt. The interior walls were bordered by long narrow buildings, still scarred from a rain of Indian fire arrows that once threatened to burn the fort to the ground.[14]

White Eyes and Morgan rode the final two hundred feet under the watchful eyes of uneasy soldiers. Only a skeleton force of one hundred rowdy Virginia volunteers held the fort at that time, under the command of Captain John Neville. The commandant's aristocratic red brick mansion stood in stark contrast to the austere barracks. Morgan walked up the cut stone steps and was greeted by Captain Neville, a forty-five-year-old former sheriff from Winchester, Virginia. Since he had assumed command shortly after the battles at Lexington and Concord, Neville's war experience had been a nightmare. Plagued by desertions and disease, the captain was testy over the constant brawls between his soldiers and the trappers. Waiting for the real war to erupt on the frontier placed everyone's nerves on a razor's edge.[15]

Morgan showed Captain Neville the instructions from Congress, penned by

John Hancock and sent by special courier. Neville and Morgan would work closely during the following month. The travelers were hungry and tired. Vegetables from local gardens, fruit from the orchards, wild game from the forest, and giant sturgeon and catfish from the river made a formidable feast. The hearty meal was toasted with rum and port. The men spent the night in wooden bunks, four-by-six-feet in size, the rooms warmed by stone fireplaces.[16]

Early the next morning Morgan assumed command from temporary Indian agent Richard Butler, an Irish immigrant who had grown up in the Cumberland Valley at a time when Daniel Boone ventured through the Gap. Butler and his brother, William, joined forces in 1770 to carry on trade with the Indians. Richard was a staunch patriot who stood up for the American cause when Lord Dunmore and the Tory doctor John Connolly were caught scheming to incite the Indians against the revolutionaries. Butler was preparing to embark on a career as a revolutionary officer, which would eventually earn him a commission as brigadier general and a future appointment as Superintendent of Indian Affairs.[17] Morgan and Butler were both strongly opinionated, and the day would come when the two would lock horns.

Before departing for the East, Butler handed over to Morgan a satchel containing secret intelligence reports. Morgan sat down to read the latest news. The first document was Butler's recent report to Pennsylvania Congressman James Wilson:

> Sir,   Fort Pitt   8th April, 1776
>   I send this by express to inform you that Kiasola [or Guyashusta, a Seneca chief representing the Iroquois Confederacy in the Ohio River Valley] & two other Indians, Messengers [arrived] from [British Colonel John] Butler, the King's agent at Niagara. . . . Kiasola delivered the wampum he [received] with a speech from the [Iroquois] Six Nations desiring his attendance at the [British] treaty to be held at Niagara & one from [Colonel John] Butler & the [British Commandant] to the same purpose.[18]

The British were one step ahead of the Americans in organizing a treaty conference with the powerful western Indian nations. Morgan would have to act quickly, or the British agents could seize the advantage by convincing the Indian leaders to attack the American revolutionaries.

During the next few days, Morgan worked at a feverish pace on a plan to infiltrate—and perhaps sabotage—the upcoming British treaty conference at Niagara Falls. If the Americans could not prevent the British from meeting with the Indians, at least some counterintelligence scheme might be set into motion. Morgan hoped for cooperation from key western Indian chiefs.

Guyashusta, the most powerful Iroquois in the Ohio River Valley, was a possible American ally. However, the Seneca chief was a shrewd leader who knew how to sit on the political fence and play both sides to his advantage. According to Richard Butler's appraisal of Guyashusta:

> He seemed determined to go although he asked Capt. Neville and my advice, & as we saw it would be of no use to attempt to stop him, we thought it best to send him off pleased; therefore delivered him a string [of wampum] with a small speech from yourself [Congressman James Wilson] & the other Commissioners.[19]

Morgan was determined to intercept Guyashusta and implement a more active plan. Indian leaders must realize that the American Indian policy firmly advocated peace and friendly relations, and that the Indians must stay out of the Revolutionary War.

The groundwork for the American Indian peace policy had been laid at the Fort Pitt treaty conference in 1775, where Guyashusta strongly supported the Seneca nation's call for peace. Richard Butler believed their chief remained an advocate for peace and neutrality: "[Guyashusta] desires me to inform you that he has but one heart & that he will say or do Nothing Contrary to his Engagements last fall that he does not doubt [the advantages] of preserving peace."[20] To be of "one heart" implied loyalty to one's convictions. Guyashusta eloquently expressed his sentiments in favor of the Americans, but Morgan knew the chief's first loyalty would be to the Senecas, as "Keepers of the Western Door" of the Iroquois Six Nations.

The Iroquois Grand Council recently had met at Onondaga, capital of the confederacy. They sent a special ambassador with news that a bountiful supply of vital trade goods was now being offered by the British after the recent defeat of Benedict Arnold and the American forces in Canada. The American agent reported:

> The Onondaga man, one of the messengers says that after Montreal was reduced there came a great [quantity] of goods round by the North side of Lake Ontario and . . . to Niagara & that great presents will be made there to the Indians. . . . I think they now know their own Importance & Expect their friendship shall be purchased as well as Courted. . . . The Indians are not a little alarmed . . . at the Exorbitant

Price of goods that our [American] traders charge them & the great scarcity of ammunition & goods.[21]

Morgan realized that the economic realities of the frontier posed perhaps the greatest threat to peace. A serious interruption of trade relations could impoverish Indian nations.

The British were investing heavily in Canada to ensure a strong northern defense. Their agents would do everything in their power to obtain supplies so the Indians would trade with, and perhaps go to war in support of, the British. Some Indian leaders, like Guyashusta, might seek to capitalize on the opportunity by courting both sides. British and American agents recognized that the powerful Indian nations represented a key force in the balance of power. Although many elders advocated peace, they were determined not to be taken advantage of by American traders.

Wars have long attracted opportunists in search of quick profits. Some American merchants were inflating the prices of goods, as demand soared to support a wartime economy. Some traders wondered why they should risk their lives carrying supplies to the Indians, when the American and British armies offered a ready market. From Morgan's perspective, the Indians must be supplied, or their growing hunger might force them to choose sides. The Americans tried to appease Chief Guyashusta with hopeful promises:

> Friend [Guyashusta], it is true it is hard just now, but our great men [have] your welfare at Heart as well as Ours & will remedy that Inconvenience as soon as possible. [The reason for the high price of goods] is that we used to buy our goods from the people of England, but the present dispute hinders us. [However, we] have sent to France and other [countries for trade goods, so we soon] will be both plentifully and reasonably supplied.[22]

This was the best the Americans could offer at that time. How long would the Indians wait before they were forced to take action? Surely Indian women were reminding their husbands of their families' needs.

The American agent also reminded Guyashusta of past treaty promises confirming peaceful U.S.–Indian relations. At the 1775 Fort Pitt Treaty the Seneca chief had been entrusted with a great belt of wampum that symbolized the American peace proposal. Guyashusta and Captain Pipe, the Lenape Wolf Clan chief, were supposed to carry the great belt to the leaders of the western Indian nations. Furthermore, they were to convince the Indians of the good intentions of the Continental Congress.

To support the diplomatic effort, pro-American trader John Gibson had been recruited as a temporary Indian agent and official observer. Chief Guyashusta now explained why the peace plan had failed:

> He said he was disappointed by Capt. Pipe who was to meet him at the Moravian [missionary] town as Mr. Gibson told him, but did not, then he says Mr. Gibson promised to send two of the Delawares from Newcomer's Town to him to the Wiandot town to go with him, but after his waiting there ten days, and saw no likelihood of their coming, he thought it too difficult to attempt alone & resolved on coming back.[23]

The American peace plan was in danger. Morgan would have to open new diplomatic relations, because other western Indian nations had not received the American peace belt.

Morgan could only speculate on why the previous year's plan had failed. He did not know that Captain Pipe, a major rival of White Eyes, was secretly leaning toward the British. Gibson's hands were full with another, more dangerous assignment. Virginian slave masters had ordered him to supervise the return of their "property," runaway African slaves who were given sanctuary by the Shawnee and other tribes.

Guyashusta also may not have tried very hard to carry the belt to the other nations because his rivals might have teased him about being an American puppet. In following a safer course, Guyashusta covered himself politically by sending messengers with a simple report on what the Americans proposed:

> [Guyashusta] says he called some of the Wiandots together & charged them to be careful of their young men & see that they did no mischief . . . he sent a message by a Wiandot man to the Western Tribes to inform them that there had been a council here & that what was said was very good & that the message was to go to the Picts & then to the Northern Tribes & relate what he was charged with.[24]

Guyashusta's account differed completely from the rumor circulating on the frontier. A report had spread back to Philadelphia that he was reluctant to proceed because some the northern warriors were threatening to cut the great belt into pieces. To cut up a wampum belt symbolized the total rejection of its accompanying message. If this rumor were true, Morgan's peace mission could be in serious trouble.

In hopes that it was not too late to mend diplomatic relations at a time when the Indians were planning to meet the British, the American Commissioners for Indian Affairs sent to Guyashusta the following message:

> Brother,
> As you are called on by your Nation & by the Headmen of Niagara, we think it very right that you go to hear what they have to say, as it is highly proper that men of sense should be at all such meetings. Hearken to no speeches that tend to disturb the Peace of the Country. We also think it very proper that you take the Great Belt [of Peace] & show it to the Six Nations & the Northern Tribes [so] they may know the sentiments of the United Colonies.[25]

The American commissioners were trying to make the best of the situation. By sending in Morgan with a thirteen-diamond wampum belt, they hoped chances of keeping peace on the frontier might be improved.

They sent a similar speech to White Eyes's Lenape nation. Expressed in the eloquent style of traditional Indian oratory, the appeal called upon their Indian "brothers" to uphold the 1775 Fort Pitt Treaty:

> Hold fast the great Belt of Peace & Friendship that you took hold of last Fall, & [do] not let it slip out of your Hands. . . . Consider us and you as One People. [Do] not hearken to any speech that the [British] Commandants of either Detroit or Niagara may send as they only mean to Deceive you. [Please] sit still & Enjoy Peace.[26]

The American commissioners were trying to discredit their British enemies. In the propaganda war, each Indian person was forced to decide who was telling the truth and who was lying.

For men like Morgan, who implemented American policy on the frontier, the job was extremely dangerous. Anti-American sentiments were growing. The Virginian demands for the return of runaway African slaves remained one of the hottest issues of the day. Many Indians in the Ohio River Valley took a stand against slavery, condemning the practice as against the divine plan of the Creator. They contended that the African and Indian peoples were made equally by the same Creator who made the white people. And what about the children who were born from interracial marriages? People whose children were in danger appealed for mercy and justice.

Despite attempts by Congress to spread goodwill, anti-American sentiments were growing. The issue of slavery not only threatened the union, but also endangered the lives of American agents carrying out American policy. Pro-American Indian traders John Gibson and William Wilson found themselves caught in the middle of the controversy. Wilson, being half Shawnee, was trying to balance between two worlds. Gibson, while attempting to gather runaway slaves, was threatened by the powerful Cayuga Chief Logan Thachnechdorus, the famous Iroquois leader in Ohio who had "glutted his vengeance" after the murder of his wife and family.

In 1774 Logan's family was shot to death by white frontiersmen. His campaign for revenge resulted in Dunmore's War along the Ohio River. Gibson's confrontation with Logan opened old wounds. Peace on the frontier would be difficult for Morgan to maintain. Guyashusta warned Gibson that his life was in danger: "I then asked how Mr. Gibson came to be threatened by Logan. He said it was a report that came to the Wiandot Town by a Mingo man & he thought it might be so, therefore had word sent to Mr. Gibson for fear, & that he might take care."[27] Gibson and Wilson, despite these threats, carried out their dangerous mission of gathering runaway slaves and captive whites.

On April 9, 1776, Gibson, Wilson, and a delegation of Shawnee had arrived at Fort Pitt with the runaways and captives. They were turned over officially to Captain John Neville. Many had been living among the Indians for a long time and loved their Indian families. One of the hardest things for non-Indians to accept was that the former white captives preferred living among the Indians and actually had to be dragged back to so-called civilization. The Shawnee, under protest, had fulfilled their treaty obligations.

Captain Neville kindly granted the group one last day to say farewell to their Shawnee families and friends:

> April 9th this day, Mr. John Gibson arrived with several Shawnees to whom Capt. Neville spoke & informed them that tomorrow he would receive the White prisoners and slaves. Other [accounts] relative to them I refer you to Mr. Gibson . . . who writes by this express which I have detained four days [waiting] for his coming.[28]

Gibson's letter to Congress, in which he accepted an officer's commission in the Continental Army, briefly outlined the fulfillment of his duties. He soon departed eastward for a career on the front lines, where he was destined to win laurels for his patriotic service.

In contrast, Captain Neville and Colonel William Crawford, western land agent for George Washington, focused on the frontier to pursue a different opportunity: speculation in Indian lands. Men who schemed to control western lands sought investors in powerful political positions, including American Indian Commissioner John Harvie. One of Morgan's greatest challenges would be to mediate the conflicting interests of his superiors and the Indians. Morgan and his predecessor, Richard Butler, both insisted that real estate developers not threaten the tenuous peace on the frontier.

Morgan read with concern Butler's final urgent report to President John Hancock and the Continental Congress, which pointed out recent treaty violations:

> Sir, there has been a survey made by Colo. William Crawford, of the long island four miles below this place in the Ohio [River], for John Harvie & Charles Syms & Captn. Neville, which is in direct breach of the Treaty of Fort Stanwix & the treaty of last fall, & the consequences is much dreaded by the many people of these parts, as it is a precedent that will be apt to be followed by many.[29]

If political and military leaders were allowed to break the law, the general populace would surely follow suit. Once the legal lock was broken, the gateway to the West would be flooded with settlers, and the result would be war on the frontier. Morgan realized that if the Americans broke the treaties and encroached on Indian lands, the "Covenant Chain of Friendship" would be shattered and the Indians would fight to defend their homelands.

The land in question was called Killbuck's Island, after Lenape Chief John Killbuck, grandson of Sachem Netawatwees.[30] Lenape ambassador Chief White Eyes made it clear to Congress that the Lenape nation demanded official recognition of its national boundaries. For eight years, since the signing of the 1768 Fort Stanwix Treaty, colonial officials had promised that no lands would be taken beyond the Ohio River. This natural barrier stood as the latest boundary in a series of invisible lines drawn farther and farther west.[31]

The mere act of surveying Indian lands could be turned against the American cause by British propagandists, who might point to this as evidence of American deceit and trickery: "It will furnish the office of the [British] Crown now going to treat with the Indians with arguments that may be much to the dishonour & disadvantage of the Colonies; how we should be punctual in observing our treaties with them, if we expect they should with us."[32] The integrity of the American Revolution was on the line. Other nations were watching carefully to determine the character of the new nation.

If American revolutionaries failed to live up to their principles, American ideals would sound hollow and hypocritical. Could the Americans be trusted? If foreign nations were to have faith in America and respect American treaties, American leaders would have to keep their word. International respect was something that had to be earned. The American Revolution represented one of the most daring political experiments in world history. Leaders of the Indian nations also were closely watching the Americans to see if they were men of deeds, as well as men of words.

As agents of the Continental Congress, men like Morgan and Butler had to demonstrate regard for sovereign Indian rights to earn respect from Indian elders. The work for peace demanded courage, creativity, and respect for human rights. The present security of the nation, Butler warned Congress, rested upon the preservation of peace between Americans and American Indians: "I hope Sir you will not take amiss my reminding you that a strong attention to Indian affairs is absolutely necessary as the peace of this frontier country depends on their being quiet & be assured that I will use my utmost endeavours for the service of the Colonies."[33]

Butler was firm in his opinion that correct handling of Indian affairs was "absolutely necessary" for peace on the frontier to be maintained. He warned that the peace might be broken not by the Indians, but by white frontiersmen. He estimated that many men throughout the frontier presently supported the British: "P.S. I am sorry to inform you that party spirit prevails here as much as ever & indeed through the country in general."[34] If Butler were accurate in his assessment of the degree of pro-British loyalty, American Indian agents like Richard Butler and George Morgan could be considered by the frontiersmen to be their enemies. Butler voiced his patriotic convictions: "I am determined to do my duty & say nothing about these matters. As I know now they stand in your opinion as well as the authors of the Disputes & Rebellions."[35]

When Morgan assumed from Butler the awesome responsibilities of the Indian agency, he became privy to a recent intelligence report delivered by William Wilson, a young, half-Shawnee trader who recently had returned from a conference with several head chiefs in his mother's country. They had chosen Wilson to escort a group of white captives back to their families, as part of the terms of the 1775 Fort Pitt Treaty.[36] Before addressing this matter with Morgan, Wilson relayed one of the most serious Indian grievances—the destructive influence of the white man's liquor.

Morgan might have to confront the most corrupt inhabitants of the frontier, the white bootleggers, who were characterized by Shawnee Chief Gieschenatsi, "Hard Man," in a satiric barb:

See them coming into our towns with their rum! See them offering it to us with persuasive kindness! Hear them cry, 'Drink! Drink!' and when we have drunk, and act like the crazed, behold these good whites, these men of a benevolent race, standing by, laughing among themselves, and saying, 'Oh, what fools! What great fools the Shawanese are!' But who made them fools? Who are the cause of their madness?[37]

Few people had acknowledged publicly how liquor was used as a weapon against the Indians. Unscrupulous traders brought rum to cheat the Indians out of their furs, speculators toasted heartily to gain title over Indian lands, and colonial officials used liquor and presents to gain the necessary approval from alcoholic puppet chiefs.[38]

Morgan knew that liquor was destroying the moral fabric of Indian society. During the next few years he wrote letter after letter to the Indian commissioners in Philadelphia, advising them to order a state of prohibition on the frontier, but the barrels of rum continued to flow. Hard Man was concerned that liquor would be used to evoke in his brothers a fighting spirit which would cause them to fight in the white man's war. He called for Indians to stay out of the war and to promote peace.

Another major grievance was revealed in the biting remarks of Hard Man:

The whites tell us of their enlightened understanding, and the wisdom they have from Heaven, at the same time, they cheat us to their hearts' content. For we are as fools in their eyes, and they say among themselves, the Indians know nothing! The Indians understand nothing![39]

Years of injustice, humiliation, and exploitation had left more than injured feelings. Hard Man claimed to have been cheated by the so-called men of God, who piously looked down on Indians. He cried out against those who subjected Indians to unfair treatment: "Because they are cunning enough to detect the weak points of our character, they think they can lead us . . . and deceive us as they please, even while they pretend to seek our good."[40] How would Morgan gain the trust of a people who had been deceived again and again? Even the best of intentions could be viewed with suspicion.

On April 24, 1776, Hard Man and the two senior Shawnee chiefs, Cornstalk and Grandfather Pethamoh, sent a declaration of peace to the Continental Congress. One week later William Wilson, their interpreter, delivered their statement to Agent George Morgan:

Brothers, Here are now present two of our Chiefs who were at the great Council last Fall at Pittsburgh when you told us to sit still & to live in Peace. We listen'd to you & think of nothing else. And as the Road between us has been opened & lately cleared, we desire it may remain open & clear for our young Men.[41]

Since Morgan was planning to travel into Indian country to meet with the Shawnee, Lenni Lenape, and other western nations, the news of open diplomatic channels was welcome. All sides realized that the lines of communication had to remain intact to prevent wild rumors, childish pranks, or acts of sabotage from mushrooming into a full-scale uprising. The Shawnee chiefs recounted their mutual treaty vows:

And as you desired us last Fall at the great Council, not to let go the Chain of Friendship but to hold it fast, even tho' one or two foolish young Men may do what is wrong, so we now desire you to be strong & do the same, & that you will not listen to foolish stories as you desire we will not.[42]

When Hard Man had gone to the autumn peace talks at Fort Pitt, his attendance had marked a dramatic shift in Shawnee policy toward the European invaders. During the previous 150 years, the Shawnee had been dispossessed time and time again. From the period of their peaceful settlement along the southern Atlantic seaboard, the Shawnee had been fragmented into mobile groups of resistance fighters.[43] Most of their warriors living in the Ohio River Valley were veterans of the French and Indian War, Pontiac's War, and, most recently, Dunmore's War of 1774, when the British governor of Virginia had ordered an invasion of Ohio.[44]

Since the time when Daniel Boone led the first settlers through the Cumberland Gap, Shawnee warriors had tried to force them out of the intertribal hunting grounds in Kentucky. From the perspective of the Indian nations, these white squatters were illegal aliens who disrupted the delicate natural balance of the forest by chopping down and burning the trees and killing too many animals; they also threatened the lives of Indian people.[45] The Shawnee first asked the settlers to leave, then tried to scare them out, and finally attacked the stubborn holdouts. Scores of whites were killed, but many were arrested and brought before tribal councils to be judged for their crimes. Some were executed for murder; others were forced to run the gauntlet for lesser offenses; yet a surprising number were judged victims of circumstance and were adopted into Indian families to take the place of departed relatives. Most were treated with such human kindness and personal respect that the majority actually came to prefer the traditional lifestyle of Indian communities and ignored all opportunities to return to white society. As already noted, this fact often baffled other white people, who assumed their way of life was superior to all others.[46]

When the Shawnee sent back the so-called white prisoners with William Wilson under the terms of the 1775 treaty, they also sent a message to the Continental Congress to prove the sincerity of their pledge for peace:

> Brothers, As it was your desire that we should restore the Prisoners we had among us, we have spent the greatest part of the Winter in getting them together, & have not had time to think of anything else. We have sent them to Pittsburgh from whence we daily expect our people who went to conduct them there. We expect they will bring us some News from you, but if they do not we shall continue to sit still until we hear from you.[47]

The Shawnee chiefs were very cautious. They did not send back all the white people. Perhaps they could not all be located, as was publicly stated, but the chiefs may also have recognized that the continued presence of some whites would serve as a future bargaining chip. Hard Man explained that the remainder would be returned when the Virginians followed through with their promise for a second round of peace talks:

> Brothers of Virginia, You told us to send all your Flesh & Blood—all that we could find we have sent to you, but some have run away, & others we have since collected. We will deliver them all up, when they are called for. You told us last Fall to expect to see you at Pittsburgh this Spring, where you would finish an everlasting Peace with us. This we still look for, & wait to hear from you. We hear bad reports often but we will believe nothing but what comes from the Congress.[48]

At this time Congress was secretly designing a plan to drive an army through Ohio to take the British stronghold at Fort Detroit.[49] The British were simultaneously developing plans to lead an army with Indian allies through Ohio to take Fort Pitt, and then to sweep eastward to Philadelphia while the British Navy attacked the coast.[50] The Indian nations of the Ohio River Valley were caught in the middle, with the Americans in the East, the British in the North, the Spanish in the West along the Mississippi, and settlers to the South, whose numbers grew as people fled into the wilderness to escape the war.

Most Indian leaders reviewed all the possible alternatives in search of the best way to prevent their young warriors from becoming involved in the white man's war. Swift runners carried the latest news from village to village in an extensive communications network that had been functioning since ancient times.[51] Each runner was trained from childhood not only in physical endurance but also in precise memorization of long messages. The Indians carefully monitored both American and British troop movements, increasing fortifications, and arms build-ups. Indian ambassadors met regularly with American and British agents to hear both sides of what was happening.

During the spring of 1776 representatives from western Indian nations united in council to debate their positions on the Revolutionary War. Some war chiefs wanted to join the British, some called for an alliance with the Americans, but the majority agreed to remain neutral as long as the whites didn't invade Indian territory.

Men of mixed ancestry, like William Wilson, served important roles as translators and messengers, as Morgan realized while he listened intently to Wilson's report of his activities in Shawnee country:

> After I had left the Town & come about 12 miles, the White Fish sent a Messenger after me to return back, which I did April 26th, 1776. The Chiefs then took me to the Council and desired me to write the following Message to the [Continental] Congress; Brothers, The White Fish, one of our Head Chiefs is just return'd from the Wiandot Town where there were several Nations met in Council & we all determined to sit still & not to meddle in your Quarrel, we will look only to you.[52]

The Shawnee council had chosen one of their most experienced elders, White Fish, father of the principal war chief, Cornstalk, to attend the Indian conference sponsored by their "Uncles."

The Wyandot, an Iroquoian people known to the French as the Hurons, had long held a key position in the complex inner workings of Indian politics around the Great Lakes. Their traditional leader, called the Half King, was endowed with the right to light the intertribal council fire. Both the Shawnee and the Lenni Lenape were beholden to the Wyandot; when the two eastern nations were pushed off their lands and forced across the Appalachians, the Wyandot council had generously granted them new homes in Ohio and rights to hunting grounds in Kentucky.[53] The Wyandot nation once stood thirty thousand strong, but generation after generation of bloody battles with the rival Iroquois Six

Nations, coupled with waves of fatal epidemics, had made them increasingly dependent on British support.

Only a few miles from the main Wyandot town was Fort Detroit, a formidable British stronghold protected by eighty cannons and encircled by a moat twelve feet deep and eighteen feet wide. From this strategic vantage point on the western tip of Lake Erie, Governor Henry Hamilton extended the realm of British influence through a network of spies, informers, and soldiers who operated for hundreds of miles in every direction. Rewards of gunpowder, wampum, and rum were offered to chiefs who sent runners with information from distant centers of Indian power: the Iroquois confederacy from the East, the Wabash confederacy from the West, the Seven Nations of Canada from the North, and the Cherokee and Muskogean nations from the South. [54]

One major issue on which the British and the western Indian nations were in total agreement was their staunch resistance to possible American invasions through Indian territory. The Shawnee chiefs took a firm stance on this point in their message to the Continental Congress: "Brothers, We will be glad if you send no Army to Detroit, nor suffer any to cross the Ohio [River]. The Commandant at Detroit tells us the same [as you did] vizt: to sit still & not to meddle in the Quarrel between you. You may rest satisfied we will sit still, & mind our Hunting."[55]

Before the war was over, Governor Hamilton at Detroit would acquire a reputation as the "Hair Buyer," a man who reportedly paid for American scalps. In spring 1776, however, he was encouraging the Indians to remain neutral while the British refortified their defenses; their supply lines through the St. Lawrence River were threatened by the attempted American siege of Quebec led by Benedict Arnold and Richard Montgomery.[56] Hamilton's secret plans coincided with Dr. John Connolly's scheme to lead legions of warriors in a coordinated attack against the American revolutionaries. If influential chiefs could be convinced that the Americans were actually planning to invade and to conquer Indian country, the tribal councils might consider the benefits of attacking the Americans by surprise.

Morgan was unaware of secret invasion plans being devised by Congress as he continued to review the Shawnee message:

> Brothers, Two of our Grandfathers, the Delawares, arrived here this day from the Wabache. They tell us the Indians there have heard from you, through the Cherokee Council, and are desirous to take hold of your Chain of Friendship & to listen to none but you, and particularly

as you have assured us that none of your people shall cross the Ohio
[River] or settle on any of our Lands. This Declaration gives pleasure
to us all & we desire you to be strong in it. We wait to hear from you
& till then shall sit still.[57]

The Delawares, the Lenni Lenape, also were known as the "Grandfathers,"
keepers of ancient records that preserved their long tradition as peacemakers.[58]
While White Eyes had been in the East lobbying the Continental Congress to
keep the peace, two other Lenape ambassadors, perhaps Welapachtschiechen
and Gelelemend, had traveled to Illinois territory for peace talks with the
powerful Indian confederacy of the Wabash. News from the southern colonies
had been transmitted from Cherokees in Georgia to Cherokees south of
Kentucky, who sent messengers westward to the Wabash. The lines of communication extended across the Mississippi throughout the Great Plains, from the
Lakota in the north, to the Pawnee, Cheyenne, and Arapaho in the center, and
to the Kiowa, Comanche, and Apache in the south. From these distant Indian
nations, information was carried along old trade routes that wound their way to
the Pacific Coast. Few white people ever realized the extent of the elaborate maze
of communication lines that had been long established by Indian nations.[59]

If Morgan were to succeed in his mission, he had to tap into these
communication lines to gain advance notice of information vital to the interests
of the Revolution. He was encouraged by the favorable report from the
Shawnee, but he had had enough frontier experience to know how suddenly
political winds could change. His most important initial step at Fort Pitt was to
establish and to expand an effective intelligence network. Morgan invited
several men to his quarters, where he interviewed them one by one as prospective agents, spies, and informers. He needed to keep a watchful eye not only on
the British and the Indians but also on rowdy American settlers and traders
whose indiscriminate actions could touch off a series of revenge killings. He had
to judge each man on his ability to survive in the wilderness, his skill in slipping
behind enemy lines, and most of all, his loyalty to the cause of the Revolution.
Morgan could not possibly foresee that some of these men would eventually
defect to the British side and bring down upon the frontier a reign of terror
almost unsurpassed in American history.[60]

Inside his headquarters at Fort Pitt, Morgan discussed the state of the
frontier with William Wilson and White Eyes, who remained at the fort for days.
Although some intelligence would have to be kept highly secret, he confided a
great deal to them. However, he also asked the two men to step outside while he

interviewed prospective agents. The first man who walked through the door was a twenty-six-year-old fur trader named Simon Girty. He spoke with a rough Scotch–Irish brogue and was dressed in tattered buckskins. He was described as a "jovial ne'er-do-well rough, hard-drinking frontiersman, physically attractive but not always dependable."[61] Simon was fluent in several Indian languages, and he knew the backwoods like a seasoned veteran. As children, Simon and his two brothers, James and George, had been captured during the French and Indian War. Simon was only one year old when he was carried away from his parents' Pennsylvania farm to a Seneca Iroquois village; James had been taken by the Shawnee, George by the Lenape. Simon had been too young to remember his real mother and father. He was adopted by a Seneca family, given the name Katepacomen, and raised like any other Indian child.[62]

Morgan had met Simon when, as a teenager, he had come with his Indian brothers to the trading post at Pittsburgh. Ambitious to prove himself as a man, Girty was driven by a desire to become a military officer. Morgan was convinced that he possessed the nerve and stamina to carry out the most dangerous tasks. After a long private discussion, Morgan called William Wilson back into his office to witness Simon Girty's oath of allegiance to the United Colonies:

> To Simon Girty, Pittsburgh May 1st, 1776
>
> The Public Service requiring an Interpreter for the Six Nations [Iroquois] at this place, you are hereby appointed to the employment at the rate of five eights of a Dollar per diem during good Behaviour or the pleasure of the Honorable Continental Congress of their Commissioners or agent for the middle Department.[63]

Simon Girty was willing to risk his life for less than a dollar a day not for the money, nor for the cause of the Revolution, but because, like many adventure seekers, he was attracted by danger and the prospect of glory. Morgan's orders continued:

> You are upon all occasions to use your utmost endeavours to promote the Public Tranquility & maintain a good understanding between the United Colonies & the Indians; and inform me of all Intelligence which may come to your Knowledge. You are to obey all my lawful & reasonable Orders during my Agency & faithfully to keep secret all private Councils between the Commissioners, Agents, Indians, & yourself so far as the Public Good shall require it.[64]

Again, the relationship depended upon mutual trust. A man like Girty would be operating throughout the frontier. While he was at the fort, Morgan could monitor his activities more closely. Rapid communications were imperative: "You are to visit & confer with all Indians who shall come to this Post so early after their arrival as possible—to learn their Business here, & to immediately acquaint me."[65]

The ever-present danger of violent confrontations prompted Morgan to give Girty a sharp warning. One foolish shot from either side could jeopardize the safety of their entire peace mission:

> In case of any Discontent among the Indians you are immediately to inform me and you will take care that none of them be insulted or injured by the Inhabitants, & be equally cautious to prevent any of them injuring the Inhabitants.
> You are upon no account to be concerned in Trade . . . unless when call'd upon to see Justice done between the Traders & Indians.
> For extraordinary services you shall be entitled to further reasonable allowance as the case may be.
>
> Given under my hand at Pittsburgh
> this first day of May, 1776.
>
> Sign'd George Morgan
> Agent for the United Colonies[66]

Morgan would have to keep a tight rein on the ambitious young frontiersman. In the meantime he would have to provide one useful service himself. Even though Simon Girty could speak several languages, he could not read nor write. He signed his enlistment paper with an "X":

> Pittsburgh
>   May 1st, 1776
>
> I do engage on my part to fulfill & comply with all the Directions to the utmost of my Ability.
>
> in the Presence of me:
> Sign'd Wm. Wilson   Simon "X" Girty
>
>   his mark[67]

The document was witnessed by Morgan's other assistant, William Wilson. Wilson remained valuable to Morgan not just as an interpreter but as a crucial political figure. He was a personal friend of Chief White Eyes and several Lenni Lenape leaders, and his mother was Shawnee, which endeared him to Chief Cornstalk and his council of elders. Since these men and women were prominent figures in the American Indian peace effort, Wilson would play a key role in helping Morgan to carry out his mission.[68]

Morgan's third assistant was a young Shawnee named Silver Heels. His late father, who bore the same name, had accompanied Morgan in 1770 on a five-boat flotilla down the Ohio River on the "Grand Illinois Venture." The journey had ended in tragedy with the ghastly murder of the elder Silver Heels. Morgan had recorded an account of this in an earlier journal: "May 9th, 1770—Last Night I was disturb'd with the Indians quarreling in my Yard & about 2 O'Clock was . . . informed by the Guard that Silver Heels [the elder] was kill'd by [Andrew] Montour."[69] The murderer, a half-French and half-Indian trader, stole away into the night, never to be prosecuted. Morgan tried his best to treat the wounds of his Shawnee friend, but the gashes were too deep:

> I ordered him to be immediately brought to my Room & prepared Dressings for his Wounds[,] but in Vain as his Pulse ceased to beat....He [received] three very deep Stabs of a large Knife in his left Breast. The Villain then cut him open across his Breast from which his Intrails came out. Thus [he] expired without even a Knife to defend himself....[Silver Heels was] a most faithful & brave Friend & Ally.[70]

Andrew Montour still roamed freely throughout the northern frontier. Although Morgan never sent the young Silver Heels where he might fall prey to Montour's blade, or on any other mission where his life might be in danger, he was not afraid to risk his own life. Before the year 1776 came to an end, Morgan would be confronted once again by Montour's evil deeds.

Chapter Three

DARK CLOUDS OVER THE REVOLUTIONARY FRONTIER
British, American, and Indian Intrigues

ON APRIL 23, 1776, at the village of the "Beautiful Spring" deep in the Ohio frontier, "Honest John" Anderson, a Quaker Indian trader, scribbled a hasty note, warning that many Indians were threatening to join the British unless "White Eyes comes soon among these people. I fear they may be led to join the other Party—they seem [agitated in] great confusion & have false reports every day."[1]

The urgent message was carried from the heartland of the Lenape nation eastward to the Fort Pitt headquarters of George Morgan. White Eyes prepared to return to his people at once. But before the chief departed on his journey, Morgan penned a letter to the Reverend David Zeisberger, leader of the Moravians, the same group of German Protestant missionaries that had worked among the Indians for over twenty years. The letter began:

> Pittsburgh May 3d, 1776
>
> Reverend Sir,
> Captain [Chief] White Eyes the bearer of this has been in Philadelphia all the last Winter. He has behaved with remarkable Regularity during the whole time & has impress'd the people with favourable Ideas of the Delaware [Lenape] Nation of your Mission of which he spoke on all occasions with the highest respect.

> Enclosed are two packets of letters which I have had the pleasure
> to bring up for you. If I can render you or your Mission any services,
> it will make me very happy & I beg you will command me.[2]

Morgan hoped his kind gesture would begin a mutually beneficial relationship. As avowed pacifists, the Moravians could aid Morgan's mission to preserve peace on the frontier. Furthermore, they were privy to much inside information, because Christian Indians confided their secrets to the men in black gowns.

The missionaries preserved detailed records in their diaries, an exhaustive source of intelligence information that could prove invaluable to the American revolutionaries. Morgan tried to coax the missionaries into becoming secret informants for the revolutionary cause: "If you can inform me what you apprehend to be the real disposition of the Western Indians & of anything material which passes among them, you will render a very acceptable service to our Country, & your name shall never be made use of."[3] If the Moravians would agree to become American spies, Morgan could expand his intelligence network through their many frontier missions. They were promised anonymity, since the British would condemn such activities as acts of treason punishable by imprisonment or death.

To sway the Moravians to the American side, Morgan emphasized the higher purpose of his mission of peace:

> I have it in charge from Congress to cultivate Harmony between the
> Indians & White Inhabitants & to encourage them to promote the Arts
> & useful Knowledge among them.
>   Will you oblige me by pointing out to me the most probable
> means of being useful in this way? And I particularly need to know if
> you can hear of any discontents among the Savages & what they arise
> from.
>
> I am &ca.
>
> George Morgan
>
> To the Rev. David Zeisberger,
> Missionary among the Indians,
> At Wethexthuppek on Muskingum River[4]

Morgan needed to find out the true allegiance of the western Indian nations: who were his allies, who were his enemies, and who simply wanted no part in the

Revolution? He hoped the Reverend Zeisberger would be able to find out if the great confusion in the Lenape villages was more than an internal feud.

Morgan's overriding concern was the possibility that the British had completed the reinforcement of their defenses in the North and were launching a propaganda campaign in advance of an invasion. A two-pronged attack could come from the two main British strongholds: Fort Detroit, where Governor Henry Hamilton was in charge, and Fort Niagara, where Colonel John Butler was planning a major British–Indian conference.[5]

The British fortress at Niagara, a stone stronghold built by the French in 1726, loomed high above the waters of Lake Ontario.[6] From this mighty bastion, the Indian fur trade was controlled, with trade routes radiating out around the Great Lakes. Just as this network could be used for productive trade, it could also be utilized for destructive, war-related purposes. British gunboats now patrolled the Great Lakes. On the eastern and western tips of Lake Erie, two strategic seats of power, the British were mobilizing their forces for a dual offensive. Morgan badly needed to infiltrate behind British lines. Advance intelligence was vital.

General George Washington, who had recently moved his forces north to New York, recognized these British frontier forts as a dangerous military threat. Washington wrote to President John Hancock and pushed for a change in policy that would allow him to recruit Indian warriors and to attack the British on the western front:

> In my opinion it will be impossible to keep [the Indians] in a state of Neutrality, they soon will take an active part either for, or against us, and I submit it to the consideration of Congress, whether it would not be best immediately to engage them on our side to prevent their minds being poisoned by the Ministerial Emissaries. Would it not be advisable to send a sufficient force from the back Counties of Pennsylvania, to take possession of the Garrisons of Niagara and Detroit?[7]

Washington was short of troops and expressed concern about protecting his flanks; however, the drastic changes he proposed regarding American Indian policy were diametrically opposed to the peace plan advocated by Morgan. Many tribal elders at present favored the Americans, because the Americans were not trying to recruit young Indian men into the war. Since the Indians were part of sovereign, independent nations, involvement on either side of the war would mean they were acting as mercenary soldiers. Furthermore, if they did try to recruit Indians, the Americans would be violating their solemn promises to respect Indian neutrality. Most traditional elders would not breach their vows of peace, which had been pledged in prayers through the sacred pipe.

By contrast, men of war, such as General Charles Lee, regarded treaties as temporary expedients to be discarded when advantage could be gained, as he indicated in a letter to John Hancock: "May I, without presumption, urge to the Congress the absolute necessity of straining every nerve to possess themselves of Niagara at least, if not Detroit?"[8] If the Americans recruited Indians and sent an invading army through Indian country to attack British forts, promises made at the Fort Pitt treaty conference in 1775 would be broken. Many Indian people would consider the betrayal proof that the Americans could never be trusted. The peace chiefs would then lose their authority to the war chiefs, and the Americans might have to contend with a full-scale Indian war. The Continental Congress, therefore, decided to give George Morgan a chance to negotiate a treaty of peace.

Morgan knew many of the western Indian chiefs personally, and he still supported a policy that would keep them out of the white man's "family quarrel." The Seneca chief Guyashusta was now preparing to attend the British–Indian conference at Fort Niagara, and Morgan was determined to have one of his men accompany the chief. The Americans needed an inside man to obtain firsthand intelligence on the British–Indian strategy.

Morgan sent word for Paul Long, a trusted patriot, to come to his headquarters. They discussed the risky mission. If his identity were revealed, Long's life would be in danger. He would have to enter the walls of the fortress, avoid detection as an American spy, and memorize all that he saw. Being fluent in several Indian languages, Long would be able to understand the representatives from different Indian nations. Morgan impressed on him the importance of absolute secrecy. Finally, Long agreed to take the following oath of allegiance:

Pittsburgh   May 3d, 1776

In consideration of Thirty Dollars I engage to go hence & proceed to Niagara so as to attend there during the approaching Treaty with the Indians, & I will after that is over return from thence to this place with all Dispatch & communicate to the Agent for Indian Affairs all the Intelligence I can learn or hear there or on the Road. I further agree that if I divulge the Business I am sent upon to any Person whatsoever, my Wages shall be forfeited, & be on Oath—or that I am engaged by the Agent on any Business or pay.

Sign'd Paul Long[9]

Morgan began preparing Long for his mission to Fort Niagara, where inevitably he would be interrogated upon his arrival by Governor Hamilton or Colonel Butler. Long would have to be persuasive to fool a British officer. John Butler was at present the senior ranking agent in the British Indian Department, since Superintendent Guy Johnson and Deputy William Claus had sailed for England. With these two veteran agents temporarily out of the picture, the Niagara conference was Butler's grand opportunity to prove his superior influence over the western Indian nations.[10]

John Butler was a wealthy, hard-driving, and ambitious man. Since the death in 1774 of Sir William Johnson, the old patriarch of British–Indian affairs, an intense rivalry for power had emerged between Colonel Butler and Johnson's descendants.[11] Butler had helped Sir William wrest Fort Niagara away from the French in 1759, when he was only twenty-four years old. He now considered the stone fortress his personal domain. A fierce Loyalist, Butler also had a vendetta against His Majesty's rebellious subjects for personal reasons. His wife and children were now being held hostage at the American fort in Albany, New York. If Butler could convince the Indian warriors to join the attack, perhaps his family could be rescued.[12]

The area between Fort Niagara and Fort Albany was the heartland of the Iroquois Six Nations. The Onondaga, the "Fire Keepers," represented the executive branch, and their head chief, the Tatodaho, stood as the leader of their strong government. The Mohawk and the Seneca, the "Elder Brothers," were organized along lines similar to those of a senate. The Oneida, Cayuga, and Tuscarora, the "Younger Brothers," were the Iroquois "house of representatives." This three-part system was structured as an open, participatory democracy. Governed under the "Great Law of Peace" and united beneath the Tree of Peace, the Haudenausaunee Grand Council represented one of the oldest governments on their sacred Mother Earth. The Iroquois Confederacy remained dynamic, extending the "shade" of their peace like the Great Tree from which "White Roots" grew in the four cardinal directions.[13]

Perhaps the reason they survived so well was that the Peacemaker, a profound spiritual man, came among their people at the time of a bloody war, like the Revolutionary War. The Peacemaker convinced the warriors through logic and spiritual means to bury their weapons of war symbolically and to plant atop them a Tree of Peace. Part of the "Great Law of Peace" was that women be granted a type of veto power over war. This divine act reflected the philosophical approach of the Iroquois toward peacemaking.[14]

Iroquois diplomats, like Guyashusta, would represent their united nations.

at the Niagara treaty council. Their political decisions exerted tremendous influence not only over thousands of people in their own nations but also over scores of other nations, who looked to them as their "Uncles." If the Iroquois Grand Council advocated neutrality, a majority of their Indian allies would join them beneath the Tree of Peace. However, if the Iroquois Women's Council believed that their safety was endangered by the Revolution and the Grand Council decided that they must fight for survival, then the war hatchet would be dug up and the war chiefs would lead the attack.

Morgan reasoned that his peace mission would gain credibility if it were supported by traditional Indian leaders. For many years Morgan had nurtured a close friendship with Chief Guyashusta, and now it was crucial to strengthen the bonds of friendship. Over the decades Guyashusta had risen to great prominence as a persuasive negotiator in wampum diplomacy. In 1753 he had accompanied George Washington and Christopher Gist, who were serving as surveyors for colonial authorities at a time when the French controlled the forts along the Allegheny.[15] After the defeat of British General Braddock in 1755, Guyashusta traveled to Montreal, where his anti-British feelings were reinforced. He was a friend in peace but a powerful foe in times of war.

When the western Indian nations had been cheated and pressured by encroachment on their lands, not even Sir William Johnson could prevent the annihilation of British strongholds. Guyashusta reportedly played a decisive role in uniting a mighty Indian alliance during Pontiac's War for independence.[16] But Guyashusta's record as a warrior should be balanced against his reputation as a peacemaker. His dedication to ensuring the welfare of his people impressed colonial officials at a series of frontier peace conferences held from 1759 to 1768. As political administrations changed and Indian policies were rewritten, Guyashusta and other Indian leaders had to alter their positions toward foreign governments.

By 1776 the political tables had been turned once again. George Washington was the American commander-in-chief against the British, and the French were allied with the Americans. On May 2 King Louis XVI of France approved a request for one million livres' worth of military aid for the American revolutionaries.[17] French and Spanish assistance would help break the British embargo and reopen the flow of trade goods to the frontier. This development would help to quiet Guyashusta's major grievance against the Americans: the severe shortage and exorbitant prices of vital supplies. However, it would be months before the necessary goods could arrive, so Morgan had to delay the time for the proposed American–Indian treaty conference. This was particularly worrisome, because the British were well supplied and were preparing a huge distribution of presents to the Indians who attended the Niagara Treaty Council.

In light of the revolutionaries' shortfall, Morgan had to depend on his skill in the art of wampum diplomacy. When Guyashusta visited Fort Pitt, he was greeted warmly with all the respect due a head of state. To symbolize the call for peace between the American United Colonies and the western Indian nations, Morgan showed Guyashusta an impressive wampum belt. It featured thirteen diamonds to symbolize the thirteen colonies, and each diamond was woven among twenty-five hundred wampum beads into a broad belt six and one-half feet in length. This great wampum belt was designed to impress the Indians with the American commitment to peace and to invite the chiefs to the upcoming American–Indian treaty conference. Since Guyashusta was preparing to leave for the British treaty conference at Niagara Falls that was to start on May 29, Morgan sent the belt directly to the Grand Council of the Iroquois Six Nations.[18]

Morgan's first week on the job had been a whirlwind of activity. He laid the groundwork for the American intelligence network, opened the lines of American frontier diplomacy, and began the work of peace to prevent the horrors of war with the Indians. All this was only the beginning. Many long hours would be needed to map out his strategy for peace. When Morgan was not meeting with key people, he was writing diplomatic correspondence, policy statements, and letters to Indian leaders. He recorded everything in his private journal. Morgan also began composing a series of messages to be carried north by Chief Guyashusta, Paul Long, and Simon Girty. To learn the source of confusion in the West, Morgan drafted responses to Shawnee Chiefs Cornstalk and Hard Man. And most immediately important, Morgan sought to discover how Chief White Eyes was handling the warriors of the Lenape nation who were threatening to join the British.

Suddenly, on the morning of May 7, news of a tragedy reached Fort Pitt from the East. The grieving wife and son of Isaac Still, the trusted Indian interpreter, arrived and asked for refuge. A few days after Morgan and White Eyes had visited the family, Isaac Still died of smallpox. The news brought terror to the frontier outpost, since it meant the threat of an epidemic of a deadly disease against which there was no known defense.[19]

A second alarming report arrived that day: White Eyes's horse, which had been given to him as a present by one of the congressional Indian commissioners, had been seen in the possession of one Watson from Ligonier. White Eyes himself was nowhere to be found. If the chief had been murdered, chances for peace would be even slimmer. [20]

On May 10 the trader John Anderson slipped another message out of Lenape country. Indian ambassadors from the powerful confederacy along the Wabash, Tippecanoe, and Vermillion rivers in Indiana had arrived, but White Eyes reportedly was still missing:

> Four Messengers have been there from the Oubache [Wabash] confederacy. [They] know what pass'd [regarding the 1775 American Treaty conference] at Pittsburgh last Fall. They say, "[We hear] you have had many Meetings & we desire you [will tell us] whether you have made friendship with the white [people] there so strong that we can take hold of it.[21]

The alliance of the Wabash stood as a mighty force in the area between the Ohio and the Mississippi rivers. As a group of Algonquian tribes, they addressed the Lenni Lenape as their "Grandfathers" in diplomatic affairs. And, in keeping with tradition, since the Lenni Lenape had taken hold of the Covenant Chain of Friendship, their lead would be recognized by related tribes who considered themselves the Lenape's "Grandchildren."[22] The Wabash at present were look-ing to the Lenape for a way to improve relations with the white people: "A dark Cloud [exists] between us & them which we wish to have dispell'd, tho' they [do not] seem to pay any regard to us."[23] John Anderson reported on the meeting between the Wabash ambassadors and the Lenape council. He stressed that it was important for White Eyes to return soon so that he could attend to the diplomatic affairs of his nation at this critical time: "The Delaware [Lenape Chief White Eyes], one of their Head-men, was still at Philadelphia & so soon [as he has] return'd, [the Wabash] should hear from [the Lenape]."[24] Morgan had no way of knowing whether White Eyes was dead or alive. It would be difficult to dispel the dark cloud of white–Indian tensions without assistance from this influential chief.

In this time of peril, when Morgan most needed help in the work for peace, he thought of Alexander McKee, a local man who spoke several Indian languages like a native, had twenty years of diplomatic experience among the western Indians, and had married into the Shawnee nation. In addition, he served as the justice of the peace for several backwoods counties of western Pennsylvania. Morgan had known this modest Irishman for years; they were good friends. There was only one problem: Alexander McKee also held a captain's commission as a British Deputy Superintendent for Indian Affairs.[25]

McKee was aware that the Americans had not yet declared their indepen-dence and that some still hoped for a reconciliation. However, wars usually divide men along ideological lines, and the American Revolution was no exception. For the present, McKee had not indicated which side he would support, if the Revolution reached the point of no return.

The issue came to a head on May 10, when the guards at Fort Pitt apprehended and searched a man named Molloy. A Tory sympathizer who had recently been imprisoned in Fredericktown, Maryland, and then transferred to the Philadelphia jail, Molloy had been the cellmate of Dr. John Connolly, the notorious British agent charged with conspiring to incite a major Indian uprising. Patriot soldiers found in Molloy's possession "a message from Doctor Connolly to Mr. McKee to forward certain orders & Intelligence to Detroit."[26] Connolly had written the letter back on December 16, 1775, but it had taken almost half a year to reach McKee:

> I have more to say to you than I will commit to paper. I mentioned you in proper terms to General [Thomas] *Gage* [the British commander in chief]; and had done something to your honour and advantage could I have got up safely to *Detroit.*
> Captain *Lord,* who was to have acted under me, will now be in danger at the *Illinois.* I have, therefore, desired him to push down the *Mississippi,* and join the Earl of *Dunmore*... send an *Indian* express with my letter to Captain *Lernoult,* at Detroit. .... I write in bed, with two sentinels at the door, with hourly apprehensions of death.[27]

Molloy was locked up in the Fort Pitt brig, which already held Samuel Sample, a Connolly cohort considered "dangerous to the safety of America."[28]

With Connolly in prison and Guy Johnson, former British Superintendent for Indian Affairs, in England, Colonel John Butler had taken command of Indian affairs for the British. Butler had busied himself in early spring organizing the Niagara Treaty Council and had written to McKee for assistance at that time:

> Dear Sir, Niagara, 29th February, 1776
> I was appointed to the Care and Charge of the Indian Department in Col. Johnson's absence. He has desired me to write you to meet me here. . . .[Your orders are] to attend a meeting we propose holding at Niagara the beginning of next May. Your knowledge in the Indian Affairs, your hitherto undoubted zeal for his Majesty's Service and the duty you owe to government make your presence absolutely necessary.
> Please to make my compliments to Col. [George] Croghan.
>
> John Butler[29]

George Croghan, the grand old trader and McKee's predecessor as deputy Indian agent, had intercepted the letter and turned the matter over to the Committee of Inspection, the local civil authority. The committee was composed of a syndicate of twenty-eight influential land owners that included Croghan and his partner, Thomas Smallman, the present chairman. These men had devoted their lives to building an empire based on western land holdings, which the Revolution threatened to tear apart. The competition for lands was not only between British and Americans; the colonies of Pennsylvania and Virginia also held conflicting claims for the lands around Fort Pitt. If Great Britain won the war, loyalist land claims would override the revolutionaries' grants; but if the Americans won, the Virginians and the Pennsylvanians would continue their dispute. For these wealthy land barons, millions of acres and huge fortunes were at stake during the American Revolution. Many were shrewdly sitting on the political fence, not committing themselves and their fortunes to either side. Since many of their land claims were often contested by the Indian nations, men of great influence among the Indians, like Morgan and McKee, were key figures in determining the outcome of these disputes.[30]

The Committee of Inspection summoned McKee to attend a hearing on the matter of his position in light of his relationship with the British high command. The committee's official report of April 9, 1776, attested to the facts:

> Major Smallman communicated to the Committee a Letter from Col. Butler at Niagara Agent for Indian Affairs in that Department to Alex McKee Esq. the Agent for this place. It appears that a treaty was intended to be held in behalf of the Ministry at Niagara and that Colonel Butler and Col. Caldwell ordered Capt. McKee's attendance and assistance.[31]

If McKee attended the conference and helped enlist the Indians for the British, their armed forces might take Fort Pitt and declare martial law. These land barons might then find their property and fortunes at risk. They could not take the chance. Therefore, the committee ruled:

> Resolved that Mr. Alexander McKee be required to give his Parole in writing that he will not transact any Business with the Indians in behalf of the Crown or Ministry, that he will not directly or Indirectly correspond with any of the Crown or Ministerial officers, nor leave the neighbourhood of Fort Pitt without the Consent of the Committee of West Augusta, and on his refusal to do so that he be committed a close

Prisoner till the General Congress be acquainted and direct what further is to be done.

Thomas Smallman
Chairman[32]

McKee signed a document that day, placing himself on parole. He cooperated fully, agreeing to cease his activities in Indian affairs for the British. He was released on his own recognizance after conceding full jurisdiction to the committee.[33]

The matter eventually was also debated in the Continental Congress, with the following result:

> Resolved: That the Congress relying on the integrity and honour of Captain *A. McGee* [*sic*] order that he be permitted to go at large, on giving his parole to the Committee of *West-Augusta* not to engage or be concerned in any measure injurious to these Colonies, by stimulating the *Indian* Nations to make war against them, or otherwise.[34]

Was McKee sincere about his promises, or was he involved in Dr. Connolly's plot to incite the Indians to go on the warpath? Morgan was still in the dark about the extent of the scheme. If McKee had been sending secret intelligence reports to Niagara, Colonel Butler might be on the lookout for Morgan's spy, Paul Long. Long's mission to infiltrate the Niagara conference would be sabotaged.

The weight of responsibility on the young Indian agent's shoulders grew heavier as he tried to maneuver responsibly through the complexities of Indian affairs. Morgan's only instructions had been the general advice of John Hancock and the Continental Congress, and he was at present financing his agency with his own money. The situation had quickly become so critical that Morgan wrote a letter in May 1776 to the Indian commissioners to make certain his actions conformed with the wishes of Congress: "In order that I may not be misunderstood, I [request you will] draw up such Instructions together with such further powers as you shall think expedient."[35] (Over a month would pass before Congress responded, in June 1776.) Morgan then informed them that he had invited a delegation of chiefs to come to Fort Pitt and that they needed to set the best date for the American–Indian peace treaty conference:

> Three or four head Chiefs of the Shawnese and as many of the Delawares [Lenapes] are to meet me here the 10th of next Month. If

you have anything particular to say to them be pleased to give me
directions in time by the Bearer.

George Morgan

P.S. Mr. Butler is continuing to tell the Indians he is the person to do
Business with them & to send Messages among them, you will find to
be very prejudicial, & I believe will have no good Tendency.[36]

Not only was Morgan plagued by the uncertainty of future British plans and
the desperate need for money to support his own agency; Fort Pitt was also on
the verge of running out of gunpowder. A two-pronged British attack from the
North and the West was possible, and news could not travel fast enough for
Morgan to know that the Redcoats were also currently mounting an offensive in
the South.

A few days previously British troops led by Sir Peter Parker and General
Cornwallis had landed at Cape Fear, North Carolina, five hundred miles
southeast of Pittsburgh. To crush the "lawless Oppression of the Rebels,"
General Gage in 1775 had ordered John Stuart, the southern superintendent
for Indian affairs, to wait until the best moment to strike, then to enlist the
Indians "to make them take Arms against His Majesty's Enemies."[37] General Henry
Clinton and Stuart sought to unite British regulars with the Indians and Tory
frontiersmen for a combined thrust through the backcountry. For this purpose,
twenty-one horses carried more than five thousand pounds of gunpowder to the
Cherokee to put the plan into motion.[38] Some southern Creek warriors also were
persuaded to fight for the British. Then, from the North, a delegation of anti-
American Lenape, Mohawk, and Shawnee rode south through Kentucky, the
international Indian hunting preserve, and delivered to the Cherokee the black
wampum belts that declared war against the Americans who had encroached
upon their lands.[39]

While the British military leaders were seeking to pull the Indians into the
forefront of the battle, General George Washington slipped away from the main
lines one night in May to make a personal appeal for congressional approval of
enlistment of Indian warriors. Joined by Major General Gates and Brigadier
General Mifflin, Washington appealed to a select committee of Congress to
support his plan for securing the frontier. Under the pressure of intense
lobbying, Congress yielded to the wishes of the military. The resolution was
written by Edward Rutledge and presented by Thomas Jefferson on May 25,
1776, to the General Assembly. It said, in part:

It is highly expedient to engage the Indians in the Service of the
United Colonies. . . .
[Recommended 1.] That the Commrs. at Albany be directed to use
their utmost Endeavors to procure the Assistance of the Indians to act
against the Enemies of these Colonies, that they apply themselves
particularly to induce the Indians to undertake the Reduction of
Niagara.[40]

A drastic shift in policy was being proposed. Washington and his generals
wanted to seize the vital stronghold at Niagara before the British could make a
move. But the trail to Niagara led through Iroquois country. If the Iroquois Six
Nations refused to allow the Americans free passage through their sovereign
lands, an invasion might drive them to side with the British. How did Washington and his supporters plan to persuade the Indians to side with the Americans?
Blood money was one element of the plan: "As an Enducement so to do they
engage in Behalf of the Congress to pay them £50 Pennsylvania Currency for
every Prisoner [Soldier of the Garrison] they shall take and bring to head
Quarters or to the said Commissioners, and the free plunder of the Garrison."[41]
This bounty was a considerable sum of money at a time when the base pay for
American soldiers was only five dollars per month.

Not only did Washington want to target Niagara for attack by the Indians
covered by the Northern Department, headed by General Philip Schuyler; the
select committee also recommended that George Morgan's Indian agency be
directed against Detroit: "[Recommended 2.] That the Commissioners in the
Middle Department be directed to use their best Endeavors to procure the
Assistance of the Indians under their Care, that they prevail upon them if
possible to undertake the Reduction of Detroit."[42]

To build a force of Indian mercenary soldiers, Washington and the committee recommended that military recruiters be hired and richly rewarded for
inducing the Indians to join in the fighting:

[Recommended 3.] That the Commrs. in each of these Departments
be directed to employ one or more able Partisans, whom the Congress
will liberally reward for their Exertions in the Business. . . .
That the Commander in Chief be authorised and instructed to
employ in the Continental Armies a Number of Indians not exceeding
[blank] to be upon such Terms as he shall think most beneficial for
the United Colonies.[43]

The number of Indians to be recruited was left open. Washington at present had only eighty-three hundred soldiers in New York who were ready for combat, and they were scattered on Long Island and Manhattan Island. The troops were rowdy and undisciplined, and Washington had had to declare a prohibition against alcohol in an attempt to keep his men sober.[44]

There were also complaints against American soldiers who went skinny-dipping, "and run to the houses naked with a design to insult and wound the modesty of female decency."[45] The "Ladies of the Night" in Manhattan were doing a brisk business, as Colonel Loammi Baldwin wrote to his wife:

> The whores . . . continue their employ, which is become very lucrative . . . I was never within the doors of . . . any of them except in the execution of my duty as officer of the day . . . [and I] broke up the knots of men and women fighting, pulling caps, swearing, crying, "Murder!".[46]

An army of soldiers, whether American or British, marching into Indian country to attack frontier outposts would pose a real danger to the well-being of Indian communities. The enlistment of young Indian men would inevitably split their councils. The Americans' reputation among the Indians for not embroiling them in the "white man's family quarrel" would be sacrificed. For over a month Congress debated whether to make the change in policy, finally resolving, in June, to modify only the amount of the bounty. Congress was not only giving Washington a free hand; it raised the sum to one hundred dollars for every commissioned officer and to thirty dollars for each private soldier. It also broadened the scope from the specific targets of Niagara and Detroit to encompass the entire American frontier. The American agent in the North, General Philip Schuyler, would soon be ordered to incite the Indians into attacking the British. Even though the Americans had not yet declared independence, their actions clearly pointed toward a declaration of war.[47]

Unaware of Washington's new plan, Morgan made the final preparations for the departure of Paul Long on his undercover mission to the Niagara treaty conference. When word arrived in mid-May that Chief Guyashusta of the Seneca nation had just departed northward, Morgan immediately sent Long to catch up with the Indian delegation. Long would be much safer traveling with an Iroquois chief to the "Great Falls." However, if Washington's plan to incite the Indians to attack Niagara were to be implemented quickly, Long would be in danger of being killed by his own side. He could not carry identification papers for fear of being exposed to the British as an American spy. Morgan would not learn if Long survived his mission until more than two months later.

In the meantime, Morgan decided to send Simon Girty, the young man who had grown up among the Iroquois, north to the Six Nations to deliver the Great Peace Belt. Girty was also to translate an American peace proposal Morgan had written to the Grand Council at Onondaga:

> The United Colonies to their Brethren the Six Nations upon the Waters of the Ohio—Brothers, When we met around our Council Fires at Albany and Pittsburgh last year we buried all evil thoughts, smoak'd the Pipe of Peace & renewed the Covenant Chain of Friendship which your Forefathers & ours had made.[48]

Morgan opened the oration in a traditional way by recalling past relations. Both governments had vowed in 1775 to preserve the peace between their nations, and the agreements were sanctified through the sacred pipe. The "Covenant Chain of Friendship" represented the original peace agreement, sealed through the smoke of a pipe with a silver chain linked to the stem, symbolizing the prayers for everlasting peace between the Indians and white people.[49]

Morgan then made certain "no rust" had formed on their "Chain of Peace": "We hope nothing has happen'd to change your Hearts, for our's remain strong & we are determined to keep fast hold of the Covenant Chain of Peace."[50] Morgan may have spoken sincerely, but the fact remained that his superiors were not determined to preserve the peace.

Morgan did not know of Washington's intentions, and unleashed a fervent attack against those who tried to destroy the peace: "But Brothers we are told there is a bad Wind blowing your way & that the Evil Spirit is striving to blind your Eyes & shut your ears from all Good & to make Mischief between you & your Brethren of the United Colonies."[51] Who was the "Evil Spirit?" Morgan apparently was referring to the British, who reportedly were trying to persuade the Indians to fight against the Americans. However, now that Congress had approved Washington's request to enlist the Indians, the Americans would run the risk of being cast as the evil force.

Morgan sought to engender warm feelings between the Indians and the Americans in order to dispel the ugly pall of intolerance that had settled over the frontier: "Now as we esteem you just like our own Flesh & Blood being all the Children of this Continent, & want to live in Peace with you upon it forever."[52] If all people had shared these harmonious sentiments and lived up to such high principles, the course of American history would have been changed dramatically. Although the rich North American continent provided enough for everyone's needs, apparently even this bountiful land could not fulfill everyone's appetite for personal gain.

Morgan then explained the purpose of the Great Peace Belt:

> We send this Belt of Wampum to enquire the Truth of what we have heard and desire you will open your Minds to us by a Deputation of your Wisest Men that we may know if you have any just cause of Complaint against us, for if you have, you may rely on our Endeavours to satisfy you immediately on your application, and if you have none we hope you will tell us so that the sorrow may be removed from our Hearts.[53]

Morgan then warned the Indians against anyone who spread negative rumors about the Americans and threatened to disrupt their mutual happiness:

> In the mean time Brethren we desire you to be cautious how you listen to bad Birds who no doubt will endeavour to sing evil stories into your Ears—The happiness of you & your Women & Children as well as that of many other Nations inhabiting this Country depends upon your Prudence at this time—Therefore be strong Brethren in preserving peace.[54]

Morgan believed that the "bad birds," Colonel Butler and the British officers at the Niagara conference, would "sing evil stories in their ears" to encourage the Indian warriors to attack the Americans. Morgan warned the Iroquois that the safety of their women and children would be endangered if they made the decision to become involved in the war.

Morgan had no way of knowing his work for peace was being undermined by Congress even as he directed his words to the head chiefs: ". . . if you have not heard before from us through our Agent to the Northward, We desire this Belt & message may be delivered to the Big Cinder and other Chiefs of the Onondago Council without delay."[55] The "Big Cinder" or "Keeper of the Fire" served as the Totadaho, the head chief of the Iroquois Six Nations. The Totadaho was nominated by the clan mothers and served for life, if he did not jeopardize the welfare of his people. As was true of sachems, he could not dictate to his people, but governed instead through wisdom, humility, and implementing the wishes of his people. In Iroquois society a good leader could never place himself above his people. The Totadaho was said to have "skin the thickness of seven spans," meaning that people could speak sharply to him but that he would not be permanently harmed. In contrast to his people, a chief had to speak with soft words, guiding the people through logic and spiritual means.

Iroquois chiefs were both political and religious leaders, for the tribe did not separate, as the Europeans would say, church and state. The Americans would adamantly demand such a division for their new country, perhaps because the institutionalized churches of Europe had demonstrated that too much power had been usurped during the Inquisition and other periods of persecution, with terrifying results. If an Iroquois chief wantonly abused his power, the clan mothers would have a subchief warn him that his actions were against the wishes of the people. If he did not heed this warning, the clan mothers would strip him of his power, and overnight he would no longer be a chief.[56]

The American Revolution placed tremendous pressure on the Iroquois chiefs, who were responsible for advising their people on the best course for surviving the war. Morgan again warned them not to get involved directly in the war and to choose the path of peace: "We wish our Brothers the Six Nations may deliberate well upon the measures they will pursue, and consider it is Peace we recommend to them. We hope they will not blow the unhappy Coal nor interfere in the Quarrel which now subsists between [your American] Brethren [and] the English."[57] The Iroquois were not strangers to war. They had survived over 250 years of intermittent warfare since their first contact with the Europeans. Wars over the fur trade had been especially divisive, pitting tribe against tribe.

Morgan reminded the Iroquois chiefs that most white people were not corrupt and warlike, as evidenced by the efforts of some white peacemakers: "If they will recollect the Great [progress] we took a few years ago in accomplishing the happy Peace between the Northern & Southern Indians, they must undoubtably think it their duty as well as Interest now to promote Peace between us."[58]

Morgan concluded on a religious note by appealing to the spiritual nature of the Iroquois people, reiterating that both they and other people around the world prayed to the same Creator. If the peacemakers were to survive and the threat of war be averted, divine help would be needed to guide them through this time of peril:

> We pray that the Great & good Spirit who governs every thing in this World may look down with Pity on the Six Nations & grant them his Aid in this good Work.

A Belt of Wampum with
13 Diamonds united 10 Rows 250 long
is 2500———
        Sign'd John Nevill
        Commandant at Fort Pitt

Sign'd Geo. Morgan Agent for
Indian Affairs at Pittsburgh
Simon Girty from Philadelphia
his mark

In the Presence of John Boreman [59]

John Boreman served as a special courier who shuttled messages back and forth between the Continental Congress and the frontier.

Morgan drafted two letters on May 16 for Boreman to carry back to Philadelphia. The first letter was addressed to the American Commissioners for Indian Affairs:

> Gentlemen,
> Although copies of the [West Augusta] committee [reporting the McKee affair] at this place or parts of them have been transmitted to the members of Congress from Virginia, I take the liberty to enclose them to you as very material parts of them relate to the Indian Department. I find the [Indians] are much confused & unsettled in their Resolutions.[60]

If the Indians were confused and unsettled at present, the confusion would be increased when American agents began enlisting them for the war effort, since Morgan's speeches calling for peace and neutrality among the western Indian nations certainly conflicted with the sudden policy shift in Congress.

Morgan asked the commissioners to provide him with the latest news, especially that related to the Northern Department, where two of his men, Long and Girty, were carrying out important missions:

> As the Commissioners of the Northern Department must undoubtedly have good Intelligence from the Six Nations (which has been much wanting here), you will be better able to judge their disposition than I yet can.
> This is of great consequence to know & you will extremely oblige me by communicating to me what Intelligence you may from time to time

receive through that Channel, as the Public Service requires a proper communication between the two Departments.[61]

Morgan was being kept in the dark. During his entire tenure as agent for Indian affairs, he would not receive one letter from General Philip Schuyler, his counterpart in the North. In fact, the reason Congress allowed Morgan to continue to promote peace while others promoted war with the Indians remains a mystery.

Morgan pressed the Congressmen to set the time for the proposed American–Indian peace treaty conference:

> It will be highly necessary when the Grand Belt is forwarded through the Western Nations that a time be fixed for the promised Treaty with them—And for that purpose I recommend that the Chiefs of the Six Nations also be invited . . . two of them of the greatest influence should be requested to accompany the Belt & to call upon Keyashuta [Guyashusta].[62]

In the absence of explicit orders, Morgan had taken bold steps toward promoting peace and neutrality among the Indians. However, he could not set the treaty preparations in motion without an exact date and the necessary funds for sponsoring the conference.

In the meantime, Morgan had continued to cultivate good relations with key chiefs like Guyashusta. The young Indian agent recommended that two influential Indian ambassadors should be chosen to carry the American invitation to the treaty conference: "[Please tell] me . . . what they are to say in particular to the Western Indians which you can direct or leave [to me as] you think [best]. . . .[A Peace] Belt . . . is now in the hand of Keyashuta [Guyashusta who is on the way] to Niagera."[63]

Morgan tried to impress on the congressmen the urgency of the situation. The British were gaining the advantage by holding their treaty conference first; time could not be wasted. Morgan urged his superiors to support his mission:

> This step Gentlemen, I conceive [to be of] the highest consequence & therefore I send the Bearer to get your Answer & Orders as well as to give me Authority to transact such expenses as may be necessary for the Public Service [and General] Orders how to draw for payment. . . . He will [at once return] to send me some Money for the purchase [of supplies], Wages, &c.[64]

Morgan then wrote a more in-depth letter to Congressman Lewis Morris of New York, one of the commissioners for Indian affairs and chairman of the committee that supplied the colonies with ammunition and military stores. Perhaps because Morris had served as a key negotiator during the 1775 Fort Pitt conference, Morgan confided to him more sensitive information:

> Things are not right with the Northern Indians, particularly with the Senecas—I have now two Indians at Niagara attending the Treaty there, and no doubt proper persons are employed from the Northern Department for the same purpose, so that you cannot fail of receiving early Intelligence of the designs of our Enemies there, which as I surmise they are against Pittsburgh.[65]

Morgan suspected that his headquarters would soon be attacked. He warned Captain John Neville, the commandant of Fort Pitt, so that the small American garrison could try to prepare.

Morgan provided Congressman Morris with a brief analysis in order to emphasize the fort's dangerous predicament:

> My reasons are: 1st Their [British] force is sufficient, provided they can gain over the Indians. 2ndly They have Water Carriage all the way except Eight miles. 3rdly There is scarcely powder West of the Mountains sufficient for every man to prime his Gun & only 200 lb. wt. in the Fort here. 4thly They cannot be Strangers to our situation & 5thly It is an Object worthy their Enterprize.[66]

Morgan's first point reflected how important the Indians were in the balance of power. If the British succeeded in luring the Indian warriors to fight for them, their combined forces could paddle down in canoes and overwhelm Fort Pitt, the strategic center of the American frontier.

From this strongpoint, an army of Redcoats and Indian warriors could drive east toward the rebel capital at Philadelphia, severing the supply lines between North and South. Morgan confided to Congressman Morris:

> As this is mere suspicion in me from their having reconnoitered the Carrying place [where the canoes would have to be portaged] & the practicability of these I venture only to intimate it to you. Had I discretionary powers, I would do several things to defeat such a Plan if formed which I cannot now do, nor indeed hardly anything else, except at the risque of bearing the expense myself. I have therefore taken the liberty to point out some necessary particulars for the Commissioners or Congress to instruct me in.[67]

Realizing that if Fort Pitt were attacked his life would be in danger, Morgan referred to his wife and family. He asked Congressman Morris if he might "let Mrs. Morgan know of the opportunity" to send a letter when the special courier next rode west.

Morgan also needed to hear from Congress as soon as possible. A delegation of Indian chiefs was scheduled to arrive within a month, and Morgan was still acting without explicit instructions:

> Between the 10th & 15th [of] June, three or four of the Shawnese Chiefs & as many of the Delawares will be here & I expect the Senecas. I shall therefore depend on you to have the Bearer, Mr. Boreman, dispatched so as to arrive here by the 15th . . . with my Instructions & the time fix'd for the Treaty. . . . It is [of] very great consequence. . . . You also shall see Deputies here from the Oubache Confederacy . . . desiring to take hold . . . of the Chain of Friendship.[68]

Morgan knew his reputation, and perhaps the outcome of the Revolution, depended upon his success or failure.

Careful timing and honest diplomacy were crucial. And all could be lost, complained Morgan, because the former temporary Indian agent, Richard Butler, was refusing to recognize Morgan's authority:

> Mr. Butler [is] continuing to tell the Indians [that he is the] Agent [which] confuses them & makes all concerned appear ridiculous. I likewise flatter myself that Mr. Butler will have advice from the Commissioners not to interfere further in my Department, or I shall have leave to return home after I forward the Grand [Peace] Belt which you may rely on I will do unless Obstacles are designedly thrown in my way.[69]

Morgan suspected that some men around him were working to sabotage his mission. Around Pittsburgh there lurked political enemies, people who profited from war, as well as criminals capable of unbridled violence. Being isolated in a remote area of the frontier, protected by only a small garrison of soldiers who were almost out of gunpowder, Morgan was in a vulnerable position.

Despite the need to reinforce Pittsburgh, a company of Virginia soldiers departed downriver to protect an area near a plantation where employees of General George Washington and other western land developers were carving out settlements on lands long claimed by the Shawnee, Cherokee, and other Indian nations. Morgan tried to make the best of the situation by sending along an Indian messenger to carry a letter to nearby Indian nations:

Captain [Matthew] Arbuckle with a Company of Virginia Forces departed from hence yesterday for the Mouth of the Great Canhawa [Kanawha River], where they are to rebuild the Fort & to remain till further Orders from [the] Convention—I thought it necessary to send an Indian [Silver Heels] with them & a proper Message on the occasion to the Delawares and Shawnese accompanied by one of his officers [Captain John Galloway] which I am sure will have a good effect.[70]

After consulting with Captain John Neville, Morgan decided to take matters into his own hands by personally traveling west and appealing directly to the Grand Councils of the Indian nations.

On May 31, Morgan and Neville sent a seven-row wampum belt and an advance message to the chiefs of the Shawnee inviting them to Fort Pitt for a treaty conference:

Brethren,

We sent you a Message by our Friends, Captain Galloway & Silver Heels, a short time past—We then requested that we might see some of you here about the middle of next month to consult what we ought to do to preserve the Peace between you & us & concerning the matter we spoke to you about last Fall, for we are strong in this good work.[71]

The Shawnee leaders Sachem Kishanatathe, War Chief Cornstalk, Peace Chief Nimwha, and Clan Mother Coitcheleh could be important friends in peace or implacable foes in war. Like the leaders of the Lenni Lenape and the Iroquois Six Nations, these Indian men and women were key figures in determining the future of the frontier.

Morgan and Neville encouraged them to be patient and to postpone their travel plans so that the American peace proposal could be explained before their Tribal Council:

We now conclude to save you the fatigue of this long Journey & particularly at this time as we understand some of you are going to Council with your and our Brothers, the Six Nations at Onondaga, which might prevent your coming at the time mentioned—And as we are very desirous to speak to them before they set off, we hope you will stop them till the arrival of our Agent, Mr. [George] Morgan at your Town.[72]

In the past the Shawnee had been dispossessed from their homelands along the Carolina coast and forced inland to Ohio. They had fought many battles for their independence and did not want to become warriors in the white people's quarrel; but just because they wanted peace did not mean they were not willing and able to stand up and fight for their rights.

Neville and Morgan wrote to the chiefs of the Shawnee:

> We thought it necessary to send [Morgan, so] no time may be lost in transacting the Business we have directed him to do with you & that we may be fully informed by him of your sentiments respecting the messages [of peace] he is charged with—And we are particularly desirous that he should see our Brother Kishanatathe before his departure for the Six Nation Country, as he has something of consequence to communicate to him for your & our Welfare.
> A Belt of [Wampum] 7 rows and 240 long is 1680 [beads]
> Sign'd John Nevill[e]
> Geo. Morgan[73]

Morgan was willing to risk his career and perhaps his life by traveling personally through the frontier. As an agent of the American revolutionaries, if he were caught by the British he would probably be condemned as a traitor, and to the Indians he would be suspect as a representative of the white settlers then squatting on tribal lands. At the same time, Indians who were openly allied with the Americans, such as Chief White Eyes, were vulnerable to the same wrath and might be further endangered by Morgan's presence. But these were risks he had to take. To inspire people with "sentiments of justice and humanity," Morgan would have to earn the Indians' respect as a true man of peace.

Chapter Four

BLACK ROBES IN THE PASTURE OF LIGHT
The Christian Indian Mission

RUMORS OF THE assassination of Chief White Eyes proved false when the old Lenape ambassador arrived safely on the night of May 12 at his village near the forks of the Tuscarawa and Muskingum rivers in the center of the Ohio Valley.[1] Since he had departed without a word after the 1775 Fort Pitt treaty conference and had spent almost six months in Philadelphia lobbying the Continental Congress, many of his own people had grown suspicious of his mysterious activities. The veil of secrecy was apparently intentional; White Eyes hoped it would give him time to construct a "grand plan" for the future of his nation.

White Eyes explained that by dealing directly with the leaders of the white people, a diplomatic resolution could be negotiated to end the bloodshed and the encroachment on Indian land. Since all human beings were endowed with an ability to reason, the chief concluded that people of different colors must be able to find a way to live in peace. As a man of great ambition and optimism, White Eyes even tried to form a united Indian nation, which would exist side by side with the United Colonies. His initial goal was to form a legal and binding agreement "to guarantee to the [Lenape] the country they then possessed, which should be their home to all generations."[2]

Years before, White Eyes had originally planned to sail to England and appeal directly to King George. When the outbreak of the American Revolution made this impossible, the chief spoke out for his people's rights before the

Continental Congress. His people had suffered from being dispossessed of their ancient homelands in Delaware and Pennsylvania, and never again did he want them to be subjected to such cruel and inhumane treatment. If he failed in his diplomatic efforts, the future of his people would be uncertain. But if he succeeded, a new age in Indian–white relations would begin. One non-Indian observer remarked: "The noble aspirations of the great chieftain command our admiration."[3]

On May 3, a week before White Eyes returned home, a message from him to his people had arrived at the Moravian mission of Lichtenau, "Pasture of Light." The new Christian Indian settlement, the third Moravian mission in the area, had been established with approval from the Lenape Council two and one-half miles downriver from the capital of Goschachgunk or Cooshocking, "The Seat of Our Government." Thirty-five Indian people from eight families, led by the Reverend David Zeisberger and his assistant, John Heckewelder, constructed a log chapel with cabins radiating outward in the shape of a cross. Lichtenau was created in a beautiful meadow: "A broad level of many acres stretched to the foot of the hills, with an almost imperceptible ascent. The river-bank, swelling out gently toward the stream in the form of an arc, was covered with maples and stately sycamores . . . the rich soil promised abundant crops."[4]

While the mission was being completed that spring, Grandfather Netawatwees, the aged sachem of the tribe, and a number of people, both men and women, had come to the peaceful sanctuary and, as an act of unselfish goodwill, helped their Christian brothers and sisters build fences. They worked together, without pay, all day long:

> The women cut the needed wood, and the men carried it. All this was done very quietly and deliberately, and soon they got the work done. Before the Chief and his people left for home, a letter arrived for him which Captain White Eyes had posted in Philadelphia in March [1776].[5]

In his message, White Eyes reported that he would soon be home and that the Continental Congress had promised to send a Christian minister and a schoolmaster as well as a blacksmith and other specialists. He recommended that the Lenape begin building a schoolhouse in their national capital.[6] Since White Eyes did not reveal of what denomination the minister would be, the missionaries assumed he would be a member of the Moravian faith. Chief Netawatwees apparently made no comment.

Almost every day Indian families arrived to visit the Christian settlement. Some were merely curious and stayed to enjoy the ceremonies featuring harmonic music. Some were visiting friends or relatives. Others, overwhelmed by tragedies in their lives or inspired by spiritual fervor, rushed in to appeal for sanctuary or salvation. The men in black robes assumed a powerful position as intermediaries between the converts and the Creator.

On the morning of May 7, four days after the arrival of White Eyes's message, Lenape Chief Gelelemend, also known as John Killbuck, came to visit Brother David Zeisberger. As the grandson and designated successor of Sachem Netawatwees, Gelelemend, at the age of thirty-nine, was prepared to shoulder the weight of governing his nation and trying to ensure its future.[7] He asked Brother David for his opinion of White Eyes, and whether he thought White Eyes would bring a Moravian minister or a preacher of some other denomination. Zeisberger conceded he did not know what White Eyes had in mind, but that another Moravian brother would be appreciated. A man of another cloth would be opposed, especially if he planned to erect a church in the middle of the Lenape capital, in competition with the Moravians.

This reflected a fundamental difference between Indian religions and European-based religions: traditional medicine people rarely proselytized or overtly tried to convert people. Some Indians tried to reconcile or even embrace both Christian and traditional Lenape principles. This was not as hard as it might seem, since both recognized the existence of the Creator and the moral value of the "Original Divine Instructions." However, Brother David often urged people who were baptized to devote themselves to Jesus:

> Among those who visited today was an Indian who had been baptized in Old Gnadenhutten as a child. Brother David talked to him, and asked him if he did not occasionally think about dedicating his heart to Jesus. . . . The Indian answered . . . he often thought about that, and that he tried to live for the Lord Jesus in the world . . . the talk was of our Saviour and of his death for us. It was good and lovely to hear. Praise be to the Lord who lets his work dwell amongst us so that in due time it will bear beautiful fruit.[8]

Grandfather Netawatwees was visiting the Moravian on the morning before White Eyes's arrival. The old sachem reportedly said his "thoughts and wishes" were always with his younger Christian brothers and sisters. He wished he were able to come every day to enjoy the serenity of their environment, but he was too burdened by tribal affairs to do so.

As the trader "Honest John" Anderson had reported, a heated political, social, and religious debate was raging within the Lenape nation. Not only had the American Revolution placed political pressure on the Lenape to choose sides, but the traditional Lenape way of life was also being challenged by the increasing influence of European technology and social structures. The expansion of missionary activity posed a spiritual dilemma for Christian Indians and those who followed the traditional religion. The Lenape people were hesitating at a historic crossroad: should they preserve the ways of their ancestors or become assimilated into white society? Those who tried to maintain a balance between two worlds were now being forced by the temper of the times to choose *one* path.

The insistence of some white people that the Indians assimilate perplexed many of the traditionalists, who considered assimilation unnatural. Even Zeisberger, who was a strong believer in conversion as the best path, conceded:

> They regard the Europeans as peaceable people, created of God to live according to their own manners and customs . . . as the Indians have been created to live in their fashion. . . .They think it contrary to the will of the deity to adopt, themselves, the manner of living peculiar to Europeans, pointing to fish, animals and birds . . . [who have] never yet been observed . . . [to adopt] the habits of another. The same principle, they hold, applies to Indians and Europeans.[9]

The Indians thought that there must be a divine reason that the Creator had made people of different colored skins, manners, and customs. When Indians contemplated the vast diversity of life in the world, it did not seem natural to them that all people should be forced to be the same, in accordance with some European model. It was true that the Europeans had much to offer technologically, and the Indians wanted to be free to adopt only what they wished to; but there appeared to be a price to be paid for white technology in terms of personal liberty. While one gained status in European society by amassing great wealth, in Indian societies, a person generally earned honor and respect by sharing wealth equally among his people. Zeisberger recorded that Indians preferred their own egalitarian social structure to the European feudal class structure in which common people worked to support the wealthy and the titled:

> They admit that the whites are very ingenious, because of their ability to manufacture a great variety of things, but regard [European] manner of living as wearisome and slavish . . . if they were as free a

people and had neither government nor punishment to fear, would [the White people] not be as united and peaceable as the Indians?[10]

Despite the propaganda portraying Indians as warlike and disunited bands of nomads, the Lenape generally were peace-loving, and lived in villages with recognized boundaries. However, according to Zeisberger, they feared that some white people did not respect their rights to their territories: "[The Indians] harbor a secret enmity which they disguise in [Europeans'] presence, for [the Indians] suspect that [Europeans] will deprive them of their land and drive them within narrower confines. This suspicion is not without foundation."[11]

Unlike these suspicious Indians, White Eyes decided to place his faith in the powerful Euro-Americans, who he hoped would honor their word. White Eyes was gambling that if he supported American political leaders and they won the Revolution, Lenape land rights and their political freedom would be protected. However, many of his own people were not so trusting of the Americans and refused to assume the risk.

Hopocan, or Captain Pipe, leader of the Wolf Clan of the Lenape, recently had seceded from the nation and moved his followers north to form a traditional enclave within their hunting grounds along the Sandusky River near Lake Erie. As White Eyes's principal rival, Pipe claimed they had relocated not to escape Moravian influence, but, rather, as a protective move in response to White Eyes's daring challenge to the Iroquois during the 1775 Fort Pitt treaty conference: "[Pipe and his followers] feared, they said, the wrath of the Iroquois, which [White Eyes] had unnecessarily provoked; and they would not stay to share the punishment to be expected from that powerful League."[12] White Eyes's famous speech, in which he boldly declared Lenape sovereignty in the Ohio River Valley, was designed to impress the Iroquois and the Americans with Lenape independence.[13] His dramatic gesture, waving his arm toward the west and claiming the land across the Ohio River for his nation, was visually impressive, but the resulting rumblings were still being heard.

White Eyes finally returned to his people on May 10, confident that he had won a great diplomatic victory. However, as with any triumph, there had also been a price to pay. To win over the Christian congressmen, the Indian statesman had made several critical concessions without first consulting his people. In hopes of convincing Congress that Indians were not "savage heathens," White Eyes had agreed to the proposal that an English minister live among the Lenape people. The choice of a preacher from the Episcopal faith was intended to impress the members of Congress who were of English heritage.

As a political move, White Eyes's approach was effective, but the final judgment of his "grand plan" would be made by the Lenape in accordance with their democratic process. Would he receive their support or be condemned for this transgression? Only the Grand Council of the Lenape nation and public opinion would decide.

Before White Eyes could make a public presentation before his people, John Anderson delivered letters and reports to the Moravians and announced: "Congress had finally come to this agreement with White Eyes: He should first discuss with his nation and reach agreement on what sort of preacher they desired. Once that was done and everyone . . . agreed, they should let Congress know."[14] Anderson tried to counteract the Lenape's growing distrust of the Americans, but the prospect of foreign preachers and technicians coming into the Lenape nation resulted in an ever-larger split in public opinion. The Moravian Indians and their influential ministers were outraged by the effrontery, while the traditionalists were concerned that their ancient culture would be further eroded. Both factions pressed the chiefs and protested against White Eyes's grand plan.

Three days after White Eyes returned, the head chief of his political division of the Turkey Clan, Welapachtschiechen, or "Erect Posture," sometimes called Captain Johnny, arrived at Lichtenau with Rachel, his white wife. The sixty-year-old chief was contemplating resigning his office for a life of quiet meditation. On May 13, Welapachtschiechen reportedly said to Brother David: "When I am with you and hear about the Saviour, my heart feels so quiet, but as soon as I come back home [at Assunnunk] and have been there awhile, time seems to stretch out almost unbearably, and so I make ready to return to you here."[15] The chief spoke in his own language. He understood a little German and English, but not very much.

Zeisberger, who realized the importance of converting influential Indian leaders at this critical juncture in church history, replied to the troubled chief:

> If you can just understand and believe that the Saviour died and shed his blood for your sins, you can gain forgiveness of your sins and everlasting life. Through your faith in Jesus Christ, the source of all understanding and wisdom, everything will come to you; you will understand the evangelists and all this insight will cost you nothing.[16]

Zeisberger, however, urged the chief not to resign his position, because it was in the best interest of the Moravians at that time to have pro-Christian Indian leaders in influential tribal offices.

Two days later Chief Gelelemend, Netawatwees's grandson, arrived at Lichtenau and announced that Netawatwees had stated that he would challenge White Eyes if he tried to introduce a minister other than a Moravian:

> Do we not already see two towns of Christian Indians before our eyes and a third has already begun to convert? Where can we find another town like that among the Indians? Has anything like that ever been seen before? Is there still reason to doubt that the cause is just and true? I am convinced that the [Moravian] brothers have the right teachings, and that they preach the truth.[17]

This statement was given secondhand and recorded by the Moravian, whose future depended on just such bolstering of their precarious position. Gelelemend reportedly announced that the Lenape Grand Council would be meeting the next day to hear White Eyes and that the Moravian ministers were invited to attend. Zeisberger prepared himself to oppose White Eyes.

On the morning of May 16, Zeisberger and his converts prayed together and appealed for divine intervention. An Indian messenger soon arrived, announcing that Zeisberger and the Christian Indians should come at once. The black-robed minister and five of his native assistants paddled their canoe upstream to where the Muskingum forked into the Tuscarawas and Walhonding rivers. Goschachgunk, the new national capital and chief center of the Turtle Clan, contained many neat log cabins and a large, rectangular council house. The people had built Sachem Netawatwees a two-story frame house with a stone fireplace—as fine a residence as any on the frontier.[18]

Netawatwees and his wife welcomed the Lenape chiefs and the council of wise advisors, as well as Zeisberger and the Christian Indians, into their homes. White Eyes soon arrived and greeted everyone in a friendly fashion. Everything was quite cordial:

> We were glad to see him back home. After we ate for quite awhile, because much food was offered, and White Eyes told us of his travels and his activities in Philadelphia . . . he had had conversations with people of different opinions, including the [Moravian] brothers, and that he had been entertained most hospitably.[19]

Finally, White Eyes, who with his eloquent oratorical style could mesmerize most listeners, reached the climax of his presentation. He produced a small bundle of official documents, but before disclosing their contents, he said the council should consider the matter carefully and deliberate until a unanimous decision was reached. Zeisberger was then given the letter addressed to Sachem Netawatwees so that he could read it to the council. The letter explained to the sachem that the Moravian "would have nothing to fear, nor . . . suffer any difficulties, if an English minister were to come here."[20]

The German preacher was noticeably unimpressed. The letter's reassurances did not change the fact that White Eyes intended to bring in an English-speaking minister. To demonstrate his influence among the political leaders of the American Revolution, White Eyes next asked Zeisberger to translate an official letter from the Continental Congress that was addressed to White Eyes as the representative of the chiefs of the Lenape nation:

> A Speech delivered to Captain White Eyes in Congress
>
> April 10, 1776
>
> Brother Captain White Eyes,
>   We have not been unmindful of our promises made to you and your nation. . . .
>
> Brothers the Delawares,
>   At the council fire, at Pittsburg, last fall, and since by our brother Captain White Eyes, who hath been all the winter with us, you requested our assistance to promote peace and useful knowledge among you, particularly the knowledge of the Christian religion.[21]

Since the Reverend David Zeisberger and the Moravian missionaries had been preaching among the Lenape for many years, some question arose as to whether Congress intended to support their efforts or to undermine them by sending a minister of another Christian denomination. The Lenape council listened as Zeisberger continued to translate the document:

> We rejoice, brothers, to find you thus disposed, and will . . . provide a suitable minister, and schoolmaster, and a sober man to instruct you in agriculture . . . we wish to advance your happiness, and . . . [to promote] a lasting union between us, and that, as you express it, we may become one people. The introduction of useful arts among you will be effected, we apprehend, by encouraging handicraft men to settle and reside in your country. The method of doing this must be left to your own discretion.[22]

Congress wisely left the final decision up to the Lenape Council. While the Lenape may have requested the technical assistance of a blacksmith and a gunsmith, their agricultural methods were already very productive.

However, the Lenape and other Indian nations did desire cooperation from the Americans in order to cultivate peace on the frontier. This also was touched on in the letter:

> Brothers, we desire that you will make it known among all the Indian nations to the westward, that we are determined to cultivate peace and friendship with them, and that we will endeavour, by making the best regulations in our power, to prevent any of our people wronging them in any manner, or taking their lands; and that we will strive to put the trade between us on such a footing, as will secure the peace. We expect, that all the wise men of every Indian nation, will use their influence for the same purpose.[23]

This most important passage documented the American commitment to honor Indian land rights. Congress also promised to promote peace and trade and to recognize the sovereignty of Indian nations.

The man Congress had entrusted with the responsibility for negotiating with the Indian nations was then introduced:

> Brothers, we have named George Morgan, esq. as agent under our commissioners for Indian affairs in the middle department, and we desire you will confer with him on whatever business you may have with us. We hope you will inform him of all public matters. We recommend him to your friendship.[24]

An effective agent not only had to mediate between the Indians and the Americans, but also had to resolve differences between Indian nations. One major intertribal controversy involved the Ohio lands where the Lenape had been invited to settle after their dispossession from the eastern seaboard. White Eyes sought to gain American recognition of Lenape land rights, which Congress delineated as follows:

> Brothers, You tell us, that your uncles, our brothers, the Wiandots, have given your nation a large tract of country, comprehended between the river Ohio on the south, the west branch of the river Muskingham and Sandusky on the west, Lake Erie on the north and Presque Isle on the west [east].[25]

Although the Wyandot recognized Lenape land rights, some Iroquois people still challenged Lenape title. Congress was walking on thin ice politically when it indicated that the Lenape would have to obtain Iroquois approval before the Americans could recognize Lenape title to the land. Such an affront to Lenape sovereignty could only evoke outrage among strongly nationalistic Lenape leaders when they received the congressional "recommendation":

> Brothers, Hearken to our advice. As we are informed that your uncles, our brothers, the Six Nations, claim most of those lands, we recommend it to you to obtain their approbation of this grant to you from the Wiandots in public council, and have it put on record. Such a step will prevent uneasiness and jealousy on their part, and continue the confidence and friendship which subsists between you and them.[26]

Indeed, White Eyes had stirred up a hornet's nest by allowing the Lenape land title to be publicly brought into question. It was as if the Lenape had suggested that they wouldn't recognize American sovereignty unless the British approved it first. How would the revolutionaries have reacted to that? But Congress also made a bold proposal: "We wish to promote the lasting peace and happiness of all our brothers, the Indian nations, who live with us on this great island. As far as your settlement and security may depend upon us, you may be assured of our protection."[27] This promise was tantamount to a proposal for a defensive security alliance. If the Indians accepted such an agreement, the implications would be serious. First, an American army could invade Indian country under the pretense of "defending" their Indian allies; this potentially violent scenario was advised against by most Indian leaders. Second, they might be expected to reciprocate by defending the Americans, and such an act would inevitably draw the Indians into the Revolutionary War.

Congress concluded its message to the Lenape nation by promising that American citizens would not be permitted to steal Indian land or to injure Indian people:

> We shall take all the care in our power, that no interruption or disturbance be given you by our people, nor shall any of them be suffered, by force or fraud, to deprive you of any of your lands, or to settle them without a fair purchase from you, and your free consent. If, contrary to our intention, any injury should be offered to you by any of our people, inform us of it, and we shall always be ready to procure you satisfaction and redress.[28]

This passage was of paramount importance to the Indian people: a legally binding promise had been made by the Continental Congress that Indian land would not be taken by force or fraud. It remained to be seen if the Americans would live up to their word and honor their promises.

The final statement exhorted White Eyes to spread the word about the American policy to preserve the Covenant Chain of Friendship:

> Brother Captain White Eyes,
> We desire you will inform your nation, your uncles the Six Nations, and Wiandots, your grand children the Shawanese, and all the other nations, what you have seen and heard among us, and exhort them to keep fast hold of the covenant chain of friendship, which we have so lately repaired and strengthened. As you are now about to depart, we present you with some money to buy cloaths and necessaries, and pay your expences, and we wish you a good journey, and bid you farewell.[29]

All those present reportedly listened with great attention, but no one said anything. Profound silence followed Zeisberger's reading of the letter. White Eyes had dealt his best hand, but nobody responded. Without uttering a word, the Lenape chiefs admonished White Eyes for overstepping the bounds of the chieftainship: A Lenape political leader could not dictate or initiate a major new policy without first consulting and receiving support from his people.

One by one, the chiefs and wise people rose and walked out the door. Finally, White Eyes, dejected, also left. Only Netawatwees, two councillors, and the Moravians remained. Zeisberger broke the silence: "I see that the Council has separated without attending to the business for which it was convened. I, too, will now go home. But before I go I wish to inform you that I will have nothing to do with these plans, and will never give my consent to them; and I advise you to consider well before you sanction them."[30] Before Zeisberger left the Lenape capital, he met Gelelemend in the street and urged him to keep the Moravian posted on any future developments.

Zeisberger later reported that, the following day, the chiefs met in private council without White Eyes. Netawatwees demanded the truth from his councillors: "Who among you have conspired with White Eyes in this matter behind my back? It absolutely was not my intention to get anyone but a [Moravian] brother as a minister."[31] White Eyes's head chief, Welapachtschiechen, professed complete innocence. No one spoke in support of the "grand plan"; the public reaction was a far cry from a hero's welcome. White Eyes had suffered a major political rebuke.

On Saturday evening, May 18, the Christian Indians lined up to receive the first communion at Lichtenau. The following Sunday morning White Eyes was among the congregation crowded into the log chapel to hear the Reverend Zeisberger deliver a sermon of fire and brimstone. In Moravian theology, the Holy Spirit still wages an unending battle against the Prince of Darkness.[32]

One of the Moravian's most devout "Indian shepherds," or "national helpers," was Isaac Glickhikan, or "Sight of a Gun Barrel," a former councillor of Munsee Chief Pakanke and the partner of Anna Benigna, who had mothered his family of ten. Glickhikan had once led war parties against invading settlers in his native Pennsylvania, but for the past eight years he had acted as a pacifist and outspoken advocate for the Christian Indians.[33] He once spoke with White Eyes about becoming a Christian:

> Brother, you remember our ancient friendship. We pledged ourselves to be faithful one to another and love one another as long as we lived. We placed our *schewondican* (tobacco-pouch) between us, that each might take from it at will. We agreed to tell each other if either of us should discover the true way to happiness. . . . I wish to testify to you that I have found this way. . . . It is the Word of God. This leads to salvation and life eternal.
>
> Come, go with me; share my happiness.

White Eyes was so moved by his old friend's appeal that "tears rolled down his cheeks . . . and he assured his friend that he often thought of becoming a Christian."[34]

Glickhikan and Anna Benigna were aided in their missionary work by Wilhelm "Bill" Chilloway, a former interpreter for Sir William Johnson, the late British Superintendent for Indian Affairs. A Lenape formerly from Province Island, near Philadelphia, Bill was described as "a tall, muscular man, with ears cut so as to hang pendants, like a pair of ear rings."[35] He and his wife, Martha, served as national helpers at Lichtenau, where they raised three children. Bill would soon also serve George Morgan as a translator.

One of Netawatwees's grandsons, Gutkigamen, or Thomas Killbuck, half-brother of Gelelemend, also served as a national helper. He lived with his aunt, Old Justina the Basketmaker, who in 1749 had been one of the Moravians' first converts.[36] Now over three dozen souls came to the "Pasture of Light" to listen to Brother David teach the virtues of living a simple, humble, and peace-loving life patterned on that of Jesus Christ. Their voices then united in singing some of the rousing hymns for which the Moravian church was famous.

After the sermon, White Eyes took a stroll through the forest with Isaac Glickhikan and Bill Chilloway:

> White Eyes was very friendly and pleasant to us, but he appeared to be depressed and restless. . . . He completely got away from the main matter [of the English minister], and his spirit had become darkened. He is concentrating on . . . great enterprises which are all rather hazy. He has great plans for the Indian nation . . . to make them respected and prosperous people. He also has the forelorn hope that the great [men] of the country will help him to achieve [his grand plan].[37]

While White Eyes's progressive ideas had appealed greatly to leaders in Congress, the same flamboyant ambition now failed to impress most Indian people. Glickhikan and Bill talked firmly to White Eyes and urged him to "remember the word of God and . . . be modest." White Eyes responded, "Thank you for your concern."[38]

But White Eyes's ambitions to make his nation as mighty as the white Americans' and himself the national leader meant sacrificing the German Moravians and favoring English-speaking ministers who were more influential among the American revolutionaries. Glickhikan reportedly scolded White Eyes in terms the white missionaries "would not dared to have uttered." White Eyes then complained: "Since I have come back home, I have suffered a great deal because of suspicion. . . . I can hardly stand all the suffering I have been experiencing."[39] The Lenape chief was caught in a whirlwind of religious, political, and social upheaval. His balancing act between two worlds had suddenly failed, and he came crashing down to earth. White Eyes faced the wrath not only of the traditionalists who sought to preserve their ancient culture, but also of the progressives, who were committed to Christianity but only under the powerful influence of German Moravian missionaries. To make matters worse, the British viewed him as a traitorous, pro-revolutionary sympathizer, and many Americans saw him as a treacherous savage simply because he was an Indian. White Eyes retreated to heal his wounds. Having learned a lesson in humility, however, the Lenape chief would soon return with renewed vigor.

Toward the end of the week, Nimwha, brother of the Shawnee Chief Cornstalk, rode quickly through the missions with a dire warning. Some of the Mingo were on the warpath, planning to murder the whites.[40] The missionaries appeared unalarmed and urged their Indian disciples to have faith.

The following Sunday, May 26, the skies opened and the rain poured down. Braving the deluge, Grandfather Netawatwees and White Eyes, followed by hundreds of others, arrived at Lichtenau to celebrate the Feast of the Pentecost. The Christians congregated to commemorate the descent of the Holy Spirit on the Apostles:

> The revered Holy Ghost made his presence felt in the service. We gave him our most heartfelt thanks for the love, faithfulness, and care manifested . . . in His dealing with our hearts. He forgave us for our frequent inattention and disobedience. And when we committed ourselves anew to Him for His further care and training before the Saviour, He allowed us to feel His peace anew.[41]

Missionary John Heckewelder and some of the brothers and sisters held a long discussion with the chiefs, especially White Eyes. Chief Gelelemend of the Turtle Clan was said to have become "very much moved in his heart."[42]

Then an announcement was made that a message had arrived from the Delamatteno, or Wyandot. Just as the Lenape were influenced by the Americans from Fort Pitt and the Moravian missionaries, the Wyandot were influenced by the British from Fort Detroit and the Catholic missionaries. The progressive Christian faction among the Wyandot addressed the Christian Lenape as their "Cousins" when they wrote:

> We learned our Cousins . . . have received the word of God which will make you and your children into a happy people. We, the Delamattenoes, were very happy to learn this [news] about our Cousins . . . . Should you adhere to . . . the word of God . . . the Delamattenoes would be delighted to . . . care for your children so they would also receive the word of God.[43]

The Christian Indians were allied on a religious basis, but with the American Revolution heating up, political divisions threatened to rip apart the social fabric of Indian communities. Although Netawatwees and White Eyes were not baptized, they advocated the individual's right to religious freedom and tried to help make life more pleasant for those who followed the Christian path.

When Netawatwees learned the Moravian were planting vegetables, he appealed to everyone to help in the fields and offered a head of beef for a feast upon completion of the work: "Thereupon, a lot of Indians, including White Eyes and all his chieftains . . . helped us plant our fields in one day. . . . [Netawatwees] encouraged his people in their work. He told them to be industrious."[44] After a long day of community service, everyone enjoyed the great feast. The gesture of goodwill and unity reflected a society in which leaders maintained high positions not because of royal splendor, but because they remained humble servants of their own people.

This political and social system had survived for countless generations, but pressures from the outside world now made the chieftaincy a center of conflict that required constant mediation of disputes. Should the Indians preserve the traditions of their ancestors or assimilate into white society? Should they continue their ancient religious ceremonies or become Christians? Should they support the British or the American revolutionaries or remain neutral? Should they resist encroachment on their lands by white settlers or try to make peace concessions or retreat farther west? The dilemmas were most complex, and the pressures almost unbearable.

Chief Gelelemend and his wife came to Lichtenau for a visit on May 30 and stayed overnight. Brothers David Zeisberger and John Heckewelder listened to the chief's confession: "He told us everything that he had in his heart; that he was too tired to live any longer under the infidels; that he was tired of being bothered by the affairs of the chieftaincy . . . and he desired to live with us permanently."[45] Gelelemend had already talked to Netawatwees and told him of his desire to live with the Moravians. Netawatwees had urged him to consider the matter carefully and asked: "What will happen to the affairs of the chieftaincy and the matters of our worldly endeavours? Who will take care of these things, if you were to leave me and resign?"[46] Although a Lenape chief would be a prized convert, Zeisberger advised Gelelemend not to resign his office. Since most Lenape chiefs currently supported the Moravians, the ministers sought to keep them in positions that would allow the ministers to recruit more converts and repress their critics.

Many Lenape people still preferred their ancient religion and did not trust the missionaries, as White Eyes had pointed out to Netawatwees: "Many of [our people] do not seem to have ears for the evangelists. Many [are] actually opposed to Christianity. Therefore, [I] believe, that many of them will leave the tribe."[47] The old sachem had become outraged by these remarks. Netawatwees proclaimed to White Eyes: "If they wanted to go, they should go, because they would not have any mind for the good life anyway. Let them go. They will come back."[48] At the approximate age of ninety-nine, Netawatwees was still not inclined to be baptized, but he apparently did not wish to reject the Moravians, who had described to him in glowing terms the wondrous Christian paradise called heaven, where an eternal "good life" awaited the faithful.

In contrast, the Lenape concept of the afterworld required a long, arduous journey across the Milky Way or "Trail of Spirits" through twelve spiritual realms:

> The "Happy Hunting Ground" [is] a beautiful country where life goes
> on much as it does on earth, except that pain, sickness and sorrow are
> unknown . . . where children shall meet their parents who have gone
> before . . . where everything always looks new and bright . . . the blind,
> cripples—anyone who has been maimed or injured—will be perfect.[49]

Although their perception of heaven was in harmony with that of the Christians, the Lenape seldom spoke of a hellish place with red devils deep under the ground. They put more emphasis on their mother, the Earth, who nurtured all living things.

At this juncture in history, the perils of war surrounded the Lenni Lenape: gunfire, violence, Redcoats, and rebels threatened to destroy their natural world. One week later, on June 5, an express messenger came riding through on horseback with an important message for other Indian nations: "We heard that Mr. [George] Morgan would be here in a few days. . . . Morgan wants . . . the Indians to spread his message . . . to invite them to meet in Pittsburg at a certain time to make a treaty with [the] United Colonies."[50] Morgan was taking a daring step by personally coming to invite the Indian leaders to the American treaty conference. On this trip his life constantly would be in danger.

As one precaution, Morgan declared a temporary prohibition against alcohol, an action the Moravians supported. Morgan ordered that "the traders or white people should not bring rum or other strong drinks into [Indian] towns nor in these areas. We appreciated that, because it had happened before that traders had brought rum . . . and that had led to terrible orgies."[51] There were difficulties enough on the frontier without anyone attempting to decide issues of life and death under the influence of anything other than serious contemplation. Attempts to talk politics or religion during a wild orgy naturally would be futile.

Chapter Five

BALANCE OF POWER
The Courtship of Indian Nations
Early in the Revolution

ON THE LAST day of the month of May, George Morgan and Captain John Neville were making preparations for the first U.S.–Indian peace treaty. They commissioned two men to ride west with an urgent message intended to prevent the Lenape and Shawnee from consorting with the British and to encourage them to await Morgan's arrival. The two express riders were William Wilson, Morgan's aide and interpreter, and Joseph Nicholson, who had grown up among the Lenape and had formerly served as a guide for George Washington.[1]

The two men crossed the Ohio River and followed an ancient Indian trail that wound through lush green valleys and dense hardwood forests and then across three mountain ridges guarding the entrance to the lands of the Lenape and Shawnee nations. The 133-mile journey from Fort Pitt to the Lenape capital took six days when the creeks were swollen during the spring runoff. Finally, on June 5, Wilson and Nicholson stopped briefly at Goschachgunk and Lichtenau. They then rode another 100 miles to the Shawnee nation to deliver the American peace message:

> Brethren,
> We sent you a Message by our Friends . . . a short time past [and] . . .
> requested that we might see some of you here about the middle of next
> month to consult what we ought to do to preserve the Peace between
> you & us & concerning the matter we spoke to you about last Fall [at

Fort Pitt regarding Indian neutrality in the American Revolution], for we are strong in this good work.[2]

Since the Americans had extended their previous invitation to the chiefs to return to Fort Pitt, Morgan had had to delay the scheduled conference because of lack of supplies. Furthermore, Morgan and Neville feared many Indians would not attend both because the British were preparing to distribute lavish presents at their Niagara treaty conference and because the Iroquois were kindling the council fire at Onondaga in New York. A small showing would have made Morgan's influence seem weak.

Nicholson translated the message to the Lenape, calling for them to wait for Morgan's arrival:

> We now conclude to save you the fatigue of this long Journey & particularly at this time as we understand some of you are going to Council with your and our Brothers the Six Nations at Onondaga. . . . And as we are very desirous to speak to [your leaders] before they set off, we hope you will stop them till the arrival of our Agent Mr. Morgan.[3]

Back at Fort Pitt, Morgan wrote several messages before departing for Indian country. His greatest concern was the threat of a British invasion and an attack on Fort Pitt at a time when the garrison was dangerously low on gunpowder. To counteract this threat, Morgan concocted an ingenious bluff. The young agent wrote directly to Canadian Governor Henry Hamilton, who was engineering a British–Indian military alliance along with Colonel Butler. These men had written to Alexander McKee and other presumed Tories to solicit support for an Indian uprising. Morgan knew of the letters, but he behaved as if the documents had been destroyed before the contents were revealed. He wrote Hamilton not as the enemy, but rather as one gentleman to another:

> To the Governor & Commandant at Detroit
>
> Pittsburgh May 31st, 1776
>
> Sir,
> I am informed that several Letters from you for this place have been destroy'd on the way—what were the contents I have not been able to learn, or I would do myself the pleasure to answer them—but perhaps an exchange of sentiments between us may be mutually advantageous.[4]

In the hope that the British high command had not been informed of the difficult American position, Morgan wrote in a tone that demonstrated both confidence and diplomacy:

> You Sir have been frequently informed that an Army were on the march from the United Colonies against your Post, [and] this has been altogether without foundation; though we are indeed prepared, should the [Indians] be induced to strike our Frontier Settlements on the Ohio [River], but if they remain quiet, you will never be disturbed, unless by the general surrender of Canada.[5]

Morgan was probably unaware of some of the recent strategies of the Continental Congress; it had been decided that General George Washington and the American revolutionaries should attack Detroit and Niagara.

Canada was not even close to surrendering, since the Americans under Benedict Arnold and Richard Montgomery had taken a beating after a few minor victories. Morgan now hoped to delay Hamilton's schemes by holding out the proverbial olive branch: ". . . for this notwithstanding we have hitherto been unsuccessful before Quebec, we still flatter ourselves with, unless by the late arrival of the commissioners from England to treat with Congress, our Grievances shall be redress'd & all our differences happily settled, which all Good Men must ardently wish for."[6] Morgan was a peacemaker; he preferred negotiation to bloodshed. Even when his back was against the wall, he first sought peace through his powers of persuasion.

Morgan's defensive tactics involved painting an exaggerated picture of the American frontiersmen's potential military capability to defeat a full-scale British–Indian attack: "Our Frontier Settlements—though sufficiently numerous not only to defend themselves but to drive all the Indian Nations before them in case of a War—have been alarm'd with repeated accounts of your endeavouring to engage the [Indians] against them."[7] Morgan was close to the mark in charging Hamilton with enlisting Indian mercenaries to drive the rebels out.

The young Indian agent made it clear that the revolutionary high command was kept fully informed of British plans. Standing poised, ready to defend American interests, Morgan pointed out that it was not too late to recall the invasion plan before the frontier went up in flames: "This information has often been handed to Congress; but as the Indians still remain quiet, no force is allowed to cross the Ohio [River], nor will be permitted to do so unless in our own defense, after being first attack'd."[8] The border established by the 1768 Fort Stanwix Treaty would be defended, Morgan wrote. But while Hamilton was stationed in the middle of the western Indian nations around the Great Lakes, the Americans faced the problem of monitoring a border over a thousand miles long.

Conflicts could break out at any point along the boundary line. Morgan still remained vigilant in supporting his hopes for peaceful relations:

> I am station'd here to observe what passes in this Quarter, & to treat with the Indians. I shall be happy to have it in my power to contribute toward a general Peace, good understanding, & happy Reconciliation.—As such I shall be glad to hear from you & any Messenger you send to me may rely on being permitted to return at any Time.[9]

While the American agent's gesture in opening diplomatic channels between himself and his British counterparts seemed a wise strategic move, this document could also expose Morgan to charges of consorting with the enemy.

Since the Niagara treaty conference had started two days earlier, Morgan sought to offset the British head start. The logistics of organizing an Indian treaty were immensely complicated. Morgan reported to the commissioners on what he had accomplished since receiving congressional authorization to order the necessary treaty supplies:

> To the Honorable Commissioners for Indian Affairs
>
> Pittsburg May 31st, 1776
>
> Gentlemen,
> I have had the honour to receive your favours of the 11th & 14th inst. & in consequence thereof I have agreed with Messieurs [Bernard and Michael] Gratz & Company for their Goods, and shall draw for the amount in ten days sight, but as they are no way adequate to the purpose, I send you an account of such articles as will be wanted.[10]

The following chart is a complete list of the supplies and presents that Morgan requested for the first U.S.–Indian peace treaty conference.

> Invoice of Goods mention'd to the commissioners (in the foregoing letter) to be wanted for the proposed Treaty vizt.
>
> 20 ps. [20 pieces = 240 yards] of Match Coats, 2, 2 1/2 & 3 points
> 10 ps. [120 yds] of Indian Blankets or stripped duffels [thick woolen cloth]
> 20 ps. [240 yds] Blue}

3 ps. [36 yds] Scarlet} 7/4 Stroud
3 ps. [36 yds] Black} [woolen cloth]
20 ps. [240 yds.] Halfthicks [blankets]—most white nap or plain some
red, blue & green. . . .
800 Shirts ruffled & plain, or Linnen & Muslin to make them—
20 ps. [240 yds] of Callicoes [cotton cloth, often floral] & Cottons, low
prices,
40 lb. white & colour'd Threads
2 doz. Wool Hats
2 doz. Castor do. [beaver hats]
1 doz: laced do. [hats]
12 ps. [144 yds] emboss'd Flannell & Striped Lincey [linen and wool cloth]
6 ps. [72 yds] red Lincey
40 common saddles
100 Bridles
2 or 3 Gro: [288-432] paint Boxes
12 Gro: [1,728] Cutteau Knives
1 Gro: [144] common brass handle or other pen knives
6 Hhds [6 Hogsheads = 378 gallons] of Philadelphia Rum, Old Spirits,
Tea, Coffee, Chocolate, Sugar &c. for the commissioners
12 Gro: [1,728] Jews Harps
12 Gro: [1,728] Morrice Bells [small bells prized by dancers]
12 doz: [144] Horse Bells
20 ps: [240 yds] striped Callimancoes [wool woven with satin twill] or
other stuffs.
20 pair Men's Shoes
2 doz: Buckles
some Brass Kettles if to be had.
20 M [20,000] Needles from No. 1 to 5
12 Gro: [1,728] Women's Thimbles
6 Gro: [864] common Horn Combs
6 Gro: [864] Scissors
12 doz: [144] Looking Glasses
6 doz: [72] Tom Hawks
12 doz: [144] Hatchets
10 doz: [120] Hoes
20 Gro: [2,880] Mackasin [moccasin] Awls
20 Nests [sets] of Tin Kettles,
6 Nests of Trunks,
6 Gro: [864] Pewter Spoons
10 doz: [120] stretching Needles,
6 doz: [72] silk Handkerchiefs low price

20 Rifles if thought proper to shew
a Confidence in them ———————
10 M [10,000] Flints
20 Gro: [2,880] Bed Lace,
20 Gro: [2,880] Scarlet & Star Gartering
100 lb. Beads
20 Kegs Salt
2 Rheams [1032 pages] of good Papers
6 papers Ink Powder
2 lb Sealing Wax
100 good [writing] Quills
20 ps. [240 yds] figured Ribbon
2 ps. [24 yds] narrow white do. [Ribbon] to ornament strings of
Wampum———
60 ps. [720 yds] red, green, yellow, blue & purple Taffata do. [silk
ribbon] to ornament strings of Wampum
4 doz: [48] Arm Bands
8 doz: [96] Wrist Bands
4 doz: [48] Gorgets [crescent-shaped breastplates]
4 doz: [48] Moons
12 doz: [48] Hair Pipes
50 doz: [600] Hair Broaches
100 doz: [1,200] Shirt do. [broaches]
6 doz: [72] Hair Plates
12 doz: [144] Nose & Ear Bobs [ear rings]
12 doz: [144] large & small Crosses
2 doz: [24] Ear Wheels
20 doz: [288] Rings
1 Faggot [bundle of] Steel
1000 lb: of Iron
a Sett of Blacksmith's & Gunsmith's Tools,
Bellows, Anvil &ca:———Mr. Geo. Roberts can furnish this at about $20
[pounds] for the whole.[11]

The request for these goods represented the American revolutionaries' efforts
to prove their good faith, as was customary in an ancient Indian tradition called
the "Giveaway." Although most Europeans misinterpreted it as a form of bribery,
traditional Indian people considered it an act of generosity, goodwill, and good
faith, one that sanctified covenants made before the Creator.[12]

To be accepted into the family of Indian nations, a "Brother" could not hoard
possessions, but rather had to share everything equally. Therefore, people in Indian

society would be neither overly rich nor desperately poor. While upper-class Europeans and Americans strove to elevate their positions by amassing luxuries, most traditional Indian societies based status on different criteria. The more one gave away, the more support one's position in society would receive.

George Morgan and his British counterparts recognized the importance of honoring Indian customs. Before departing for his tour of the Indian nations, Morgan diligently worked to locate and order the necessary presents for the upcoming American–Indian peace treaty conference. He gave an accounting to his superiors in the American Indian Commission:

> Mr. [Richard] Butler & Co. have a few Goods in their store here, value about 5 or 600 Dollars—a Mr. [Alexander] Blain of Carlisle has some neat Indian Goods there, & Mr. [Bernard] Gratz Junior in Philadelphia has some excellent Match Coats, Strouds, Halfthick [blankets], &ca. The Silver work Mr. [Joseph] Simons of Lancaster can furnish a good assortment of at a short notice.[13]

Locating and purchasing trade goods during a time of severe shortages was not easy. It was even more difficult to get the supplies transported over the mountains to the remote frontier post. Morgan drew upon his contacts with Indian traders, such as Joseph Bullock, a trusted business associate and son-in-law of his partner, John Baynton: "Mr. [Joseph] Bullock of Philadelphia would be a good person to purchase the Articles you want, & to send them up here—if they arrived by the middle or latter end of August it will answer [our needs]—I shall pick up lead, Tobacco, & Sundry other articles here to the value of six or seven hundred Dollars."[14] A good Indian agent had to be skilled in handling both business and logistics. If the latter were mishandled, the agency would appear ridiculous, and with the fate of the American Revolution in the balance, there was no room for bungling. Each step demanded careful calculation and timing.

To ensure that the Indians would attend the treaty conference, Morgan informed the American commissioners:

> With regard to the time of the Treaty, I shall be under the necessity to consult the convenience of the Indians, for which purpose I shall set out for their Towns in a few days, & have already sent word of my intended Visit, & to stop the Chiefs who proposed to come here, as well as those that were about to set out for Onondaga, by way of the [Great] Lakes, to Council with the [Iroquois] Six Nations on particular appointment.[15]

The chiefs could not approve a precise time for the treaty ceremony without first consulting their people. As in all participatory democracies, Indian politics naturally functioned at a slower pace than when elected officials make the final decisions.

Morgan urged the American commissioners to delay the scheduled date of the treaty to give him time to lay the groundwork: "In the interim you may be satisfied you need be under no apprehensions from the Western [Indian] Nations till I return, and [I will] send you notice when to meet them here; for the time you have mentioned [July 20th] will by no means suit [our purpose]."[16] Morgan explained his reasoning to the commissioners and reassured them that they could trust his judgment. However, he urged the commissioners to attend at once to the powerful Iroquois Six Nations, who were being courted by the Redcoats. The American agent in the North, General Philip Schuyler, also needed time to counter the British:

> My visit will answer many good purposes, and will give the [Indian] commissioners in the Northern Department time to put the Six Nations into good Temper, for it appears to me that there is some discontent among them. . . . I am glad of the opportunity I shall have, of seeing the Western Chiefs before their departure for Onondaga, in order to send them off in a good disposition.[17]

Onondaga, where the sacred fire of the Grand Council was kindled, was a focal point for Indian affairs in the North, because it represented the seat of the Tatodaho, head sachem of the Iroquois Six Nations. Chiefs from the Mohawk, Seneca, Oneida, Cayuga, and Tuscarora, as well as surrounding Indian nations, congregated at Onondaga to discuss international affairs. Their league of nations represented one of the oldest continuously maintained governments.

Morgan estimated that the Iroquois and The Wyandot in the North, the Lenape and Shawnee in the West, and the Cherokee and Muskogean nations in the South were most influential in determining matters of war and peace on the frontier. Although White Eyes had convinced Morgan that the Lenape would remain favorably disposed toward the revolutionaries, Hard Man, the head chief of the Shawnee, who was preparing to depart for Onondaga, remained recalcitrant: "The first Chief of the Shawnee is one of them, & he has refused to Council with the United Colonies from all [the bad] treatment he received here about two years ago, which was the foundation of the last War with Virginia."[18] Morgan was referring to Dunmore's War of 1774, when the Virginians had invaded

Indian country to fight for their questionable claims to Kentucky. Hard Man's war chief, Cornstalk, had led a daring attack at the Battle of Point Pleasant in response. However, from the Shawnee perspective, Daniel Boone and hundreds of settlers were still trespassing on the intertribal hunting grounds of Kentucky, and more white people than ever were moving west with the outbreak of the American Revolution.[19]

One of the main purposes of Morgan's tour was to reassure the Indians that he was empowered to prevent frontiersmen from illegally crossing the Ohio River border. Another major purpose was to appeal for peace while the British in the north were trying to get the Indians to go on the warpath: "Whatever Intelligence comes here in my absence Captain [John] Nevill will forward to you ... the report of the Garrison at Detroit going to Niagara, arose from the Vessels sailing with soldiers on board, but there are still near one hundred men there."[20] The British were mobilizing their forces for the Niagara Treaty Council. Morgan's men had ridden north to infiltrate the Niagara conference, which was then under way.

To keep the Indians at peace, the young American agent knew he would have to employ his skills in the art of wampum diplomacy, as demonstrated in this letter: "I received the Wampum—but it was White [the symbol of peace] I principally wrote for, & shall stand in need of—yet 40 M. [40,000] more will be wanted, & I shall be glad to receive them by the earliest opportunity."[21] Morgan reassured the commissioners that he had established a network of allies and that to fulfill the promises Congress had made White Eyes:

> I have engaged good Interpreters at 5/8 of a Dollar per day, & have
> sent to Bedford for a Gun Smith with who I expect to agree to about
> 220 or 280 per Annum—but I shall not be able to find a School
> Master. Indeed I wish the engaging [of] one as well as the Minister may
> now be postponed till I can confer with you.[22]

Morgan kept to himself his reasons for requesting this postponement. Perhaps he foresaw that the Lenape would react negatively to White Eyes's proposal for an Anglican minister.

Perhaps Morgan simply did not wish to bear the expense, since he was at present financing the Indian agency out of his own pocket:

> I have contracted for the necessary Flour & Cattle for the Treaty, but
> if you do not send money up by Mr. [John] Boreman I shall be at some

loss. On my return from the Indian Country you shall hear from [me].

Yours &ca,
[George Morgan]

Be pleased to provide me with 20 large & 20 small Silver Medals with such devices as you think proper.[23]

How much would the first U.S.–Indian treaty conference cost? Morgan sent the Congress a bill on June 3. It was only the first in a long list of invoices:

To the Honorable Commissioners for Indian Affairs,

Pittsburgh June 3d, 1776

Gentlemen,

I have this day drawn on you for Goods purchased for the Indian Department,

In favour of William Trent for	$ 2774
In favour of Simon & Campbell for	$ 296 1/3
In favour of John Anderson for	$ 100
Total _____	$3,170 1/3[24]

The cost of supplies would soon skyrocket; inflation was rampant. The revolutionaries were printing money without the gold bullion to back it up. Furthermore, the wartime shortage of supplies showed no sign of abating, while opportunists sought to capitalize on the seller's market. Morgan did his best to economize without jeopardizing the revolutionary cause.

Before Morgan departed for Indian country, he finally learned from an unnamed source about George Washington's new plan for Indian enlistment in the revolutionary cause, and about the support given the plan by the revolutionary delegates, as evidenced by the *Secret Journals of the Acts and Proceedings of Congress*: "Resolved . . . it is highly expedient to engage the Indians in the service of the United Colonies."[25] Morgan considered soliciting Indians as mercenary soldiers wrong. Furthermore, the young Indian agent learned that the Virginia convention had jumped the gun and was sending an agent to enlist a force of Indians at once. Before leaving for the West, Morgan drafted a formal protest to the American Indian commissioners:

I shall depart this Evening for the Indian Country, but am sorry to find that the Honorable Convention of Virginia have adopted a measure

which I fear will be highly injurious to the interest of the Colonies &
particularly to their own Frontier at this critical juncture if attempted
to be carried into execution vizt: that of sending an Agent to engage
two hundred of the Western Indians to act in Conjunction with their
Troops.[26]

Morgan's work for peace was in jeopardy. Not only did he have to counteract the
treacheries of the British and possible outbursts by injured Indians, but he also
was being undermined by his own superiors.

While the Americans might gain a few hundred recruits, thousands of
Indian warriors could become their enemies almost overnight. The enlistment
of Indian warriors might be judged a betrayal by the chiefs and clan mothers.
Morgan appealed for saner minds to prevail, before the frontier went up in
flames:

> ...for beside the improper method taken & the disappointment they
> will meet with, I apprehend it may occasion Hostilities against our
> Frontier Settlements to our infinitely greater damage than the value
> we can possibly expect from the service of... [a few Indians who] may
> engage themselves [in the American army].[27]

American military leaders were clearly desperate, and political leaders
apparently lacked confidence in their existing troops, or they would not have
tried to enlist Indians. Since the first shots had been fired at Lexington and
Concord, the American commissioners had told the Indians to remain neutral
and not to get involved in the white people's "family quarrel." Now the American
high command was doing an about-face. Morgan concluded that the enlistment
plan was not only unethical, but also illegal, because it broke the terms of the
1775 Fort Pitt Treaty:

> It's breaking in on the [peace] Plan I have pursued in all my Messages
> ... & Conversations with them, agreable to the late Treaties. ... [This
> change in policy] will confuse my Negotiations with them—And I
> cannot but wish the measure had been deferr'd till the ensuing
> Treaty, when if it should be thought at all expedient by Congress, it
> would be the most proper time.
>
> I am &ca.
> [George Morgan][28]

Morgan tried to delay the change in policy. If he could succeed in building a peaceful alliance with Indian nations, perhaps the military brass would back off. Men like General George Washington would have to be convinced that there were greater advantages to following Morgan's course. Indian neutrality was a real option, since it was favored by the majority of chiefs. However, only firm evidence could change the general's presumption that the Indians would fight either for the Americans or for the British, so it had better be the Americans.

The evidence that most Indian leaders favored peace, as long as the Americans did not break the treaty, was now being seen firsthand by Paul Long, Morgan's spy at the Niagara Indian council. Several weeks earlier, Morgan had sent Long northward secretly to catch up with Seneca Chief Guyashusta, who had suddenly departed to attend the British conference. Morgan remained in the dark about the success of the mission until Long returned two months later to give the following eyewitness report:

> To George Morgan Esq:
>
> Sir,
> Agreable to your orders I left this place privately the [11th] of May
> . . . & proceeded alone for Niagara with the paper you gave me. . . . I
> overtook [Guyashusta] with a number of other Chiefs of the Senecas,
> a few Shawnese, & some Munsies making in all one hundred & thirty
> six, on their way to the Treaty at Niagara.[29]

By traveling with the chiefs, Long's chances of infiltrating the British conference were greatly enhanced. It was a dangerous mission, because if he were detected as an American spy, he would be judged a traitor by the British and executed.

A consummate actor, Long played his role so well that he served as an interpreter between the British and the Indians:

> I joined their Company & conducted myself agreable to your direc-
> tions. When we arrived at Fort Erie . . . , where Lieut. Burnett
> commands & has about 40 Men, I acted between him & the Indians for
> there was no Person there [who] could speak to them. He furnish'd
> us with Provisions & Boats to the Big Falls & from thence we went by
> Land to [Fort] Niagara.[30]

While Indian delegations arrived from all directions, Indian trader James Heron observed the May 28 arrival from Detroit of Captain Hugh Lord, former commander of Fort Chartres on the Mississippi River, with two companies of the

Royal Irish Regiment.[31] Part of the garrison from Michilimackinac, a fortress on the channel between Lake Michigan and Lake Huron, also arrived in armed vessels for the British–Indian conference at the Big Falls. Apparently Governor Hamilton and Colonel Butler were calling in their big guns to impress the Indians with British military might.[32]

Surrounded by a spike-tipped palisade with heavy cannons projecting outward, Fort Niagara loomed high overhead, an awesome testament to colonial imperialism, ready to defend the waterway between Lake Ontario and Lake Erie. Within the fortress British officers resided in a huge white mansion that was three stories high with ten chimneys, while hundreds of other Redcoats, products of strict British discipline, were quartered in a formation of barracks.[33] Colonel John Butler lived outside the fort in a private residence that had stood silent since his wife and children had been kidnapped and held hostage at the American fort in Albany.

Butler, resplendent in his crimson coat with shiny brass buttons, greeted the Indian chiefs and Paul Long:

> On our arrival there I accompanied the Chiefs to Col. Butler's house which is out of the Fort & deliver'd him your paper. He told me he would talk to me after he had done with the Indians—He then welcomed them to Niagara, gave them Provisions & said he would be ready to speak to them the next day.[34]

Morgan had coached Long for this critical moment. His interrogation by the British was inevitable, so Morgan had prepared responses for Long to give in answer to Butler's probable questions:

> When the Indians had left Col. Butler, he began to question me, as follows: Who sent that Paper to him? Why Captain [Alexander] McKee did not write? Why I brought no Letters from Col. [George] Croghan? Why I left Pittsburgh without informing Col. Croghan? Who commanded at Pittsburgh? The number of Men & Cannon there?[35]

The "paper" referred to was not preserved in Morgan's journal, but was apparently part of Long's cover. Captain McKee, the British Indian agent at Pittsburgh, was on parole because Butler's invitation to him to attend the treaty conference, on behalf of the British, had been intercepted. Colonel George Croghan was now retired near Fort Pitt.

Long's responses were recorded by Butler, but although that document has not been located, Long was evidently able to convince Butler he was not a spy:

> My answers were conformable to your Lessons & I was directed to attend on him [the] next day—As he had wrote down my answers to all his questions, he now cross examined me & finding I was not a Spy as he at first suspected. This day & the next I was examined & re-examined by four different Officers of the Garrison, all of whom took my answers in writing & comparing them together found them to agree.[36]

The interrogation was grueling, but Long kept his head and stuck to his story.

However, the British still had a few tricks up their sleeves to flush out traitors, as Long later reported to Morgan:

> A Serjeant was then sent to me as I suppose, who proposed to desert & accompany me back to Pittsburgh, but I was on my guard—I was sent for by Col. Caldwell the Commandant who attempted to frighten me to a confession but finding me consistent in all I said, he & Col. Butler united in opinion that I had a very honest countenance and gave me a suit of clothes out of the King's Store.[37]

Thanks to his own courage and to Morgan's coaching, Paul Long succeeded in fooling the British. In fact, Long seems to have been practiced at hiding his true identity; even his name may have been an alias, since he apparently does not appear anywhere else in the historical record. However, once he was safely inside the walls of the British stronghold, Long played a heroic role in support of the American Revolution.

On the morning of May 29, shortly before the opening ceremonies of the Niagara Treaty Council, Butler invited Paul Long and a group of the chiefs to his home. The British had sent belts of wampum to invite delegates from the Iroquois Grand Council at Onondaga as well as to Indian nations in the Ohio River Valley. Now dozens of leaders gathered to consider the British position. Paul Long reported: "Col. Butler . . . began to abuse the Americans & particularly for their intentions of extirpating the Indians & for their deceiving them & telling them so many Lies at the Treaty last Fall at Pittsburg."[38] The Americans had promised the Indians peace, respect for their sovereign land rights, and noninvolvement in the Revolutionary War. These vows would be broken if George Washington and the Continental Congress proceeded with their plans to enlist the Indians. This would be playing right into Colonel Butler's hands, as Long reported: "He then ask'd me if I could read & answering in the Affirmative, he put into my hands a quire of written paper saying this is an exact copy of all their damned [American] Treaty held at Pittsburgh last Fall—I open'd it & read many parts of it & found it was so."[39] How did Colonel Butler obtain a copy of the American treaty? Apparently the British also had spies operating around their enemy's forts.

If Morgan were to succeed in his mission, he would need to expose the Tories who were working undercover to subvert the Revolution. Long picked up a clue regarding this crucial facet:

> Col. Butler then put into my hands a Letter wrote to him in a rough black hand I think I know the hand tho' the name was defaced—It was on a whole Sheet two Sides full & dated at Pittsburgh the 22d of April. . . . The contents of the Letter so far as I read & understood was giving information of the situation and strength of the Country at & near Pittsburgh & expressing great sorrow for the Mad proceedings of the [Revolutionary] people which the Writer said his influence could not prevent.[40]

Long did not reveal in his report who he suspected the man with a "rough black hand" to be. But the intelligence on the vulnerability of Fort Pitt must have encouraged the British in attempting to get the Indians to attack frontier settlements at a time when the Americans were almost out of gunpowder.

This "opportunity" was one of the principal motives for the convening of the Niagara Conference: "Before I had read this Letter out, the Indians had assembled in the Council House & Col. Butler was sent for. . . . I accompanied him as usual to act as one of the Interpreters. . . . The first day of the Treaty was taken up in the usual Ceremonies."[41] Hundreds of Indians crowded inside the council house and formed a great circle. In accordance with traditional custom, a "pure fire" was lit. The sacred pipe was passed around, and prayers to the Creator were given in order to sanctify the proceedings. Each spokesman presented strings of wampum, "to open their eyes, to cleanse their ears, to wipe the sweat from their bodies, to bury all evil thoughts, and to polish any rust from the Covenant Chain of Friendship."[42]

On the following day, May 30, Colonel Butler was ready to unveil his plan for discrediting the Americans and to try to enlist the Indians in His Majesty's service:

> Brothers, Your Father the King has taken pity on you & is determined
> not to let the Americans deceive you any longer—tho' you have been
> so foolish as to listen to them last year & to believe all their wicked
> Stories—they mean to cheat you & should you be so silly as to take their
> advice & they should conquer the King's Army, their intention is to
> take all your Lands from you and destroy your people, for they are all
> mad, foolish, crazy & full of deceit.[43]

Was Colonel Butler a mere propagandist or a prophet? The answer would depend on how well the Americans and the Indians honored their treaty promises. Morgan's mission was to nurture the Tree of Peace, an ancient covenant inspired by the Peacemaker in accordance with the "Great Law of Peace."[44] But many events were not subject to his control.

At the 1775 Fort Pitt treaty conference, the American and Indian leaders had symbolically buried all their weapons of war beneath the Tree of Peace. In accordance with the Great Law, sacred vows were made to the Creator to honor their commitment to preserving the peace. In a daring attempt to break this treaty, Colonel Butler proclaimed:

> They [the Americans] told you last Fall at Pittsburgh that they took the
> Tom Hawk out of your Hands & buried it deep & transplanted the
> Tree of Peace over it. I therefore now pluck up that Tree, dig up the
> Tom Hawk, and replace it in your hands with the Edge toward them
> that you may treat them as Enemies.[45]

There was dead silence throughout the council house. To dig up the tomahawk from beneath the Tree of Peace signified an act of war. Colonel Butler was asking the Indians to become mercenary soldiers, the same proposal George Washington and Congress would soon be advocating. Congress had authorized Washington to offer a cash bounty of $100 for the head of a British officer such as Colonel Butler; the British were also willing to offer the Indians blood money.

For three days and nights the Indians deliberated in private council. The future of the American Revolution depended on the outcome of their talks. Finally, on the morning of June 2, the chiefs sent word that a decision had been reached. Colonel Butler and Colonel Caldwell arrived "full of expectations." Once all were seated, Chief Guyashusta rose to speak on behalf of all present:

Brother,

It is three nights since you told me the Americans with whom you are at War, are all mad, foolish, crazy & full of deceit, & that their intentions toward us are all bad—You then told us we were foolish for listening to their Speeches which were all lies.[46]

In accordance with the customs of Iroquois diplomacy, Guyashusta first repeated the previous statements. Therefore, if anything had been misinterpreted, the matter could be cleared up. Butler and Caldwell remained silent as Guyashusta continued: "You say that you pluck up the Tree of Peace, they planted over the Tom Hawk which they bury'd & that you now replace that Tom Hawk in our hands with the Edge toward them & you direct us to make use of it."[47] The Seneca chief paused. All were silent.

No one questioned the accuracy of his account of what had been said. Guyashusta then voiced the Indian response, directing his words at Colonel Butler:

Brother,

I now tell you that you are the mad, foolish, crazy & deceitful person—for you think we are fools & advise us to do what is not our interest—The Americans on the contrary are the wise people so far as they have yet spoke to us—for what they advise us [to be peaceful] is our Interest to follow—they tell us your quarrel [in the American Revolution] is between yourselves. . . . [The Americans] desire us to sit still & they tell us right.[48]

Guyashusta echoed the peace policy advocated by George Morgan. As long as the American treaty was honored, the authority of the peace chiefs would prevail. Their reputations as honorable men were on the line. The well-being of their families, clans, and nations depended on their wise counsel.

Guyashusta and the other chiefs firmly rejected Butler's proposal: "But you want us to assist you which we cannot do—for suppose the Americans conquer you . . . what would they then say to us?"[49] This question went to the heart of the matter. The Americans would inevitably take their revenge on their enemies and punish them severely. Guyashusta concluded: "I tell you Brother, you are foolish & we will not allow you to pluck up the Tree of Peace nor raise the Hatchet— We are Strong & able to do it ourselves when we are hurt."[50] Colonel Butler and Colonel Caldwell reportedly lost their composure, for rarely had British officers been so shamed in public. The council abruptly adjourned.

The unanimous opinion of the chiefs was clear: they were firmly dedicated to peace. Only if the Americans broke the treaty and "hurt" the Indian nations would warriors strike back in self-defense. As long as the Americans honored their word, the Indian leaders would advocate peace.[51]

Ironically, on the following morning, the American political leaders, hundreds of miles from the Niagara conference, moved another step closer to breaking the treaty. According to the *Secret Journals of the Acts and Proceedings of Congress*, the American delegates had expanded the powers of George Washington: "Resolved, That the general be empowered to employ in Canada a number of Indians, not exceeding two thousand."[52] If Colonel Butler had been armed with this evidence when he made his speech, the outcome of the meeting could have been quite different.

The best Butler could do without this information was to find one unnamed Mohawk man, who cried out:

> Brothers,
> We have been call'd here by desire of our Father, the great King who has taken Pity of us & promises to assist us in driving the Americans out of the Country they have cheated us of. I now call on you to be strong & united in this good work.—Let us drive all the Americans into the great Sea.[53]

The Mohawk, defenders of the "Eastern Door" of the Six Nations territory in New York, had suffered the main brunt of incursions by American land grabbers. A few Mohawk warriors, without authorization from the council of chiefs, recently had joined the British in fighting against the American invasion forces crossing Indian lands into Canada.

The Mohawk warrior urged the chiefs to strike while the Americans were weak: "We are able to [drive the Americans off our lands,] for what did a handful of our young Men & the King's Troops do the other day. . . . They kill'd & took no less than 536 of their Warriors—what then shall we not be able to accomplish, if we unite in this good work?"[54] (On May 16, British Captain Forester and some Indian allies had encountered the American troops of Major Isaac Butterfield retreating from Quebec. About thirty miles downriver from Montreal at The Cedars, the force of over five hundred Americans was surrounded, and surrendered with little resistance.)[55]

The Mohawk orator at the Niagara conference then turned to address the Munsees, a tribe long affiliated with the Lenni Lenape nation:

> Brothers, I desire you will go after your return home to a little Town
> in the Delaware [Lenape] Nation.... Captain White Eyes is Chief. Tell
> him his heart is all over Virginian & that if he does not alter it you will
> fling him away entirely.—Captain Pipe at Kaskaskies is almost the
> same.[56]

By charging that White Eyes's "heart is all over Virginian," the Mohawk orator
meant the Lenape chief was allied with the American revolutionaries. Furthermore, he implied that while White Eyes might have been an Indian by heritage,
his deeper sentiments had been shaped by the white man. (Today, such an
Indian is called an "Apple," one who is red on the outside, but white on the
inside.)

After urging the Munsees to incite a coup that would overthrow the political
leaders of the Lenni Lenape nation, the Mohawk orator then turned to the
Shawnee representatives and challenged them to follow a similar course:

> And you our young Brethren, you have one among you who was once
> a Man, but now is a perfect Virginian—I therefore desire you will
> change his heart or that you will disregard him—I mean Colesquo
> [Chief Cornstalk]—Be strong Brothers & let us play the Man.[57]

Neither the Munsee nor the Shawnee responded; the council house was silent.
The conference then adjourned for the day.

Early the next morning, Colonel Butler called for the chiefs to reassemble.
The Redcoat officer made a second, more fervent attempt to encourage the
Indians to join the British:

> Brothers,
>   I have endeavoured to open your Eyes that you might see your
> own Interest & act accordingly.—You seem to be fearful & doubtful
> that the Americans may be able to conquer the Troops of the King
> your Father.—I tell you they are but as a Boy—they are few in
> comparison to our Warriors who are all Men & able to fight being
> trained to it.[58]

Butler sought to impress the Indians by making a display of might while also
challenging them to face the Americans in battle. In a shrewd bit of psychologi-
cal warfare, he played on the male ego by hinting that they were afraid.

Butler then proclaimed that the Indians had nothing to fear, since the

British were well supplied for war: "[We British] are well provided with Arms, Ammunition & every thing necessary, whilst the Americans are destitute of all these they have not one pound of powder, where we have a thousand, nor a pound of Lead where we have ten thousand, nor do they know how to fight."[59] Although Butler was exaggerating, there was more than a grain of truth in his statements about the Americans' shortage of gunpowder. Morgan's complaint to Congress that each man had barely enough powder to prime his gun had resulted in an immediate special order. Unfortunately, the military pack train loaded with two thousand pounds of gunpowder had been hijacked en route to Fort Pitt. To alleviate the critical shortage of gunpowder, the Virginia Committee of Safety had recently dispatched two officers, Captain George Gibson and Lieutenant William Linn, on a secret mission to New Orleans. They were ordered to buy up to ten thousand pounds of powder from the Spanish and then to sail up the Mississippi and the Ohio back to Fort Pitt.[60]

Colonel Butler decided that while the Americans were still weak and vulnerable he should get the Indians to attack. He tried to provoke the chiefs further by saying:

> [The Americans] make a little Powder among themselves 'tis true—
> but it is no better than dirt. It is rotten & they cannot kill a Man with
> it—You therefore need not be afraid, but take up the Hatchet & your
> old Men & Women, your Wives & Children shall be well taken care of.
> They may live in our Forts—We will both feed and cloathe them.[61]

Butler was offering to support thousands upon thousands of Indian people. If they all actually moved into the forts and the British tried to fulfill Butler's promises, the cost would be exorbitant. However, the Indians did not want welfare; most were too independent and self-sufficient. The chiefs said nothing to Colonel Butler before again discussing the matter privately, this time taking the new developments into account.

While the Indian leaders at Niagara were debating their future course of action, George Morgan had departed on horseback from Fort Pitt on June 4, 1776, to invite the Indian nations in the West to the upcoming American–Indian treaty conference. He was armed with strings and belts of wampum as well as with orders from John Hancock, instructing that he promote peace and harmony. Morgan could only hope that Congress would take his advice and continue to honor their promises "to keep fast hold of the Covenant Chain of Friendship."[62]

On the morning of June 5, the eighth day of the Niagara Indian conference, the chiefs called for Colonel Butler and Colonel Caldwell. Once all were assembled in the council house, Cawcowcaucawketeda, or Flying Crow, head war chief of the Seneca, spoke:

> Brother,
>   You have call'd us here to open Our Eyes, to break the peace we live in with our American Brethren & to ask our help to fight them— You tell us they have blinded us, that they have cheated us & will continue to do so & that we must not expect to live long if you are conquered. You tell us you are double their numbers, that you are Men & Warriors [and] that they are weak Boys—that you are provided with good Arms, & plenty of Powder, Lead & every thing necessary, & that they are destitute of all these except a little bad Powder which can do no harm—That they are mad, foolish, wicked & deceitful & that they will kill us all if they conquer you.[63]

Chief Flying Crow paused. In accordance with tribal custom, he had faithfully recited what had already been said about the matter at hand.

Flying Crow was an intelligent and courageous man. He knew danger well; he had nearly been assassinated at the 1775 Fort Pitt treaty conference. Over 650 warriors were under his leadership. He addressed Colonel Butler directly:

> Brother,
> We have now lived in Peace with [the Americans] a long time & we resolve to continue to do so as long as we can—when they hurt us, it is time enough to strike them—It is true they have encroach'd on our Lands, but of this [matter] we shall speak to them—If you are so strong Brother, & they but as a weak Boy, why ask our assistance?[64]

A most logical question had been posed by Flying Crow. Although he was a war chief with many marks of distinction, he preferred to seek peaceful solutions.

But if the Americans refused to resolve their differences reasonably and instead violently broke the treaty, Flying Crow proclaimed, his warriors, as a last resort, would fight for their freedom: "It is true I am tall & Strong, but I will reserve my Strength to strike those who injure me—If you [British] have so great plenty Warriors, Powder, Lead, & Goods, & they so few and little of either [then you] be strong & make good use of them."[65] Flying Crow had called Butler's bluff. The Indians were not gullible, as Butler had assumed they would be.

> The elders were known for their wisdom, and although it was too early to judge the true nature of the Americans, they realized that Colonel Butler clearly had lied. Flying Crow charged: "You say their

Powder is rotten—We have found it good—You say they are all mad, foolish, wicked & deceitful—I say you are so & they are wise for you want us to destroy ourselves in your War & they advise us to live in Peace—their advice we intend to follow."[66]

Although Flying Crow and Guyashusta were head chiefs, their positions did not empower them to dictate to their people. Several other chiefs, however, also spoke in support of preserving the peace. In the end, each man chose which path he wished to follow. The vast majority of Indians declared themselves in favor of peace.

Colonel Butler then rolled out his secret weapon: barrels of rum. A small minority, emboldened by drink, finally sounded the war whoop. Paul Long recalled the moment:

Several other Chiefs spoke to the same Effect [in favor of peace]; but Adongot and Soyouca & one other Seneca Chief agreed to all Col. Butler required with regard to joining the King's Troops in Canada— and by their influence a number of Six Nation, Chipwas, & Ottawas embarqued & crossed the Lake for that purpose [of attacking the Americans].

But the majority declared against it, or [against] having any thing to do in the dispute—Tho' Col. Butler daily renewed his application in & out [of] Council.[67]

The peace chiefs were upset that a minority faction had joined the British, but knew it would not be fair to condemn all Indian nations because of the "foolish acts of a few young men." As the peace chiefs later pointed out to Colonel Morgan, even the Americans had dissidents called "Tories," but this fact should not result in the condemnation of an entire nation.

The overwhelming majority of Indians at Niagara stood steadfast in their determination to preserve the peace. Colonel Butler finally conceded, as Paul Long attested:

But [Colonel Butler] at last gave it over & made a Speech to them to the following Effect,

Brothers of the Six Nations,
   The reason of Kindling this Council Fire was that we might consult with all Nations how to preserve the Peace & Friendship & assist each other in cases of Distress, & that we might lay a good

foundation for the happiness of our Women & Children after our old
men are dead & gone.[68]

Colonel Butler appeared to speak with a "forked tongue." His sweet words of
conciliation seemed hypocritical, since he had just sent out a war party.

His professed concern for the Indian women and children after "our old
men are dead & gone" may have been interpreted by the Indians as a veiled
threat against the elderly peace chiefs. In his desperation, Colonel Butler gave
the chiefs a few months to reconsider his offer: "I desire Brothers you who have
not fully determined to join your hands with the great King's your Father,
will think well of it again next Fall when you may expect all nations will be called
to meet us here."[69] The time had come to pass out the customary presents.
Despite Colonel Butler's earlier claims that the British were supplied a thousand
times better than the Americans, the British officer now made excuses for
his meager offering: "As the Rivers and Roads have been stopp'd by the
American Troops, your & our Enemies, we have but this handful of Goods
to deliver you—but in the Fall you may expect every Man to receive as much
as he can carry away as the Roads will then be open'd."[70] As often proved the
case when the Indians dealt with Europeans, they were promised much but
received little.

Paul Long reported the following inventory of the British presents to the
Indians: "The Goods were then distributed tied up in little Bundles which
consisted of a Match Coat, a stroud, Leggings, one quart of Powder, 2 lb. Ball,
1 Knife, 1/4 lb. Paint & 3 Flints to each Man, & as much to each woman, with
about a Barrel of Rum."[71] Many Indians began to drink from the big barrel. The
more they drank, the more aggressive they became, until what had begun as a
party escalated into a wild orgy.

Late the next morning, Long reported, a small Indian party returned from
a bloody attack. A frenzied commotion erupted, and Colonel Butler called for
the Indians to assemble in the chapel inside the fort: "The Council was held in
the Church or Chappel—A number of Chipwas & about 30 Senecas [who had]
embarqued from Niagara to go against our Army in Canada under one ____
Johnson—part of them return'd & brought in three Scalps & a Prisoner."[72] Colonel
Butler and Colonel Caldwell pointed to the scalps as proof that the Americans
would squirm for mercy. Long reported the scene inside the chapel:

[The] Three Scalps which were brought in the sixth of June from our
[American] Army in Canada were hung up in the middle of the

Council . . . on which Col. Butler & Caldwell exulted highly and Said,
"The Fiddle was now getting in Tune for the Americans to dance by."[73]

The balance of power at this point in history clearly rested in the hands of
the mighty western Indian nations. As he rode west to meet face to face with the
chiefs and clan mothers, George Morgan knew that the Niagara Indian conference was probably concluding, but he was unaware of its outcome. All the young
Indian agent knew for certain was that he was riding into the frontier on one of
the most dangerous and important missions of the early days of the American
Revolution.

Chapter Six

BROTHER TAMANEND'S MISSION TO THE LENNI LENAPE

ON THE EVENING of June 4, 1776, Morgan left Fort Pitt on his mission of peace. He was accompanied by Alexander McKee, the former British Indian agent, who had offered to join him. The two men had been friends since first working together in the Indian trade years before. However, their continued collaboration at the outbreak of the American Revolution was surprising, to say the least, since two months earlier McKee had been placed on parole by local authorities because of his involvement with the British. The handsome thirty-six-year-old Irishman with long blond hair displayed remarkable skill in balancing between Americans, British, and Indians. Perhaps quite apart from reasons of friendship, Morgan had concluded that it would be better to keep McKee close at hand. McKee also was married into the Shawnee nation, and had considerable influence with those chiefs who were wavering on the issues of war and peace.[1]

The two men would have covered 468 miles by the time they returned home forty-five days later. After sleeping the first night on Shirties Island, they followed the Great Trail twelve miles to Schwickley Bottom, on the north side of the Ohio River. On the morning of June 6, they stopped briefly at Logstown, a former Shawnee and Iroquois village called Shenango, which had been visited by the young George Washington in 1753.[2] This village of log cabins was a traders' outpost in 1776, run by John Gibson. Captured during the French and Indian War and adopted by an Indian mother, who had taught him Indian languages and customs, Gibson had recently enlisted as a captain in the Continental Army.

111

On May 13 he reportedly had arrived at Williamsburg, the capital of Virginia, where he warned, "there is a great Probability that the Wyandott, Taway [Ottawa] & other Indians will be Troublesome this Summer."[3]

After leaving Logstown, Morgan and McKee rode up the ridge ten miles to where they could ford Big Beaver Creek and then pressed on for another nine miles before camping at the forks of the Little Beaver. The next morning big storm clouds boiled up from the northern horizon, the direction in which Colonel John Butler was concluding the Niagara treaty council. Thunder rumbled as rain poured from the heavens. However, the urgency of Morgan's mission soon forced the men back into the saddle. They rode twenty-three miles through the downpour before nightfall prompted them to seek shelter at White Oak Camp.[4]

Unknown to Morgan and McKee, a radical political movement was taking final shape three hundred miles to the east in Philadelphia. Delegate Richard Henry Lee of Virginia put forth the following proposal, accepted by Congress on Friday, June 7, 1776:

> Resolved, That these United Colonies are, and of right ought to be, free and independent States, that they are absolved from all allegiance to the British Crown, and that all political connection between them and the State of Great Britain is, and ought to be, totally dissolved.[5]

There could now be no turning back; the break was irrevocable. Work would soon begin on what was to become the Declaration of Independence.

The storm on the Ohio frontier intensified the following morning, but Morgan and McKee pushed forward another sixteen muddy miles. They camped at Salt Licks, a place where animals of the forest regularly gathered. Finally the rainfall ended during the night. The riders picked up their pace on Sunday and covered twenty miles. Late in the day they waded across a swollen tributary of the Muskingum, or Elk Eye River, and arrived at the Moravian Indian mission called Schonbrunn, or Welhik-Tuppeek, the "Beautiful Spring."[6] This settlement of log cabins with a little chapel was located in the middle of a veritable paradise:

> On both sides of the river were bottom-lands interspersed with small lakes, reaching, on the western bank, to the foot of a precipitous bluff. . . . Near the base . . . the spring gushed in a copious stream from beneath the roots of a cluster of lindens and elms, and fed a lake nearly a mile long . . . [where] the Indians could paddle their canoes.[7]

Morgan and McKee were greeted warmly, fed well, and given beds for the night. Messengers were sent out to announce their arrival.

Schonbrunn was the home of the Reverend David Zeisberger, whom Morgan had attempted to solicit as an undercover informant for the American revolutionaries. The settlement was also home to over four hundred Christian Indians, representing the largest of the three Moravian missions in the valley:

> Schonbrunn had two streets laid out in the form of a T . . . about the middle of it . . . stood the church [which held up to 500 people]. . . . At the northwest corner of the main street was the school-house. The bottom, from the foot of the bluff to the river, was converted into cornfields. The town contained more than sixty houses of squared timber, besides huts and lodges.[8]

The next morning, on June 10, William Wilson, the Indian trader who was also Morgan's assistant, and four other white men and some of the Shawnee joined Morgan and McKee, and they all rode west together. Four miles downstream they swam their horses across the river and arrived for lunch at the second Moravian mission, Gnadenhutten, or "Huts of Grace."

This settlement had been established by Zeisberger and 132 Christian Indians—mostly Mohicans, but also a few Munsee and Iroquois. Morgan and McKee were welcomed and invited to share a humble meal. After lunch they inspected the mission:

> Such settlements were remarkable not merely as towns, built with surprising regularity and neatness, but also as communities governed, without the aid of Colonial magistrates, by a complete code of laws. In order to administer these, a council was set over each village . . . that reconciled personal liberty, which the Indian prizes so highly, with restrictions tending to the common good.[9]

This form of government was an adaptation of the traditional Lenape style of government, which had survived for perhaps thousands of years. The major difference was that the German missionaries retained the right to make final decisions. They also regulated the important agricultural work of the community:"Their plantations covered hundreds of acres along the rich bottoms of the valley; herds, more numerous than the West had ever seen, roamed through the forests or were pastured in their meadows."[10]

Morgan reportedly was impressed by the productivity of the Moravians. Heckewelder later wrote that:

> He was astonished at what he had seen in our towns. That the improvements of the Indians bespoke their industry; and that the cleanliness, order, and regularity which were everywhere observable . . . gave them a claim to be ranked among the civilized part of mankind. That they deserved to be set up as an example to many of the whites.[11]

In the afternoon, Morgan and McKee said a friendly good-bye and again swam their horses across the river. They followed the bank twenty-two miles downstream, where they once more crossed the river and arrived at White Eyes's village. White Eyes, his wife, and their son, along with the rest of their extended family of the Turkey Clan, lived nine miles from the Lenape national capital of Goschachgunk.

White Eyes joined Morgan, McKee, Wilson, and the others the following morning, June 11, as they rode to the Lenape capital. The large town of log cabins and bark longhouses was buzzing with activity, for "all their Chief and principal Men" had arrived from throughout the Lenape nation. Chief Welapachtschiechen—Erect Posture or Captain Johnny—represented the western Turkey Clan, White Eyes's political group. Chief Hopocan, also known as Captain Pipe, represented the northern Wolf Clan. Sachem Netawatwees, or "Skilled Advisor," and his grandson Chief Gelelemend, or John Killbuck, represented the Turtle Clan. Together with the Council of Wise Men known as the Lupwaaeenoawuk, the grandmothers, and other influential members of society, they assembled in the Grand Council House.[12]

Morgan entered the Lenape Xi'ngwikan, or Big House, a log building fifty feet long and twenty-four feet wide.[13] According to Lenape ceremonial custom, two council fires were lit with a pump drill in order to make a "clean fire"—one facing the East, the other the West. The flicker of the flames illuminated twelve wooden posts that were topped with carved Misi'ngw faces with slanted eyes and flared noses painted red on the right and black on the left, representing the duality of forces embodied in the Manitou. These spirit guardians watched over everything and carried prayers to the Creator. Four faces were carved on the center post, which stood for the staff of the Great Spirit, placed in the center of the world. The four walls of the big house were aligned with the four quarters of the universe, with the eastern door open to face the rising sun, which symbolized the beginning of things. The floor suggested the back of Turtle

Island, and the roof arched like the sky, leading to the realm of the Creator. The entire Big House symbolized the universe.[14] The Lenape people gathered here not only for important political meetings but also for the Ga'muing, an annual twelve-day ceremony of thanksgiving, during which they recited their dreams and prayed for peace, harmony, and the preservation of the whole world.[15]

Following Lenape custom, the Wolf Clan women sat to Morgan's right, with Captain Pipe and the Wolf men lining the north wall. The Turkey Clan women sat to Morgan's left, with Captain Johnny, White Eyes, and the Turkey men lining the south wall. The Turtle Clan women sat along the west wall, with Grandfather Netawatwees, Gelelemend, and the Turtle men positioned in the southwest corner. Many of the Lenape elders knew Morgan, one of the few honest traders during the decade of his activities in the Ohio River Valley. Their young white brother was now assuming an important role in an unfolding frontier drama.

Important meetings were opened with the sacred pipe being smoked to purify the thoughts of those involved and to communicate their prayers to the Great Manitou. The long moment of silent meditation was intended to clear their minds and open their hearts as a prelude to the work for peace. As head sachem of the Lenape nation, Netawatwees welcomed Morgan in a traditional way by conducting a condolence ceremony with a cluster of strings of white wampum shell beads. He said:

> Brother,
>   We wipe your eyes so you may see us all as Brothers and find your way clear. We cleanse your body after the fatigues of your Journey. We make you appear fair and white to all people. We remove all bad reports from your heart and open your ears to hear our good words.[16]

Morgan responded by revealing a long string of white wampum as he rose to speak.

To preserve an accurate record of this historic meeting, Morgan noted the details in his personal journal:

> Tuesday June 11th, 1776
> In the Delaware Council at Coochocking
>
> Present all their Chiefs & principal Men,
>
> The usual Ceremonies having pass'd I address' them as follows:
>
> Brothers,
>   I thank you for your kind Reception of me into your Towns, & Council House at this place, which from the Friendship you have now

shewn to me, I see appears fair & clear like that of our Ancestors. You have wiped my Eyes that I may see you all as Brothers & find my way clear. You have cleansed my Body after the fatigues of my Journey, & made me appear fair & white to all people. You have removed all bad reports from my Heart & open'd my Ears to hear your good Words. I thank you for this kindness. And I feel myself refresh'd & much at ease.[17]

Morgan was following the tradition of Indian oratory, in which the speaker recounted the previous statements before making his own original speech. He spoke with confidence, praising the Lenape elders for their dedication to promoting friendship between the Americans and Lenape people:

It pleases me to meet you thus as it is a sure Testimony of your remembering the Friendship you made with your Brethren of the United Colonies last year at Pittsburgh. That Friendship I hope will last forever. To promote it is the business of my present visit to you. I therefore now clear your Ears & remove all bad Reports from your Hearts that what I am going to say from the Wise Council of the United Colonies may have due Impression on your Minds.
A String 400 [Wampum][18]

Morgan was recalling the 1775 American–Indian treaty conference at Fort Pitt, when Lenape ambassadors had proclaimed their commitment to peace and friendship.

Morgan also brought up the matter of White Eyes's journey to Philadelphia to speak before the Continental Congress. This was an important achievement, according to Morgan:

Brethren,
Our Brother Captain [Chief] White Eyes was all the last Winter on a visit among us [in Philadelphia]. I make no doubt but he has told you how desirous all our Wise Men are to promote your Happiness & to live in fast Friendship with you forever—He assured the Wise Council at Philadelphia that you intended to live in Peace with us & to keep fast hold of the Covenant Chain of Friendship you & we entered into last Fall—This made their Hearts glad & all your white Brethren of the United Colonies rejoice in the hope of living with you on this great Island as true Friends and Brothers for ever.[19]

Morgan's eloquent plea for peace was intended to strengthen the bonds of unity. Since White Eyes represented an important link in the diplomatic relations between the white and Lenape peoples, Morgan sought to reinforce the credibility of the Lenape statesman before his own people. If true peace were to be achieved, both sides would have to trust each other and make an effort to preserve sincere friendship.

To symbolize the American commitment to peace and friendship, Morgan held up an impressive belt of wampum interwoven with thirteen stripes that symbolized the thirteen United Colonies (soon to become the thirteen United States). The young agent then invited the chiefs to come together for the treaty conference to be held at Fort Pitt:

> Brothers,
>   Last Fall you were told to expect another Treaty at Pittsburgh this year. You have lately been desired to send to all the Western Nations to hold themselves ready to meet us or send some of their Wise Men to Pittsburgh as they might soon expect to be called there to meet some of our wise Counsellors who are appointed to hold a Treaty there.[20]

As the Grandfathers of the Algonquian family of nations, the Lenni Lenape held a key position in frontier political and social affairs. Morgan recognized that many other nations would follow their lead, so he asked the Lenape to invite their intertribal relations to attend the treaty conference. For this effort to succeed, careful timing would be critical: "I was directed to consult you, when would be the most suitable time, & for that purpose I lately sent a Message to request I might see two or three of your Wise Men to advise with them on that matter, & on what was necessary to be done to make our Friendship lasting."[21]

Morgan proposed a tentative date for the Indians to meet with the commissioners to negotiate the terms of a lasting peace plan: "I have since received Instructions from Congress to call all Nations to meet their Commissioners at Pittsburgh the 20th of next month when they proposed to hold the Treaty, or as soon as you & all the Nations could be assembled there."[22] The final decision about the time for the treaty conference rested with the Indians.

If the Americans tried to rush things, the main chiefs and leaders might not attend the conference, and that would be a disaster. Morgan therefore humbly requested the advice of the Lenape council:

I was directed to consult you on this Business & to desire that you would join your Endeavours with ours to call the Chiefs of all the Western Nations to this Treaty to be held so soon as you think the Lake Indians, & the Oubache Confederacy can have notice & arrive there—for these reasons Brothers, I thought it best to come here to see you myself as I was not sure of my Message coming in time—Beside I now have the good Council of all your wise men here on which I shall depend & thank for it.

A Belt 13 Stripes 2350 [Wampum][23]

Resembling the first version of the American flag, with the circle of stars, this valuable belt of wampum represented the Americans' pledge to promote peace and friendship with the Indian nations. For a lasting peace to be established, dozens of the nations would have to be involved, including the Lake Indians, the Wyandot, Ottawa, Chippewa, and Potawatomi, as well as the Wabash Confederacy, the Miami, Pict, Kickapoo, Muscouton, and many more. Together with the Lenni Lenape, Shawnee, and Iroquois Six Nations, the western Indian nations represented a force that had to be respected.

Morgan again asked the Lenape for their help to spread the news of the upcoming treaty:

Brothers,

When you fix the time you think will best suit to hold the Treaty, I desire you will join me in sending a Belt through the Western Nations informing them thereof & that you will request their Chiefs to meet us at the time appointed.[24]

The acceptance of this point was critical. Morgan could personally address some nations, but Lenape runners would more effectively reach remote tribes, some of them hundreds of miles away.

Morgan concluded by stressing the importance of the Lenape people taking an active role in the work for peace. His strategy involved enlisting the Indians not as soldiers, as George Washington proposed, but rather as peacemakers: "I must for this reason request you will appoint three of your wisest young Men to follow me to the Shawanese Town in two or three days in order that they may be joined by a number of your Grand Children to go with the Belt of Invitation to the different Nations."[25] The Lenape Council concluded for the day and retired to deliberate on Morgan's proposal.

On this same day in Philadelphia a delegation of Six Nations ambassadors was also taking a bold step by appearing before the Continental Congress. They wanted the American revolutionaries to recognize the Six Nations confederacy and realize that they were dedicated to the preservation of peace. Beyond opening diplomatic relations with the revolutionary council, the Iroquois also sought to open up trade and commerce and obtain American recognition of the Indians' territorial sovereignty.

Led by an Onondaga chief, the delegation was invited into Independence Hall to meet President John Hancock, Thomas Jefferson, John Adams, and the other members of the Congress. After some ceremony, Hancock spoke from a prepared speech:

> Brothers,
> We hope the friendship that is between us and you will be firm, and continue as long as the sun shall shine, and the waters run; that we and you may be as one people, and have but one heart, and be kind to one another like brethren.[26]

In the classic style of Indian oratory, Hancock voiced the original promises that had been made to the Indians. If these vows were honored, the future relationship between the Americans and the Indians would be founded on the "Great Law of Peace." Hancock also explained why war had broken out between the Americans and the British:

> Brothers,
> The king of Great Britain, hearkening to the evil counsel of some of his foolish young men, is angry with us, because we will not let him take away . . . our land, and all that we have, and give it to them, and because we will not do every thing that he bids us.[27]

A phrase that was crossed out of the speech stated that "he hath taken up the hatchet to strike us, and given money to a people [German Hessian mercenaries] who are strangers to us, to come from a far country, and fight against us."

Hancock also failed to mention that the Congress was preparing to enlist the Indian warriors as mercenaries to fight the British. It was ironic that what Hancock claimed was the main cause of the conflict—that the king wanted to take away the Americans' lands—was also a major complaint of the Indians against the settlers who were usurping their homelands. Hancock continued: "[The King] . . . hath hindered his people from bringing goods to us; but, we have made provision for getting such a quantity of them, that we hope we shall be able to supply your wants as formerly."[28] The Iroquois did not want a handout, just a free and equitable trade relationship. The British economic blockade was taking its toll on the Americans, who were running low on supplies.

Unknown to both parties at this juncture, on the previous day, King Louis XVI of France had approved loans to the Americans that would help finance the Revolution. But for the time being supplies were hard to get, and when supplies ran low, tempers tended to grow short. During this potentially explosive period, Hancock appealed for peaceful cooperation:

> Brothers,
> We shall order all our warriors and young men not to hurt you or any of your kindred, and we hope you will not suffer any of your young men to join with our enemies, or to do any wrong to us, that nothing may happen to make any quarrel between us.[29]

It was true that a few young Iroquois men had taken the British side at the Niagara treaty council, but the Grand Council would soon send two chiefs to recall and scold all of those warriors. The Six Nations appealed to the Americans not to condemn all Indians because of the impetuous actions of a few hotheads.

The Iroquois were impressed by the promises of the Continental Congress. In acknowledgment of the vows of friendship voiced by the president, the Onondaga chief addressed John Hancock by the honored title the Indians had given him, Karanduawn, the Great Tree of Liberty.

Soon after the Iroquois delegation departed, the Continental Congress appointed a committee to draft the Declaration of Independence. Steps were being taken to create a new government, "the form of a confederation to be entered into between these colonies" whose democratic structure would be patterned in part on that of the confederation of the Iroquois Six Nations.

Meanwhile, at Cooshocking, Morgan was advocating the creation of a peaceful society that combined the best qualities of European and Indian cultures. He was especially impressed by the Iroquois and the Lenni Lenape, whose governments represented perhaps the most ancient forms of participatory democracy on earth. With regard to the specific matter before him, he met with the Lenape elders the morning of June 12 to hear their response to his invitation to the peace treaty:

In Council   June 12th 1776

Captain [Chief] White Eyes spoke as follows [to George Morgan]

Brother,
  This string was sent to us by our Uncles the Wiandots a few days
ago.—It is to thank us for our Intelligence that the United Colonies
and we are in strict friendship & that we join our desires to live in Peace
with all Nations—They say, "Let us all who are of one colour look up
to Heaven for ability to live in Friendship & be strong in doing so as
it will promote our lasting Happiness."[30]

The spiritual foundation of the American Indian peace effort was articulated
clearly in this statement by the Wyandot nation. As the "Uncles" of the Lenni
Lenape in the family relationships of Indian politics, the Wyandot and their
policies carried considerable weight. Since the Wyandot capital was located near
the British fortress at Detroit, the headquarters of Governor Henry Hamilton,
the Wyandot stood in a pivotal position to sway the tribes from the area around
the Great Lakes.

After his opening words, White Eyes held up another string of wampum and
recited the Wyandot response to the opening of diplomatic relations with the
American revolutionaries: "On this other String [of Wampum] they [the
Wyandot] add—'We are glad Nephews that you have been to the Great Council
of the United Colonies [meaning White Eyes's visit to Philadelphia] the
Speeches you have sent us are very good & we take fast hold of them."[31] The
approval by the Wyandot of White Eyes's bold diplomatic efforts before the
Continental Congress helped to strengthen the Lenape ambassador's reputation. If they had disapproved, White Eyes would have been responsible for
disrupting Lenape–Wyandot relations. This would have been especially serious,
because for Lenape land title to be secure, they needed to remain on coopera-
tive terms with their powerful allies in the North.

Anyone who jeopardized the national territory would inevitably be condemned. But White Eyes had safely navigated the troubled political waters, and
he continued to read the Wyandot message:

> Last year we [the Wyandot] were invited by them [the Americans] to
> meet them at Pittsburgh on which five of us attended without advising
> with our Head Chiefs & that was the reason of our Silence at the
> Treaty. But we will not do so again for we will consult with them when
> we are invited again.[32]

Half King Daunghquat, Old Calotte, Tarhe Crane, Abraham Kuhn, Tegasah, and Bawbee served as the main chiefs and medicine people of the Wyandot Nation. If they could be persuaded to remain neutral and to resist the political and economic pressure being applied by the British, the chances for peace on the frontier would be enhanced.[33]

The message from the Wyandot concluded: "We are now determined to listen to our Wise people in future—And we desire that whenever our Brethren of the Colonies have anything to say to us you will lead them by the hand to us that we may see their own Faces & hear themselves speak that we may declare to all Nations with certainty what they say to us."[34] The diplomatic door now appeared to be open, but certain dangers still remained. The Wyandot invitation could, for instance, be a trap to capture Morgan. During this troubled period, the risk of being double-crossed or assassinated made many people constantly look over their shoulders.

White Eyes held up and began to translate another string of wampum from Chief Conneodico, an Onondaga living at Salt Licks in Ohio:

> This String Brother is from Conneodico enquiring what Speeches were sent from the Six Nations & White People to us, as he was jealous that something was going on against him—We told him to go to the Fort & hear for himself, for there was no ill intended to him.
>
> Our Uncles the Wiandots refuse to have anything to do with him as they think him a troublesome person, & recommend that we should speak to him ourselves for we had desired them to do it.[35]

The reason Conneodico was living so far away from his nation, which was centered around the Finger Lakes in New York, remains a mystery. But regardless of whether he was an outcast, an outlaw, or a resistance leader, Conneodico and a small party of warriors were spreading threatening rumors and pounding the war drums.

White Eyes then picked a small belt of wampum that symbolized the policy of the Lenni Lenape toward the American revolutionaries. He said:

> Now Brother listen to us—The Delaware Council,
>
> We thank you for your good words spoke to us from the Congress yesterday—We receive everything you have said as the strongest Testimony of their Friendship towards us—You desire our assistance in promoting a lasting Peace between the United Colonies & all the

Indian Nations—Your request is good and we take it into our Hearts—
We will afford you what you desire all in our power for our wishes are
the same as yours vizt: That all Nations may live in Peace.

A little Belt [of Wampum][36]

Morgan had succeeded in getting from their chiefs a strong affirmation of
the Lenape commitment to peace. The Lenape were not merely inclined to
remain neutral, but were willing to help actively in the work for peace. If Morgan
could win similar support from other Indian nations, the chance for the frontier
to stay free of the Revolutionary War would be much greater.

White Eyes proposed that Morgan carry the message of peace to neighboring nations:

> Brother,
> You are now going to see our Grand Children the Shawanese, we
> desire you will not stop there but will speak to our Uncles the Wiandots
> yourself or send some of your own people with our's who we have
> appointed to accompany & assist you in this good work—We now clear
> the Road for you that nothing may interrupt your Journey.[37]

The Lenape were willing to lend their skills in wampum diplomacy in order to
communicate the American peace message and were offering Morgan free
passage and protection through all the Lenape territory. However, the long
distances that needed to be traversed and the delicacy of the negotiations at
hand would require more time for Morgan's work to succeed. White Eyes held
up another string of wampum and suggested:

> We think the time you propose holding the Treaty is much too soon
> for the Western Nations—they cannot come in less than sixty days
> though our Uncles, the Wiandots will be best able to fix the time
> themselves and whatever time they fix will be agreeable to us—We for
> our parts are determined to keep fast hold to our good Friendship and
> desire you will be strong to do the same—We have already sent [a
> message] to the Oubache Indians to expect to be called to Pittsburgh.
> A string [of Wampum][38]

The timing of the treaty was left up to the Wyandot. Out of respect for their
Uncles, the Lenape deferred the choice to them. Lenape messengers raced west
to spread the news of Morgan's mission to the more distant nations.

The young agent summarized in his journal the main points of the response he had thus far received:

> Answer to the foregoing,
>
> 1st. Thanks for the Intelligence & String from the Wiandots.
> 2nd. Thanks for sending to them & to the Oubache,
> 3rd. Thanks for the three Men appointed to accompany me,
> 4th. And for their good advice & promises to be strong in holding fast to our Friendship
> 5th. Repeated to them the Message sent [during the] last Treaty to Conneodico & requested them to join me once more, that if he should act wrong hereafter, he only may be blamed.[39]

The message sent to Conneodico and the Mingo among whom he lived in the Ohio River Valley called upon them to "bury in Oblivion all that has past" regarding previous conflicts and to "brighten the Chain of Friendship."[40]

Conneodico obviously refused to accept these terms. The belts of wampum that symbolized the Covenant Chain of Friendship represented political and spiritual agreements of unity. Morgan referred to the eloquent ceremony to reinforce their mutual commitment to peace:

> Brothers,
>   It is necessary to examine our Covenant Belts & if any dirt or rust comes thereto, to have them brightened—Now we desire you will do this often, & if You find the least spot tell us of it that we may assist you in rubbing it off & in strengthening our Friendship—[41]

Morgan sounded like an old Indian diplomat as he drew upon the poetic imagery of traditional Indian oratory.

To ensure that any future conflicts would be resolved peacefully, Morgan called upon the Lenape to express themselves freely, for only through an active and continuous dialogue could disagreements be resolved. Morgan appealed for principles of international cooperation to be honored:

> For this purpose we desire you will open your Hearts & speak freely & kindly to us for if you have any doubts or Jealousies or any uneasiness or just cause of Complaint against your Brethren of the United Colonies or against your Brethren of them & will now inform us therof you may depend the great Congress will be prepared to do you Justice

when we meet you next in Council at Pittsburgh—this we likewise promise to all Nations & we desire you will tell them so.[42]

Morgan extended his hand in friendship and made a commitment on behalf of the American revolutionaries to promote the everlasting happiness of the Indian people:

> Brothers,
> We not only incline to do you Justice in all things but we wish to promote your happiness & to render you every service in our power if you tell us what you want—We therefore desire your Wise people will consider this matter well, for we wish to see you a happy People & to live with you in Friendship forever. Speak your minds free when you come to the Treaty that we may understand you.
> A String 400 [Wampum][43]

After Morgan had told the Lenape elders, "I should proceed on my Journey tomorrow," the national council deliberated on the remarkable nature of this young white man. When a person performed an exceptional service for the betterment of society, the elders occasionally conveyed a special honor. In recognition of George Morgan's dedication to peace and harmony, the Grand Council of the Lenni Lenape nation bestowed on him the title of an honorary chief, Brother Tamanend, the "Affable One":

> This Gentleman [George Morgan] was much beloved & admired by the Indians for the addresses he continually made to them to remain Peaceable, yea he had their Confidence to Such a Degree, that they honoured him with a Name [Brother Tamanend] which was one of their Chiefs . . . 100 years ago, who was known by every one, as a good & Peaceable Man.[44]

The conferment of this title represented one of the greatest honors a white man ever received from an Indian nation. Tamanend was not just any chief. He was perhaps the most important and revered leader in Lenape history. He was the "Great Peacemaker," and was said to have been reincarnated three times. The first Tamanend, a man of nobility and goodness who lived in ancient times, sealed bonds of friendship through the power of his sacred pipe. The second Tamanend reportedly formed an alliance between the Iroquois and the Lenape to end a terrible, bloody war of revenge. The third Tamanend was said to have joined hands with William Penn beneath the Tree of Peace in 1682 at Shackamaxon, "The Place Where Chiefs Are Made," which later became Philadelphia.[45] The name of Tamanend had come to symbolize for the Lenape ideal human qualities:

> He was in the highest degree endowed with wisdom, virtue, prudence, charity, affability, meekness, hospitality, in short every good and noble qualification that a human being may possess. He was supposed to have had an intercourse [discussion] with the great and good Spirit; for he was a stranger to everything that is bad.[46]

The reason the Lenape so honored Morgan was explained as follows:

> The [Lenape] conferred on him [Morgan] the name of Tamanend in honor and remembrance of their ancient chief, and as the greatest mark of respect which they could shew to that gentleman, who, they said, had the same address, affability and meekness, as their honoured chief, and therefore, ought to be named after him.[47]

Along with the name of the Great Peacemaker, the new Brother Tamanend assumed the weight of responsibility of living up to his title. After receiving the honor, Morgan prepared to ride west the next morning to meet with the chiefs and clan mothers of the Shawnee nation. Despite his great success with the Lenape nation, he knew that his greatest challenges were still ahead.

Chapter Seven

THE WHITE DEER'S MISSION
TO THE SHAWNEE

ON THE MORNING of June 12, George Morgan departed from the Lenape capital of Goschachgunk and rode southwest toward the Shawnee and Mingo nations. He was accompanied by former British agent Alexander McKee, interpreters Joseph Nicholson and William Wilson, and four Lenape escorts.[1] After crossing the Muskingum River, they briefly visited Christian Indians at Lichtenau, the "Pasture of Light":

> Two and a half miles below Goschachgunk . . . a broad level of many acres stretched to the foot of the hills, with an almost imperceptible ascent. The river-bank, swelling out gently toward the stream in the form of an arc, was covered with maples and stately sycamores.[2]

White Eyes and John Killbuck's father, Hi La Japen, followed the men to Lichtenau, where a discussion of importance took place after Morgan's departure.

Brother Wilhelm Chilloway, a supervisor of Moravian Christian Indians, took White Eyes aside for a pointed discussion: "You have heard the speech that Mr. Morgan made that you should carefully consider your request to Congress, so what are you supposed to consider?"[3] A former interpreter for Sir William Johnson, the late British Superintendent for Indian Affairs, and now a devout Christian Indian, Chilloway launched into a fiery sermon. White Eyes stood silent as he said in a commanding tone:

Well, I will tell you. Consider very carefully what you intend to do and what you have already done. You have declared that you intend to accept the word of God, and after that you have declared that the word should be preached amongst you. You have that now. The [Moravian] brothers are there. You have made a mistake.[4]

White Eyes's proposal to bring an Anglican minister into the Lenape nation was being challenged in the strongest terms.

While the Lenape council had merely turned a deaf ear to the issue, Chilloway spoke out angrily:

You have deviated from the right path, and have forgotten what you feared in the beginning. . . . As soon as you give up your intention to call another minister, and remain with the [Moravian] brothers, you will be helped and the purpose of your wish [to make the nation great] will be achieved. However, if you continue in your present intent . . . you will fall into even greater confusion.[5]

Few men had ever so addressed White Eyes. Although they were pacifists, the Protestant Moravians were indeed a power not to be underestimated. White Eyes appeared to submit to their influence:

White Eyes now appeared to have found the thread that would lead him out of the labyrinth. He recognizes now that he, because of his manipulations, has drawn upon himself the hatred of the Indians . . . he intended to be their regent and wanted to order them around. . . . They would prefer to cut his throat.[6]

What caused the Indians' wrath against White Eyes was not only that he planned to bring in an English minister, but also that by "opening the door" a little, he risked allowing a flood of white people onto Indian lands. The Indians feared that once their boundaries were penetrated, their territory would be overrun.

While this encounter was taking place, Morgan's entourage made progress along the Coshocton trail, passing an old town and a fine spring and fording a small creek to the burned rubble of Waketameki, a Shawnee town destroyed in 1774 during Dunmore's War. This was the former home of Morgan's old Shawnee friend Silver Heels, who had been stabbed to death years before in Illinois country. The charred remnants of Waketameki were a grim reminder of the horrors of white–Indian war.[7]

By nightfall Morgan's party had covered twenty-one miles, arriving at Licking Creek. Along the banks, they found shelter at the old village of a Lenape wise man named Wingenund:

> This great and good man was not only one of the bravest and most celebrated warriors, but one of the most amiable men of the Delaware nation. To a firm undaunted mind, he joined humanity, kindness and universal benevolence; the excellent qualities of his heart had obtained for him the name of *Wingenund*, which . . . signifies *the well beloved*.[8]

Morgan would later appeal to Wingenund for his support, but for the time being he had to move on quickly in order to carry out his mission. The riders made good time on the ancient trail that led them into a cultural center of the old Adena and Hopewell cultures, known as the "Moundbuilders."[9] Indian people had lived in this area for over ten thousand years.[10]

To the right of the Coshocton trail were numerous burial mounds along a two-and-a-half-mile corridor that was centered around a remarkable earthenwork effigy of an eagle. The impressive ruins of a people the Lenape called the Tallega included huge embankments, geometric plazas, and pyramids made of earth. The pioneer archaeologist Ephraim Squier later wrote: "In entering the ancient avenue for the first time, the visitor does not fail to experience a sensation of awe, such as he might feel in passing the portals of an Egyptian temple."[11] The dense forest of centuries-old trees was full of wildlife, a huge bubbling spring was circled with salt licks, and the "Great Buffalo Swamp" was overgrown with tangled vines and spring flowers. Near the water's edge, Flint Ridge, a sacred site covered with Indian petroglyphs, extended fifty feet into the sky:

> There is an Indian [legend] that the tribes, gathering to get material for arrowheads at Flint Ridge, were so inclined to war that the Great Spirit ordained it neutral ground. The local residents assert that no war points are found, and that the Indians agreed to abide by the tradition.[12]

Morgan and his men rested at the head springs of the Hockhocking and Muskingum rivers, called Pipe's War Marks, before riding the last leg of the day's journey. For the next eight miles, the trail rolled up and down like long waves. By nightfall the day's trek had taken them thirty miles, a formidable distance through such rugged terrain. The men slept that night at Snake Egg Camp.[13]

On Saturday morning, June 15, Morgan's entourage crossed Hockhocking River to the western banks and visited the village of Assunuck, the "Place of the Standing Stone."[14] On a high plateau northeast of the Shawnee confederacy resided the chief of the Turkey Clan, Welapachtschiechen, also known as Captain Johnny or Erect Posture, a sixty-year-old Lenape leader originally from Pennsylvania.[15] He shared his humble home with his white wife, Rachel, who had been captured during the French and Indian War in 1757 and adopted into the clan.[16] Since their recent visit to the Moravian mission, she had been pressuring her husband to resign from the chieftaincy and to join the Christians. If Chief Welapachtschiechen resigned, his people would lose a valued leader and the Lenape's political strength would be decreased. The responsibilities of the chieftaincy during this difficult period were complex and demanding. As yet undecided, Welapachtschiechen remained atop the red sandstone cliffs in his village, which had a view of Pickaway Plains and a string of mesas leading off into the distance. The well-being of his wife and three children, as well as the fate of his people, depended upon his decision. Perhaps with the arrival of Brother Tamanend, the young American Indian agent, a safe passage could be formulated to ensure their survival against those who might assassinate a peace chief to incite war.

Morgan and his party rode for another nineteen miles before crossing the Scioto River and continuing on for two miles to Old Kiskapoo, an abandoned Shawnee village. The Shawnee had built a series of villages along the Scioto when scattered tribes from Georgia, Alabama, the Carolinas, Maryland, Illinois, and Pennsylvania had reunited in Ohio in the 1750s.[17] Morgan and his men rested for the night at Old Kiskapoo before completing the final part of the day's journey.

Early Sunday morning Morgan's group rode south on the "Warriors' Path" along the Scioto River. Most of the Shawnee nation was now consolidated downstream. The first major population center, inhabited by a few thousand people, was at the United Towns: "Traditional Shawnee towns, semi-permanent settlements inhabited in summer, consisted of bark-covered lodges resembling Iroquois longhouses . . . also . . . one-room log huts roofed with bark and buildings made of boards or shingles."[18]

Shawnee society was composed of twelve main clans—Turtle, Raccoon, Bear, Wolf, Snake, Turkey, Hawk, Deer, Elk, Great Lynx, Buffalo, and Tree. They were organized around two main political parties, one for peace and one for war. The peace party represented an alliance of five divisions, each headed by a peace chief who could be male or female. There was also a woman's council organized in a similar style. Most addressed the Creator as "Our Grandmother," who was accompanied by her grandson, called Rounded Side or Cloudy Boy. The spiritual intermediaries who carried divine messages included tobacco, fire, water, and eagles. Our Grandmother was said to have taught Shawnee people a set of ten sacred laws about the importance of preserving a peaceful and harmonious society.[19]

By nightfall Morgan and his entourage had arrived at Chillicothe, "Home of the People." In the center of the town stood the large wooden council house, sixty feet square. This building was used on both political and religious occasions by roughly three hundred people living in Chillicothe.[20]

For the introductory meeting, the Shawnee chose to take Morgan to a nearby council house at Kiskapoo. The sachem of the nation, Old Kishanatathe or Hard Man, was accompanied by head war chief Cornstalk or Colesquo, his sister, Clan Mother Coitcheleh, and his brother, peace chief Nimwha. Since Morgan had come on a mission of peace, Nimwha was the first to speak:

> In Council at Kiskapoo a Shawanese Town Monday June 17th, 1776
>
> Present: The Chiefs & Head Men of all Tribes
>
> The Chiefs having been assembled sometime in Council sent to inform me they were ready to receive me—Being seated sometime— Nimwa in behalf of the whole spoke as follows:
>
> Brother,
> You are welcome to our Council Fire, we are well pleased to see you—We cleanse your Eyes, Mouth, Ears, etc. We wash your Body with sweet Oil & wipe it with a white Cloth sent from God for that purpose.[21]

Nimwha was following rituals of wampum diplomacy by welcoming Morgan in the traditional manner. Like other Indian societies, the Shawnee were striving to preserve their culture and heritage. Their people had suffered greatly from past conflicts with Americans, and they were now especially concerned with protection of the intertribal hunting preserve in Kentucky. The Shawnee were prepared to fight for their survival, but they were also willing to try first to open a path for peaceful and equitable relations: "We tell you again we rejoice to see our Brother from the Great Council [of the Continental Congress]—It looks as if we may now take hold of the end of that [Covenant Chain of] Friendship which has been so long bury'd. We gladly do it & we will not let it go."[22]

The Shawnee did not immediately accept the Covenant Chain of Friendship, but Nimwha was nonetheless encouraging, indicating that his nation might yet embrace such an opportunity. If a fair and honorable agreement could be negotiated, Nimwha assured Morgan, the Shawnee sincerely desired peace.

When it was his turn to speak, Morgan rose and held up a string of wampum beads:

> I am much pleased Brothers with your kind welcome into your Towns & Council & that I have found the Road so clear. It convinces me your Hearts are good, like mine, & will enable me to deliver to you what I have to say from the Great Council of the United Colonies with great pleasure—It does my heart good to meet you thus & to see your Wives & Children in Friendship.[23]

After decades of being called savages, heathens, and other degrading names, the Shawnee welcomed Morgan's address, for he spoke to them as brothers and treated them like human beings. The expression of kindness toward Shawnee women and children went to the heart of their concerns, since protection of their families' security and happiness was foremost on their minds.

Morgan also made an appeal for strengthening of intertribal family relationships, noting that the Shawnee had recently reestablished bonds with their Grandfathers, the Lenni Lenape:

> On my way hither I met my Brothers, your Grand Fathers the Delawares [Lenape] in Council at Coochocking. Their Wise Men received me just as you have done & sent four of their Young Men to assist me in the good work I am come on. They sit now here before you. As it is now late I will tomorrow deliver to you what I have in charge from the Great Council.
> A String 400 [Wampum][24]

At that very moment, unknown to Morgan, as well as to the British, who were winding up their Indian conference in Niagara, the "Great Council" in Philadelphia was finalizing and expanding the powers of General George Washington to enlist Indian warriors as mercenary soldiers.

In direct violation of the 1775 Fort Pitt Treaty, Congress passed the following formal resolution:

> That General Washington be permitted to employ the Indians. . . . In any place where he shall judge they will be most useful; and that he be

authorized to offer them a reward of one hundred dollars for every commissioned [British] officer, and of thirty dollars for every private soldier of the Kings's troops that they shall take prisoners in the Indian country, or on the frontiers of these colonies.[25]

This action gave Washington authority not only to enlist Indians fighting in Canada, but now virtually anywhere on the vast American frontier. While Congress approved the plan to pay Indians a one-hundred-dollar bounty for every British officer, delegates struck down a proposal to raise the pay of American soldiers from five dollars to six dollars per month.[26] Washington and Congress were clearly banking on the military potential of the Indian nations.

In contrast to Congress's sudden change of direction, Morgan continued to pursue the original policies and promises that President John Hancock had instructed him to follow. When the Shawnee leaders reconvened, Morgan spoke like a wise elder:

> In Council Wednesday June 19th, 1776,
> Present as before——[G. Morgan said,]
>
> Brothers,
>   You have wiped the Sweat off my Body, cleansed me with Sweet Oil & wiped me down with a clean Cloth sent from Heaven for that purpose, you have wiped my Eyes & open'd them that I may see clear & look at you as Brothers—You have removed all bad Stories from me, & have open'd my Ears that I may hear what is good—I now feel comfortable & much at Ease.[27]

Morgan did not sound like a young white man. He was so well versed in tribal manners and customs that his orations resounded with a traditional Indian eloquence.

In addition, Morgan's knowledge of Indian history made him mindful that certain promises to promote peace and friendship had been made previously, and such sacred vows should not be broken:

> I thank you Brothers for this Kindness & for your very friendly reception of me into your Towns & into your Council House at this place—This is just like the happy Meetings of our wise Ancestors in former times as every thing looks fair & clear—it pleases me Brothers to meet you thus, & to find the Road between us is kept so clear—It is a sure Testimony that your Hearts are good.—I now widen the Road that we may all travel it often & with safety. A String 400 [Wampum][28]

The fact that the "road" was clear meant diplomatic relations were now open. As long as their ambassadors continued to speak freely, the chance for peace appeared "fair and clear." It was only when talks broke down and nations ceased to communicate that the future seemed dark and threatening.

Morgan held up another string of white wampum and professed:

> Brothers,
> I wipe your Eyes that you may see me clear. I remove all idle stories from you. I cleanse your Hearts & open your Ears that you may hear distinctly & understand what I have to say to you from the Great Council of the Thirteen United Colonies, representing all your White Brothers who have grown out of this same big Island with yourselves— What I have to say, Brothers, is intended to promote the old good friendship of our Ancestors which we renew'd last Fall at Pittsburgh & which we hope will last forever.[29]

Morgan recalled agreements made at the 1775 Fort Pitt treaty conference. Both sides had vowed to promote peace and friendship between their people. Their bonds had particular significance in light of the fact that both Indians and Americans were born on this continent and therefore should live in harmony upon "Turtle Island." Morgan made a special point of this in order to distinguish the Americans from the British and other foreigners.

The early history of the relationship between white people and Indians was fraught with conflict. However, a series of treaties—such as when Tamanend and William Penn joined hands beneath the Tree of Peace—had established a precedent for peaceful cooperation. Morgan acknowledged that many treaties had been broken, but quickly pointed out that it was not too late to revive the original vows of peace:

> Brothers,
> The dark Cloud which had intervened between us for sometime is now dispell'd. There are many of our wise Men still living who remember the Wise Councils of our Ancestors & the Friendship which they entered into with your Great Grand Fathers—they . . . wrote down all these Wise Councils for us to read—It is this same good old Friendship we now want to promote & strengthen by brightening the [Covenant] Chain.
> A String 400 [Wampum][30]

Morgan sought to freshen the memories of Shawnee elders so that they might recall that the pages of their history were not all covered with the blood of war.[31] Morgan then symbolically purified the environment, so that the work for peace could be revived:

> Brothers,
>   I now cleanse your Council House from all dirt. I sweep it clean, that it may appear white & fair like that at Philadelphia from which I am sent—& like that which your & our Wise Men formerly sat in there. A String 200 [Wampum][32]

Actually, Congress at that time was confronted not with images of peace, but rather with gruesome depictions of war. The delegates in Philadelphia were outraged by recent reports from Canada that Brigadier General Benedict Arnold was taking a beating and American soldiers were being tortured and killed:

> On the 24th day of May . . . a party [600] of the enemy . . . attacked a post at the Cedars, held by a garrison of 350 Continental forces . . . on the third day [of the battle] the garrison surrendered themselves prisoners of war . . . the said enemy murdered two of them, butchering the one with tomahawks and drowning the other; and left divers others exposed in an island naked and perishing with cold and famine.

Congressional delegates passed a resolution that such horrors were a "gross and barbarous violation of the laws of nature and nations."[33]

The British officer in command of the Cedars, Captain Forester, was targeted for prosecution once he was captured. Desire for revenge burned in the hearts of some American congressmen.[34] The crimes committed in this incident were indeed horrible, but if the Continental Congress ordered American soldiers to commit the same acts in revenge, how would Americans appear to the world? The Shawnee knew well the horrors of war, which was why the elders were working so hard with Morgan to prevent the Revolution from spreading throughout the frontier.

Morgan next held up a white belt of twelve hundred wampum beads and proclaimed:

Brothers,

This Belt is sent by the Great Council of the United Colonies to our Brother Kishanatathe [Hard Man]—Our Wise men know his Father was a very wise & good Chief of your Nation & that during the time of his taking care of the Friendship nothing happened to interrupt it—Therefore they send this Message to him which I will now read to you.[35]

Morgan's acknowledgment of Hard Man's father, the former sachem Hawcawohcheykey, was a most sensitive and thoughtful gesture. For Morgan to recall the work of a former chief who had been dedicated to preserving the well-being of the Shawnee nation was a small but very important gesture as far as the Shawnee were concerned.

Morgan then produced an official letter from Congress and began to read:

To Kishanatathe—Head Chief of the Shawanese Nation, from his Brethren of the Thirteen United Colonies, who have grown out of the same great Island with him, by their Representatives met in one great Council.

Brother Kishanatathe:

Our Commissioners whom we appointed to hold a Treaty with our Indian Brethren last Fall at Pittsburgh, have informed us that you did not meet them there, owing to the conduct of foolish people who were instigated by the evil Spirit.[36]

A special effort was being made to win cooperation of Sachem Kishanatathe or Hard Man because he was an elder chief who was looked up to by many Indians. If Hard Man approved the proposed treaty between the Americans and the Indians, chances for its success would be greatly improved. Morgan continued to read the congressional message:

Brother,

It is a long time since you have sat in the Council of our Wise Men in the place of your father, Haw, caw, oh, chey, key, by whose wise Councils whilst he had the care of our Friendship our Brothers the Shawanese & we always lived together in strict Friendship.[37]

The Shawnee's ancestors were known to have lived in the late seventeenth century around Delaware Water Gap upon an invitation from their grandfathers, the Lenni Lenape. In 1728 Sachem Hawcawohcheykey, or Kakowatcheky, led his people to Wyoming Valley in Pennsylvania. Fifteen years later, they returned to their ancient homeland in Ohio, where sachem Hawcawohcheykey's son, Sachem Hard Man, helped to reunite many Shawnee tribes into one main nation.[38]

Congress was concerned that the Shawnee, who—as has been noted earlier—were severely treated by the Virginians, might join the British side, so Sachem Hard Man was warned not to listen to "foolish people":

> Brother,
>
> We are sorry for what has been done by foolish people to interrupt your & our Friendship—The dark Cloud which has interven'd between us for sometime is now dispell'd & we can see each other clear. Therefore with this Belt which we send [by Mr. Morgan] we now cleanse your Heart & place it just like your Fathers & those of our Wise Men. We rub & wipe your Body down, we cleanse it from every spot & stain, make all Nations to see you white & fair & remove every sorrow from your Heart.[39]

A firm gesture was being made by Morgan on behalf of the Congress to end the longstanding feud between the Shawnee and the white people. This traditional condolence was intended to soothe hard feelings and to introduce an age of peace and cooperation:

> Brother,
>
> We now desire you will remember the good Councils of your Wise Father—take fast hold of our Covenant Belt of Peace & Friendship, as he always did, strengthen every Link of the Chain, keep it bright & clean, never let it slip out of your hands—That by your example all our Brothers of your Colour of all Nations may be strong in preserving Peace and Friendship with us.[40]

The Covenant Chain of Friendship was a powerful image for Indian people. If both sides kept fast hold of their ends of the agreement, peace was possible. However, if one promise was broken, the peaceful alliance would prove only as strong as the weakest link. Therefore, it was important that great care be taken to honor every point in the efforts for peace.

Morgan concluded reading the message from Congress:

Brother,

The Road is clear for all Nations to come to us & particularly for your & our young Men & your Grand Fathers the Delawares [Lenape] & your Brothers the Six Nations [Iroquois] to pass & repass whenever they please; we desire to widen it, & that you will assist us in Keeping it clear from all bad Weeds, Thorns, & Briars, & that you will never let the evil Spirit blind the Eyes of your people again nor suffer him to rule them.

A White Belt about 1200 [Wampum][41]

Congress had made it clear that it wanted to keep diplomatic channels open. However, it was concerned that the British would try to create discord between Americans and Indians. Clearly the "evil spirit" was the British, and the Indians would be wise not to be "blinded" by their designs. The spiritual dimension of the Americans' plea demonstrated a perceptive approach to the art of wampum diplomacy. This might enhance their image among the tribes, but the Americans' reputation as a people following divine laws of the Great Spirit would be maintained only as long as they kept their word and honored their treaty promises.

Morgan then held up a larger belt of twenty-five hundred wampum beads interwoven with thirteen figures to symbolize the thirteen United Colonies, a belt similar to the one he had given the Lenape. The young American Indian agent then made a personal appeal to the Shawnee to join him in the work for peace:

Brothers,

I am sent to you from the great Council of the Thirteen United Colonies (representing all your white Brethren) who have grown out of this same Island with yourselves to consult with you on the best means to preserve the Peace & Friendship which our Wise Ancestors enter'd into, & which we lately renewed at Pittsburgh [in the 1775 Treaty,] and I ask your good Council & assistance in establishing Peace between us & all the Western Nations.[42]

After the opening ceremonies and formalities, Morgan had arrived at the main purpose of his mission. Morgan sought to construct a solid foundation for peace based on equality for both societies:

Brothers,

Last Fall we began this good work—We continue strong in it—We then had a good Council with you at Pittsburgh—We hope nothing has happened since then to change your Hearts for our's remain firm & we are determined to hold fast the Covenant Chain of Friendship which our wise Ancestors entered into and which we then renew'd with you our Brothers & with the Six Nations and Delawares.[43]

An equitable judicial system was needed to deal with criminal activity on the frontier. This was one of the issues to be discussed at the proposed treaty conference. Morgan had two months to organize the meeting. He would need the help and cooperation of the chiefs if many distant nations were to be informed in time. And their presence was essential, since the treaty conference could only have a real impact if leaders of a vast majority of western Indian nations united in agreeing to stay neutral. Morgan continued:

> I therefore desire you will not only come yourselves, but that you will join with me & with your Grand Fathers the Delawares in sending to our Brothers the Hurons & the Nations of the Wabache Confederacy—who are desirous to take hold of our Friendship, and we desire you will invite them all to meet our Wise Men at Pittsburgh at that time, and that you will particularly take the Picts & Wabache by the hand & lead them to us & put their hands to our Covenant Belt of Friendship that we may enter into an everlasting Peace with them.[44]

All Indian nations from the Mississippi River to the Allegheny Mountains and from the Great Lakes to the Ohio River were to be invited.

If the Shawnee agreed, their ambassadors would help carry the Grand Wampum Belt from village to village in order to spread the word that peace was to be seriously sought at Fort Pitt. Morgan concluded his message to the Shawnee:

> Brothers,
>   We desire you will shew this Belt & Message to all the different Indian Nations immediately & bring them by the hand to us.
> Message in Writing
> Large Belt, 13 Figures, in imitation of the Grand Belt [with] 2500 Wampum.[45]

Morgan presented the wampum belt to Sachem Hard Man. It was an exact duplicate of the belts that had been presented to the Lenni Lenape and the Iroquois Six Nations. The wampum belts were an Indian version of a legal covenant equal in importance to a Declaration of Independence or a Constitution. The Shawnee were also given a written copy of the speeches, since past experience had shown that Europeans often did not recognize anything other than a written document as being legally binding.

Morgan then briefed the Shawnee on the American plan to invite other western Indian nations:

> Brothers,
> This is our Message to the Lake Indians & Wabach Confederacy. We desire you will join us & your Grand Fathers the Delawares in shewing it to them, & that our Brothers the Mingoes in your Neighbourhood may see it & be invited to the Treaty.[46]

Morgan recognized the importance of maintaining an open diplomatic policy.

Trust could not be built on secrecy, so Morgan read the Shawnee the speech he hoped they would help him spread far and wide.

> To all the Western Nations,
>
> —A Message from the Thirteen United Colonies in Council
> —June 1776
>
> Brothers,
> We who have grown out of this same big Island with yourselves are desirous to live in peace & Friendship with you,—for that purpose the Great Council of the United Colonies & several Indian Nations our Brethren now send this Message & Belt to invite your Wise Men & War chiefs to a Conference & Treaty appointed to be held at Pittsburgh in the middle of next August—[47]

As previously acknowledged, it would be impossible for Morgan to carry the message personally to all western Indian nations. The only way to reach these remote societies would be by a network of Indian runners carrying the invitation from village to village.

Furthermore, Indian tribal councils logically would be reassured by hearing the message directly from respected Indian ambassadors. Morgan continued reading his message to the western Indian nations:

> There [at the treaty please unite with us] to join your hands with our Brothers the Six Nations, Shawanese & Delawares to a firm Covenant, Belt of Peace & Friendship, that your & our Women & Children may ever enjoy the Benefit of it, & that the Road between us may be made

& kept open for our Young Men to travel with Ease & Safety. We desire you will rise & come to us with our Brothers the Shawanese & Delawares, that we may open your Eyes to see us clear & pick your Ears to drive all bad reports from them & make you hear what is good.[48]

Morgan's reference to "bad reports" acknowledged that with the escalation of the American Revolution, another propaganda war would surely rage this summer of 1776 on the frontier. Rumors inevitably would be spread by those who would profit by the war, a group that included not only the British but also western land speculators and vengeful settlers, who could easily become involved in schemes to provoke Indians.

The Revolution also was placing extraordinary demands on supplies of vital goods. Prices were rising, and Morgan knew that the Indians' reliance on the now-diminished fur trade often left them in desperate straits. He tried to reassure them that their needs would be addressed at the treaty conference.

Brothers,
You need not fear being hungry or dry We have plenty of Provisions . . . to give you with Cloathes for your Wives & Children.

By order of Congress,
Geo. Morgan[49]

The invitation to the first formal American–Indian peace treaty conference had been fully presented for the consideration of the Shawnee Council. The chiefs did not respond at once. They deliberated among themselves, then informed Morgan that before they accepted the proposal, he would have to speak with the Mingo chiefs of the Iroquois living in the Ohio River Valley. The Shawnee clearly did not wish to upset bonds of intertribal relations. Anticipation grew stronger on all sides as Morgan and the Shawnee awaited the arrival of the powerful Iroquois chiefs and head warriors.

Chapter Eight

THE COUNCIL HOUSE
AND THE MINGO NATION

ON JUNE 20, 1776, the chiefs and head warriors of the Mingo arrived in canoes at the Shawnee village of Kiskapoo on the Scioto River, to speak with the new American Indian agent. George Morgan was prepared for a most challenging round of wampum diplomacy. The Mingo had engaged in a series of bloody conflicts with American settlers in Kentucky, and their desire for revenge remained strong.[1]

Over a century earlier Iroquois warriors from the area of present-day upstate New York raided the country south of Lake Erie and claimed the Ohio territory for their expanding fur trade. By 1748 Iroquoian settlements along the Cuyahoga, Sandusky, and Scioto river valleys totaled over 1,200 people, including 650 Seneca, 300 Mohawk, 140 Onondaga, 80 Cayuga, and 60 Oneida.[2] In 1750 these Mingo appealed to the Iroquois Grand Council at Onondaga for political independence, but the confederacy stood strong in asserting its continued jurisdiction, despite the fact that enforcement subsequently proved to be nearly impossible.[3]

Although the Mingo gained notoriety for their daring raids against white settlements in Kentucky, most of their energies actually were devoted to hunting and agricultural activities. During the springtime, they conducted a Sun Dance and Green Corn Ceremony, then worked through the summer in their farming communities, cultivating corn, beans, and squash, the "Three Sisters."[4] In late fall they held another Sun Dance, to give thanks to the Sun and the Thunder

Beings for the blessings of fertility and for protecting them from destructive storms. Twelve medicine men wearing startling face masks, accompanied by six others wearing Corn Husk Faces, also circulated through villages in the spring and fall to perform the ceremonial duties of their Medicine Society. Then the Mingo loaded their canoes and embarked in small groups for remote winter hunting camps, later performing a Midwinter Ceremony to usher in the New Year. In the spring they packed up their furs and deer skins, and either sold them at trading posts or returned home to await the arrival of white traders, who would provide colorful cloth, metal tools, gunpowder, hunting and farming equipment, and a variety of other goods.[5]

Morgan originally had met the Mingo during his circuits through the valley as a trader. The reputation he established as an honest man certainly was in his favor, but this joint conference with the Mingo and the Shawnee would require him to answer some hard questions. Morgan recorded the meeting in his journal:

> Thursday June 20th, 1776
>
> The Chiefs & Head Warriors of the Six Nations settled in this Country, having been sent for, came in—I invited them all to my Cabin where having presented them with some Refreshments & a few Twists of Tobacco, & having smoaked our Pipes an Hour & shook hands, I address'd them as follows:
>
> Brothers,
> I am rejoiced that you have come as I requested to hear the good Talks I have brought from the United Council of all your white Brethren who have grown out of this same big Island with yourselves.[6]

Morgan began the meeting in a traditional way by smoking the Pipe of Peace. By meditating first for an hour, the minds of participants were to be focused on the good work so that their prayers for peace would be carried aloft in the smoke from the sacred pipes. After the pipes had been smoked, Morgan spoke to the chiefs confidently: "Before I deliver'd these talks I waited three days for your coming, and had you not now arrived I was determined to visit you at your own Town, that I might open your Eyes, cleanse your Hearts & set them at ease by removing all evil from you & letting you see what is true & what is good."[7] Morgan's introductory speech to the Mingo touched on the ancient custom of purifying the body and spirit. Once the darkness of evil was cleared away, truth and goodness would appear.

Morgan then repeated some of the information he had earlier given the Shawnee, since he had initiated his talks with their chiefs. He presumed that they had briefed the Mingo to some degree on his mission of peace: "I suppose our young Brothers the Shawanese have repeated to you all the Strings & Belts [of wampum] which the Great Council have sent to them, & as you are settled here in their Neighbourhood & we look on your Councils but as one, you are to consider all these Talks as delivered to yourselves."[8] Morgan was careful not to appear as though he favored the Shawnee over the Mingo. Since he had addressed the Shawnee first, the proud Mingo might have been offended. Morgan assured both the Mingo and Shawnee that the American revolutionaries looked upon them as equals.

He then impressed upon the Mingo that their relatives of the Grand Council of the Iroquois Six Nations had already accepted the American peace belt:

> Our Brothers the Six Nations & we are in strict Friendship & we take care to keep the [Covenant] Chain [of Friendship] bright—I therefore desire you will be strong in the good work—& if you have any thing which lays heavy at your Hearts, you must tell me that I may remove all Evil from them & make them just like the Hearts of your Wise Ancestors.
>
> A String 400 [Wampum][9]

Morgan had invited the Mingo to express their sentiments openly. One of the most famous leaders of the Mingo, Logan Tachnechdorus, or "Spreading Oak", a fifty-year-old war chief who was the son of the late Shickellamy and one of ten Cayuga sachems, spoke first. The tall, imposing leader was described as "a man of superior talents but of deep melancholy," to whom life "had become a torment."[10]

Logan had suffered a great deal, having seen many of his relatives murdered, and he had taken his bloody revenge during Dunmore's War of 1774. Thomas Jefferson later recorded "Logan's Lament" in his *Notes on the State of Virginia:*

> I appeal to any white man to say if ever he entered Logan's cabin hungry, and he gave him not meat; if ever he came cold and naked, and he clothed him not.
> During the course of the last long and bloody war, Logan remained idle in his cabin, an advocate for peace. Such was my love

for the whites, that . . . I had even thought to have lived with you, but for the injuries of one man . . . [who] last spring, in cold blood, and unprovoked, murdered all the relations of Logan; not sparing even my women and children.[11]

Logan initially suspected that the mass murderer was a Colonel Cresap, but the murders were never fully investigated.

Some people charged the crimes to a white settler named Baker, while other evidence pointed to a notorious frontiersman, Jacob Greathouse. He and his men reportedly invited Logan's family across the Ohio River for a friendly visit, proposing that they engage in a marksmanship contest. The Indians shot first. Then, supposedly, Greathouse and his men suddenly turned their muskets on the Indians and shot to death thirteen members of Logan's family, including his sister and her baby.[12] A war of revenge soon erupted, as Logan described:

> There runs not a drop of my blood in the veins of any living creature. This called on me for revenge. I have sought it: I have killed many: I have fully glutted my vengeance. For my country, I [now] rejoice at the beams of peace. But, do not harbour a thought that mine is the joy of fear. Logan never felt fear. He will not turn on his heel to save his life. Who is there to mourn for Logan? Not one.[13]

However, a glimmer of hope for a more peaceful future was being offered by the Indians' young white brother, George Morgan, and Logan was willing to listen:

> They consulted together a little time & spoke by Logan as follows:
>
> Brother,
>   We of the Six Nations settled near our young Brothers the Shawanese have never till now heard any good Talks—Everything we have heard [previously] has been bad; for our part we are satisfied to live in Peace since the Wise Men have renewed the old Friendship— What you have now said brings that good old Friendship strong into our Minds—Your Business here Brother is very good—you say that all your talks shall be repeated to us in Council tomorrow—We will then speak our Minds.[14]

Logan paused for a moment, and then decided to bring up some of the Mingo's serious concerns.

Conneodico, an Onondaga chief living among the Mingo, had heard rumors that Americans were planning to assassinate several Indian leaders. Logan called for the truth to be brought out into the open:

> Brother,
>   Conneodico & we have never heard any thing from you [White people] but what was very bad—You tell me to inform you why we can't sit still & take hold of your Friendship—This is good Brother, for without you know the cause of our uneasiness you cannot remove it.[15]

Logan's reasonable attitude, his willingness to discuss causes of the conflict, was fortunate for Morgan. The Mingo people had been treated harshly in the past, seldom receiving a fair hearing, and white authorities rarely prosecuted crimes committed by white people against Indians. In the absence of an effective judicial system, Indians like Logan found that there was no alternative to taking justice into their own hands. The fires of revenge, once ignited, proved difficult to extinguish. Many Indian killers—like the infamous Greathouse and others— were still running free, mysteriously exempt from legal prosecution.

Logan spoke candidly with Morgan about the danger of Indian leaders being assassinated:

> Brother,
>   Some of us have been hardly dealt by [the White People], but since the Friendship is begun, we are satisfied—Yet we still hear bad news—Conniodico and some of us are constantly threatened and the Bearskin a Trader from Pennsylvania among others say a great Reward is offered to any Persons who will take or entice either of us to Pittsburgh where we are to be hung up like Dogs by the Big Knife [Virginians].[16]

The mere rumor of a planned mass hanging of Indian leaders, whether true or not, clearly could be enough to destroy Morgan's whole peace mission, and perhaps even put his life in jeopardy. Logan continued to be direct: "This being true, how can we think of what is good.—That it is true we have no doubt & you may depend on it that the Bearskin told Metompsica every word of what I have mentioned."[17] Little has been recorded about Bearskin, the source of these charges, other than that he was a trader from Pennsylvania and that he later accused people of committing murders through black magic.[18]

Although Bearskin may have been an unreliable source, the danger of

Indians being murdered was real. Logan appealed to Morgan to consider the historical record:

> Brother,
> I have lived much among the White people. I leave to them to say how I have behaved among them—but I was tired of seeing & hearing my Friends & Relations being murdered by them. It would be too much to mention the particulars of the horrid Massacre in Lancaster & the frequent Murder of our People returning from War through Virginia when they happened to be scatter'd or wounded.[19]

Logan's mention of the Lancaster Massacre recalled one of the most horrifying incidents in American Indian history: the 1763 murder of Conestoga Indians by the Paxton Boys, a vigilante group.[20]

Hundreds of unsolved murders had been committed against Indians, but local authorities rarely apprehended or prosecuted the criminals. Logan questioned Morgan about this obvious injustice:

> But of late years several most infamous Massacres have been committed on our People by our white Brethren in cold blood and the Murderers if they have not been rewarded are protected.—Pennsylvania that is under many obligations to us now harbours Frederick Stump who made the Strawberry & his Family of Eight Women & Children drunk & then knock'd all their Brains out with an Ax—Does this look like wanting to live in Friendship with us?[21]

Logan was referring to events eight years before, when, on Sunday morning, January 10, 1768, Frederick Stump had invited an Indian family to a party at his cabin near Harrisburg, Pennsylvania. After Stump got them drunk, he burst into a manic rage and hacked the Indians to pieces with an ax. Aided by an accomplice, John Ironcutter, he dragged the mangled bodies to the river and pushed them through a hole in the ice. The next day, parts of frozen bodies floated ashore at Harrisburg, alerting the community to the atrocity. Stump and Ironcutter were arrested on March 23, but a company of settlers surrounded the Carlisle jail and set them free. They were never prosecuted for this brutal massacre because the so-called authorities did not consider killing Indians a crime.[22]

Chief Logan and his fellow Indians clearly had cause for complaint. But how were the killings to be stopped? Logan explained that he personally had restrained his warriors from striking back in revenge for Stump's atrocities, because the chief was determined to prevent a full-scale war over the acts of a crazy man:

> Had it not been for me, that Affair would have cost the lives of hundreds, perhaps thousands—I prevented the Blow—Yet this did not stop Jacob Greathouse & some others of your people (Virginians I call them) from murdering my Mother & my Cousin [& my Sister] altho' the latter was then married to a white Man & then had his Child on her Back.[23]

Despite Logan's extraordinary self-control after the Stump massacre, violent men like Jacob Greathouse continued to carry out a reign of terror against Indians with complete immunity from prosecution. Logan's sister had been married to a white trader, John Gibson, so her child was half white, but even this fact failed to prompt the "officers of the law" to take action.

The lack of justice in the area around white frontier settlements appalled and angered the Indians, and when the authorities refused to prosecute Greathouse, Logan and his warriors attacked Kentucky frontiersmen in revenge. Morgan noted in his journal: "Logan's Sister, her Child, & some others of his Family, were the first persons murder'd in cold Blood, at the commencement of the late Disturbances—before that he was firmly attach'd to the White people & had render'd them many Services."[24] Logan and other Indians had found that it was not easy to maintain peace and friendship with white people. While most Indians were friends in times of peace and enemies only in war, an alarming number of white frontiersmen harbored such deep-seated prejudices that they were bent on killing Indians as they slaughtered wildlife.

Logan was quick to remark that violent men were a minority in both societies and that wise leaders should continue to exhibit tolerance. The chief further noted that his people had once had many friends among the whites, and that it was not too late for Morgan and the American authorities to restore justice to the frontier.[25] It remains a mystery whether Logan ever caught up with Greathouse, who seems to have disappeared from the historical record. However, as long as Frederick Stump escaped prosecution—reportedly having received amnesty in Virginia—the Mingo would question the veracity and integrity of American agents.

Morgan never recorded his immediate response to the Mingo interrogation, but he later wrote in his journal:

Logan & his company being thus free & open gave me an opportunity to remove all their Jealousies—Which I did so effectually that after a short Council together, they express'd themselves as follows,

Brother,
      You have open'd our Eyes that we see all clear around us . . . you have set our Hearts at ease—for we believe you—And from this time forward, we will think of nothing but our hunting & having pity on our Women & Children.[26]

Morgan apparently struck a chord in the Mingo by bringing up the question of the well-being of their families. Despite their reputation as mighty warriors, the Mingo were family men, dedicated to the protection of their wives and children.

Morgan succeeded in his appeal because peace and friendship between all nations represented the highest aspiration of the Mingo's wise elders. Chief Logan proclaimed:

We will take hold of the old Friendship & be govern'd by our Wise People. But with regard to coming to Pittsburgh we will consult with Conniodico, after you send him your good Talk & we have further time to consider of it—If I come I will be strong to bring him & all his people along—I must tell you three or four foolish people are gone off privately to the Big [Ohio] River, we suppose on bad intentions.[27]

With this affirmation of peace, and the advance warning of an impending act of war, the council concluded for the day.

Morgan spent the night composing a letter to the Onondaga chiefs Stone and Conneodico, two powerful leaders in the Ohio River Valley. The Onondaga chiefs in New York served as final arbitrators of international affairs, and apparently these two in Ohio occupied a similar political position. Morgan's message summarized the essence of his mission of peace:

To the Stone, Conneodico &c.—said the Head Chiefs of the Onondagoes and other Six Nation Indians settled at the Salt Licks.

Brothers,
      All your white Brethren who have grown out of this big Island desire to live in Peace & Friendship with you & all Nations, And have sent Belts & Speeches; which our Brother Logan will . . . repeat to you—You & all your people are particularly invited to Pittsburgh to a Treaty to be held there by Wise Men appointed by our Great Council,

in order to remove all bad thoughts from your Heart & place it like your wise Ancestors with whom we always lived in strict Friendship.

A String 400 [Wampum][28]

Morgan was exaggerating when he claimed that their respective ancestors had "always" lived in peace, but his message projected a sense of optimism about prospects for peace. The fact that some past generations had witnessed interludes of friendly cooperation proved peace was possible. As long as they continued trying, a chance for peace remained. Of course, there would continue to be acts of violence, but prudent leaders would not condemn an entire nation for the violent transgressions of a few criminals. The establishment of some form of international court headed by both Indian and white judges with power to enforce their decisions seemed imperative.

Morgan's speeches advocating peace and justice so impressed the Mingo that they, like the Lenape, bestowed on him an honored name: Shanashase, or the "Council House." This title represented the political, legal, and spiritual center of Indian societies. The Shawnee also honored Morgan by conferring on him the name Weepemachukthe, or the "White Deer." The color white symbolized the "Land of the White Eastern Light" in the East, where Grandfather Sun rose to light the new day; the deer moved freely through the forest, a gentle and graceful creature. The "White Deer" was considered sacred, a blessing from the Great Spirit.[29]

The next morning the joint council of the Mingo and the Shawnee reconvened. Shawnee wampum keepers began by reciting all belts and strings previously presented by Morgan. After careful consideration of the American proposals, the time had come for the chiefs to deliver their decisions. The first to speak was the great Shawnee strategist, Cornstalk or Colesquo, who had led Indians in the Battle of Point Pleasant in the 1774 war to revenge the murders of Logan's family and other grievances, and who later played so prominent a role at the Fort Pitt treaty conference in 1775. Cornstalk's eloquent style of oratory was described by a Virginia officer who was present at the joint council that ended Dunmore's War:

> When he arose he . . . spoke in a distinct and audible voice without stammering or repetition and with peculiar emphasis. His looks . . . were truly grand and majestic; yet graceful and attractive. I have heard the first orators in Virginia, Patrick Henry and Richard Henry Lee, but never have I heard one whose powers of delivery surpassed those of Cornstalk.[30]

The Shawnee chief now applied his oratorical talents to promoting peace on the frontier. Speaking on behalf of his sachem, the elder Hard Man, his sister, Clan Mother Coitcheleh, and the people of the Shawnee nation, Cornstalk recited the American peace proposal.

He then turned and addressed his elder Brothers of the Mingo nation, as Morgan reported:

> Friday June 21st, 1776
>
> All the Speeches being repeated by the Shawanese to the Chiefs of the Six Nations settled in this Country in my Presence—The Cornstalk spoke to them as follows,
>
> Our Elder Brothers the Mingo,
>   You have heard the good Talks which our Brother [Morgan]** Weepemachukthe [The White Deer] has delivered to us from the Great Council at Philadelphia representing all our white Brethren who have grown out of this same Ground with ourselves for this Big [Turtle] Island being our common Mother, we & they are like one Flesh and Blood.[31]

When Cornstalk spoke of Turtle Island as their "Mother," he was reflecting a fundamental world view shared by the tribal people. In this perception, the Earth was alive with a maternal spirit that nurtured all forms of life. To Native Americans, the Earth was not simply an inanimate mass; to them, Mother Earth was sacred and alive. She was the common mother of both the Indian people and other Americans who were born on this continent, creating a special kinship between these peoples.

Cornstalk reminded the Mingo of their previous commitments to preserving peace on Earth. He recalled earlier treaties made with Sir William Johnson, former superintendent for British Indian affairs:

> Brothers,
>   I see several sitting among you who were sent to us some years ago by Sir William Johnson & by the Council at Onandago to desire us to keep fast hold of our Friendship with our White Brethren & to do nothing to disturb their Peace.[32]

At the outbreak of the Revolutionary War, Cornstalk had considered both Americans and British to be "White Brethren." This neutral stance was imperative because if the Indians favored one side, the opposing force would consider them enemies.

Now, however, Cornstalk acknowledged that they had been blinded by the influence of an "evil spirit": "It is true the evil Spirit has been among us, but the Great Council of our White Brethren have now opened our Eyes so that we can see all around us fair & clear, and when we turn our Eyes toward them we can discover the Wise Councils of our Ancestors & our Hearts are now cleansed & made like theirs."[33] Morgan's council for peace was being described as if it were a ritual of exorcism. But the actual purification ceremony—the peace treaty itself—was still ahead.

Continuing his address, Cornstalk placed his faith in Morgan and the Continental Congress:

> Brothers,
>   The Wise Council desire to live with you & us & with all Nations of our Colour, as Brethren—What they desire makes us glad—Our old Men—young Men—Our Women & Children rejoice to hear this good Talk—It reminds us all of what our Fathers used to tell us of their Strong Friendship & good Councils with the old wise Men of our white Brothers.[34]

The whole of humanity united through spiritual bonds of friendship—this was an ideal that inspired Cornstalk and many Indian people. Most of their ancient religious ceremonies focused on the restoration of balance and harmony between forces of the cosmos. If these sacred designs could be followed by people of different cultures, a peaceful coexistence such as their ancestors once shared could be achieved.

Chief Cornstalk appealed to the Mingo to embrace this great effort, so that coming generations might enjoy the blessings of a peaceful future:

> We therefore now in our turn desire you to put away all evil thoughts far from you, as you came here formerly to advise us to do—Be strong in this & let us preserve the Peace of our Country that our young Men may hunt without fear or danger & that we may take pity on our Women & Children & provide for them as we ought to do—for these reasons we hope that you will join with us in this good work—Consider what I have said & let us know your Minds.[35]

Cornstalk's eloquent oration resounded through the Council House; it was an appeal that seemed timeless and universal.

But attention shifted to the Mingo chiefs as everyone awaited their response:

The Chiefs of the Six Nations settled among the Shawanese after deliberating on the Messages which were repeated to them by the Shawanese Chiefs accompanied with a spirited Speech from the Corn Stalk. [A Mingo chief then] spoke on a String of Wampum as follows—

Brothers the Shawanese,
　　Our Brother [Morgan] *Shanashase [the Council House] who is come from the great Congress at Philadelphia has set our Minds at ease—The talk he has brought & which you & he have repeated to us are all very good.[36]

Morgan's message was thus accepted. The peace process had progressed beyond a formidable barrier through successful efforts to bring the chiefs of the Mingo, Shawnee, and Lenape nations together. Although they were still some distance from their goal of true peace, the formation of a strong coalition of Indian and white leaders was a good first step.

The Mingo asked the Shawnee to be their spokesmen, and extended their appreciation to the Americans for initiating this effort:

They have removed all evil from our Hearts & made us see all around us fair & clear. The evil Spirit has govern'd us too long—We will now take care & do nothing to prevent a perfect establishment of our ancient Friendship—We therefore desire that you will speak for us as well as for yourselves & be strong in taking hold of the ancient Friendship with our Brethren of the United Colonies which we will join with you to promote by every means in our power.[37]

The Mingo expressed a strong commitment to peace; their words appeared to "come from the heart and not from the lips." The sincerity of what was expressed in council was reinforced by the religious communion of smoking the sacred pipe because the Great Spirit was said to be able to witness all that passed during that ceremony.

In recognition of the revival of the work for peace originally initiated by their ancestors, Cornstalk lamented the passage of his wise ancestors while expressing joy for the dawning of a new age of peace and friendship: "We therefore thank you for repeating to us the wise Councils of our Ancestors, which have made our Hearts rejoice, & dispell'd all darkness.—The Clouds are now pass'd away, & we see every thing fair & clear when we look toward you.—We thank you Brothers for all this;—Our old & young men, Women & Children have heard & are pleased with what you have said."[38]

Cornstalk's poetic words on behalf of his people conveyed their dedication to peace.

The reestablishment of a warm friendship with the Americans was symbolized through restoration of the Covenant Chain:

> We gladly take fast hold of our ancient [Chain of] Friendship with you
> & will never let it go for we spring from one Mother, we have all grown
> out of this big Island & therefore are Brothers; and you may depend
> we will do all we can to promote your Friendship with all the Western
> Nations, as you have desired.[39]

The Mingo's acceptance of Morgan's request for help in spreading word about the treaty ceremony would aid in the successful completion of his mission.

Cornstalk also recommended to Morgan that particular attention be paid to an alliance of fourteen nations around the Great Lakes, headed by the Wyandot: "But Brothers as you have ask'd our advice & assistance in this good work & as we are sincere in it we recommend to you to keep your Eyes on our Elder Brothers the Wiandots who are in strict Friendship with fourteen different Western Nations, [and] have more influence then we have."[40] Although Cornstalk did not identify member nations in the Wyandot confederacy, the circle of lake tribes included the Ottawa, Potawatomi, Sauk, Fox, Kickapoo, Mascouten, Chippewa-Ojibwa, Menominee, Winnebago, Nipissing, and Algonquin.[41]

Originally called Hurons by the French before they were defeated by the Iroquois in the mid-seventeenth century, the Wyandot retained the organizational skills necessary to form complex alliances from their trading center around Detroit. And since the British were stationed at the fort, winning the support of the Wyandot would not be easy. Cornstalk offered diplomatic aid to Morgan:

> Therefore we will accompany your Messengers & deliver all your
> Wampum to them & will join our interests with theirs to promote the
> good work you have desired your peace Belt shall pass through all
> Nations—Our Grandfathers the [Lenape] Delawares who have come
> with you & our Brothers of the Six Nations settled among us, promise
> to be strong & join us in promoting this good Friendship.[42]

The southern alliance, composed of the Shawnee, Lenape, and Mingo, thus agreed to serve as intermediaries between Morgan and the northern Wyandot confederacy as well as with the western Wabash confederation.

However, it would take time for delegations of Indian ambassadors to cover the great distances to reach the western Indian nations. Cornstalk therefore recommended that Morgan's conference be delayed somewhat:

> But Brothers we think the time you have appointed for our Meeting at Pittsburgh is too short to answer the good purpose you intend—for this reason we advise you to look toward our Brothers the Wiandots, as we will, for they know best what time it will take to assemble the Wise Men of the Western Nations whom you wish to live in Peace & Friendship.[43]

The Wyandot in 1776 were a small Iroquoian-speaking nation estimated to number only twelve hundred people, including three hundred warriors. Before the introduction of smallpox and the onset of devastating wars, their population may have been over thirty thousand. Half King and other chiefs wielded amazing power, given the size of their nation. Even the Lenni Lenape, Grandfathers of the Algonquian family of nations, addressed the Wyandot as their Uncles. They exhibited an ability to bring together Indian nations of different languages and cultures while serving as intermediaries for the Europeans, especially in matters of trade.[44]

Cornstalk gently reminded Morgan that the Americans would have to do something to improve the flow of trade goods and to hold down prices because peace was dependent on economic stability:

> Now Brothers we have no more to say but to desire that you will take pity on your young Brothers & on our Women & Children, for Goods are very dear, & that you will be strong in holding fast to the old Friendship & good Councils of our Great Grand Fathers which you have repeated to us & which begins to sound very sweet in our Ears for it is a long time since we have heard them mention'd till now.[45]

Cornstalk's message of support for the Americans was concluded on the best terms. All the chiefs present had agreed to cooperate in working toward a peace treaty.

Cornstalk then expressed a final courtesy to their young brother, the White Deer:

> Brother Weepemachukthe [George Morgan],
> We shall be glad if you will stay & rest yourself with us—Whenever you desire to return some of our young Men shall accompany you to provide Meat on the Road.[46]

Morgan accepted the kind gesture. Although he was young and white, he had won the respect and friendship of the Indian elders. They now shared a common bond as leaders in the peace effort. The White Deer held up a string of four hundred wampum and announced:

> Brothers,
>   I thank you for what you have said & for your readiness to join with your old Brothers in promoting our ancient Friendship and for your promise to do all you can to bring in all Nations to take hold of our Friendship—Your advise to look toward our Brothers the Wiandots is very good & what we shall observe.[47]

Morgan's speech of thanksgiving touched upon the Indians' highest aspiration, to bring all nations into a state of peace.

Morgan accepted the advice of the elders and promised:

> You may depend what I have said from the Great Council comes from the Heart & not from the Lips & that your White Brethren who were raised out of this same Island with you, are determined to be strong in holding fast to our ancient Friendship—On my return home I will inform the Wise Council of your kindness to me & of all you have said, which I am sure will give them great satisfaction as it has to me.[48]

Morgan reassured the Indians that the Continental Congress would be satisfied with the supportive position of the chiefs, so that peace and friendship were nearly at hand. Morgan then accepted the chiefs' invitation to relax for a few days before departing to make the final preparation for the treaty conference:

> Brothers,
>   I propose to rest myself here a few days longer & then set out for Pittsburgh where I shall be wanted to prepare the Goods & Provisions for the Meeting—Whenever you are ready to send [your ambassadors] to our Brothers the Wiandots, Mr. [William] Wilson & Joseph Nicholson & our Brothers, your Grandfathers the [Lenape] Delawares will set out with your Messengers.[49]

Morgan concluded the council meeting on a spiritual note. Appealing for divine help from the Creator, he prayed for them to be blessed with spiritual unity in their work for peace: "... and I am glad that our Brothers the Six Nations here will join us.—I pray to the great Spirit to bless their Undertaking & to make the Hearts of all Nations like our's are, strong for Peace & Friendship. A String 400 Wampum."[50]

In less than two weeks the Declaration of Independence would be signed. Congressman Thomas Jefferson and a group of assistants were developing a document based on the "Laws of Nature and of Nature's God" to declare that "all men are created equal, that they are endowed by the Creator with certain unalienable Rights, that among these are Life, Liberty and the pursuit of Happiness."[51] Were American Indians intended to be included among "all men?" Certainly the Indian elders whom Morgan was uniting in the Covenant Chain of Friendship shared a common desire to preserve their rights; they were determined to retain the freedom and happiness of all colors. It remained to be seen, however, if the signers of the Declaration of Independence would share this vision.

While Morgan and the chiefs were trying to create a harmonious relationship between their nations, three Mingo warriors were crossing the Ohio River on an illicit raiding party. Their target was the small settlement of Lee's Town, a mile below Frankfort on the Kentucky River. The Mingo sought revenge against a group of Pennsylvanian settlers and Virginian veterans of the 1774 Indian war who were claiming squatters' rights within the international Indian hunting preserve.[52]

One of the settlers, Andrew McConnell, had arrived in the summer of 1775 to plant corn and to build a log cabin. The next winter he sent for his wife, daughter, and twin sons, Adam and William. They brought cattle from Westmoreland County, Pennsylvania, and were determined to carve out a permanent settlement in the middle of Indian territory.[53] As the sun was setting on the evening of June 23, 1776, Mrs. McConnell sent her twin boys and an indentured servant to herd the cows in the pasture. A few hundred yards outside of town, Mingo warriors from Pluggy's Gang were spying on the group. Suddenly, from out of the dark shadows, a burst of gunpowder exploded from the barrel of a musket. The twins and their servant turned in panic. In a split second, an iron ball whizzed across the meadow and hit with a thud.[54] The servant was knocked to the ground, clutching his breast. Where a puff of blue smoke billowed from the bushes, three Mingo warriors rose up and raced toward their prey. The twins and the wounded servant turned and ran for their lives.[55]

The servant miraculously escaped, but he died a short while later after gasping a warning to the settlers. Mr. and Mrs. McConnell were frantic. Their boys had been kidnapped. A search party combed the surrounding area for tracks up to the southern shore of the Ohio River. No trace was found. Any chance of recovering the boys seemed remote.

Two weeks later, George Morgan reported from Chillicothe, Ohio: "Whilst I was at the Shawnese Towns, three Mingoes from Pluggy's Town . . . return'd & pass'd by where I was with the two Boys Prisoners."[56] Morgan's interpreter, Joseph Nicholson, recognized the prisoners as the sons of his friend, Andrew McConnell. Nicholson alerted Morgan. Mingo warriors also were warned of the presence of an American Indian agent, as Morgan reported: "Hearing of my being at the Council House, they [the Mingo Warriors] did not enter the Town. I therefore followed & arrived at the Mingo Town before them & in time to save the boys from the Gauntlet."[57]

The gauntlet was a test of courage and endurance. Two rows of Mingo men and women would line up with switches ready. The captives were then ordered to run as fast as possible to reach a designated post. The purpose of the gauntlet was to determine how a person would react to pain. If he passed the test, he would be judged worthy to be adopted by an Indian family who had lost a loved one. Morgan saved the boys from this ordeal.

The young Indian agent rode into the middle of Pluggy's Gang. Mingo warriors surrounded him. Morgan boldly demanded that they surrender the boys into his custody, "unless they intended this breach of the peace as an open declaration of war."[58] The Mingo chiefs and warriors entered the Council House to debate Morgan's ultimatum.

Later in the day, Morgan's Indian allies began arriving on the scene. According to an article published later in the *Pennsylvania Packet:* "All the headmen of the Six Nations, Shawanese & Delawares, who were called together on this occasion, behaved in a very friendly manner, and joined with Mr. Morgan in his demand made to these warriors."[59] The willingness of the chiefs to help mediate the case in a just manner reflected their determination to support a system of frontier justice.

Morgan and his Indian allies interrogated three Mingo warriors to learn their side of the story. Morgan obviously was not impressed: "The Villains say they did no other Injury except they wounded a young man [the servant] they fired at, which they are not certain of, as it was in the Evening and he out ran them."[60] The Mingo attempted to hold the boys as hostages, and suggested they would return them at the proposed U.S.–Indian peace treaty. Morgan found this proposal totally unacceptable. He refused to budge. If the Mingo did not return the boys at once, Morgan insisted, the incident would be considered an act of war against the United Colonies.

Finally, Morgan and his interpreter, Joseph Nicholson, worked out a compromise: the McConnell twins were ransomed for the price of a rifle, and the three Mingo warriors were "promised forgiveness on condition of future good behavior."[61] The boys were released into the custody of Morgan and old Buckshenutas, an elderly chief who aided in their release.

Morgan helped the twins onto a spare horse and headed for home. He noted his route in a travel log:

> July 10th: to Captain Johnny's Town;
> 11th: to the great Licks of Licking Creek; 12th: to Lower Moravian Town;
> 13th: to the Delaware Council, & then to Captain White Eyes;
> 14th: to Canhaudenhauden in a high Fever; 15th: to Walehaketuppan, Rain, a Little Fever;
> 16th: very ill—let Blood—Rain; 17th: a little Feverish—Rain. . .[62]

Morgan was very sick. The notation that he "let blood" referred to a widespread belief in eighteenth-century white societies that one would get better by letting out some of the "bad blood."

Morgan and the twins finally made it safely back to Fort Pitt on July 22. Morgan's journey to the Indians had been a success. The boys were freed and cheerfully reunited with their uncle, William McConnell. Diplomacy had won over brute force. The major chiefs and clan mothers had accepted the invitation to attend the fall treaty. Morgan had won respect from his adversaries and admiration from his supporters. Furthermore, the Lenni Lenape nation had adopted him and made him an honorary chief, complete with an Indian name, Brother Tamanend. Preparations for the treaty needed to be completed. The work for peace was moving forward.

Chapter Nine

THE 1776 U.S.–INDIAN
PEACE TREATY

IN THE AUTUMN of 1776, George Morgan and the commissioners from the Continental Congress gathered at Fort Pitt on the Forks of the Ohio, to negotiate the first formal U.S.–Indian peace treaty. Despite Morgan's efforts during his summer tour of Indian country to invite the sachems and chiefs of the western Indian nations, prospects for a peace treaty seemed dim when urgent reports arrived warning that some Indians were on the warpath.[1]

During the summer, Jemima Boone, daughter of famed frontiersman Daniel Boone, and Betsy and Fanny Callaway, daughters of Colonel Richard Callaway, had been kidnapped while they were paddling a canoe downstream from Boonesborough. A Pennsylvanian named James Cooper was scalped. The girls were saved in a daring rescue by Daniel Boone and his men, but Cooper and two unidentified Indians were killed.[2]

Subsequently, more blood was spilled on both sides. On August 31, an Indian trader named Matthew Elliott arrived at Fort Pitt with a hair-raising tale of his escape from Mingo warriors. He swore to the commissioners:

> I have heard from different Indians (some of them Chiefs) . . . that a general Confederacy was form'd among the Indian Nations, & that the Ottawas & Chippawas were to make an attack at Pittsburgh, [while] the Wiandots, Delawares, Shawanese, Picts & part of the Six Nations were to cross the big [Ohio] River. . . . I am convinc'd that an

Indian War is inevitable: if the Indians should come to the Treaty, they will come in very large numbers . . . with the intention of destroying the Fort & Town.³

What the commissioners and Morgan did not know was that Matthew Elliott was working as a secret agent for the British.

Elliott's rumor spread like wildfire, alarming settlers from Pennsylvania to Kentucky, lands long claimed by the Indian nations. The American commissioners for Indian affairs, Colonel John Montgomery and Jasper Yeates from Pennsylvania and Dr. Thomas Walker and John Harvie of Virginia, sent riders racing from village to village, crying out a call to arms:

> Pittsburgh   August 31, 1776
>
> We Yesterday Evening received Intelligence by a Gentleman from the lower Shawanese Towns, which is very alarming, a General Confederacy of Western Tribes seems to have been form'd, in order to Strike our Frontier Settlements. . . . The danger of the Times demand . . . [we] defend ourselves from the Incursions and repel their attack. . . . Chippawas and Ottawas, two numerous Tribes, should attack this place, and the Shawanese the Settlements on this side of the Ohio.⁴

During the following month, hundreds of guns and thousands of pounds of gunpowder, as well as other provisions, arrived on the frontier from the East. Militiamen rallied for the upcoming battle, and barrels of rum were rolled out to put the men in a fighting spirit.

With the arrival of new intelligence from trader "Honest John" Anderson at the Lenape capital, the commissioners sent riders out to spread a second alarm to the troops and militia along the Ohio:

> Pittsburgh   September 29th, 1776
>
> On the 20th inst. [of September] eighteen Wiandots, two Mingo and one Ottawa Warriors passed the standing Stone, they said they were going to view the Forts and Roads, and that they were to be joined by a large party of Wiandots about the full of the Moon.⁵

The commissioners assumed that Indians were preparing to attack the frontier, but in fact they were probably only scouting the area before bringing their chiefs and elders to the peace treaty conference.

On this same day, Grandfather Netawatwees, the revered old sachem of the Lenni Lenape nation, paused at the Moravian Christian settlements on his way to Fort Pitt. He appeared to be optimistic about the American treaty conference, proclaiming: "Soon there will be peace in this neighborhood among the Indians."[6]

Chief White Eyes and John Killbuck also passed through the missions with their wives and children, as did hundreds of other Indian families on their way to Fort Pitt. If the Indians had been planning to go to war, would they have brought their wives and children?

When Chief Cornstalk and ninety Shawnee arrived at one of the missions in a "heavy down-pour," the Christians provided them with food and refuge from the rain in ten houses, and the missionaries reported:

> Throughout the night all was as quiet and as peaceful as though no stranger were here. . . . Chief Corn Stalk visited us and was very friendly . . . [then spoke through a translator,] an old mulatto . . . who has lived among them for twenty years and can speak English and Shawanee well and acts as his interpreter.[7]

The Shawnee had long provided a safe haven for runaway black slaves—a fact that had brought about the Shawnee trouble at the 1775 Fort Pitt conference. The "old mulatto" who accompanied the war chief translated Cornstalk's speech to the Reverend John Jacob Schmick, one of the missionaries, as follows: "I am very glad to see you and your wife; it is always a pleasure for me to visit you. Especially I cannot forget how, two years ago, I came here very ill and all that you did for me then. For that reason, I shall consider you and your wife my parents and shall from now on adopt you."[8] Schmick and his wife were overwhelmed. Adoption into an Indian family was the highest honor an Indian could bestow. Cornstalk's mention of his illness primarily referred to Mrs. Schmick, who was renowned for her medical skills; she had once saved the Reverend John Heckewelder's life using herbal remedies.

The Reverend Schmick humbly responded to Chief Cornstalk: "That is too much. But if you are willing to adopt me as your brother and my wife as your sister, that suffices us."[9] Chief Cornstalk appeared most pleased by this response and gave the Schmicks his hand to symbolize their bonds of fellowship. To signify that his proposal was more than an idle gesture of goodwill, Cornstalk said: "I will make this friendship we have entered upon known to all my friends."[10] Their families—including Cornstalk's brother, Nimwha, and two of his uncles—shared a big feast together. Cornstalk's elderly mother embraced

Mrs. Schmick and exclaimed, "So you, too, are my daughter." Later in the evening Cornstalk introduced his son, Ellinipsico, and a young chief to Schmick, saying, "Brother, this young chief is my grandchild and now yours too; the other is my real son and now your son."[11]

The two young men greeted the missionary in a friendly manner and began to talk about the present situation. They were concerned about the Revolutionary War and expressed their wish that "peace might come." Regarding this, Chief Cornstalk commented: "Surely there soon will be peace among the Indians; you shall see it."[12] With the arrival of more people, the Shawnee delegation now totaled more than a hundred, including most of the head chiefs and councillors with their mothers, wives, and children.

But while hundreds of Indians were arriving at Fort Pitt to make peace, American soldiers were patrolling the frontier armed for war. One fatal musket shot could easily lead to a catastrophe. And there was nothing Morgan himself could do to prevent it, for he had no command over the military and his authority as Indian agent had been superseded by the commissioners themselves.

Word that American soldiers had crossed the Ohio River, thereby violating the international border and invading Indian territory, reached Fort Pitt in September. The Indian commissioners and the new commandant at Fort Pitt, Captain Andrew Wagoner, finally heeded Morgan's warnings and ordered their men to restrain themselves:

> Pittsburgh   October 1st, 1776
>
> The Commissioners for Indian Affairs in the middle Department, and the Commanding officer of the Garrison at Fort Pitt . . . received information that some of the Scouts appointed to range on the Ohio and its waters have crossed the Ohio and ranged the Northwestern Banks in the Indian Country in order to discover the motions of the Savages.
>
> The said practices may tend to embarrass the negotiations of the ensuing Treaty, and . . , precipitate an Indian War. . . . The Officers of the Regular Forces and Militia [are hereby] . . . ordered not to cross the Ohio or range through the Indian Country, unless in the pursuit of a party of Savages who have committed actual Hostilities.[13]

The temporary invasion of Indian territory by American soldiers was observed by Indian scouts. The transgression was serious, because it broke the terms of the 1768 Fort Stanwix Treaty.[14] The American military buildup appeared to substantiate the rumors repeated to Morgan by Logan, that the Americans were planning to assassinate all Indians at the treaty by "hanging them up like dogs."[15]

Just as some Americans were overreacting to the situation, a few Indians were meeting violence with violence. To avenge the deaths of Indians killed by whites when they crossed the border, bands of young warriors, anxious to prove their manhood, were now heading south to defend their territory against the Long Knives. The commissioners reported on October 8 that small groups had been seen heading for the Canhawas River, where General George Washington had himself claimed lands along Grave Creek, the site of sacred Indian burial grounds:

> Parties from these different [Indian] Nations have frequently joined our Enemies and some few of them we now fear, have passed the Ohio at the mouth of Hochocking in order to attack the Settlements on the Canhawas—whether they are to be considered as a mere Banditti whose conduct is not authorized by the Chiefs of their Nation, or whether they are about making a pretence for an Indian War, are points we cannot at present determine.[16]

The question of whether the Indian attackers acted alone or with the permission of their chiefs was a crucial one. Hot-headed young men on both sides were almost impossible to control. Unfortunately, entire Indian nations were too often blamed for unauthorized acts of violence committed by outcasts called "banditti." As the result of such actions, the Ohio River Valley was in danger of becoming another battle ground for the Revolutionary War.

Morgan attempted to mediate between the commissioners, soldiers, and Indians. The rumors were growing ever wilder and tensions higher, especially since the treaty conference had been delayed twice. Morgan was concerned that the Indians would turn around en route and go home without attending the conference. All his work would then have been for nothing, and the outcome of the Revolution would be jeopardized. On October 9, Morgan composed and sent a letter by messenger to reassure the Shawnee chiefs:

> To Kishantathe & all the Chiefs & Warriors of the Shawnese Nation
>
> Brothers,
>   I have taken your advice in all things relating to the Treaty you have been invited to at this place. The wise Men of your Grand Fathers the [Lenape] Delawares gave me the same Council you did & I found it to be good....We now only wait for you & them to help us uncover

the Council Fire. The commissioners from Congress think the time long & want to return home—I therefore desire you will hasten your steps & be strong in every good Resolution as I am—Don't let Evil Stories keep any of you back.

A String 400 [wampum][17]

Morgan seemed confident that the Lenape were coming to the treaty conference, but he feared that the Shawnee might be wavering. If both nations attended, then the odds that other western Indian nations would follow their lead would be increased. The Indian commissioners were growing restless, and Morgan intimated to the Shawnee that the American authorities might return to the East, if the Indians did not arrive soon. "Evil stories" were being spread by British agents and anti-American Indians playing on the human tendency to presume the worst to be true. Good communications were essential if rumors were to be dispelled. The many different languages of the participants created a further complication, so Morgan urged the Shawnee to bring Cosar, an old mulatto interpreter:

> Brothers,
>   I spoke to you in your Towns for Cosar to come up with you—I hope to see him that we may understand each other perfectly for the commissioners have a great deal to say to you & every thing is good. If this [message] meets you on the Road, as I expect it will & Cosar is not with you, I desire you will send for him. G.M. [George Morgan]
>
> [P.S.] If this [message may] fall in Mr. Anderson's way at Cochocking he will explain it to the Delawares.[18]

Three days later "Honest John" Anderson arrived at Fort Pitt. He had returned from a mission undertaken at the direction of the commissioners during which he was to gather intelligence and to invite the Lenape chiefs to come at once for the conference.

Anderson now reported that a small Wyandot war party was outraged about the American soldiers who had invaded Indian territory:

> October 12th, 1776
>
>   On the 30th. September being at the New Town two miles from Coochocking there came to that place Six Wiandots Warriors who said that they had been near the head of Middle Island Creek to look at the

white people, but had seen none, that the reason of their going was, that the Shawanese had informed them that the white people had encroached on their Lands on the other side of the River.[19]

Because they believed the Americans were planning a western military offensive, young warriors had organized an Indian resistance movement and begun to sharpen their tomahawks for striking at the Long Knives.

Most of the chiefs and elders hoped to resolve the potential conflict through peaceful negotiations, but if talks broke down, warrior societies among western Indian nations were prepared to defend their homelands to the death. Anderson conveyed the concern of the chiefs:

> John Killbuck a [Lenape] Delaware Chief informed me that [warriors among] the Cherokees, Wiandots, Tawas, Chippawas, and Pootawatomies were all united as one Nation and that the Wiandots had received the Tomahawk from the Mingoes . . . he also informed me that the Pootawatomias had made a Tomahawk and gave it to the Orvachtonese to strike the Big Knife.[20]

If this information were true, the situation was truly desperate. Peace on the frontier depended partly on the success of the treaty conference, and the peace chiefs and elders could only hold back their young warriors if American authorities restrained their young soldiers. With tensions so high, isolated acts of violence could easily escalate overnight into a full-scale war. If negotiations broke down and the treaty conference failed, the authority of the peace chiefs, in accordance with tribal law, would be turned over to the war chiefs.[21]

The specter of the combined forces of over ten thousand warriors among the western Indian nations tipping the balance of power and thereby crushing the American Revolution was again raised: "Mr. Anderson says that the Delawares have frequently told him that it was impossible for us to stand against England, and at the same time against the Cherokees, Wiandots, and all the other Tribes of Indians that would come against us, and we should certainly fall."[22] Because of the fear of a major Indian war, Major—formerly Captain—John Neville, previous commandant at Fort Pitt, led a body of troops downstream to a little log stockade called Fort Randolph to reinforce the border. At the same time, the Virginians were determined to defend their claims to Kentucky, the ancient Indian hunting grounds. Since the incident involving the kidnapping of Daniel Boone's daughter, hundreds of settlers had fled east, leaving three communities of diehards behind: Boonesborough, Harrodsburgh, and McClelland's Station. Four small Mingo and Wyandot war parties were frightening these white squatters, attempting to get them to leave the Indian hunting grounds. One group of sixty Mingo was reportedly led by young Mohawk Chief Pluk-kemeh-notee; this was the notorious Pluggy's Gang.[23]

In violation of previous treaty agreements, Captain Matthew Arbuckle, "one of the most experienced woodsmen and Indian fighters," ordered a covert action to be undertaken:

> I immediately . . . Sent two Spies across the Ohio [River] . . . they saw some Indian Signs & was immediately fired on by an Indian not above eight yards Distance. Just at the very moment the foremost of the Spies was jerking his Gun off his shoulder in order to Shoot . . . the Indian Bullet [struck] the Box of his Gun (just Opposite his Breast).[24]

As illegal aliens trespassing on Indian land north of the Ohio River, the American spies were attacked, and a skirmish ensued: "The Spy [was] . . . grazed on the Arm in two or three Places. . . . The Spies shot at him [the Indian] as soon as Possible . . . he fell. But recovered immediately & he & his Partners Cleared themselves as quick as Possible . . . the Damned Savages . . . I intend keeping out Spies both up, Down & over the Ohio."[25] Arbuckle persisted in executing these foolish covert operations. His secret actions were apparently unauthorized, but they were also left unchecked. His spies gave the false—and very dangerous— appearance of being advance scouts for an American invasion. Retaliation followed swiftly.

On the night of October 7, a seven-man scouting unit led by Robert Patterson was driven from its Kentucky camp near the mouth of the Hockhocking River:

> When the men awaked, the Indians were amongst them with their tomahawks and war clubs; a scuffle ensued . . . the men were obliged to run . . . one was cut with a tomahawk by the side of his back bone to the hollow of his body, another cut under the shoulder to the ribs . . . [James Wernock] was killed on the spot & scalped; [Joseph McNutt was] shot through with two bullets, of which he died the next day; two of the men had an arm broken . . . the other two not hurt.[26]

Pluggy's Gang was in the area, but no immediate identification of the murderers was made. However, the crime was unauthorized and illegal under tribal law, and would later be prosecuted by the peace chiefs.

On the morning of October 12, terrifying news arrived at Fort Pitt, as Morgan reported:

> A letter arrived from Major Neville at Chartiers to Captain Wagoner informing him that Eleven People were kill'd by the Indians on Fish Creek near Grave Creek three Hours after he passed by on his Way up from the Canhawa—He does not say how he obtained the Information, from whom, who were the People murder'd nor by what Indians.[27]

The white people around Fort Pitt responded with fear and rage; soldiers were ready to "kill the savages." They wanted the blood of *any* Indian.

Morgan called for the people to calm down, trying to enlist the official authorities in an effort to prevent a violent backlash: "Immediately on being informed of it & hearing the Sentiment of People, I recommended to John Gibson Esq. Chairman of the Committee to speak to [commissioners] Doctor Walker & Mr. Harvey to order the Garrison & militia not to insult or injure any Indians on account of the above Intelligence."[28] The fact remained that they did not know who had committed the murders. However, when an Indian or group of Indians was guilty of a crime, the white public often lashed out blindly against all Indians in their desire for revenge.

Morgan spoke directly to the American commissioners and to the commandant of Fort Pitt:

> I also applied in Person to the commissioners for Indian Affairs & recommended to them to assure such orders to the Garrison & Militia (as above proposed) as they had informed me the whole were under their Command & I apprehended Danger.—
>
> Geo. Morgan
>
> NB: I also applied to Captain Wagoner, Commandant of the fort on the above Subject this Morning about 11 O'Clock—Present Lt. [Presley] Nevile & John Boreman.[29]

Morgan cautioned the authorities not to overreact. The killings were a terrible crime, but blame had to be directed at the criminals, not at whole Indian societies. After all, such crimes also were committed in white societies, but not all Americans were condemned. Before some rash action was taken, an investigation to discover the facts should be conducted.

However, the source of the initial report, Major John Neville, arrived at Fort Pitt an hour after Morgan had spoken, reporting that eleven people had been killed.[30] When the official report was sent later to Governor Patrick Henry in Virginia, only two people were listed as having been killed and one child kidnapped. The identity of the criminals remained a mystery:

> On the 9th of October two women were killed at the mouth of Fish Creek, & a little boy was taken prisoner. The husbands of the women were in canoes moving home from the fort at Grave Creek; one of the men upon hearing the women [screaming,] fired on, ran ashore & discharged his gun at one of the Indians, & it was thought wounded him.[31]

When the crime was reported in the *Pennsylvania Gazette*, the exaggerated figure of eleven dead was cited. Despite the fact that the identities of the murderers were unknown, the newspaper charged "the Tawahs [Ottawas], Wyandots, Mingoes, and other disaffected Indians."[32] This amounted to a blanket condemnation of the Indians living in the Ohio River Valley, when less than one percent of the Indian population actually was involved in the raids.

Each succeeding act of wanton violence threatened to destroy the treaty before the council fire could be lit. Morgan, however, did not give up hope that peace was still possible. He urged the commissioners to restrain their anger and to send a special invitation to the chiefs:

> October 12th. Recommended to the commissioners to send a Person to meet the Shawnese & Delawares coming to the Treaty to tell them not to be alarm'd at the Intelligence of our People being kill'd on Fish Creek that we guess who has done the Mischief & desire they will listen to no bad Stories but hasten up to the Treaty.[33]

A small delegation of advance men from the Shawnee nation arrived at Pittsburgh. Their assignment was to scout the situation before the chiefs and elders appeared. The sight of Indians inside the fort evoked a desire within some whites to take revenge for the recent killings. Morgan reported how a few of the soldiers suddenly lost control: "October 13th. Two Shawnese Indians made complaint—One that a Soldier had struck him in the Back with a Stone yesterday—The other that a Soldier had without the least offence or reason drawn a Knife & offer'd to stab him but was hindered by another Soldier."[34] Another tragedy had been narrowly averted. Morgan raced about trying to put out the fires of vengeance. He appealed to the commissioners to maintain law and order:

> Promises were made by the Gentlemen Commissioners to inquire into & punish the Offenders & the Strongest Assurances were made of our Friendship, &c. The Party of Shawnese inform'd the Commissioners that they would leave two of their People & the rest return home to their Hunting. . . .They expressed their Resolutions to hold fast of our old Friendship.[35]

To allow matters to cool off, the commissioners agreed to this plan. What they did not realize was that the British had a secret agent inside the fort, planting seeds of unrest.

The same man who had initially started the rumors of impending doom that had ignited the conflict now sought to spread dissension outside the fort. As cover for his scheme he offered to take his trading goods directly to the Shawnee for their convenience: "[The Shawnee delegation] desired that Mathew Elliot who has a small Parcel of Goods might be allowed to go to their Town & trade with them—that they would conduct him & bring him & his Effect Safe back— The commissioners agreed to this & made some small addition to their Presents."[36] Matthew Elliott, the undercover British agent, rode freely out of the gates of Fort Pitt with his two men and his black slave. From a safe vantage point, he began to breed dissension among Indians coming to the peace treaty conference.

Hundreds of miles to the east, General George Washington was also surrounded by the storms of war. British General Sir William Howe, a military strategist known for his great courage, was deploying his troops under the leadership of General Charles Cornwallis around Manhattan Island in New York, intending to trap Washington. On the morning of October 12, four thousand Redcoats navigated the East River in eighty boats under cover of a dense fog. Slipping up Frog's Neck to the rear of Washington's lines, the Redcoats met heavy resistance at the King's Bridge. According to American General William Heath, the Redcoats were thwarted by the ingenuity of a handful of revolutionaries:

> Colonel [Edward] Hand's [thirty] riflemen took up the planks of the bridge . . . and commenced firing with their rifles. . . . Colonel [William] Prescott, the hero of Bunker Hill, with his regiment [brought two cannons] . . . all of which was promptly done to the . . .

disappointment of the enemy. . . . The [American] riflemen and [Hessian mercenary] jagers kept up a scattering popping at each other across the marsh.[37]

Despite the momentary standoff, General Washington avoided entrapment by evacuating his troops from Manhattan.

Unlike Washington, who knew when he was outnumbered and thus had to retreat, the military officers on the frontier, who were also outnumbered, decided to go on the offensive. Morgan urged the authorities to have faith in the desire of the Indian chiefs to restore the peace, but Colonel Dorsey Pentecost, magistrate of Westmoreland County, called a council of war. A body of fifty-five militiamen under Captain William Harrod was ordered down the Ohio River to "chastize the savages": "Scour up the river . . . and if you find any Indians . . . which have Hostile Intentions you will Treat them as open & avow'd Enemys . . . overtake and Chastize them . . . those Rasculs that may attempt to Attack our Lives, Libertys or property."[38] Pentecost's orders constituted an act of war. An Indian had only to exhibit "intentions" of hostility—as if it were possible to read another's mind—for him to be condemned as an enemy. The soldiers were empowered by the chief legal authority of the area to take the law into their own hands and dispense summary justice. Pentecost set into motion acts that could end in catastrophe.

Four days later, on October 18, two Mingo chiefs arrived at Fort Pitt to talk with Morgan and the American commissioners. They conceded that a few of their young men had gone on the warpath, but they also said that these actions were unauthorized and did not represent a general act of war. Chief Kanaghragait, also known as White Mingo, who had carried an American peace belt to the Indians around the Great Lakes, explained what had happened: "I delivered your Message to the Wiandots informing them that you were their Brothers, and held fast the old Chain of Friendship. . .wished them well, and invited them to the Treaty to be held here. I delivered your Belt to them."[39] Despite the backlash against the Mingo, at least two of their chiefs were still working to promote peace between Americans and Indians. White Mingo had performed a laudable service by traveling to the western tip of Lake Erie, where the Wyandot capital was located, next to the British Fort Detroit.

The Wyandot Half King, or Danghquat, who was a veteran of the French and Indian War, had responded to the American peace belt as follows:

Brother,
What you desire is very hard, we do not know when to believe you. I hear ill News every day. I am afraid to let my old Men go to your Council Fire: You have two Mouths: at one time you speak good, at another bad.[40]

British propaganda was apparently having an effect. Fort Detroit, which was under the command of Governor Henry Hamilton, was a vital trading center for the Indians. If they were to side with the Americans, it was quite possible that the British would punish them by imposing a trade embargo. Half King was also concerned about encroachments on the international hunting preserve from the Kanhawa to the Cherokee River.

Since Mingo Chief Pluggy was actively trying to force white people out of Kentucky, Half King speculated that the Americans might invade north to press a war of revenge: "I do not like what has been said of Kanhawa; a Letter came from thence to us, which passed through our Towns to Detroit, intimating that you knew where the ill disposed Indians lived, & would cutt off Pluggy's Town, and lay it in Ashes."[41] Pluggy's Town was located in the upper Scioto River Valley, less than a hundred miles from Wyandot communities. If the Americans invaded Ohio to burn it, the soldiers might continue the offensive and raze Wyandot communities.

Half King pointed to documentary evidence supporting this theory: "It was wrote by your Commanding Officer when a Shawanese Man told him of the designs of Pluggy's Party, he said if they struck his people he would return the blow, and root out the Indians, he told the Shawanese to wait with heads down, he was their Friend and would not hurt them."[42] The "commanding officer" may have been either Major John Neville or Captain Andrew Wagoner. The specific document referred to by Half King has not been located among available sources. It would have been foolish for the Americans to put a secret plan in writing and give it to the Shawnee. Whether or not the document was a forgery planted by the British is unimportant, however, when one considers the impact the threat had.

White Mingo reported that the Wyandot now refused to accept the invitation to the American peace treaty conference and returned the wampum belt:

They returned your Belt which I now deliver. The old Wiandot Chief [Calotte?] then rose up and spoke to me:

Uncle,
I hope your Mind is not disturbed; many bad Birds have whistled

> in your Ears and I beg of you not to believe the Chippawas intend
> differing with the Six Nations—The Chippawas now at Pittsburgh are
> not Chiefs;—They live below at Guyahoga.[43]

The Chippewa, or Ojibwa, an egalitarian, Algonquian-speaking society spread throughout the Canadian forests north of the Great Lakes, reportedly had over five thousand warriors.[44]

The old Wyandot chief's statement that the Chippewa going to the treaty conference at Pittsburgh were not chiefs constituted a serious charge. It would not be the first time, nor the last, that some unauthorized Indian fooled the commissioners. The old Wyandot then reassured White Mingo:

> Uncle, do not mind what they say, be easy and set your minds at rest,
> the Chippawas have no notion of striking you. He sat down, and then
> getting up spoke further to me. We are glad to see you, the Wiandots
> have no ill will toward you, we hope your mind is good towards us.
> He delivered me a String of Black and white Wampum.[45]

A move to boycott the American peace treaty conference had been set in motion. The principal reasons were as follows: first, the Virginians were encroaching on the international hunting preserve in Kentucky and other lands along the frontier; second, the British were applying economic pressure on the Indians by threatening to cut off vital trade goods; third, although the Americans were promising improved trade and political justice, they were raising prices and breaking the policy of neutrality by trying to recruit Indians as mercenary soldiers; and fourth, the revolutionaries were suspected of plotting to assassinate Indian leaders and invade sovereign Indian territory in a war of conquest.

Chief White Mingo countered the Wyandot charges by concluding that it was better to settle differences between nations through diplomacy than through violence: "The day following I convened the Wiandots and said, I cannot disapprove of your not attending the Treaty at Pittsburgh; you have reason to be afraid, as your young men have taken up the Tomahawk against the Americans, but I will go thither."[46] White Mingo and many other leaders were still determined to attend the American peace treaty conference in the hope that justice would prevail. As an Iroquoian chief and an Uncle of the Wyandot, White Mingo used his authority to urge his Nephews to call back their young warriors.

By proclaiming an intertribal ceasefire, diplomats would be granted time to see if peace were possible:

Now be strong; I speak to you not for myself, but for all the Six Nations. When your young men come from War, tie them together in a strong Knot, and prevent them from going out again till I see you; you cannot tell whether Virginia means either good or ill until you have heard them, after the Treaty is over, I will come to your Towns & tell you every thing is said there, you can then judge for yourselves.

I gave them a String which you delivered to me.[47]

White Mingo's logic was sound, and the Wyandot chiefs were reasonable men as well, as indicated by their response.

If the American leaders were honorable men and acted in good faith at the treaty conference, the Wyandot chiefs would unite in the work for peace:

A Head Counsellor of the Wiandots got up and spoke to me:

We thank you for your kind intentions and offers of communicating to us what passed at Pittsburgh; we will follow your advice. When our young men return from War, we will prevent them from going out again, until we see you.[48]

White Mingo had achieved a vital diplomatic concession at a critical point.

He then turned to the tribal elders of the Chippewas, Potawatomies, and other surrounding nations, for their consent was also essential. White Mingo appealed to them to unite behind the temporary ceasefire:

I then spoke to the Counsellors beyond the Lake, & desired them to be strong and not to listen to ill Birds who spread false News; I told them to be strong and not to think of War until I returned to them: I would then communicate to them what the Virginians said at the Council Fire.[49]

White Mingo successfully gained some time for the Americans to prove their sincerity to the Indian nations. However, if the American peace treaty conference at Pittsburgh failed, thousands of warriors would strike in force.

The American commissioners were then briefed on the course of events that had precipitated the recent crisis: "The White Mingo then proceeded to inform the Commissioners that sometime ago the Alarm Halloo passed thro' the Wiandot Towns by a Shawanese who told them the Virginians were coming to attack them."[50] The threat of an American invasion had provoked a call to arms: painted warriors raced south to defend their country, while women and children prepared to evacuate to the north. This was probably the result of Captain Matthew Arbuckle's foolish spy missions north of the Ohio. By the time the report of his incursions reached the Great Lakes, it had been grossly exaggerated.

At the last moment, a messenger had arrived and announced that this was all a false alarm: "The Warriors rose up in order to meet the Enemy; but a Runner shortly after undeceived them; many returned back, but some young Men went on to War and would not be restrained by their Chiefs."[51] Once the winds of war had started to blow, it proved difficult to quell the storm.

British officials and their Indian allies, who were fighting back Benedict Arnold and the American invasion forces in eastern Canada, kept stirring up the commotion:

> The minds of the Indians have been set in a ferment by some Senecas who went to the Shawanese Towns and told them that Scalps were daily coming in to their Castles, having been brought from Canada; this had an ill effect, as it stirred up the ambition of their young Men ...about one half of the Indians are desirous of Peace, particularly the Wiandot Chiefs who are averse to War—but the rest care not what happens—the young men cannot be kept back by their Chiefs.[52]

A violent minority of young warriors was gaining new recruits and challenging the authority of the peace chiefs and wise elders.

The tribal counselors advised White Mingo to tell the American authorities to restrain themselves and to give the chiefs time to restore order, or the whole frontier could well go up in flames: "Several of the Indians told [White Mingo] in conversation that the Virginians should not return the blow even if they were struck—they had better put up with it; and wait a while before they attack the Indians."[53] Although many of the Americans were avowed Christians, most exhibited little inclination to turn the other cheek.

A revolution was in the making, and violence inevitably would be met with violence. White Mingo reported: "There are now five Parties of Warriors out against the Frontier Settlements; but their number cannot be ascertained. Three of them consist of Wiandots, and two of Mingoes."[54] White Mingo's account was confirmed in part by Moravian missionaries who were settled between the Wyandot and Fort Pitt. The Reverend John Jacob Schmick wrote in the Gnadenhutten Diary on October 19: "Three more Shawanes arrived here early with the report that the Mingoes are very much incensed at the Shawanes who have gone to the treaty and are now on the warpath intending to kill many of them on this account."[55] This report was not substantiated, but the mere rumor might prevent some chiefs from attending the peace treaty conference.

Later in the afternoon the Reverend John Heckewelder returned to the mission and related an even more disturbing rumor that had been relayed by two messengers from the Lenape capital:

> We heard a terrible report . . . that the governor in Detroit [Henry Hamilton] would cross the lake in four days and land here with two armies of English and Indians . . . one army is to march to Pittsburg and the other on Canhawa. . . . We rely . . . in these outwardly disturbed times, upon our dear Lord and upon His gracious help . . . peace, joy, salvation, and life.[56]

Hundreds of Indians began amassing in camps across the river from Fort Pitt. Whether they had come for peace or war could not immediately be ascertained.

Finally, two Lenape chiefs, White Eyes and John Killbuck, paddled across the Ohio River and walked through the gates of the fort. George Morgan and the American commissioners greeted the Indian ambassadors, who requested to speak privately with their Brother Tamanend:

> In private Council   Pittsburgh   October 24th, 1776
>
> Present:
> Captain [Chief] John Killbuck
> Captain [Chief] White Eyes
> the latter spoke as follows,
>
> Brother,
>   We have come to talk to you about the Clouds which seem to threaten your & our peace—Yesterday two Messengers arriv'd with Wampum to Capt. Pipe who keeps Secret from us all the News he hears—we cannot learn what these Messengers have come about— they are to return tomorrow.[57]

Was Captain Pipe, White Eyes's chief rival, plotting with pro-British Indians to attack during the American peace treaty conference? White Eyes urged Morgan to investigate:

> We therefore recommend to you to send for them and Capt. Pipe and enquire their Business; for we fear they are not doing what is good— We have been told that a stroke is intended against you here from the English at Detroit while we are talking of Peace, and that Guy Johnson is to come by way of Prisque Isle, and the Western nations are to cross

the Ohio with the English Army—This may be all Lies but there seems to be something bad abroad.[58]

British Superintendent of Indian Affairs Guy Johnson had recently returned from England, where he had taken Joseph Brant in order to court the Mohawk warrior's favor. Since their arrival in New York, Brant had reportedly "distinguished himself by his steadiness and courage" at the Battle of Long Island against Washington's troops. The heroic Mohawk warrior then began proclaiming to the Indians that "their own Country and Liberty" were "in danger from the Rebels."[59]

Chief White Eyes reported to Morgan that sharp threats had been made to the effect that the American peace treaty conference was targeted for a bloodbath:

> We hear the Wiandot told the Shawnese it was a Folly for them to come here to talk to dead people, that if you were not dead already, you would soon be so they had better not come—We shall however know the truth of this when the Shawnese arrive which will be in three days. After you talk to Capt. Pipe we shall be glad to hear from you—'tis best that you talk to him yourself.[60]

Captain Pipe, head chief of the Lenape Wolf Clan, whose traditional name was Konischquanoheel, "Maker of Daylight," arrived later that day. Pipe was accompanied by Checalese and Pukangehela or Buckungahelas, "One Whose Movements Are Certain."[61] Morgan met privately with the three Lenape leaders:

> Pittsburgh   October 24th 1776
>
> In private Council with Capt. Pipe, Checalese, and Pukangehela. Frederick Ferry, Interpreter
>
> Captain Pipe spoke as follows,
>
> Brother,
>   You told me on this giving of Wampum that you heard I had News from the Wiandots with a Belt, by Wandoohala's son, and have repeated to me what you were informed of. . . . I tell you there is no truth in what you have heard except with regard to the Belt I mention'd to you some days ago, it was a white Belt which I will show you from our Uncle the Wiandots brought by Wandoohala's son, merely to clear the Road agreable to our Custom as it appears lately

to have been fill'd with Brush. . . .With regard to the two men who arriv'd two nights ago—they brought no message to Wandoohala's son to return home, nor are they going home till after the Treaty—The Wampum they brought was sent to me by Wandoohala, who collected it from his Friend, and Children; it was a present to me.[62]

Wandoohala, "Council Door," was the father of Pukangehela. Pipe spoke on their behalf, denying all charges that had been made by White Eyes. Pipe's reference to the "Road Belt" was an example of the tradition of protocol in wampum diplomacy. His poetic reference to the road having been "fill'd with Brush" had to do with the recent breakdown in diplomatic communications. Captain Pipe was said to be "a very artful and designing man and a chief of considerable ability and influence."[63] The truth of his present statements was difficult to ascertain. However, it was known that Pipe could be a strong ally in peace and an awesome foe in times of war.

Morgan did not provoke the Wolf Clan chief, who proceeded to make a point of his integrity: "I indeed received a Belt near three Months ago from the Sennecas to desire me and my People to continue to hold fast our Friendship with our white Brethren and not to take hold of anything but what is good—Pametamah a Munsey Chief brought this Belt to me on his return from Niagara."[64] Three months earlier, at the Niagara Indian conference, Seneca Chief Guyashusta had in fact spoken strongly for peace despite Colonel Butler's attempts to incite the Indians to violence. Therefore, Pipe might very well have been telling the truth at this point. But his claim that he had not heard about the Wyandot war parties seemed implausible:

> In answer to your enquiry about our Uncles the Wiandots having struck you, I do not know nor have I heard that they have, or that they intend to do it. The whole of our disturbance, have arose from the Mingos of Scioto, and a few bad people about seventy in number,—including the Mingos who have associated with Conneodighes that bad man I am told is now gone with evil intentions to cross the Ohio.[65]

Conneodico, the Onondaga Mingo chief allied with Stone from Salt Licks and perhaps with Mohawk Mingo Chief Pluggy, indeed had a bad reputation. The Wyandot considered him "troublesome." He was the same man who told Cayuga Mingo Chief Logan that everyone who came to the treaty conference would be "hung like dogs."

Morgan had invited Conneodico to the treaty conference, but the chief had apparently decided to raid Kentucky instead. Pipe reported that Conneodico had lost most of his followers:

> You have heard he has sixty Warriors, but there are only four besides himself—if he is gone which to me is doubtful; they crossed the path near the big lick, between the standing stone and the Shawnese Town just as two of our young men did who arrived yesterday—that was eight days ago; by their course they meant for the Ohio about Hockhocking.[66]

Pipe's report placed Conneodico in the general area of recent attacks, kidnappings, and murders against American frontiersmen.

If Pipe's revised estimate of Conneodico's followers was correct, and if these five men were in fact guilty of the crimes, it was amazing how much damage could be done by a small number of warriors. Pipe urged Morgan to be reasonable:

> The reports you hear about us Indians are much like those told to us about you—but I hope the wise people of neither side believe them— there are many people on both sides who to answer their own purposes endeavour to raise evil reports and to sow discord between you and us, let us not listen to such people.[67]

Pipe proposed that they keep the lines of communication open in order to avoid future misunderstandings: ". . . but when we hear news of any Importance which may be depended on, let you and I communicate it to each other—for my part I am determined to do so and you may depend on what I have said to be the truth."[68] Pipe's gesture of goodwill was truly laudable. By initiating an "open road" policy similar to a present-day hotline between national leaders, violent incidents that could provoke warfare might be quelled.

The second step to peace involved the establishment of trust. As present-day Mohawk Chief Jake Swamp explains: "The expression of trust is achieved through the sharing of responsibility and equality in all areas of existence."[69] Chief Pipe accepted this responsibility, then conveyed to Morgan and the Continental Congress an expression of mutual trust:

> Brother,
>   I believe your Heart to be good toward all the red people . . . you say the Great Council of all our white Brethren have placed you here to promote and preserve Peace—[You say] that they even desire not

to be obliged to strike those who have struck you . . . provided they will do no more [acts of war] and will now accept of your proffered friendship before it be too late.[70]

This provision required continuous restraint on both sides. As peacemakers, Morgan and the chiefs were empowered with a moral responsibility to apply their strength through "spiritual means, reasoning, and logic to transform a warring people into a peaceful existence."[71]

As a representative of his people, Captain Pipe could not dictate to tribal members, but instead had to consult with them and carry out their wishes:

> You ask my advice and assistance to bring this about—this shews that the Hearts of the Great Council are good—But Brother this [is] a matter of so great consequence that I cannot answer you until I consult some of our men. . . . I will advise with them and will then speak to you.[72]

With these concluding remarks, Chief Pipe returned to his people.

Later in the day, White Eyes and John Killbuck, representatives of the Lenape Turkey and Turtle clans, returned to speak to Morgan. Political rivalries within the Lenape tribe were complicating matters, and Morgan was caught in the middle. Even after he had related Pipe's positive statements, White Eyes remained suspicious:

> In private Council the same day
>
> Present Captain White Eyes and his Cousin
> and Captain John Killbuck
>
> Captain White Eyes spoke.
>
> Brother,
>   I desired you would talk to Captain Pipe—You have related to me what passed between you, but I fear there is something going on which is not good, therefore let us keep a good lookout and tell each other what we hear.[73]

White Eyes may have been justified in his fears, or he may have been attempting to repair his political reputation, which had been damaged by his proposals in favor of partial assimilation. Killbuck was also a questionable figure to the traditionalists because of his leanings toward the Moravians. For his part,

Captain Pipe had gained supporters from the Turkey Clan elder Wandohela, "Council Door," and the Turtle Clan elder Weliechsit, "He Speaks the Language Well," who was also known to the whites as Delaware George. As son of the late Chief Tamaque, called "King Beaver," and nephew of the late war chief Shingas, "The Terrible," Weliechsit was particularly influential. He, Wandohela, and Captain Pipe formed a powerful trio in the affairs of the Lenape.[74]

Since their national sachem, Grandfather Netawatwees, was now ninety-nine years old, a power struggle was bound to break out. White Eyes saw his authority slipping, as he reported to Morgan:

> Captain Pipe, Delaware George, Wandoohala his two Brothers, seem to be the only persons in our Nation who know what is going forward among other people—for our part we can hear nothing forward . . . our Ears are stopt. Delaware George was last night overheard when in liquor to say your Council would be broke up by a stroke which would be made whilst we were talking of peace.[75]

It was not clear whether White Eyes was telling the truth or simply trying to discredit his political rivals. He did not reveal who had overheard Delaware George, or whether the suspected plot had been supported.

White Eyes himself was in the dark, his "ears stopt," which further implied that chiefs of other nations were not confiding in him either. Even in negotiations of peace, there were political strategies that had to be kept confidential. But White Eyes promised openly that he would inform Morgan of anything that happened: "You may depend that we have determined to have nothing to do or say, in any thing that is bad; and whatever we hear or see, you shall be immediately informed of it.—Beside the people over the Great Water have never asked us to do any thing but to sit still."[76] The "people over the Great Water" were of course the British, not the Americans, who were "grown out of this same Island." However, since the British were actively recruiting Indians to fight in the Revolutionary War, White Eyes's statement appeared to contradict the facts.

White Eyes proceeded to berate his rivals by questioning the actions of Pukangehela, "One Whose Movements Are Certain": "If Wandoohala's son had nothing but good Messages to Captain Pipe, why keep them secret from us? Why did they hide their Wampum under their Cloathes when one of us approach'd their Camp?"[77] The reason Pipe had excluded White Eyes from his private councils remained a mystery. However, it may have had something to do with the fact that in the past White Eyes had sometimes acted without first consulting his people. He repeated this folly in his attempt to win Morgan's favor:

Brother,

> We are determined to desire them to speak their minds out aloud as we will that they may have no excuse hereafter. . . Our Grand Children the Shawnese and we are of opinion we should open a path for you whenever you are obliged to strike those who strike you.[78]

This was untrue. The Shawnese chiefs would soon speak against the proposal to "open the path" for an American army to invade Indian territory in order to strike the Mingo. Shawnee villages lay in the path of such an attack.

White Eyes was speaking out of turn when he proclaimed: "It is our desire to do so and to shew my friendship you shall have liberty to pass even through my Doors for that purpose and I will accompany you—We will talk more of these matters another time after we make further search after the Truth."[79] White Eyes was offering to join the American army in a war of revenge against certain the Mingo, British, and other foes. By inviting the Americans to invade Indian territory without first gaining the consent of his people, White Eyes was taking perhaps the biggest gamble of his career. If such a plan were made public at this critical juncture, the chances for peace might be lost.

Two days later, on the morning of October 26, 1776, the first U.S.–Indian peace treaty conference began. Morgan counted 644 Indians crossing the river in canoes, including leaders of the Lenni Lenape, Munsee, Mohican, Shawnee, and Iroquois Six Nations.[80] Most of the Wyandot, Lake nations, and the Mingo from Upper Scioto boycotted the conference, but a significant number of other head chiefs, clan mothers, and medicine people attended this historic meeting. As was the custom, they wore deerskin and woven clothing with floral beadwork and ribbon appliqué; their faces were painted with colorful designs, and eagle feather headdresses identified honored members of the tribes.[81]

In accordance with tradition, muskets were fired to symbolize the unloading of all weapons, then a ceremony was performed, representing the Covenant Chain of Friendship:

> The dance of peace [is] called also the calumet or pipe-dance, because the calumet or pipe of peace is handed about during the dance. . . . The dancers join hands, and leap in a ring. . . . Suddenly the leader . . . springs forward, and turns round, by which he draws the whole company round [spiralling inward and outward symbolizing] . . . the chain of friendship. A song . . . for this solemnity, is sung by all.[82]

The eldest member of the assemblage, Grandfather Netawatwees, was granted the honor of lighting the council fire, as was customary. Everyone formed a large circle around the Tree of Peace, "all took their places according to seniority, and a profound silence ensued for the space of ten minutes."[83] Prayers of peace were then offered through the smoke of the sacred pipe.

After Morgan and the American commissioners for Indian affairs formally greeted the Indians, the Shawnee were designated the opening speakers:

> Saturday October 26th 1776
>
> Present
>
> Col. John Montgomery}
>
>   } Commissioners
> Jasper Yeates Esq.}
>
> George Morgan Esq. Agent for the United States.
>
> Shawnese Chiefs, Koketha, Colesquo [Cornstalk], Johnny, Nimwa, and some others,
>
> The Corn Stalk who had been sent by Mr. Morgan with other Chiefs to the Wiandots, Ottawas, &ca. said he would relate to us, the result of his Embassy, which he did to the following effect. . . .[84]

Three months earlier Chief Cornstalk had traveled north to help deliver the American peace message. He had invited his Uncles of the Wyandot nation to come to the first U.S.–Indian peace treaty conference:

> On my arrival at the Wiandot Towns I told the Chiefs I had a very good talk to deliver to them from our eldest Brothers of the United States. I deliver'd the Speeches and Wampum with which they were much pleased but said they must consult their Father . . . Governor [Henry Hamilton] of Detroit on them. . . . When they were deliver'd and explain'd to him, he tore the written Speeches and cut up the Belts in pieces which were thrown about the Council House. The people said they could do nothing but what was agreeable their Father the Governor, but it was their opinion and desire that all Nations should live in Peace with the United States.[85]

Cornstalk had been accompanied on the peace mission by Chief White Eyes; an interpreter, John Montour; and Morgan's representative, William Wilson. The authenticity of Cornstalk's account was corroborated by Wilson's own testimony to the commissioners. The Wyandot Half King had told Wilson: "There is my Tomahawk. I will never lift it, nor shall any of my family fight against the Big Knife if I can help it, unless [the Americans] come into my house."[86] Half King meant that as long as the Americans did not invade Indian territory, the Wyandot would promote peace. However, Montour, who stayed two days longer than Wilson, reported, "when the Half King got a little in Liquor he told him that the Big Kife need never expect him to be friends. . .[and] he should follow nothing but breaking their heads."[87]

Chief Cornstalk's report continued:

> [The Wyandots said] That their father the Governor had often told them and others, he did not want the Indians to strike the Inhabitants on the Ohio but to sit still That there were but few of the bad people who created trouble by crossing the Ohio and striking the white Inhabitants.[88]

It was true that Governor Hamilton had told the Indians to "sit still" for the moment, but after Guy Johnson returned, "they perceived the waters to shake." Some of the Cherokee and Mingo warriors had already accepted "Black Tomahawk Belts" of war. Moreover, the governor had ordered White Eyes "to leave Detroit before the Sun set" if he "regarded his head."[89] White Eyes was thus publicly humiliated. Possibly the underlying reason that White Eyes proposed an American attack against the Mingo was that he also wanted to direct the army against the British governor at Fort Detroit. White Eyes wanted revenge.

Cornstalk assured the commissioners that the Wyandot were also troubled by the Mingo:

> The Wiandots said they had repeatedly spoke to these bad people who are associated together at Pluggy's Town and in that Neighbourhood and desired them not to continue in their evil conduct for it would bring their younger Brethren the Shawnese into trouble again for they were near Neighbours to the white people.[90]

The Shawnee had tasted war in 1774, and they wanted to avoid being the victims of an American invasion. Since their villages lay on the route an American force would take on its way north from Kentucky to attack the Mingo, it was possible that invading soldiers would not distinguish between Shawnee villages and those of the Mingo and would burn both indiscriminately.

Cornstalk presented his version of the Wyandot position: "[The Wiandots said] that they the Mingoes had been instrumental in promoting the last disturbances and deserted the Shawnese in the day of Trial at the mouth of the Canhawa and took shelter behind them the Wiandots."[91] This comment referred to the Battle of Point Pleasant, during which Cornstalk had served as the war chief. A skillful military strategist, Cornstalk could have had all the whites killed, but he pulled back instead and called for a council of peace. Cornstalk wanted to continue the work of conciliation, and attested to Governor Hamilton's statements against further raids:

> The governor of Detroit spoke to the Indians in my presence and told them he did not desire they should strike the white Inhabitants on the Ohio, and I tell the truth when I say that, if you blame him or the people at Detroit for what is done you are wrong for no persons are to blame but a Banditti of Mingoes and those with whom they have intermarried at and near Pluggy's Town.[92]

But how could they bring Pluggy's Gang to justice? While White Eyes said he and the Shawnee wanted an American attack, Chief Cornstalk had a different proposal. Since the Mingo were an Iroquoian people, Cornstalk was determined to have the Six Nations take control of their relatives: "I intend now to speak to the Six Nations at this Council to remove these people from us—they threaten our lives as well as your's and we are daily insulted by them—The Six Nations at this Council are the Proper Persons to remove these bad people for they belong to them."[93] Flying Crow and Guyashusta, two prominent Iroquois chiefs, were present at the treaty conference. Cornstalk wanted them to assert the authority of the Grand Council.

Cornstalk recommended that if the Mingo failed to listen to their own chiefs, "they should be cutt off [banished], for we can never live in Peace whilst they remain there—To have this matter settled is part of my Business up here, and we the Shawnese will join you in this good work."[94] With Cornstalk's concluding statement, the public council ended for the day. The Shawnee chief had made a bold pronouncement, since the Mingo from Pluggy's Town would soon receive word of his speech and from then on would consider Cornstalk their enemy.

After three days of heated debate, Cornstalk and the Shawnee chiefs asked to speak privately with Brother Morgan, the "White Deer":

After the Publick Council broke up all the Shawnese Chiefs desired I would accompany them to some convenient place where they could speak to me alone, I did so, and they addressed me as follows viz:

Brother,
    It is you who have open'd the Road for us to this place—you have raised up our old Chief who lay dead and neglected you have made him white [pure and just] to all Nations—this we shall forever thank you for.[95]

To be thus singled out by the Shawnee chiefs for a private discussion was clearly a mark of their confidence in George Morgan.

Chief Cornstalk also expressed his appreciation for recent positive exchanges between his own people and the Americans:

We have lately experienced so much kindness from the people of Virginia and Pennsylvania that it makes a strong impression in our hearts.—We are a people who cannot forget good Offices.—
    When Nimwa and others went to Virginia they were treated by everybody there and along the Road, like Brothers—every one gave them a kind welcome.[96]

Cornstalk's brother, Nimwha, and other Indians had traveled east as diplomatic envoys, and Morgan himself had hosted Indian delegations during his career. Cornstalk certainly seemed willing to extend the hand of friendship:

When our two young Brothers Wenthissica and Pelaiwa went with you to Philadelphia and New York they were treated in the same manner—These things we will never forget—such kindnesses will tie us to our white Brethren forever; and we are resolved that nothing shall break our Friendship.—This is from our Hearts and not from our Lips only—therefore believe us.[97]

Cornstalk's sincerity inspired trust. He then turned to the main issue—the steps that needed to be taken for peace to be secured. The Shawnee chief first addressed the immediate problem of the "banditti":

Brother,
    You have lately spoke to the Chiefs of the different Nations respecting the Mingoes and Banditti who have been striving to break

our Friendship. You have asked our advice and assistance to prevent the designs of the evil spirit—It has been our resolution before we came from home to speak to you on this business and we will join you and our grandfathers, the Delawares therein with all our might.[98]

The Shawnee chiefs were united in their conviction that the problem had to be dealt with effectively.

Cornstalk elaborated on the diplomatic solution he had proposed earlier:

It is our advice that we shall all speak to the Six Nations in Publick Council—Let us be strong and tell them from whence all the mischief has arisen. When your Younger Brother, the Shawnese and our Grandfathers, the Delawares have spoke, do you support them?—don't let them stand alone, but speak loud and strong that you may make the Six Nations hear and comply with what you ask.[99]

Cornstalk could not have been more emphatic: Morgan had professed his brotherhood; it was time for him to prove his good faith. The Shawnee chiefs then briefed Morgan on their appeal to Flying Crow and chiefs of the Six Nations. If the Iroquois refused to deal with the Mingo, a violent conflict appeared inevitable.

Cornstalk soon rose before the treaty council to voice the united position of the Shawnee:

Our eldest Brothers the Six Nations,
We are rejoiced to meet you at this Council—you who are from the Head Castles and are the Head Chiefs of Warriors of the Sennecas— Listen to us.
Last Fall when we met here you gave us good advice. You told us not to be foolish any more but to be strong and preserve our Friendship with our white Brethren.[100]

As the "Keepers of the Western Door" of the Iroquoian Confederation, Flying Crow and the Seneca chiefs were the appropriate authorities in this case. Furthermore, because they represented the largest of the Six Nations, they had the manpower to back up their word.

The Shawnee had followed the advice of the Seneca chiefs to remain peaceful, and it was time for the Senecas themselves to do the same. Cornstalk appealed to them for their support:

Brothers,

    We took your advice and have behaved as you then desired us. We have done nothing to interrupt our Friendship or to stop the path between our white Brethren and us.—But we had scarcely got home from [that] Council fire, and thrown off our Bundles, before we heard a great noise like Thunder which when we listen'd to, we found to be no other than some of your foolish young Men who had been to strike the Virginians.[101]

"Thunders" of war rumbled through the Ohio River Valley; Pluggy's Gang was on the warpath. Armed with muskets, tomahawks, and war clubs, small parties of warriors employed hit-and-run tactics along the frontier. In fact, George Washington had learned the same tactics as a young frontiersman, and was now harrying the Redcoats in much the same way.

    Cornstalk was concerned that the Revolutionary War would spread to the frontier, because raids against illegal white settlers in Kentucky were increasing: "We had frequent repetitions of this great noise—at one time it was owing to our eldest Brethren of the Six Nations arriving with the Tomhawk, which they also carried to the Cherokees & Creeks, in order to induce us and them to strike the Virginians."[102] South of Kentucky, the Overhill Cherokee (led by Great Warrior and Dragging Canoe) and the Middle Cherokee (following Raven and Oconostota) as well as the Upper Creeks (under War Chief Emistisigno) and the Lower Creeks (led by Pumpkin King and Tallassee King) collectively represented many thousands of warriors.

    In the summer of 1776 a delegation of Mingo and other northern warriors had reportedly arrived in Cherokee territory to call for war: "Painted black and bringing belts of black wampum, the trans-Ohio tribesmen reported Patriot designs against all the Indians and urged the Cherokee to join the common resistance."[103] British gun runners were covertly supplying southern warriors with arms and gunpowder. The legitimate grievances of Indians were clearly being manipulated to further the designs of the British in the Revolutionary War.

    Chief Cornstalk challenged Flying Crow and the Iroquois chiefs to state publicly whether or not they condoned the killings, kidnappings, and other acts of war:

At another time some of your young men who had been to look at the Virginians, brought two Boys Prisoners from thence and passed through some of our Towns. Now you are some of the head men of our

eldest Brothers the Six Nations. We desire you will speak out and tell
us whether your young Men have done these things with your knowledge or approbation Aye, or No.[104]

Cornstalk was referring to the kidnapping by three Mingo of the McConnell
boys, whom Morgan and Pukangehela, "One Whose Movements Are Certain,"
the Lenape counselor, had saved during the previous summer.

Since the Shawnee villages were south of Pluggy's Town on the Warriors'
Trail along the Scioto River leading to Kentucky, the Shawnee were clearly in a
position to observe what was going on. Cornstalk appealed to the Iroquois chiefs
by recalling their original instructions when the Mingo had come to settle in
central Ohio:

> When they first came to sit down by our side, you told us that we should
> give them good advice and take care of them, but they would never
> listen to us but have brought us into great trouble—when any mischief
> has been done to our white Brethren by them they have whisper'd
> about it is the Shawnese—The Shawnese have done it.[105]

To be falsely accused of crimes outraged the Shawnee.

Cornstalk reminded the Iroquois that when the family of Mingo Chief
Logan was murdered, precipitating Dunmore's War of 1774, it was the Shawnee,
not the Mingo, who had been drawn into the battle: "This has brought us into
great trouble, and when we met the Big Knife, these very people, who occasion'd
the War, refused to fight—Well, no sooner was Peace made but these people
wanted us to break it again, and they are constantly telling us bad News."[106] Cornstalk continued to berate Mingo troublemakers, charging the Virginians also
with threatening two Shawnee chiefs, including Cornstalk's own brother. The
Shawnee had suffered the repercussions of the Mingo's activities long enough,
Cornstalk charged:

> They [the Mingo] have even come in our Towns to injure the Traders;
> & because we concealed them, they [the Mingo] have threatened to
> tie and carry off Nimwa and Wry Neck, two of our Chiefs who were
> active in preserving our white Brethren—those Chiefs and others of
> us they call Big Knife, because we are determined to hold fast our
> Friendship.[107]

Cornstalk did not appreciate being insulted for promoting peace; he had proved himself as a war chief in the past. The Shawnee had tasted war, and found it bitter. The ever-present threat of violence had long hung over their heads. Now they were determined to live in peace with integrity.

Cornstalk concluded by giving the Iroquois chiefs an ultimatum: "Now our eldest Brothers, You who are Chiefs and Warriors of the Six Nations we desire you will come and take these bad people from among us or make them sit still— It is our opinion they have made a Tomhawk of their own—but you can tell how this is."[108] The treaty council ended for the day with the Iroquois being given time to consider Cornstalk's demand.

George Morgan pressed the Iroquois in a personal diplomatic effort. This white man, whom the Iroquois called the "Council House," soon received their response:

> In Council in the Six Nation Camp
>
> Present—all their Chiefs
>
> The Flying Crow spoke to me as follows,
>
> Brother,
> I thank you for what you have said it is very good—Your uneasiness respecting our people at the Salt Licks shall be put an end to, we shall speak to you tomorrow in Publick Council on this matter—We are determined to send the White Mingo and others to make them sit still—if they do not take our advice they shall repent it.[109]

The Iroquois chiefs had spoken. If the Mingo warriors failed to heed the warnings of the peace chiefs, the matter would be turned over to the Iroquois war chiefs. And in fact, before the year was out, the Mingo warrior Pluggy would be killed.

Although men were leaders and spokesmen in the effort among American Indians to preserve peace on the frontier, the women had an important role behind the scenes in promoting the good work. Moreover, among the Iroquois and other Indian societies, women had the power to veto any decision to go to war. The position of Clan Mother Coitcheleh and the Shawnee women was presented by Chief Cornstalk upon a string of white wampum:

Pittsburgh   October 30th, 1776

Received a String of Wampum from Coitcheleh the Head Shawnese
Queen by her Brother—she says,

Brother,
     Agreeable to your desire I have spoke to our head-Men—they
have got up, and are on their way to meet you at Pittsburgh—I have
exhorted them and all our Nation to keep fast of your Friendship.[110]

Coitcheleh stayed back in her village, because she had recently given birth
to a baby. The future of this child now depended on the success of the
peacemakers.
     Perhaps Indian women were entrusted with veto power over war because, as
mothers and grandmothers, they valued the precious gift of life in a way that was
difficult for some men to perceive. Coitcheleh explained to Morgan:

I would come up myself but have been lately delivered of a son.—Yet
I hope you will not forget me in the distribution of your goods.

Brother,
     If the white people entertain designs to strike us I beg you will tell
me—I depend upon you that I may remove out of danger with my
children.[111]

In return for this help, Coitcheleh pledged to warn her white brethren so that
their children could be saved from destruction: ". . . and you may rely you shall
not be ignorant of what passed among the red people—I will give you constant
notice and will never deceive you. For our part, we the Shawnese are determined
to preserve our Friendship with our white Brethren inviolable."[112]
     Coitcheleh also helped Morgan by identifying warriors who were the cause
of the present conflict and reporting on their most recent movements: "The
Mingoes who live near to us are the only people who appear to have bad
intentions against you—several parties of them have been to the Great River, all
of them are now return'd but one consisting of three Persons only—they had
three scalps with them."[113] Coitcheleh and other Shawnee leaders did not con-
done the scalping of white settlers in Kentucky, even though they were deliber-
ately trespassing on ancient hunting grounds of the Shawnee south of the Ohio
River. Instead, she recommended that leaders of the Americans and Shawnee
unite in working toward a swift solution: "I hope your and our Chiefs will agree
to have these bad people removed from us or make them sit still for they have

often shook the Tomhawk over our heads and call us the Big Knife—When I am able to travel I will come and see you."[114]

Coitcheleh concluded by giving the disturbing report that Pluggy, leader of the Mingo "banditti," had gone to Detroit to consult with British officials. The governor of Detroit, Henry Hamilton, who had gained a notorious reputation as the "Hairbuyer," and Colonel John Butler, commander of Fort Niagara, were both implicated in the scheme to incite Indian warriors. Coitcheleh revealed to Morgan: "Pluggy has been sometime at Detroit, where he went to know the will of the Governor there—he is not yet returned; some think he is gone or will go to Niagara."[115]

In the wake of foreign intervention, elders such as Grandfather Netawatwees had witnessed firsthand the destructive effects of being caught in the middle of the European contest to control America. The Lenape had encountered the Dutch, Swedes, Italians, French, Germans, Swiss, and English, as well as their descendants the Americans. In the process of trying to coexist with these foreigners, the Lenape had lost thousands of people while being forced to move first from their Delaware lands to Pennsylvania, and then from Pennsylvania to Ohio. Having lived almost a century and risen to the position of head sachem of the Lenni Lenape nation, Netawatwees, the "Skilled Advisor," had survived countless wars and enjoyed interludes of peace. He had been a young boy when the great Lenape Sachem Tamanend joined hands with William Penn beneath the Shackamaxon Tree of Peace. Now a very old man, Netawatwees addressed another as Brother Tamanend, George Morgan, who had been thus honored for reviving the tradition of the peacemaker.

The journey to the peace conference had been long and arduous for the old sachem, and by the end of October Grandfather Netawatwees was greatly weakened and was beginning to slip away. His last words were reportedly a prayer for peace—a desire that Indian people remain neutral in the Revolution and a hope that faith in the Creator would prevail. On October 31, 1776, Grandfather Netawatwees died. In accordance with his wishes, he was buried at the Forks of the Ohio beneath the Tree of Peace.[116]

In the following days Indian nations from far and wide sent delegates to express their condolences to the Lenape people, who were in mourning. Even the distant Cherokee, who had boycotted the treaty conference and warred against the Americans, sent an embassy of fourteen led by two principal chiefs. The Lenape, Grandfathers of many nations, expressed their appreciation to their Grandchildren on a string of wampum.[117] Some days later, on a November morning, they all gathered in the forest to conduct a memorial service. The ceremony began by "raising a melancholy song," and then "silence prevailed for about half an hour and all present cast their eyes on the ground."[118]

One of the Cherokees, Chief Crow, "rose, and with an air of sorrow, and in a low voice, with his eyes cast up to heaven, spoke":

> One morning, after having arisen from my sleep. . . . I observed at one place in the horizon a dark cloud projecting above the trees; . . . it neither disappeared, nor moved from the spot. . . . Seeing the same cloud successively every morning. . . I began to think . . . the cloud was lying in the direction that my grandfather dwelt . . . [and] something might be . . . causing him grief.[119]

The Cherokee chief had followed the path to the north toward the "dark cloud" until he came to the land of their Grandfathers, the Lenni Lenape: "I arrived at my grandfather's, whom I found quite disconsolate, hanging his head, and the tears running down his cheeks! . . . Even I cannot help weeping with my grandfather, seeing in what a situation he is! I cannot proceed for grief!"[120] Chief Crow sat down. There was silence for about twenty minutes during which time the Cherokee appeared "deeply afflicted."

Then, after receiving a string of wampum from a fellow chief, Crow rose again and exclaimed:

> Grandfather! Lift up your head and hear what your grandchildren have to say to you! These having discovered the cause of your grief, it shall be done away! See grandfather! I level the ground on yonder spot of yellow earth [Netawatwees's grave] and put leaves and brush thereon to make it invisible! I also sow seeds on that spot, so that both grass and trees may grow![121]

New hope for the future was being planted. The young grass and trees, like Netawatwees's children, grandchildren, and great-grandchildren, would live and enjoy the fruits of peace sown by their Grandfather.

Chief Crow held up another string of wampum and soothed the Lenape people:

> Now my grandfather! The cause of your grief being removed, let me dry up your tears! I wipe them from your eyes! I place your body, which by the weight of grief and a heavy heart is leaning to one side, in its proper posture! Your eyes shall be henceforth clear and your ears open as formerly! The work is now finished![122]

Gelelemend, or John Killbuck, grandson of Netawatwees and the new sachem of the Lenape nation, accepted the strings of wampum. The Lenape and Cherokee people stepped forward and shook hands. Then, when everyone had sat down again, Sachem Gelelemend responded: "Grandchildren! You did not come here in vain! You have performed a good work, in which the Great Spirit assisted you! Your grandfather makes you welcome."[123] The chiefs of different nations formed a sacred covenant to strive together toward achieving everlasting peace for the coming generations. The work commenced by Grandfather Netawatwees would be continued by those who were now united in the Covenant Chain of Friendship.

At the close of the first U.S.–Indian peace treaty conference, Chief Cornstalk asked George Morgan to send the following message to President John Hancock and the delegates of the Continental Congress:

> Pittsburgh   November: 7th. 1776
>
> The Corn Stalk desiring to speak to me I listen'd whilst he spoke as follows—which he desired me to commit to writing and forward to Congress.
>
> Brothers,
>
> You have several times desired our Chiefs to inform you what occasion of uneasiness we and other Nations complain of against our white Brethren of the United States—We always thought your Wise men could see into the causes thereof, but since they desire to know I will now tell you.[124]

Cornstalk proceeded to list the causes of conflict as he saw them. If a firm and lasting peace were to be established, both sides would have to recognize a common code of rights and liberties. Prejudice would have to end, as would injustice. Different cultures had to be preserved. Furthermore, spiritual and political sovereignty had to be respected.[125]

The Americans were engaged in a revolution to establish a sovereign, independent nation. The original people of this land were also struggling to preserve their independence, their cultures, and their homelands. If Americans and Indians were truly to be brothers, they had to recognize their mutual rights to "life, liberty and the pursuit of happiness." In addition, they had to recognize and respect their mutual rights to a sovereign homeland, as Cornstalk articulated: "We never sold you our [Kentucky] Lands which you now possess on the Ohio between the great Kenhawa and the Cherokee River, and which you are settling without ever asking our leave, or obtaining our consent. Foolish people have desired you do so, and you have taken their advice."[126]

Over twenty-five million acres lay between the Great Kanhawa and the Cherokee or Tennessee River. This land was an ancient intertribal hunting ground shared by the Shawnee, Cherokee, Creek, Lenape, Wyandot, Iroquois, and other Indian nations. No legal or just treaty of sale had ever been contracted. Chief Cornstalk humbly asked Congress for justice:

> We live by Hunting and do not subsist in any other way—That was our hunting [grounds] & you have taken it from us. This is what sits heavy [on our] Hearts & on the Hearts of all Nations, and it is impossible [that we] work as we ought to do whilst we are thus oppress'd [of our] right. Now I stretch my Arm to you my [Brothers] of the United States met in Council at Philadelphia.[127]

Most leaders of the American Indian peace effort had made a fair and equitable appeal to Congress, and George Morgan faithfully conveyed their messages to his superiors. Now it was up to President John Hancock, to members of the Continental Congress, and, ultimately, to the American people to decide how they would treat the original people of this land in the coming years.

Chapter Ten

"THE RIGHT TO LIFE, LIBERTY AND THE PURSUIT OF HAPPINESS"

THE ANCIENT TRIBAL relics and records, long preserved by the late Sachem Netawatwees, were passed on in trust to his grandson, Killbuck, who with White Eyes and George Morgan, vowed to fulfill the old chief's death wish. Peace might one day be achieved through the power of the Creator. However, from 1776 to 1789, powerful political and military forces were setting into motion plans to control the country from "sea to shining sea."

British officials, wealthy land barons, revengeful frontiersmen, political extremists, and intertribal rivals were splintering the people of the country into bitter factions. In March 1777 Lenape Wolf Clan leader Hopocan (Captain Pipe) and his allies challenged Killbuck and White Eyes to change political directions, away from the United States of America. Pipe advocated normalizing relations with the Iroquois Confederacy. When White Eyes protested, Pipe charged him with being disloyal to the nation.

White Eyes reached out to the deepest sentiments of his people. With tears streaming down his face, the Lenape statesman appealed to the Grand Council: "You know what our aged chief believed . . . that the Word of God is true. . . I take my young people and children by the hand and kneel before that Being. . . I pray that he may have mercy upon us all."[1] Out of respect for George Morgan, the only American Indian agent present, the tribal council asked him, "Brother Tamanend, we want your advice what we shall do?"[2]

Morgan could do little, because his authority was being undermined by one of George Washington's generals, Edward Hand, a hardened soldier who was determined to "chastise the savages."[3] He made no secret of his undiscriminating hatred for Indian people. Morgan was forced to warn the Indian ambassadors not to come to Fort Pitt, because they were in danger of being murdered. Hand soon ordered American soldiers to invade Indian country in the Ohio River Valley.

During the summer of 1777, a circle of pro-American Lenape and Shawnee leaders was left isolated in efforts to keep the peace. From out of the north, Indian war parties armed with British muskets reportedly were advancing against American frontier settlements. Shawnee Chief Cornstalk and his counselor, Red Hawk, rode south and swam across the Ohio River to warn the settlers. When the two men arrived at one Kentucky fort, the American commandant, Matthew Arbuckle, arrested Cornstalk and Red Hawk, put them in the brig, and held them as hostages. The chief's young son, Ellinipsico, soon came to see if his father were all right. He also was thrown into jail. On the same day, the body of a scalped soldier was brought into the fort. Panic gripped the community. A vengeful cry rang out to kill the three Indian hostages.

According to eyewitness accounts, Chief Cornstalk turned to his weeping son and calmly consoled him: "My son, the Great Spirit has seen fit that we should die together. . . . It is His will and let us submit; it is for the best."[4] The Shawnee chief and his son then rose with an air of dignity to meet their assassins' bullets. Red Hawk tried desperately to escape through the chimney, but he was dragged out and hacked to pieces. All three were killed and their bodies mutilated.

Morgan later tried in vain to comfort his Indian friends who grieved over this horrid affair: "Brothers, I am ashamed of the conduct of our young foolish men. . . . Now I see there are foolish people among all Nations."[5] In the wake of such shocking acts of violence, White Eyes continued to express remarkable sympathy for the American dream of independence predicated upon democratic principles of liberty. A plan was designed to protect the freedom of the Lenape nation and to ensure official recognition of Lenape land title. Other Indian nations pursued their own plans to ensure their survival and to promote good relations with the United States.

During the harsh winter, when Washington's troops were starving at Valley Forge, the general appealed in vain for supplies to feed his men. Local farmers and merchants refused to give him credit, nor would they accept continental dollars devalued by inflation. In the freezing cold and delirious from hunger, Washington's men spotted a band of Indians advancing from the North and prepared for battle. At the last moment, the soldiers realized that the Indians were not carrying guns, but rather baskets of corn and other food. The Oneida

Indians saved the lives of Washington's men at Valley Forge. The soldiers reportedly were so ravenously hungry that they had to be held back from eating uncooked dried corn which would have bloated their bellies. To honor the elder Indian woman, Polly, who stayed on and cooked for the general's troops, Martha Washington gave her a shawl, which is still in the possession of the Oneida nation. Through part of the Revolution, Washington, Lafayette, and other Americans employed Indian bodyguards. Several Oneidas and Tuscaroras enlisted in the Continental Army, and some became high-ranking officers. Many Indians contended that they thus earned the right to be treated as equals in American society.[6]

While Morgan envisioned a form of democratic city-state, White Eyes supported the creation of a "fourteenth Indian state" to be admitted into the American union. He soon appeared before the Grand Council to advocate political reform and unity. Lenape citizens were urged to reunify around the Lenape capital at Coshocton, Ohio. White Eyes wanted his people to elect tribal members as congressmen to represent Indian interests in the United States Congress.[7]

When his political rivals voiced strong opposition, White Eyes made a daring speech and then resigned his chieftaincy. Supporters rose to his defense. The people debated which direction to take at this political fork in the road. White Eyes's bitter rival, Captain Pipe, warned everyone that the Americans were plotting to steal all Indian lands and to destroy Indian communities. The Lenape nation split permanently into two parties at this point in history. Outraged by White Eyes and his allies' pro-American stance, Pipe and his followers packed up their belongings and resettled farther to the north between the Seneca nation and Fort Detroit.[8]

The plan for Indian statehood posed a threat not only to the British, but also to private land speculators. Some viewed White Eyes and Morgan as dangerous men who had to be eliminated, because official recognition of Indian land rights would result in the loss of millions of dollars in potential profits to be made through westward expansion. Several covert schemes were set into motion by rival special interest groups to sabotage Indian sovereignty. Morgan's political enemies spread false rumors that he was conspiring with the British, and General Hand placed him under arrest. A congressional investigative committee summoned Morgan to Philadelphia, where he would eventually be cleared of these charges.[9]

But while Morgan was fighting for his political life, federal Indian policy was being changed from peace and neutrality to war and alliance. Congress secretly authorized ten thousand dollars for a new treaty with the Lenape. General

Lachlan McIntosh and Colonel Daniel Brodhead were placed in command. While Morgan was still in Philadelphia, McIntosh promised White Eyes Indian statehood for the Lenape, if they would allow the Continental Army to attack the British at Fort Detroit. White Eyes accepted a colonel's commission, put on a blue uniform, and led thirteen hundred American troops against his old enemy, British Governor Henry Hamilton. The mission turned out to be a hoax; White Eyes had been tricked. This great chief, who had always remained true to the Americans, was assassinated by General McIntosh's soldiers. They tried to cover up the murder by claiming White Eyes had died of smallpox, but Morgan's subsequent investigation concluded that the Lenape chief was "treacherously put to death." Morgan condemned the vicious murder of Chief White Eyes and denounced General McIntosh before Congress. Of the 1778 U.S.–Lenape Treaty—still recognized as the first federal Indian treaty—Morgan remarked: "There never was a conference with the Indians so improperly or villainously conducted."[10] Thus began the infamous series of broken treaties.

Although Morgan's political rivals were pressuring him to resign, he felt a deep responsibility to help the Indian people avoid a fate of poverty, subjugation, and dispossession. Morgan arranged in the spring of 1779 for Chief Killbuck and representatives of the Lenape Grand Council to express their predicament to the Continental Congress. The delegation brought with them an eight-year-old boy named George Morgan White Eyes, son of the late chief. Little George believed his father was a great man who had died of smallpox while faithfully serving his American friends.

At home in Princeton, Morgan and his wife, Mary, were entertaining their Lenape guests when a messenger arrived with an invitation from General George Washington:

> To Colonel George Morgan at Princeton
>
> Sir,
>   I received your favor of the 9th Inst. by Captain Dodge—It will be convenient for me to see the Delaware [Lenape] Chiefs and those who attend them at Head Quarters tomorrow Evening at 5 O'Clock. The whole or a part will come as may be most agreeable to them and you will be pleased to accompany them.
> I am Sir
> Yr Most Obedt. Servant,
>
> G. Washington
> Head Qrs., May 11, 1779 [11]

The next day Chief Killbuck explained to Washington that the Indian people only wanted justice: "We do not mean to beg," but they were certain that honest men would do what was right and fair toward the Lenape nation.[12]

In a bold, spirited voice, General Washington proclaimed:

> Brothers,
>   I am a warrior. . . . 'Tis my business to destroy all the Enemies of these States. . . . I am sorry to hear that our people have not dealt justly by you. . . . I will do every thing in my power to prevent your receiving any further injuries.[13]

Washington then warned Morgan about various plots to assassinate the Indian leaders. A heavily armed guard escorted them to Independence Hall, where the Lenape delegation appealed for justice before the Continental Congress.

Chief Killbuck and the Lenape received little encouragement from the congressmen, who were planning to dispossess Indian tribes. Faced with mounting bills from the American Revolution, Congress planned to sell Indian land to help pay off the national debt. Had the tribes known the truth and united at that time, they could have crushed the revolutionaries. Killbuck explained to Congress that one man, George Morgan, was "the cause of our friendship with the states . . . he is the wisest and best man I ever had anything to do with."[14] Chief Killbuck and the Lenape could not understand why Morgan was being pressured to resign his position as Indian agent.

George Washington and many members of Congress had invested in western lands. A man like George Morgan, who wanted the Indians to live as equals with white Americans, was standing in the way of so-called progress. Morgan conceded that he was powerless to prevent the inevitable. However, he offered the Lenape one thread of hope. If the younger generation of Indians could be educated in American universities, perhaps they would achieve a new era of understanding between white people and Indian people.

The tribal council decided to entrust to Morgan's care three boys: John Killbuck, the sixteen-year-old son of Chief Killbuck; Thomas Killbuck, the chief's eighteen-year-old half brother; and little George Morgan White Eyes. Morgan treated them like his own sons while they attended Princeton University. School officials initially were skeptical, but the Lenape boys demonstrated amazing aptitude, especially in mathematics, geography, and foreign languages. Young George learned Greek, progressed through Virgil, and won a prize for academic excellence. Unfortunately, achieving social acceptance and balancing between two worlds proved more difficult. The boys were harassed by some students and negatively influenced by others. Thomas Killbuck was introduced to rum and became a teenage alcoholic. John lost interest in his studies after falling in love with one of Morgan's maids. Their secret affair was exposed when the maid became pregnant.[15]

Then something unexpected and far more devastating occurred. The Pennsylvania legislature passed a bill offering one thousand dollars for Indian scalps. The result was mass murder. Indian men, women, and children were massacred by bands of white scalp hunters, including the infamous Captain Sam Brady. Morgan tried to protect the three Lenape boys, whose lives were in danger from bounty hunters during their trek through Pennsylvania en route to New Jersey.[16]

Chief Killbuck made a desperate attempt to prove Lenape loyalty to the United States. He and his men offered to enlist in the Continental Army. Congress responded unfavorably, placing an embargo on all trade with Indians. Without gunpowder, Indian men could not hunt for enough game to feed their families. They had no alternative but to trade with the British. This relationship was used as justification for charging Indians with consorting with the enemy. A minority of Indian men sided with the British in Cherry Valley and carried out other attacks in defiance of the neutrality policy that was maintained by most tribal councils. When George Washington ordered an invasion of Iroquoia, Seneca Chief Cornplanter sent an urgent message to the general:

> Father,
>   You have said that we are in your hand and that by closing it you could crush us to nothing. Are you determined to crush us? If you are, tell us so that those of our nation who have become your children and have determined to die so, may know what to do. But before you determine on a measure so unjust, look up to God who made us as well as you. We hope He will not permit you to destroy the whole of our nation.[17]

Washington ordered a series of invasions to attack and burn Indian villages. The Iroquois retreated, and General Sullivan's soldiers destroyed over a million bushels of corn, cut down orchards, and poured salt over the fields. In response, the Haudenausaune gave George Washington a new name, which translated as "Destroyer of Villages." The title has been inherited by every United States president down to George Bush.[18]

The name Brodhead would forever be a black one to the Lenape. Colonel Daniel Brodhead and his soldiers attacked, looted, and burned the Lenape capital at Coshocton, Ohio, to the ground. A group of Lenape women, who were making salt beside a spring, were raped and murdered by General Edward Hand's soldiers in the notorious "Squaw Campaign." However, the darkest page in the history of the Lenape was yet to come.[19]

In 1782, a second regiment led by Colonel Crawford committed what became known as the Gnaddenhutten Massacre. Almost a hundred elderly men, women, and children—all Christian pacifists of the Moravian faith—were condemned to die. Their only crime was that a group of Mingo Indians, who had kidnapped a woman in Kentucky, had ridden their horses through the mission on their way northward. A piece of the woman's dress purportedly was found, and the whites decided to kill the entire village. They were led two by two into their church. The soldiers took turns clubbing them to death upon their sacred altar. Among these people were some of the true Mohicans who had been adopted into the Lenape nation and then converted to Christianity. Only two Lenape boys survived the massacre. One had hidden under the floor, drenched by his mother's blood as it dripped through the cracks. The second boy was scalped, but he survived. When the chapel was torched and the soldiers were riding away, the two boys tried to crawl out from under the roaring fire. Unfortunately, one boy was too overweight to get through a tight space, and he burned to death.[20]

For 208 years, the Lenape people have returned to the Gnaddenhutten "Huts of Grace" Mission and conducted religious ceremonies. Red Cedar incense is burned to purify the air, and they speak softly to the departed spirits of their ancestors. In the summer of 1988, over a hundred Lenape people from Oklahoma to Canada reunited at Gnaddenhutten. Representatives were also present from the Cherokee, Munsey, Choctaw, and Iroquois nations. When the medicine people arrived, one of the residents of the old mission asked for help. In one of the log houses rebuilt over the actual site, something that looked like blood was coming up between the cracks of the floor. Later in the afternoon, a Tree of Peace was planted, and the children tied onto the boughs ribbons colored red, white, yellow, and black. Prayers were offered to bring peace to people of all colors in every continent on earth, as the breeze blew the ribbons into rainbows. People hugged each other, shook hands, cried, and laughed together. The Lenape nation was once again reunited along with representatives from the Iroquois, Cherokee, and Choctaw nations.[21]

The ancestors of these nations and many more entered into a series of treaties with the U.S. government which recognized their sovereign rights. In an effort to preserve their rights, these nations have fought to defend their liberty, from the battlefields of the western frontier to state and federal courts across this land. One of the crucial issues has been the extent of their jurisdiction, the right to legally control activities within their sovereign territories.

It was a policy of the federal government from 1785 to 1795 that non-Indians who entered Indian territories were subject to Indian jurisdiction. This policy was confirmed for the Lenape, Iroquois, Ottawa, Wyandot, Chippewa, Potawatomi, and Sauk nations by the 1789 Treaty of Fort Harmar, and this interpretation has been supported by Felix Cohen, author of the *Handbook of Federal Indian Law*.[22]

The United States recognized the supremacy of Indian jurisdiction over Indian land for a variety of reasons:

1. Indian nations truly controlled the law of the land within their territorial boundaries.[23]

2. The United States conducted an economic analysis and determined it was cheaper to negotiate than to go to war. By recognizing Indian jurisdiction, it temporarily kept whites out of Indian territory and thus limited the number of expensive border conflicts.[24]

3. Certain U.S. officials were buying themselves time to promote their future economic interests. At the time of the 1789 treaty, U.S. geographer Thomas Hutchins was surveying lands in the Ohio River Valley for future U.S. settlement. Federal officials hoped the Indians would sell out cheaply, so they could make large profits in the future.[25]

4. The United States recognized Indian jurisdiction to win favors at a time when British agents were also courting Indian allies. The United States remained concerned that Indians would unite with the British in an offensive.[26]

5. The United States recognized the jurisdiction of distinct Indian nations, because it feared the Wabash Confederacy, the Delaware and their allies, as well as the Iroquois Confederacy might form one Great Indian Confederacy. Unification of the Indian nations was in fact later advocated by Tecumseh, Black Hawk, and others.[27]

6. The United States also recognized the jurisdiction of Indian nations, because as nations they could sign treaties and transfer to the United States jurisdiction and land title. The United States wanted ultimately to achieve supreme authority. One way to achieve this goal was through treaties, which is why the U.S. Constitution states: "Treaties are to be judged the supreme law of the land." While it recognized Indian jurisdiction by treaties, Congress did so with the intent of later getting tribes to sign these jurisdictional powers back over to the United States in subsequent treaties. However, the Sauk and some other

nations signed the 1789 treaty in which the United States recognized their jurisdictional authority, but never signed another treaty giving up this power.[28] Moreover, Congress gave itself absolute authority over the states in negotiating treaties and land transfers and formalized its position in the 1790 Non-Intercourse Act. By recognizing Indian jurisdiction, the United States was clarifying that the states did not have jurisdiction.[29]

Congress also claimed exclusive right to regulate trade and commerce with Indian nations. This right was important from its perspective for financial, political, and legal reasons. It wrote its authority into the Commerce Clause of the U.S. Constitution, and it is from this clause that Congress to this day claims authority in drafting laws regarding Indians.[30] However, the United States has expanded its authority into a paternalistic role far greater than the Constitution actually defines. This change in attitude is reflected in the diplomatic correspondence, where the president stopped calling Indians "Brothers," and started calling them "Children." Thus was born the idea of the "Great White Father."

The U.S. Constitution also includes the phrase, "Indians not taxed." Indian nations were not to be taxed, and federal income tax was not imposed on the Indians until after the 1924 Indian Citizenship Act. Congress also made it quite clear that the states were not to interfere in Indian affairs.[31]

Today, many traditionalists among the Iroquois, Lenape, Sauk, and Hopi are still protesting and refuse to pay taxes. They contend that one nation does not have the authority to force the people of a second nation to become the citizens of the first. To assert their sovereign rights, some Iroquois and Hopi traditionalists have been traveling to foreign countries not with a U.S. passport, but rather with an Iroquois or Hopi passport. Many foreign countries have accepted Indian passports.[32]

On July 13, 1787, Congress passed the Northwest Ordinance, an important law regarding the relationship between the U.S. government and Indian nations:

> The utmost good faith shall always be observed towards the Indian; their lands and property shall never be taken from them without their consent; and in their property, rights and liberty, they shall never be invaded or disturbed, unless in just and lawful wars authorized by Congress; but laws founded in justice and humanity shall from time to time be made, for preventing wrongs being done to them, and for preserving peace and friendship with them.[33]

Congress clearly was assuming control of Indian affairs over the states, a law which should have prohibited the states from taking Indian lands without both federal and Indian consent. Written largely by Nathan Dane of Massachusetts, the Northwest Ordinance provided for interim governance of the territory by congressional appointees (a governor, secretary, and three judges), creation of a bicameral legislature once there were five thousand free white males in the territory, and ultimate establishment of three to five states on an equal footing with the states already in existence. Freedom of worship, right to trial by jury, and public education were guaranteed, and slavery prohibited. Upon achieving statehood, the inhabitants would become citizens of the United States.[34]

Some traditional Indians take the position that they hold "dual citizenship," meaning they are citizens of both the United States and their own Indian nation. They contend that they should not be taxed for income generated on Indian land. This position is attractive to owners of tribal businesses, such as smoke shops and gasoline stations. Major battles are presently raging in New York and other states over this issue.[35]

What happened to the treaty signed by George Morgan? When the author testified before the U.S. Senate Select Committee on Indian Affairs, on December 2, 1987, along with Onondaga Chief Oren Lyons and Professor Vine Deloria, we were asked by Senator Daniel Inouye, "I have been advised that since 1778— I believe that is the first treaty—we have had a total of 370 treaties between the United States Government and Indian nations. Am I also correct that provisions of every one of these treaties have been violated?"

Vine Deloria, author of *Trail of Broken Treaties* and *Custer Died for Your Sins*, responded in part:

> I think the spirit of all the treaties has certainly long since been destroyed. . . . There are probably close to 800 treaties all told, about 430 of them being unratified. So, not only have ratified treaties been violated, but the United States has claimed to own lands based on treaties that it itself refused to ratify or admit as a legal document.[36]

Senator Inouye went on to clarify that during the past two hundred years treaty violations have resulted in Indian nations losing five hundred million acres of land. When he asked how U.S. policy developed to force Indians from their lands, I explained:

The policy changed actually quite early on. The original policy early in 1776 was one of peace and neutrality.

George Washington needed soldiers to fight in the Revolutionary War, so he and . . . his generals went secretly to Philadelphia and lobbied the Continental Congress to change the policy to one of war and aggression. He in a sense was saying Indians either have to join us and join the United States Army or they will be against us.

At that point in time, a policy began to change, and the original position was that the United States encouraged peace and neutrality among Indian nations, and the Grand Council agreed with that. In fact I found [in the Morgan Papers] that the Grand Council of the Iroquois Confederacy in 1776 called all the warriors in at a time when the British were offering bounties for American scalps.

Two of the chiefs went out and actually brought warriors back in, and they said the British are trying to get us involved in war. The Americans are not. They are saying remain in peace and neutrality and within friendship. That is what is within our best interests.

When the policy changed and the United States officials began to actively try to get Indians involved in war, that is when the Confederacy began to question whether or not these promises that were made for "as long as the sun shines" were really true.[37]

And what of George Morgan? After his retirement from the Indian agency, Morgan moved to his farm, Prospect, near Princeton, New Jersey, and pursued his love of science and nature. He focused his enthusiasm on the creation of a model farm, developed through experiments in scientific agriculture, where he and his family could live in peace. He published his findings with the Philadelphia Society for the Promotion of Agriculture, for which he was awarded a gold medal. Morgan used a microscope to study organic farming, natural pest control and fertilizers, bee culture, selective breeding of farm animals, herbal medicines, and the value of trees. He even donated a hundred elm trees to restore the square in front of Independence Hall. Morgan read his research papers on American Indians, featuring ancient settlements along the Mississippi River, to the American Philosophical Society. Furthermore, he wrote newspaper articles criticizing U.S. policy in conjunction with Benjamin Franklin, George Washington, Samuel Adams, and various members of Congress, and his literary contributions earned him recognition as an American intellectual.

After a decade of scientific experiments, extensive research, and reevaluation of his revolutionary experience, Morgan could have rested on his laurels as a gentleman farmer. However, history took a turn he could not ignore, which challenged his democratic principles about the right to liberty. He believed U.S. national security and honor were threatened by military intervention in Indian country and the trail of broken treaties which resulted in war. Justice and integrity, not deception and force, were keys to peace, as Morgan wrote to Samuel Adams: "National honesty must be the fundamental Principle of our Politics with the Indian Nations."[38]

His political theories fell upon deaf ears. In 1789, when the old Articles of Confederation had expired and the new Constitution was not yet in force, George Morgan boldly espoused a new plan of action. He ventured west of the Mississippi River, outside of U.S. jurisdiction, to create a model community, the fulfillment of his ultimate dreams. His dynamic new plans, still preserved in the Library of Congress and the National Archives, called for a true, representative democracy, greater human rights, and a civic government free to make its own laws. Two years in advance of the Bill of Rights, Morgan proposed total freedom of religion, a liberal school system, and free trade. Moreover, Morgan invited the Lenape and other Indians to come and live with equal rights in America's first racially integrated community.

Morgan held a provisional Spanish grant to fifteen million acres of land south of St. Louis, Missouri. He called his community New Madrid to please the Spanish Crown, and started construction near the mouth of the Ohio River. For forty-eight Mexican dollars, settlers received 320 acres, providing they built a house and became responsible citizens. Morgan's city of New Madrid represented a vision of future planning, designed with balanced geometry and offering free land for community parks, places of worship, and public schools. A natural lake graced the center of the city, with radiating roads lined by rows of trees and parkways.

As a conservationist, Morgan was ahead of his time. Not even one tree could be cut down without permission from the magistrates. Commercial hunting was outlawed "for the preservation of those animals, and for the benefit of neighboring Indians."[39] Morgan made certain that no tribes had claims to the lands around New Madrid, then invited Indians from as far away as Pennsylvania to come and live in peace. He promised them that no white men would be allowed to trap for furs, hunting being restricted to feeding one's own family in accordance with Indian custom. In short, Morgan's democratic plan of union offered greater security, better economic incentives, and more religious and political liberty.

Almost overnight, groups of powerful men began plotting New Madrid's destruction. The selfish ends that motivated men to use devious means to destroy Morgan's dreams have been well documented by Max Savelle.[40] In particular, the Spanish government absolutely refused to grant the people freedom of religion. Morgan was informed that only Catholicism would be permitted. Furthermore, the Spanish governor of Louisiana, Estevan Miro, told Morgan the King wanted him to grow huge fields of hemp "for the sake of the royal navy." If Morgan found these terms to be unacceptable, he did not blurt it out, but rather returned to Pennsylvania and stood his ground in hopes the king would approve his original plans. Had his plans been accepted, others may have patterned similar integrated communities based on the best of Euro-American and Native American cultures. Perhaps almost a century of Indian wars could have been avoided by living out Morgan's vision of peaceful coexistence founded upon the principles of liberty. But it was not to be. Before he passed away on March 10, 1810, Morgan eloquently described the free nature of the American spirit: "Our love of Liberty, Civil and religious, is our ruling Passion: Give us these & all Princes or Rulers & all Countries are alike to Us."[41]

During 1811–1812 a series of earthquakes rumbled through the heart of the country, climaxing with perhaps the most violent earthquake in American history. The Mississippi River actually stopped and changed its course. Giant trees crashed to the ground, producing so much dust, that the sky looked blood red. Reported from coast to coast, the earthquakes were so devastating that a Catholic mission was damaged in Santa Barbara, California, and simultaneously the Liberty Bell was said to ring from the jolt in Philadelphia, Pennsylvania. The powerful quake ironically was centered in New Madrid, Missouri, the site of George Morgan's proposed utopian community. Surely it was just a coincidence, but is it possible that there are greater forces at work in the history of the world?

NOTES

Chapter One

1. The official response of the Continental Congress to Chief White Eyes, hereafter cited as Speech to Captain White Eyes, was printed in *Journals of the Continental Congress, 1774–1789*, ed. Worthington C. Ford et al., 34 vols. (Washington, DC: Government Printing Office, 1904–37), 4:269–70. It can also be found in Papers of the Continental Congress, National Archives M247, r37, i30, pp. 347–50. Citations to these records follow the format used in John P. Butler, comp., *Index: The Papers of the Continental Congress, 1774–1789*, 5 vols. (Washington, DC: Government Printing Office, 1978), giving Microfilm Publication (M) number, roll (r) number, item (i) number, and volume, page, or frame numbers.

2. An excellent analysis of American revolutionary reactions to British colonial oppression is Bernard Bailyn, *The Ideological Origins of the American Revolution* (Cambridge: The Belknap Press of Harvard University Press, 1967); see especially pp. 94, 143. Compare the roots of oppression of Native Americans recorded by Wilbur R. Jacobs, "British Indian Policies to 1783," in Wilcomb E. Washburn, ed., *History of Indian–White Relations,* vol. 4 of *Handbook of North American Indians* (Washington, DC: Smithsonian Institution, 1988), pp. 5–12; and *Dispossessing the American Indian: Indians and Whites on the Colonial Frontier* (New York: Charles Scribner's Sons, 1972), pp. 4–5, 103, 110–12, 118, 123–25, 140–41.

3. An eyewitness account of the Lancaster Massacre by local resident William Henry was recorded by the Reverend John Heckewelder, *Narrative of the*

Mission of the United Brethren among the Delaware and Mohegan Indians, from its Commencement in the Year 1740, to the close in the Year 1808 (Philadelphia: McCarty and Davis, 1820; reprint, New York: Arno Press and the New York Times, 1971), pp. 78–80. For a report of the subsequent investigation, consult Benjamin Franklin, *A Narrative of the Late Massacres, in Lancaster County, of a Number of Indians, Friends of this Province, by Persons Unknown* (Philadelphia, 1764), in *The Papers of Benjamin Franklin*, ed. Leonard Labaree et al., 27 vols.– (New Haven: Yale University Press, 1959–), 11:42–69. For an account of the murders of Indians by Frederick Stump in 1768, see a report by Chester Sipe, *The Indian Wars of Pennsylvania* (Harrisburg, PA: Telegraph Press, 1931), pp. 484–86.

    4. A collection of original documents related to the murder of Logan's family and the subsequent War of 1774 was preserved by Lyman Draper. See Reuben Gold Thwaites and Louise Phelps Kellogg, eds., *Documentary History of Dunmore's War, 1774* (Madison: Wisconsin Historical Society, 1905).

    5. For an analysis of original documents on William Penn's meeting with Chief Tamanend and the Lenape nation, see Granville Penn et al., "The Presentation to the Historical Society of Pennsylvania of the Belt of Wampum Delivered by the Indians to William Penn, at the Great Treaty under the Elm Tree, in 1682," *Memoirs of the Historical Society of Pennsylvania* (1858), 6:205–82. For an account of George Morgan receiving the name "Tamanend," see John Heckewelder, *History, Manners and Customs of the Indian Nations Who Once Inhabited Pennsylvania and the Neighboring States,* rev. ed. (Philadelphia: Historical Society of Pennsylvania, 1876), pp. 300–301.

    6. For a synonymy of Shackamaxon and related stories, see George Donehoo, *A Story of the Indian Villages and Place Names in Pennsylvania* (Harrisburg, PA: Telegraph Press, 1928), pp. 175–85. An excellent biography of Penn and an analysis of the "Holy Experiment" was written by Harry Emerson Wildes, *William Penn* (New York: Macmillan, 1974).

    7. Wildes, *William Penn*, pp. 121–82, 255–58, 327–59.

    8. Mark Harrington, *Religion and Ceremonies of the Lenape* (New York: Museum of the American Indian, Heye Foundation, 1921).

    9. Ibid., 81–120, 195.

    10. For an analysis of the importance of Indian sovereignty, see D'Arcy McNickle, Mary Young, and W. Roger Buffalohead, *Captive Nations: A Political History of the American Indian* (Washington, DC: Government Printing Office, 1977), pp. 1–22.

    11. For an account of Morgan's activities in Philadelphia, see Max Savelle, *George Morgan: Colony Builder* (New York: Columbia University Press, 1932; re-

print, New York: AMS Press, 1967), pp. 111–40; a scholarly account of his career as an Indian trader can be found on pp. 18–19. For an index of the original papers of his trading partnership, Baynton, Wharton and Morgan, see the microfilm directory prepared with support from the National Historical Publications Commission, *Baynton, Wharton and Morgan Papers in the Pennsylvania State Archives,* Donald H. Kent, project director (Harrisburg, PA: Pennsylvania Historical and Museum Commission, 1967).

12. Report on Indian Affairs in the Middle Department, Philadelphia, April 10, 1776, *Journals of the Continental Congress,* 4:267–70.

13. Savelle, *George Morgan,* p. 186.

14. Ibid.

15. Robert Secor, ed., *Pennsylvania 1776* (University Park, PA: Pennsylvania State University Press, 1975), pp. 159–73; Edwin Wolf II, *Philadelphia: Portrait of an American City: A Bicentennial History* (Harrisburg, PA: Stackpole Books, 1975), pp. 68–93.

16. Compare Savelle, *George Morgan,* pp. 1–75; and Edmund S. Morgan, *The Birth of the Republic* (Chicago: University of Chicago Press, 1956), pp. 1–77.

17. Wolf, *Philadelphia,* pp. 68–93.

18. Savelle, *George Morgan,* pp. 39–59. For an excellent collection of essays on Franklin, see Wilbur R. Jacobs, ed., *Benjamin Franklin: Statesman–Philosopher or Materialist?* (New York: Holt, Rinehart and Winston, 1972).

19. Savelle, *George Morgan,* pp. 1–20, 130–66.

20. For an anthropological study of Eastern Woodland cultures, see Bruce G. Trigger, ed., *Northeast,* vol. 15 of *Handbook of North American Indians* (Washington, DC: Smithsonian Institution, 1978), hereafter cited as *Handbook of North American Indians: Northeast.*

21. The Lenape were addressed as "Grandfathers" by the Shawnee, Potawatomi, Mohegan, Cherokee, and many other nations.

22. For an interesting analysis of wampum diplomacy, see Paul A. W. Wallace, *Indians in Pennsylvania* (Harrisburg, PA: Pennsylvania Historical and Museum Commission, 1968), pp. 53–55ff.

23. Papers of the Indian commissioners are indexed in Butler, comp., *Index: The Papers of the Continental Congress,* 2:2519–23.

24. See the original engraving by J. Trenchard after Charles Willson Peale, *A Northwest View of the Statehouse,* 1778, Historical Society of Pennsylvania, Philadelphia.

25. *Journals of the Continental Congress,* June 11, 1776, 5:430. For a colorful description of John Hancock, see Richard M. Ketchum, "Men of the Revolution

XIV—John Hancock," *American Heritage* 26 (February 1975):65, 81–82.

26. For a cross-cultural analysis of this theme, see Edwin Oliver James, *The Tree of Life: An Archaeological Study* (Leiden: E. J. Brill, 1966). The relationship between the Tree of Peace as a universal symbol and cosmological parallels in Native American religions was articulated by the author in a paper delivered to the United Nations: Gregory Schaaf, "The History of the American Indian Peace Movement—A Presentation in the Pacem in Terris Society," notice cited in *Secretariat News,* New York, April 29, 1983, p. 11.

27. Bailyn, *Ideological Origins of the American Revolution*, pp. 23–29.

28. For a biographical sketch of Charles Thomson, see *Appleton's Cyclopedia of American Biography.*

29. George Washington to the President of Congress, Cambridge, March 27, 1776, *The Writings of George Washington from the Original Manuscript Sources, 1745–1799,* ed. John C. Fitzpatrick, 39 vols. (Washington, DC: Government Printing Office, 1931–44), 4:437–38.

30. George Washington to Major General Philip Schuyler, Cambridge, January 27, 1776, ibid., 280.

31. George Washington to Joseph Reed, Cambridge, April 1, 1776, ibid., 456.

32. George Washington to the President of Congress, Cambridge, April 1, 1776, ibid., 456–57.

33. Whitfield Bell, *John Morgan: Continental Doctor* (Philadelphia: University of Pennsylvania Press, 1965), pp. 182–88.

34. Albert T. Volwiler, ed., "William Trent's Journal at Fort Pitt, 1763," *Mississippi Valley Historical Review* 11 (December 1924):400.

35. Bell, *John Morgan,* p. 184.

36. George Washington to Joseph Reed, Cambridge, April 1, 1776, *Writings of George Washington,* 4:454–55.

37. Albert T. Volwiler, *George Croghan and the Westward Movement, 1741–1782* (Cleveland: Arthur H. Clark Co., 1926), p. 324.

38. Dr. John Connolly to the Congress, Philadelphia, February 8, 1776, *American Archives,* ed. Peter Force, ser. 4, 6 vols.; ser. 5, 3 vols. (Washington, DC: M. St. Clair Clarke and Peter Force, 1837–55), ser. 4, 5:1122.

39. George Morgan to Lewis Morris, Pittsburgh, May 16, 1776, Papers of the Continental Congress, National Archives M247, r180, i163, pp. 237–40.

40. On the western land dealings of George Croghan and his associates, compare Volwiler, *George Croghan and the Westward Movement,* pp. 300–324; D'Arcy McNickle, *Native American Tribalism: Indian Survivals and Renewals* (London:

Oxford University Press, 1973), pp. 41–47; and Senator James Abourazk et al., *American Indian Policy Review Commission: Final Report* (Washington, DC: Government Printing Office, 1977), 1:51–52. For a scholarly analysis of Morgan's land dealings, see Savelle, *George Morgan*, pp. 76–110.

41. Richard Smith, Diary, Philadelphia, December 16, 1775, *Letters of Members of the Continental Congress*, ed. Edmund C. Burnett, 8 vols. (Washington, DC: Carnegie Institution, 1921–36), 1:278. Smith's account describes the first appearance of White Eyes before Congress.

42. John Adams to General Horatio Gates, Philadelphia, April 27, 1776, *American Archives*, ser. 4, 5:1091.

43. Ibid.

44. Francis Russell, *Adams: An American Dynasty* (New York: American Heritage Publishing Co., 1976), pp. 13–14.

45. Thomas Jefferson, quoted in Cornel Lengyel, *Four Days in July: The Story Behind the Declaration of Independence* (Garden City: Doubleday, 1958), p. 221.

46. "Treaty with the Delawares, 1778," Pittsburgh, September 17, 1778, Charles J. Kappler, ed., *Indian Affairs: Laws and Treaties*, 5 vols. (Washington, DC: Government Printing Office, 1904–41; reprint, New York: AMS Press, 1971), 2:3–5; White Eyes to George Morgan, Cushitunk, July 19, 1778, Papers of the Continental Congress, National Archives M247, r98, i78, v. 14, p. 239.

47. Benjamin Franklin, *The Interest of Great Britain Considered, with Regard to Her Colonies, and the Acquisitions of Canada and Guadaloupe* (London, 1760), *Papers of Benjamin Franklin*, 9:66.

48. Franklin, *Narrative of the Late Massacres*, ibid., 11:55.

49. Ibid., 65.

50. Benjamin Franklin, quoted in Lengyel, *Four Days in July*, p. 98.

51. James Wilson, quoted in ibid., 101.

52. For a discussion of the congressional debate on slavery, see Bailyn, *Ideological Origins of the American Revolution*, pp. 232–46.

53. For further information on the subject of cultural conflicts and prejudice, see Vine Deloria, Jr., *We Talk, You Listen* (New York: Macmillan, 1970), pp. 33–44; and Edgar S. Cahn, ed., *Our Brother's Keeper: The Indian in White America* (Washington, DC: New Community Press, 1969).

54. *Journals of the Continental Congress*, April 10, 1776, 4:267.

55. Ibid.

56. Ibid., 268.

57. Ibid.

58. The sacred nature of "All Our Relations"—meaning we pray for all

creations—represents a fundamental tenet of many Indian religions.

59. Donehoo, *Indian Villages and Place Names*, p. 267.

60. Ibid., 185.

61. William Penn, "On Peace with the Indians," *Pennsylvania Archives*, ser. 1:239–40; cited in C. A. Weslager, *The Delaware Indians: A History* (New Brunswick, NJ: Rutgers University Press, 1972), p. 186.

62. Weslager, *Delaware Indians*, pp. 344–45.

63. Secor, ed., *Pennsylvania 1776*, pp. 364–66.

64. For an excellent study of the Conestoga Road and other trails, see Paul A. W. Wallace, *Indian Paths of Pennsylvania* (Harrisburg, PA: Pennsylvania Historical and Museum Commission, 1965), p. 36.

65. Secor, ed., *Pennsylvania 1776*, p. 365.

66. For a full account of the Lancaster Treaty of 1744, see *Pennsylvania Colonial Records*, 4:698–737. For a secondary interpretation see Sipe, *Indian Wars of Pennsylvania*, pp. 121–26.

67. William Henry, an inhabitant of Lancaster, recorded this account of the Lancaster Massacre, which appears in Heckewelder, *Narrative of the Mission of the United Brethren*, pp. 78–80.

68. *Pennsylvania Journal*, March 21 and 28, 1765, cited in Savelle, *George Morgan*, p. 21.

69. For the Papers of Jasper Yeates, consult the Pennsylvania Historical Society in Philadelphia.

70. For information on Indian interpreter Isaac Still, see George Morgan to John Hancock, Carlisle, Pennsylvania, April 22, 1776, Papers of the Continental Congress, National Archives M247, r180, i163, pp. 233–34.

71. For the papers related to Franklin's Indian negotiations in Carlisle, consult *The Writings of Benjamin Franklin*, ed. Albert H. Smyth, 10 vols. (New York: Macmillan, 1907), 1:375–95 and 3:343–53.

72. For the papers of Ephraim Blaine, the future Commissary General of Purchases, see Butler, comp., *Index: The Papers of the Continental Congress*, 1:463–66.

73. John Hancock to George Morgan, Philadelphia, April 19, 1776, Morgan Papers. These revolutionary era documents, part of the papers of George Morgan, were passed down through a branch of the Morgan family that settled on the West Coast. The manuscripts eventually came into the possession of Mrs. Susannah Morgan, the widow of one of Morgan's great-great-grandsons, and were made available to the author in 1976. Thereafter they were preserved initially by the George Morgan Document Preservation and Marketing Company

and later sold at Sotheby's in New York on April 25, 1989. Microfilm copies of the Morgan Papers are deposited in the Special Collections, University of California, Santa Barbara; the Special Collections, California State University, Chico; and the Grand Council, Iroquois Confederacy, in the care of Chief Leon Shenandoah, Onondaga Nation, via Nadrow, New York.

74. Ibid.

75. Ibid.

76. Ibid.

77. George Morgan to John Hancock, Carlisle, Pennsylvania, April 22, 1776, Papers of the Continental Congress, National Archives M247, r130, i163, p. 233.

Chapter Two

This chapter attempts to unravel the events surrounding Morgan's initial stage of establishing the first U.S. department of Indian affairs on the Ohio frontier. The legacy of over two hundred years of U.S.–Indian relations now may be traced back to these early origins.

1. The primary sources of information on the establishment by the Continental Congress of an Indian agency in the Middle Department are the records of agent George Morgan, found in his Personal Journal and Letterbook (Pittsburgh, April–November 1776, 73 pages), Morgan Papers, hereafter cited as Morgan's Journal. Over 350 additional pages of Morgan's journal and letterbook are located in the holdings of the Andrew Carnegie Library, Pittsburgh; the Pennsylvania State Library, Harrisburg, has typescript copies. The sections of Morgan's journal and letterbook in the Carnegie Library are identified as Morgan's Journal I, II, and III. Sections from the latter part were published in two volumes: Reuben Gold Thwaites and Louise Phelps Kellogg, eds., *The Revolution on the Upper Ohio, 1775–1777* (Madison: Wisconsin Historical Society, 1908) and Louise Phelps Kellogg, ed., *Frontier Advance on the Upper Ohio, 1778–1779* (Madison: State Historical Society of Wisconsin, 1916). Many historians have relied on these documents to reconstruct U.S.–Indian history during the period 1775–1782. The relationship of this period to the larger historical framework was established by Randolph C. Downes, *Council Fires on the Upper Ohio: A Narrative of Indian Affairs in the Upper Ohio Valley Until 1795* (Pittsburgh: University of Pittsburgh Press, 1940). Downes first recognized Morgan's important role in Indian affairs in an earlier article, "George Morgan, Indian Agent Extraordinary, 1776–1779," *Pennsylvania History* 1 (October 1934):202–16. Downes expanded a previous sketch of Morgan written by Walter R. Fee, "Colonel George

Morgan at Fort Pitt," *Western Pennsylvania Historical Magazine* 11 (October 1928):217–24.

The same primary sources were used in a chapter on Morgan by Savelle in *George Morgan.* Savelle's contribution focused on Morgan's land dealings and his attempt to establish an interracial colony at New Madrid, Missouri. Anthropologist C. A. Weslager referred to the published letterbooks, characterizing Morgan as "a capable executive, fur trader, and colonizer," in *Delaware Indians,* pp. 295–317. Barbara Graymont also touched upon Morgan's activities in her study of northern Indian affairs, *The Iroquois in the American Revolution* (Syracuse: Syracuse University Press, 1972).

Among the more recent studies of Indian affairs during the American Revolution, two works figure prominently. Both were published during the Bicentennial: Francis Jennings, "The Indians' Revolution," *The American Revolution: Explorations in the History of American Radicalism,* ed. A. F. Young (DeKalb: Northern Illinois University Press, 1976), pp. 320–48; and Edward G. Williams, "Fort Pitt and the Revolution on the Western Frontier," *Western Pennsylvania Historical Magazine* 59 (January 1976):1–38, (April 1976):129–52, (July 1976):251–88, (October 1976):379–410, a four-part series on Morgan's headquarters, Fort Pitt.

2. For a description of the trails between Philadelphia and Pittsburgh, see Wallace, *Indian Paths of Pennsylvania,* pp. 145, 159, 166, 198. Morgan's classical studies began at an early age and continued through his involvement with the American Philosophical Society, a learned club established by his neighbor, Dr. Benjamin Franklin. For an example of Morgan's use of classical metaphors, see George Morgan to Thomas Morgan, July 4, 1807, Morgan Papers.

3. The treaty papers of the "Great Peace" between William Penn and Tamanend, along with the original wampum belt, were presented by Penn's great-grandson, Granville J. Penn. See "Presentation to the Historical Society of Pennsylvania of the Belt of Wampum," 6:205–82. For an excellent secondary account see Wildes, *William Penn.*

4. John Heckewelder, Diary (1762), in Paul A.W. Wallace, ed., *Thirty Thousand Miles with John Heckewelder* (Pittsburgh: University of Pittsburgh Press, 1958), p. 40. The original manuscript is in the Moravian Mission Archives, Bethlehem, Pennsylvania. Most of the collection has been reproduced on microfilm and indexed by the Reverend Carl Fliegel, *Index to the Records of the Moravian Mission among the Indians of North America* (New Haven, CT: Research Publications, 1970).

5. The official orders of the Continental Congress pertaining to the establishment of the Indian agency at Fort Pitt were written by John Hancock to George Morgan, April 19, 1776, Morgan Papers. For further documentation, see *Journals*

of the Continental Congress, 4:294–95. For a secondary account, refer to Savelle, *George Morgan,* pp. 137–38.

6. A history of the Indian place names in the Pittsburgh area can be found in Donehoo, *Indian Villages and Place Names.* Several well-documented articles on the findings of archaeological studies of the area were published in the *Handbook of North American Indians: Northeast.* See James A. Tuck, "Regional Cultural Development, 3000 to 300 B.C.," 28–43; James E. Fitting, "Regional Cultural Development," 44–57; and James B. Griffin, "Late Prehistory of the Ohio Valley," 547–59.

7. Donald Jackson et al., eds., *The Diaries of George Washington,* 6 vols. (Charlottesville: University Press of Virginia, 1976–79), 1:132.

8. The history of colonial Indian affairs from 1750 to 1775 has been the subject of hundreds of books and articles. Among the earliest studies are Samuel P. Hildreth, *Pioneer History, Being an Account of the First Examinations of the Ohio Valley* (Cincinnati: For the Historical Society of Cincinnati by H. W. Derby and Co., 1848); and the famous narrative by Francis Parkman, *History of the Conspiracy of Pontiac, and the War of the North American Tribes against the English Colonies after the Conquest of Canada* (Boston: Little, Brown and Co., 1851). Popular accounts were dramatized in James Fenimore Cooper's "Leatherstocking Tales." Modern scholarship has presented a more balanced portrayal of native perspectives, particularly the work of Jacobs, *Dispossessing the American Indian,* and *Diplomacy and Indian Gifts: Anglo-French Rivalry along the Ohio and Northwest Frontiers, 1748–1763* (Stanford: Stanford University Press, 1950; reprinted as *Wilderness Politics and Indian Gifts: The Northern Colonial Frontier, 1748–1763* (Lincoln: University of Nebraska Press, 1966), hereafter cited as *Wilderness Politics and Indian Gifts.*

9. One of the most in-depth studies of western land speculation by George Washington and others was written by Thomas Perkins Abernethy, *Western Lands and the American Revolution* (New York: Russell and Russell, 1959). His research reveals that many of the founding fathers had invested in western land grants and that the Revolution was deeply influenced by economic considerations.

10. George Morgan was elected secretary of the land company formed by the "Sufferers of 1763," involving lands granted to traders by the Iroquois signers of the 1768 Fort Stanwix Treaty. For the original transcript of the 1775 meetings in which Morgan became secretary, see George Morgan, Minutes of the Indiana Land Company, Pittsburgh, September 21, 1775, and Carlisle, November 15, 1775, Morgan Papers. A copy of this transcript is in the holdings of the Historical Society of Pennsylvania in Ohio Company Manuscripts, 2:9–29. For a secondary account see Savelle, *George Morgan,* pp. 82–85.

11. Most of George Morgan's early records and journals as an Indian trader

are available on microfilm: see *Baynton, Wharton and Morgan Papers.*

12. Uncited quotation in Donehoo, *Indian Villages and Place Names,* p. 155. A series of eyewitness descriptions of this early frontier settlement was compiled in a book by Leland D. Baldwin, *Pittsburgh: The Story of a City, 1750–1865* (Pittsburgh: University of Pittsburgh Press, 1937). An earlier study was completed by George Thornton Fleming, *History of Pittsburgh and Environs: From Prehistoric Days to the Beginning of the American Revolution,* 2 vols. (New York: American Historical Society, 1922). An interesting cultural history of frontier life in this area is J. E. Wright and Doris S. Corbett, *Pioneer Life in Western Pennsylvania* (Pittsburgh: University of Pittsburgh Press, 1940).

13. A series of biographies of the men who served at the fortress from the time of its construction to the revolutionary era was written as a joint effort by the Daughters of the American Revolution, Bicentennial Committee, Pittsburgh Chapter: *Pittsburgh Patriots* (Pittsburgh: The Chapter, 1974).

14. The details of the description of Fort Pitt are the result of a meticulous study by Charles Stotz, "The Fort Pitt Museum," *Western Pennsylvania Historical Magazine* 52 (October 1969):30–35 and 53 (January 1970):36–39. The text was later rearranged and numerous illustrations were added for a special booklet: *Point of Empire: Conflict at the Forks of the Ohio* (Pittsburgh: Historical Society of Western Pennsylvania, 1970). The old blockhouse is still standing, and there is a diorama of the former appearance of the area on display in the Fort Pitt Museum. Life-sized reconstructions of some of the rooms, complete with wax figurines and tape-recorded voices, help to give the visitor a vision of the old frontier fortress.

15. A biographical sketch of John Neville is offered by Elizabeth Curll Kahl et al., *Pittsburgh Patriots,* pp. 54–55.

16. Stotz, "The Fort Pitt Museum," 53:36–39.

17. For a biographical sketch of Richard Butler, see Helen Hultz et al., *Pittsburgh Patriots,* pp. 12–14.

18. Richard Butler to James Wilson, Fort Pitt, April 8, 1776, Papers of the Continental Congress, National Archives M247, r69, i56, p. 217.

19. Ibid.

20. Ibid.

21. Ibid., 218.

22. Richard Butler to Kiosola (Guyashusta), Fort Pitt, April 1776, Papers of the Continental Congress, National Archives M247, r91, i78, v. 2, p. 41.

23. Butler to Wilson, Fort Pitt, April 8, 1776, Papers of the Continental Congress, National Archives M247, r69, i56, p. 218.

24. Ibid.

25. Butler to Kiosola (Guyashusta), Fort Pitt, April 1776, Papers of the Continental Congress, National Archives M247, r91, i78, v. 2, p. 41.

26. Ibid., 42.

27. Butler to Wilson, Fort Pitt, April 8, 1776, Papers of the Continental Congress, National Archives M247, r69, i56, p. 219.

28. Butler to Wilson, Fort Pitt, April 8–9, 1776, Papers of the Continental Congress, National Archives M247, r91, i78, v. 2, p. 21.

29. Ibid., 22.

30. For a map of the island, see Baldwin, *Pittsburgh*, p. 345.

31. For a map entitled "Proclamation Line of 1763, Indian Cessions and the Land Companies," see Jacobs, *Dispossessing the American Indian*, pp. 98–99.

32. Butler to Wilson, Fort Pitt, April 8–9, 1776, Papers of the Continental Congress, National Archives M247, r91, i78, v. 2, p. 22.

33. Ibid., 26.

34. Ibid.

35. Ibid.

36. For a biographical sketch of the well-known Indian trader William Wilson, see Thwaites and Kellogg, eds., *Revolution on the Upper Ohio*, p. 202, n. 41.

37. Hard Man to the Shawnee Council, Waketameki, Ohio, 1773, recorded by the Reverend David Zeisberger in Edmund De Schweinitz, *Life and Times of David Zeisberger: The Western Pioneer and Apostle of the Indians* (Philadelphia: J. B. Lippincott, 1870; reprint, New York: Arno Press and the New York Times, 1971), p. 393. De Schweinitz translated many of Zeisberger's German diaries preserved in the Moravian Church Archives, Bethlehem, Pennsylvania. Perhaps no other weapon has dealt a more devastating blow to the lives and well-being of native peoples than alcohol. Since the age of first contact with Europeans to the present day, alcohol has been used and abused, weakening the power of the people and the coherency of their traditional social structures. For recent statistics and medical information, refer to the *American Indian Policy Review Commission, Final Report*, 1:373–74.

38. One statement that illustrates the impact of alcohol was made by a critic of King Sassoonan, a Delaware man who in 1732 "drank the land away." See Governor Patrick Gordon, Sassoonan, Elalapis, Ohopamen, Pesqueetamen, Mayemoe, Partridge and Tepakoasset, "Conference Transcripts," June 1732, *Pennsylvania Archives*, ser. 1, 1:344–46, quoted in Sipe, *Indian Wars of Pennsylvania*, pp. 95–97. Sipe's study highlights colonial Indian affairs from 1755 to 1795. Although sometimes outdated in his interpretations, Sipe offers a formidable analysis of hundreds of original documents published in the *Pennsylvania Archives*.

39. Hard Man to the Shawnee Council, in De Schweinitz, *Life and Times of*

David Zeisberger, pp. 391-92.

40. Ibid.

41. Hard Man and the Shawnee Council to the Continental Congress, Lower Shawnee Town, April 24, 1776, narrated by William Wilson and recorded in Morgan's Journal, p. 10.

42. Ibid.

43. A summary of Shawnee history and an interesting map tracing their movements since the 1690s were prepared by Charles Callender, "Shawnee," *Handbook of North American Indians: Northeast,* pp. 622–35.

44. For original documents and biographical sketches of many of the Indian leaders during this period, refer to Thwaites and Kellogg, eds., *Documentary History of Dunmore's War, 1774;* and Chester Sipe, *The Indian Chiefs of Pennsylvania* (Butler, PA: Ziegler Printing Co., 1927).

45. Many of the original documents related to Daniel Boone were compiled by Reuben Gold Thwaites in *Daniel Boone* (New York: D. Appleton and Co., 1902).

46. Henry Bouquet to John Penn, Forks of the Muskingum, November 15, 1764, *Minutes of the Provincial Council of Pennsylvania,* 8:207. For two secondary accounts, compare Weslager, *Delaware Indians,* p. 249 and Sipe, *Indian Wars of Pennsylvania,* pp. 475–85. In regard to native systems of justice, Shawnee society was governed by twelve sacred laws that formed a covenant among all living things. For further information see Charles Ovegelin, John F. Yegerlehner, and Florence M. Robinett, "Shawnee Laws: Perceptual Statements for the Language in and for the Content," *Language in Culture,* ed. Harry Joijer (Chicago: University of Chicago Press, 1954), pp. 32–46.

47. Hard Man and the Shawnee Council to the Continental Congress, Lower Shawnee Town, April 24, 1776, narrated by William Wilson and recorded in Morgan's Journal, p. 10.

48. Ibid.

49. *Secret Journals of the Acts and Proceedings of Congress,* 4 vols. (Boston: Thomas B. Wait, 1820–21), 1:43. The secretary recorded on April 29, 1776: "Resolved, That the committee appointed to consider the state of Indian affairs, in the the middle department, be instructed to prepare a plan of an expedition against Fort Detroit, and an estimate of the expense."

50. The first British agent employed to carry out this plan was Dr. John Connolly, who was captured and jailed in Philadelphia in the early spring of 1776; he later escaped. See Samuel Hazard, ed., "Intelligence Received by Congress," Philadelphia, April 2, 1775, *Pennsylvania Archives,* ser. 1, 4:728–29.

51. A unique book on the history of Indian runners has been written by Peter

Nabokov, *Indian Running* (Santa Barbara: Capra Press, 1981).

52. Hard Man and the Shawnee Council to the Continental Congress, Lower Shawnee Town, April 26, 1776, narrated by William Wilson and recorded in Morgan's Journal, p. 10.

53. The relationship between the Lenape and the Shawnee with their "Uncles," the Wyandot, Huron, or Talamatan, began long before the coming of Europeans, according to ancient legends. One account was recorded by Heckewelder, *History, Manners and Customs of the Indian Nations*, pp. 48–49. For a summary of Wyandot ethnohistory, see Elisabeth Tooker, "Wyandot," *Handbook of North American Indians: Northeast*, pp. 398–406.

54. Unsigned letter, "Information regarding Detroit," Detroit, April 2, 1776, doc. 3U580, Thwaites and Kellogg, eds., *Revolution on the Upper Ohio*, pp. 147–51.

55. Hard Man and the Shawnee Council to the Continental Congress, Lower Shawnee Town, April 26, 1776, narrated by William Wilson and recorded in Morgan's Journal, p. 10.

56. For two secondary accounts of the Canadian campaign, see Francis F. Bierne, "Mission to Canada, 1776," *Maryland Historical Magazine* 60 (1965):404–20; and John F. Roche, "Quebec Under Siege, 1775–1776: The 'Memorandums' of Jacob Danford," *Canadian Historical Review* 50 (March 1969):68–85.

57. Hard Man and the Shawnee Council to the Continental Congress, Lower Shawnee Town, April 26, 1776, narrated by William Wilson and recorded in Morgan's Journal, p. 11. The Wabache or Wabash refers to the Oubache confederacy of Indian nations in present-day Indiana and Illinois.

58. The early history of the Lenni Lenape is the subject of a study in process by the author, entitled "The Grandfathers." The mention of ancient records refers to the *Wallam Olum*, considered the tablets of their history by traditional Lenape people. As the late Lenape elder Winnie Poolaw once said to the author, "The *Wallam Olum* is like our Bible."

59. The extent of Indian trade routes throughout the North American continent was one of the subjects discussed by traditional elders at "The Symposium in Honor of the Ancestors," Hotevilla, Arizona, September 1981. Several elders recounted traditions of international Indian trade which began long before the coming of Europeans. There are many good books on Indian trails for almost every state in the country.

60. Three of Morgan's assistants defected to the British during the autumn of 1778. These men previously had been on British as well as American payrolls. Their identities will be revealed in a later chapter.

61. Simon Girty was a complex personality in frontier history, and more

scholarship and even psychoanalysis would be necessary to unravel his many-sided character. Two early sketches were attempted by John MacLeod, "A Sketch of the Life of Simon Girty," *Amherstburg Echo,* Amherstburg, Ontario, November 21, 1884, later reprinted in *Michigan Pioneer Collections,* 7:123–29; and T. L. Rogers, "Simon Girty and Some of His Contemporaries," *Western Pennsylvania Historical Magazine* 8 (July 1925):148–58.

62. Rogers, "Simon Girty and Some of His Contemporaries," p. 149.

63. George Morgan to Simon Girty, Pittsburgh, May 1, 1776, Morgan's Journal, p. 11.

64. Ibid., 11–12.

65. Ibid., 12.

66. Ibid.

67. Simon Girty, "Enlistment Paper," Pittsburgh, May 1, 1776, Morgan's Journal, p. 12.

68. George Morgan, "Memorandums," Ohio River, May 9, 1770, in *Baynton, Wharton and Morgan Papers,* microfilm roll 1, frames 497–524. For an excellent analysis, see Robert F. Oaks, ed., "George Morgan's 'Memorandums': A Journey to the Illinois Country, 1770," *Journal of the Illinois State Historical Society* 69 (August 1976):185–200.

69. Morgan, "Memorandums," frame 512.

70. Ibid.

Chapter Three

1. John Anderson, "Extent of a Letter," Walehachehucppache, April 23, 1776, Morgan's Journal, p. 1.

2. George Morgan to David Zeisberger, Pittsburgh, May 3, 1776, Morgan's Journal, pp. 6–7.

3. Ibid., 7.

4. Ibid.

5. The author's understanding of British–Indian affairs has been enhanced by the perceptive research of Dr. Paul L. Stevens, who graciously shared his knowledge during many months of personal correspondence.

6. Fort Niagara has been preserved at its original location near Niagara Falls. The work of many dedicated professionals and volunteers to restore historic structures has helped to preserve our heritage.

7. George Washington to the President of Congress, New York, April 19, 1776, Papers of the Continental Congress, National Archives M247, r186, i169, v. 1, pp. 291–96.

8. Charles Lee to John Hancock, Williamsburg, Virginia, May 10, 1776, Papers of the Continental Congress, National Archives M247, r177, i158, pp. 59–61; see also *American Archives*, ser. 4, 6:403.

9. Paul Long, Oath of Allegiance, Fort Pitt, May 3, 1776, Morgan's Journal, pp. 12–13.

10. For a report on British–Indian affairs during the spring of 1776, see *American Archives*, ser. 5, 1:867–68.

11. Howard Swiggett, *War Out of Niagara: Walter Butler and the Tory Rangers* (New York: Columbia University Press, 1933), pp. 12–13, 27, 35, 65.

12. Ibid., 65ff.

13. I wish to thank Iroquois chiefs Leon Shenandoah, Oren Lyons, and Jake Swamp for introducing me to the political structure of the Six Nations Confederacy. Speaking before their Grand Council in the spring of 1983 was a memorable experience.

14. My knowledge of the traditions of the Iroquois Peacemaker also has been based upon the teachings of the Iroquois elders.

15. For early biographical information on Guyashusta, see Frederick Webb Hodge, ed., *Handbook of American Indians North of Mexico*, 2 vols. (Washington, DC: Government Printing Office, 1907–10), 1:682.

16. For an excellent analysis of Guyashusta's role in Pontiac's War, see Jacobs, *Dispossessing the American Indian*, pp. 86–87. For further information, compare the following accounts: Parkman, *History of the Conspiracy of Pontiac* and Howard Peckham, *Pontiac and the Indian Uprising* (Princeton: Princeton University Press, 1947).

17. Charles Dumas to John Hancock, Utrecht, April 30–May 9, 1776, Papers of the Continental Congress, National Archives M247, r121, i93, v. 1, pp. 18–29.

18. The location of the "Great Wampum Belt with 13 diamonds and 2,500 wampum beads" remained a mystery for almost two hundred years. I once received a call from an Indian woman who recalled her grandmother's story of such a belt being shown to her. Then in December 1987 I traveled to the Tonawanda Seneca Nation with Onondaga Clan Mother Alice Papineau. She introduced me to Seneca Chief Corbett Sundown. While reading sections of Morgan's Journal to the elder chief, I asked him if he had ever heard of the Thirteen Diamond Wampum Belt. Surprised, the chief revealed that his people had it, and that it was over six feet long. When asked how the Seneca nation came to preserve the belt, the chief revealed that it had been kept for many years in a safety deposit box along with some old treaty papers.

19. Henry F. Dobyns, *Their Number Become Thinned: Native American Population*

Dynamics in Eastern North America (Knoxville: Published by the University of Tennessee Press in cooperation with the Newberry Library Center for the History of the American Indian, 1983).

20. George Morgan to Lewis Morris, Pittsburgh, May 16, 1776, Morgan's Journal, pp. 4–5.

21. John Anderson, Delaware Towns, May 10, 1776, ibid., 1.

22. For further information on the Oubache, see Alexander McKee, Journal, Plains of Scioto, April 8, 1773, Papers of the Continental Congress, National Archives M247, r52, i41, v. 10, pp. 508–11.

23. Oubache ambassadors to Lenape Council, reported by John Anderson, Delaware Towns, May 10, 1776, Morgan's Journal, p. 1.

24. Ibid.

25. John H. Carter, "Alexander McKee, Our Most Noted Tory," *Northumberland County Historical Society Proceedings* 22 (1958):60–75; Walter R. Hoberg, "Early History of Colonel Alexander McKee," *Pennsylvania Magazine of History and Biography* 58, No. 1 (1934):26–36; Hoberg, "A Tory in the Northwest," *Pennsylvania Magazine of History and Biography* 59 (January 1935):32–41.

26. George Morgan to Lewis Morris, Pittsburgh, May 16, 1776, Morgan's Journal, p. 6.

27. John Connolly to Alexander McKee, Fredericktown, Maryland, December 16, 1775, *American Archives*, ser. 4, 4:617.

28. In Committee of Safety, April 2, 1776, *American Archives*, ser 4, 5:734.

29. John Butler to Alexander McKee, Niagara, February 29, 1776, Papers of the Continental Congress, National Archives M247, r83, i69, v. 1, pp. 121–31. For further information on the disposition of Indian lands, compare Abernethy, *Western Lands and the American Revolution* and George E. Lewis, *The Indiana Company, 1763–1798: A Study in Eighteenth Century Frontier Land Speculation and Business Venture* (Glendale: Arthur H. Clark Co., 1941).

30. Savelle, *George Morgan*, p. 84.

31. West Augusta District (Virginia) Committee, Resolve re Alexander McKee, April 9, 1776, copy by Thomas Smallman, Papers of the Continental Congress, National Archives M247, r83, i69, v. 1, p. 119.

32. Ibid.

33. Alexander McKee, Parole, April 9, 1776, Papers of the Continental Congress, National Archives M247, r83, i69, v. 1, p. 123.

34. Continental Congress, Resolution Regarding Alexander McKee, *American Archives*, ser. 4, 5:1692, cited in Hoberg, "Early History of Colonel Alexander McKee," p. 33.

35. George Morgan to Congress, Fort Pitt, May 1776, Morgan's Journal, p. 1.

36. Ibid.

37. Thomas Gage to John Stuart, September 12, 1775, *The Correspondence of General Thomas Gage*, ed. Clarence Carter, 2 vols. (New Haven: Yale University Press, 1931–33), 1:246; Stuart to David Taitt, December 15, 1775, British Public Record Office, London, Colonial Office, ser. 5, 77:30, hereafter cited as CO. For an excellent account of this area, see James H. O'Donnell III, *Southern Indians in the American Revolution* (Knoxville: University of Tennessee Press, 1973), pp. 30–53. O'Donnell's study provides perceptive analysis of obscure original sources.

38. Alexander Cameron to John Stuart, June 3, 1776, CO, ser. 5, 77:175 cited in O'Donnell, *Southern Indians*, p. 37.

39. Henry Stuart, Report, August 20, 1776, CO, ser. 5, 77:126–29. For a critical analysis of drafting Indians into war, see Jack M. Sosin, "The Use of Indians in the War of the American Revolution: A Re-Assessment of Responsibility," *Canadian Historical Review* 46 (June 1965):115–16.

40. Congress, Report of Committee re Indians in Canada, Philadelphia, May 25, 1776, Papers of the Continental Congress, National Archives M247, r27, i19, v.4, p. 77; printed in *Journals of the Continental Congress*, 4:394.

41. *Journals of the Continental Congress*, 4:394–95.

42. Ibid., 395.

43. Ibid.

44. For a documentary study of eyewitness accounts of the American Revolution, especially during the tenure of American troops in New York, consult George Scheer and Hugh Rankin, *Rebels and Redcoats* (Cleveland and New York: World Publishing Co., 1957), pp. 159–81.

45. General Order issued by Nathanael Green, quoted in ibid., 147.

46. Loammi Baldwin to his wife, June 17, 1776, Baldwin Papers, Harvard College Library, quoted in ibid., 146.

47. *Journals of the Continental Congress*, June 17, 1776, 5:452.

48. United Colonies to the Six Nations, Pittsburgh, May 19, 1776, Morgan's Journal, p. 13.

49. The meaning of the Covenant Chain of Friendship was explained to the author by Leon Shenandoah and Oren Lyons, chiefs of the Onondaga nation.

50. United Colonies to the Six Nations, Pittsburgh, May 19, 1776, Morgan's Journal, p. 13.

51. Ibid.

52. Ibid.

53. Ibid.

54. Ibid., 13–14.

55. Ibid., 14.

56. The role of the chieftaincy in Iroquois society was explained to the author by Leon Shenandoah and Oren Lyons from the Onondaga and Chief Jake Swamp from the Mohawk nations. Chief Swamp presently is an organizer of the Akwesasne Freedom School, where Mohawk children learn their history, culture, and other subjects taught in the Mohawk language.

57. United Colonies to the Six Nations, Pittsburgh, May 19, 1776, Morgan's Journal, p. 14.

58. Ibid.

59. Ibid.

60. George Morgan to the Commissioners for Indian Affairs, Pittsburgh, May 16, 1776, Morgan's Journal, p. 2.

61 Ibid.

62. Ibid.

63. Ibid.

64. Ibid.

65. George Morgan to Lewis Morris, Pittsburgh, May 16, 1776, Morgan's Journal, p. 5. For further information see Thwaites and Kellogg, eds., *Revolution on the Upper Ohio*, pp. 158–59.

66. Morgan to Morris, Pittsburgh, May 16, 1776, Morgan's Journal, pp. 5–6.

67. Ibid., 6.

68. Ibid.

69. Ibid., 4, 6.

70. Ibid., 6.

71. John Neville and George Morgan to the chiefs of the Shawnee, Pittsburgh, May 31, 1776, Morgan's Journal, p. 14.

72. Ibid.

73. Ibid., 14–15.

Chapter Four

1. A daily chronicle of events on the Ohio frontier was preserved in the diaries of German Protestant Moravian missionaries to the Indians; see Fliegel, comp., *Index to the Records of the Moravian Mission*. Part of the manuscripts were translated and analyzed by De Schweinitz, *Life and Times of David Zeisberger*. Zeisberger and his assistant, John Heckewelder, were the principal Moravian missionaries during the

late eighteenth century in Ohio. The papers of the younger missionary were edited by Wallace, *Thirty Thousand Miles with John Heckewelder.* Heckewelder also wrote an account of this period of history, *Narrative of the Mission of the United Brethren.* Although the Moravians recorded the most exhaustive body of eyewitness accounts among the Indians, scholars interpreting this material must consider their cultural and religious world view, which influenced their mission to convert the "heathens" to Christianity. The Moravians were devout pacifists who provided a place of refuge for hundreds of dispossessed Indians. Because some key Moravian journals have never been translated or published, I am greatly indebted to Dr. Horst M. Lorscheider from Santa Barbara, California, who graciously translated materials from old German into English. I also wish to thank Dr. Abraham Friesen, Professor of History, University of California in Santa Barbara, who recommended Dr. Lorscheider and agreed to be a member of my doctoral committee. For the reference to Chief White Eyes's arrival in May 1776, see Anonymous, Diary from April to September 1776, in Lichtenau, May 11, 1776, box 141, file 8, item 1, manuscript 3, p. 5, Records of the Moravian Mission, Bethlehem, Pennsylvania, translated by Dr. Lorscheider, hereafter cited as Lichtenau Diary.

2. For an analysis of White Eyes's "Grand Plan" see Sipe, *Indian Chiefs of Pennsylvania,* pp. 415–16.

3. Ibid., 416.

4. De Schweinitz, *Life and Times of David Zeisberger,* p. 438.

5. Lichtenau Diary, May 3, 1776, pp. 3–4.

6. White Eyes, Speech, Philadelphia, March 18, 1776, original in the private collection of Mrs. A. G. Happer of Washington, Pennsylvania, cited in Savelle, *George Morgan,* p. 135, n26. Reference to the receipt of this document by Lenape Sachem Netawatwees and a summary of its contents can be found in Lichtenau Diary, May 3, 1776, p. 3. The author has not examined the original document and therefore did not quote it directly.

7. For a biographical sketch of Gelelemend (1737–1811), see Sipe, *Indian Chiefs of Pennsylvania,* p. 419.

8. Lichtenau Diary, May 8, 1776, p. 5.

9. *David Zeisberger's History of Northern American Indians,* ed. Archer Butler Hulbert and William N. Schwarze (Columbus, OH: Press of F. J. Heer, 1910), p. 121, hereafter cited as *Zeisberger's History.*

10. Ibid., 122.

11. Ibid.

12. De Schweinitz, *Life and Times of David Zeisberger,* pp. 433–34.

13. White Eyes to the Iroquois, Fort Pitt, October 9, 1775, Thwaites and Kellogg, eds., *Revolution on the Upper Ohio*, pp. 86–87; see also Heckewelder, *Narrative of the Mission of the United Brethren*, pp. 140–41.

14. Lichtenau Diary, May 13, 1776, p. 6.

15. Ibid.

16. Lichtenau Diary, May 13, 1776, p. 7. This quote has been edited from third person to first person to preserve continuity.

17. Ibid.

18. Thwaites and Kellogg, eds, *Revolution on the Upper Ohio*, p. 46, n72.

19. Lichtenau Diary, May 16, 1776, p. 8.

20. Ibid.

21. Speech to Captain White Eyes, Philadelphia, April 10, 1776, *Journals of the Continental Congress*, 4:269.

22. Ibid.

23. Ibid.

24. Ibid.

25. Ibid., 269–70.

26. Ibid., 270.

27. Ibid.

28. Ibid.

29. Ibid.

30. David Zeisberger, quoted in De Schweinitz, *Life and Times of David Zeisberger,* p. 438.

31. Lichtenau Diary, May 17, 1776, p. 7.

32. Ibid., May 19, 1776, p. 12.

33. For a biographical sketch of Glickhikan, see Wallace, *Indians in Pennsylvania,* p. 173.

34. Glickhikan to White Eyes, 1773, quoted in De Schweinitz, *Life and Times of David Zeisberger,* p. 404.

35. Sipe, *Indian Wars of Pennsylvania,* p. 548. For further information see De Schweinitz, *Life and Times of David Zeisberger,* pp. 289, 389, 518, 560, 629.

36. See Thomas Killbuck and Old Justina entries in Fliegel, comp., *Index to the Records of the Moravian Mission.*

37. Lichtenau Diary, May 19, 1776, pp. 11–12.

38. Ibid., May 19, 1776, p. 12. Tense has been changed from third person to first person for continuity.

39. Ibid.

40. Gnadenhutten Diary, May 24, 1776, box 144, file 7, p. 18, Records of the

Moravian Mission, translated by Dr. W. N. Schwartz.

41. Ibid., May 26, 1776, p. 18.

42. Lichtenau Diary, May 26, 1776, p. 13.

43. Ibid. Tense has been changed from third person to first person for continuity.

44. Ibid., May 17, 1776, pp. 13–14.

45. Ibid., May 30, 1776, p. 14.

46. Ibid.

47. Ibid., 15.

48. Ibid.

49. Harrington, *Religion and Ceremonies of the Lenape,* p. 53.

50. Lichtenau Diary, June 5, 1776, p. 16.

51. Ibid.

Chapter Five

1. The principal document on American Indian affairs at Fort Pitt during the summer of 1776 is Morgan's Journal. An account was reconstructed by Hildreth, *Pioneer History,* pp. 95–110. For information on interpreter William Wilson, see Morgan's Journal, pp. 9–12, 33, 55, 57; also Thwaites and Kellogg, eds., *Documentary History of Dunmore's War, 1774,* pp. 408, 422; and *Revolution on the Upper Ohio,* pp. 202–203. For information on interpreter Joseph Nicholson, see Morgan's Journal, pp. 33, 56ff; *Documentary History of Dunmore's War, 1774,* pp. 12, 154, 285; *Revolution on the Upper Ohio,* pp. 176, 202; and Wallace, ed., *Thirty Thousand Miles with John Heckewelder,* p. 243.

2. George Morgan and John Neville to Shawnee Chiefs, Pittsburgh, May 31, 1776, Morgan's Journal, p. 14.

3. Ibid.

4. George Morgan to Governor and Commandant at Detroit, Pittsburgh, May 31, 1776, Morgan's Journal, p. 17.

5. Ibid., 18.

6. Ibid.

7. Ibid.

8. Ibid.

9. Ibid.

10. George Morgan to the Commissioners for Indian Affairs, May 31, 1776, Morgan's Journal, p. 15.

11. Morgan's Journal, pp. 16–17. For a scholarly analysis of Indian presents, see Jacobs, *Wilderness Politics and Indian Gifts,* pp. 46–60.

12. "Giveaways" and generous acts of charity have been documented extensively in ethnohistorical literature. For a bibliographic essay on this custom among Eastern Woodland cultures, see Regina Flannery, *An Analysis of Coastal Algonquian Culture* (Washington, DC: Catholic University of America Press, 1939), pp. 143–44.

13. Morgan to the Commissioners for Indian Affairs, May 31, 1776, Morgan's Journal, p. 15.

14. Ibid.

15. Ibid.

16. Ibid., 15–16.

17. Ibid.,16.

18. Ibid.

19. Thwaites and Kellogg, eds., *Documentary History of Dunmore's War, 1774*, pp. 12ff.

20. Morgan to the Commissioners for Indian Affairs, May 31, 1776, Morgan's Journal, p. 16.

21. Ibid.

22. Ibid.

23. Ibid.

24. George Morgan to the Commissioners for Indian Affairs, June 3, 1776, Morgan's Journal, p. 18.

25. Congressional Resolve, May 25, 1776, *Secret Journals of the Acts and Proceedings of Congress*, 1:44.

26. Morgan to the Commissioners for Indian Affairs, June 3, 1776, Morgan's Journal, pp. 18–19.

27. Ibid.

28. Ibid., 19.

29. Paul Long to George Morgan, Pittsburgh, July 23, 1776, Morgan's Journal, p. 41.

30. Ibid.

31. James Heron to George Morgan, Detroit, July 27, 1776, Morgan's Journal, p. 49; for information on Hugh Lord, see Clarence Alvord, ed., *Kaskaskia Records, 1778–1790* (Springfield: The Trustees of the Illinois State Historical Library, 1909), p. 4, n4.

32. For a historical map of the frontier forts around the Great Lakes in the eighteenth century, see James Truslow Adams, *Atlas of American History* (New York: Charles Scribner's Sons, 1943), p. 40.

33. For a photograph of the main building at Fort Niagara, see Graymont,

Iroquois in the American Revolution, p. 202.

34. Long to Morgan, Pittsburgh, July 23, 1776, Morgan's Journal, p. 41. For further information on the activities of John and Walter Butler, compare Ernest Cruikshank, *The Story of Butler's Rangers and the Settlement of Niagara* (Welland, ONT.: Tribune Printing House, 1893) and Swiggett, *War Out of Niagara*.

35. Long to Morgan, Pittsburgh, July 23, 1776, Morgan's Journal, pp. 41–42.

36. Ibid., 42.

37. Ibid.

38. Ibid.

39. Ibid. For a transcript of the 1775 Fort Pitt Treaty, see Thwaites and Kellogg, eds., *Revolution on the Upper Ohio*, pp. 125–26.

40. Long to Morgan, Pittsburgh, July 23, 1776, Morgan's Journal, p. 42.

41. Ibid.

42. These are formalized phrases derived from the Condolence Ceremony and often used in wampum diplomacy, as explained in Wilbur Jacobs, "Wampum, the Protocol of Indian Diplomacy," *William and Mary Quarterly*, ser. 3, 6 (October 1949): 596–604.

43. Colonel John Butler to Western Indian Nations, Fort Niagara, May 30, 1776, recalled by Paul Long and recorded by George Morgan, Pittsburgh, July 21, 1776, Morgan's Journal, pp. 42–43.

44. For an explanation of the significance of the Tree of Peace, see Mohawk Nation, *A Basic Call to Consciousness* (Akwesasne, New York, 1977) and Wallace, *Indians in Pennsylvania*, pp. 90–100.

45. Butler to Western Indian Nations, Fort Niagara, May 30, 1776, Morgan's Journal, p. 43.

46. Guyashusta to Colonel Butler, Fort Niagara, June 2, 1776, Morgan's Journal, p. 43.

47. Ibid.

48. Ibid.

49. Ibid.

50. Ibid., 43–44.

51. Chief Oren Lyons, "Iroquois Principles," Onondaga Nation, 1979, in *Akwesasne Freedom School Newsletter* (Mohawk Nation, 1982), p. 2.

52. Congressional Resolve, Philadelphia, June 3, 1776, *Secret Journals of the Acts and Proceedings of Congress*, 1:45.

53. Mohawk Speaker, Fort Niagara, June 3, 1776, Morgan's Journal, p. 44.

54. Ibid.

55. Commissioner of Canada to John Hancock, Montreal, May 17, 1776, Papers of the Continental Congress, National Archives M247, r183, i166, v. 2, p. 49.

56. Mohawk Speaker, Fort Niagara, June 3, 1776, Morgan's Journal, p. 44.

57. Ibid.

58. John Butler to Western Indian Nations, Fort Niagara, June 4, 1776, Morgan's Journal, p. 44.

59. Ibid.

60. Cumberland County (Pennsylvania) Committee, Shippensburg, Resolve re gunpowder, June 7, 1776, Papers of the Continental Congress, National Archives M247, r83, i69, v. 1, p. 135. For a summary of the Gibson–Linn expedition, see John E. Selby, *A Chronology of Virginia and the War of Independence, 1768–1783* (Charlottesville: Published for the Virginia Independence Bicentennial Commission by the University Press of Virginia, 1973), p. 278.

61. Butler to Western Indian Nations, Fort Niagara, June 4, 1776, Morgan's Journal, pp. 44–45.

62. George Morgan, Travel Record, Shirties Island, June 4, 1776, Morgan's Journal, p. 39.

63. Flying Crow to John Butler, Fort Niagara, June 5, 1776, Morgan's Journal, p. 45.

64. Ibid.

65. Ibid.

66. Ibid.

67. Long to Morgan, Pittsburgh, July 23, 1776, Morgan's Journal, pp. 45–46.

68. Butler to Western Indian Nations, Fort Niagara, June 5, 1776, Morgan's Journal, p. 46.

69. Ibid.

70. Ibid.

71. Long to Morgan, p. 42.

72. Butler to Western Indian Nations, p. 46.

73. Long to Morgan, p. 42.

Chapter Six

1. George Morgan kept a daily log of his Journey through Indian Country, June 4–July 19, 1776, Morgan's Journal, pp. 39–40. The mileage traveled and the locations visited were recorded meticulously. The entire tour encompassed 468 miles. Although Morgan did not note expressly that he was accompanied by Alexander McKee, that fact was recorded by Moravian journalists, Gnadenhutten Diary, June 10, 1776. For a biographical sketch of Alexander McKee (1735–

1799), see Carter, "Alexander McKee, Our Most Noted Tory," pp. 60–75.

2. A historical description of the "Great Trail" was composed by Frank Wilcox, *Ohio Indian Trails: A Pictorial Survey of the Indian Trails of Ohio*, ed. William A. McGill (1933; reprint, Kent, OH: Kent State University Press, 1970), pp. 43–47. Further information on Logstown can be found in Thwaites and Kellogg, eds., *Revolution on the Upper Ohio*, pp. 26–27, n52.

3. Patrick Lockhart to the Chairman of the Botetourt Committee, Williamsburg, Virginia, May 14, 1776, Thwaites and Kellogg, eds., *Revolution on the Upper Ohio*, p. 155. For biographical information on John Gibson (1740–1822), see Wallace, ed., *Thirty Thousand Miles with John Heckewelder*, p. 410.

4. Journey through Indian Country, Morgan's Journal, p. 39.

5. Richard Henry Lee, Resolution on Independence, Philadelphia, June 7, 1776, *Journals of the Continental Congress*, 5:425.

6. Journey through Indian Country, Morgan's Journal, p. 39.

7. De Schweinitz, *Life and Times of David Zeisberger*, pp. 375–76. Soon after white settlement encroached upon these lands, the "Beautiful Spring" dried up and the lake was reduced to a marsh choked with water lilies.

8. Ibid., 380, n1.

9. Ibid., 423–24.

10. Ibid., 424.

11. John Heckewelder, *Report of the Indian Mission to the Society for Propagating the Gospel*, quoted in De Schweinitz, *Life and Times of David Zeisberger*, p. 425, n1. See also Gnadenhutten Diary, June 10, 1776, pp. 19–20.

12. Considerable confusion over Lenape political and social organization has complicated the historiography. The initial misconception was recorded by Heckewelder, *History, Manners and Customs of the Indian Nations*, p. 250. This Moravian missionary erroneously equated the Turtle, Turkey, and Wolf socio-political divisions with the early geo-political divisions Unami, Unalachtigo, and Munsee. This mistake was repeated by later writers such as De Schweinitz, *Life and Times of David Zeisberger*, pp. 35, 348–49. Frank Speck subsequently recognized that the latter terms represented territorial divisions; see *A Study of the Delaware Indian Big House Ceremony* (Harrisburg, PA: Pennsylvania Historical Commission, 1931), pp. 75–76. I would like to thank the Lenape elder and herbalist Nora Thompson "Touching Leaves" Dean from Oklahoma for explaining the structure of their society.

13. The dimensions of the Big House were estimated by the Baptist Minister David Jones, *A Journal of Two Visits Made to Some Nations of Indians on the West Side of the River Ohio, in the Years 1772 and 1773* (Burlington: Printed and sold by I. Collins, 1774), p. 104.

14.   Perhaps the earliest description of the Lenape Big House was preserved by Peter Lindestrom, *Geographia America, with an Account of the Delaware Indians, Based on Surveys and Notes Made in 1654–1656,* trans. and ed. Amandus Johnson (Philadelphia: The Swedish Colonial Society, 1925), p. 211. Later accounts were recorded by William Penn to Free Society of Traders, Shackamaxon, August 16, 1683, *Narratives of Early Pennsylvania, West New Jersey, and Delaware, 1630–1707,* ed. Albert Cook Meyers (New York: Charles Scribner's Sons, 1912), pp. 230-33; Charles Beatty, *The Journal of a Two Months Tour, with a View of Promoting Religion among the Frontier Inhabitants of Pennsylvania and of Introducing Christianity among the Indians to the Westward of the Alegh-geny Mountains* (London: Printed for W. Davenhill, 1768), p. 72; David McClure, *Diary of David McClure, Doctor of Divinity, 1748–1820,* with notes by Franklin B. Dexter (New York: Knickerbocker Press, 1899), p. 61; Harrington, *Religion and Ceremonies of the Lenape,* pp. 828–83, 119, 148–50, plate vi, drawing by Ernest Spybuck, December 23, 1912. For analysis of the Big House symbolism see Speck, *Study of the Delaware Indian Big House Ceremony,* pp. 22–23, 85–87; Jay Miller and Nora Thompson Dean, "A Personal Account of the Unami Delaware Big House Rite," *Pennsylvania Archaeologist* (1977):39–43; Herbert Kraft, "Model of the Big House by Ruben Wilson," *Bulletin of the Archaeological Society of New Jersey* (1978):40.

15.   An extensive historiography exists for the Ga'muing or Big House Ceremony of Thanksgiving. Most of the early sources were analyzed by Speck, *Study of the Delaware Indian Big House Ceremony.* The last time the ceremony was known to have been performed was during World War II, to pray for the Lenape soldiers. All reportedly returned safely. A brief account subsequently was composed by H. L. McCracken, "The Delaware Big House," *Chronicles of Oklahoma* 34 (Summer 1956): 183–92. The best recent oral history account was narrated by Dean to Miller, "A Personal Account of the Unami Delaware Big House Rite," pp. 39–43.

16.   Netawatwees to George Morgan, Cooshocking, June 11, 1776, Morgan's Journal, p. 20. This speech was edited from Morgan's recitation of the opening greeting.

17.   George Morgan to Lenape Council, Cooshocking, June 11, 1776, Morgan's Journal, p. 20.

18.   Ibid.

19.   Ibid.

20.   Ibid., 20–21.

21.   Ibid., 21.

22.   Ibid.

23.   Ibid.

24.   Ibid.

25. Ibid.

26. John Hancock to Iroquois Ambassadors, Philadelphia, June 11, 1776, Papers of the Continental Congress, National Archives M247, r37, i30, p. 350; also printed in the *Journals of the Continental Congress*, 5:430.

27. Ibid.

28. Ibid.

29. Ibid.

30. White Eyes to George Morgan, Cooshocking, June 12, 1776, Morgan's Journal, pp. 21–22.

31. The Wyandot to Lenape Nation, narrated by White Eyes, Cooshocking, June 12, 1776, Morgan's Journal, p. 22.

32. Ibid.

33. For further information see Tooker, "Wyandot," *Handbook of North American Indians: Northeast*, pp. 398–406.

34. The Wyandot to Lenape Nation, Cooshocking, June 12, 1776, Morgan's Journal, p. 22.

35. Conneodico to Lenape Nation, narrated by White Eyes, Cooshocking, June 12, 1776, Morgan's Journal, p. 22.

36. White Eyes to George Morgan, Cooshocking, June 12, 1776, Morgan's Journal, p. 22.

37. Ibid., 23.

38. Ibid.

39. George Morgan, Summary of Response to Lenape Nation, Cooshocking, June 12, 1776, Morgan's Journal, p. 23.

40. Ibid.

41. Ibid.

42. Ibid.

43. Ibid., 24.

44. Heckewelder, *Narrative of the Mission of the United Brethren*, pp. 156–57.

45. Documentary evidence of the first two Tamanends was recorded by the Lenape recordkeeper, Olumapi, in the legendary wooden tablets called the *Wallam Olum* or "Radiant Record." The controversy surrounding the Lenape saga has been analyzed in the most recent translation by David McCutchen, "The Radiant Record of the Original People: The Wallam Olum of the Lenni Lenape, Indians of the Delaware," unpublished manuscript (Santa Barbara, 1980). The history of the third Tamanend was debated in Penn et al., "Presentation to the Historical Society of Pennsylvania of the Belt of Wampum," 6:205–82.

46. Heckewelder, *History, Manners and Customs of the Indian Nations*, p. 300.

47. Ibid., 301.

Chapter Seven

1.   The primary source of information for George Morgan's mission to the Shawnee and Mingo is Morgan's Journal, pp. 20–40. A brief secondary account was written by Edgar Hassler, *Old Westmoreland: A History of Western Pennsylvania during the Revolution* (Cleveland: Arthur H. Clark Co., 1900), pp. 20–23. Hassler's account was based principally on the report of William Wilson published in *American Archives*, ser. 5, 2:514–18. The Moravian missionaries also reported Morgan's visit through their towns: see Lichtenau Diary, June 1776. Another brief secondary account was recorded by Savelle, *George Morgan*, pp. 136–39. Savelle based his version on brief references in the Records of the Moravian Mission. No detailed accounts of Morgan's mission were possible until the eyewitness version became available in Morgan's Journal.

2.   The geographic description of Lichtenau was composed by De Schweinitz, *Life and Times of David Zeisberger*, p. 433.

3.   Lichtenau Diary, p.17.

4.   Ibid., 17–18.

5.   Ibid., 18.

6.   Ibid.

7.   Morgan's Journal, p. 40. For a brief sketch of Waketameki, see Wallace, ed., *Thirty Thousand Miles with John Heckewelder*, p. 443.

8.   Heckewelder, *History, Manners and Customs of the Indian Nations*, p. 285.

9.   For scholarly summaries of the archaeological studies of ancient Northeast Indian sites, see Elisabeth Tooker, "History of Research"; James E. Fitting, "Prehistory: Introduction"; Robert E. Funk, "Post–Pleistocene Adaptations"; James A. Tuck, "Regional Cultural Development, 3000 to 300 B.C."; and James E. Fitting, "Regional Cultural Development, 300 B.C. to A.D. 1000," *Handbook of North American Indians:Northeast*, pp. 4–57.

10.   Olaf Prufer and Raymond Baby, *Paleo-Indians of Ohio* (Columbus: Ohio Historical Society, 1963); James Adovasio et al., "Excavations at Meadowcroft Rockshelter, 1973–1974: A Progress Report," *Pennsylvania Archaeologist* 45 (1975): 1–30.

11.   Ephraim Squier and Edwin H. Davis, "Ancient Monuments of the Mississippi Valley, Comprising the Results of Extensive Original Surveys and Explorations," *Smithsonian Contributions to Knowledge*, no. 1 (1848). For an excellent, well-illustrated popular account, see James Maxwell, ed., *America's Fascinating Indian Heritage* (New York: Reader's Digest, 1978), pp. 34–41.

12.   Wilcox, *Ohio Indian Trails*, p. 91, n3.

13. Morgan's Journal, p. 39.

14. Wilcox, *Ohio Indian Trails*, pp. 93–94; Morgan's Journal, p. 39.

15. For biographical information on Welapachtschiechen, see De Schweinitz, *Life and Times of David Zeisberger*, p. 436, n2, 543; Wallace, ed., *Thirty Thousand Miles with John Heckewelder*, p. 416.

16. De Schweinitz, *Life and Times of David Zeisberger*, p. 436, n2.

17. For a historical overview and map of Shawnee migration, see Charles Callender, "Shawnee," *Handbook of North American Indians: Northeast*, pp. 622–35.

18. Ibid., 625.

19. Ibid., 626; Vernon Kinietz and Erminie W. Voegelin, *Shawnee Traditions: C. C. Trowbridge's Account*, Occasional Contributions from the Museum of Anthropology of the University of Michigan, no. 9 (Ann Arbor: University of Michigan Press, 1939), pp. 16–17; Charles Voegelin, "The Shawnee Female Diety," *Yale University Publications in Anthropology* 10 (1936): 3–15.

20. William Galloway, *Old Chillicothe: Shawnee and Pioneer History: Conflicts and Romance in the Northwest Territory* (Xenia, OH: Buckeye Press, 1934), p. 73.

21. Nimwha to Morgan, Kiskapoo, June 17, 1776, Morgan's Journal, p. 24.

22. Ibid.

23. George Morgan to Shawnee Nation, Kiskapoo, June 17, 1776, Morgan's Journal, p. 24.

24. Ibid., 24–25.

25. *Journals of the Continental Congress*, Philadelphia, June 17, 1776, 5:452.

26. Ibid.

27. George Morgan to Shawnee Nation, Kiskapoo, June 19, 1776, Morgan's Journal, p. 25.

28. Ibid.

29. Ibid.

30. Ibid., 25–26.

31. For the historical causes of the breakdown in relations with the Shawnee, see Charles Thomson, *An Enquiry into the Causes of the Alienation of the Delaware and Shawanese Indians from the British Interest and into the Measures taken for Recovering their Friendship* (London: Printed for J. Wilkie, 1759).

32. Morgan to Shawnee Nation, Kiskapoo, June 19, 1776, Morgan's Journal, p. 26.

33. *Journals of the Continental Congress*, June 17, 1776, 5:455–56.

34. Ibid., 458.

35. Morgan to Shawnee Nation, Kiskapoo, June 19, 1776, Morgan's Journal, p. 26.

36. Congress to Kishanatathe, Philadelphia, no date, narrated by George Morgan, Kiskapoo, June 19, 1776, Morgan's Journal, p. 26.

37. Ibid.

38. For a summary of seventeenth- and eighteenth-century Shawnee history, see Sipe, *Indian Wars of Pennsylvania*, pp. 45–50.

39. Congress to Kishanatathe, Philadelphia, no date, Morgan's Journal, pp. 26–27.

40. Ibid., 27.

41. Ibid.

42. Morgan to Shawnee Nation, Kiskapoo, June 19, 1776, Morgan's Journal, p. 27.

43. Ibid., 27–28.

44. Ibid.

45. Ibid.

46. Ibid.

47. United Colonies to Western Indian Nations, June 1776, Morgan's Journal, p. 28.

48. Ibid., 28–29.

49. Ibid., 29.

Chapter Eight

1. The main documentation of George Morgan's meeting with the Mingo was preserved in Morgan's Journal, pp. 29–40. A second eyewitness account was reported by interpreter William Wilson to American Indian Commissioners, September 20, 1776, Morgan's Journal II, pp. 48–57, Andrew Carnegie Library, Pittsburgh. Brief secondary references to Morgan's mission to the Mingo were mentioned by Hassler, *Old Westmoreland*, pp. 20–23; Savelle, *George Morgan*, pp. 136–39; and Downes, *Council Fires on the Upper Ohio*, pp. 189–90. These accounts are based primarily on Morgan's summary report, which was reinterpreted in Indian Commissioners to Congressional Committee on Indian Affairs, July 30, August 2, 1776, Morgan's Journal II, pp. 1–4. The present chapter represents a unique contribution by analyzing the original speeches of the Indian leaders transcribed in Morgan's Journal.

2. Population estimates for the Mingo were compiled by Erminie Wheeler-Voegelin, *An Ethnohistorical Report on the Indian Use and Occupancy of Royce Area II, Ohio and Indiana,* in *Indians of Ohio and Indians Prior to 1795,* 2 vols. (New York: Garland, 1974), 1:129–463 and 2: 9–468.

3. Ibid., 2:167, 413–21.

4. For an excellent ethnohistorical summary of the Mingo, see William C. Sturtevant, "Oklahoma Seneca–Cayuga," *Handbook of North American Indians: Northeast*, pp. 537–43. Information on the "Three Sisters" was given to the author by Chief Jake Swamp, Mohawk nation, Akwesasne Freedom School (1984).

5. Sturtevant, "Oklahoma Seneca-Cayuga," pp. 539–42.

6. George Morgan to the Mingo, Kiskapoo, June 20, 1776, Morgan's Journal, p. 29. For information on the peace pipe see Hodge, ed., *Handbook of Indians North of Mexico*, 1:442–43; and Wallace, *Indians in Pennsylvania*, pp. 71–72.

7. Morgan to the Mingo, Kiskapoo, June 20, 1776, Morgan's Journal, p. 29.

8. Ibid.

9. Ibid.

10. For biographical information see Sipe, "Logan, Chief of the Mingoes," *Indian Chiefs of Pennsylvania*, pp. 437–48; and Wallace, *Indians in Pennsylvania*, pp. 155–58, 175, 178.

11. Thomas Jefferson, *Notes on the State of Virginia*, ed. William Peden (Chapel Hill: Published for the Institute of Early American History and Culture by the University of North Carolina Press, 1955), p. 63.

12. Logan to George Morgan, Kiskapoo, June 20, 1776, Morgan's Journal, pp. 29–30.

13. Jefferson, *Notes on the State of Virginia*, p. 63.

14. Logan to Morgan, Kiskapoo, June 20, 1776, Morgan's Journal, pp. 29–30.

15. Ibid., 30.

16. Ibid.

17. Ibid.

18. Records of the Moravian Mission, January 7, 1804, box 162, file 15.

19. Logan to Morgan, Kiskapoo, June 20, 1776, Morgan's Journal, p. 30.

20. For a collection of contemporary studies on these "barbarous outrages" see Wilbur R. Jacobs, ed., *The Paxton Riots and the Frontier Theory* (Chicago: Rand McNally, 1967), pp. 3–14.

21. Logan to Morgan, Kiskapoo, June 20, 1776, Morgan's Journal, p. 30.

22. Alexander McKee to George Croghan, February 13, 1768, *Collections of the Illinois State Historical Library*, 16:170, cited in Savelle, *George Morgan*, p. 34, n6; see also Sipe, *Indian Wars of Pennsylvania*, pp. 484–86.

23. Logan to Morgan, Kiskapoo, June 20, 1776, Morgan's Journal, p. 31.

24. George Morgan, "Note on Logan's Family," Kiskapoo, June 20, 1776, Morgan's Journal, p. 30.

25. Logan to Morgan, Kiskapoo, June 20, 1776, Morgan's Journal, p. 31.

26. Ibid.

27. Ibid.

28. Morgan to Stone and Conneodico, Kiskapoo, no date, Morgan's Journal, p. 35.

29. Morgan's Journal, pp. 31–32.

30. Colonel Benjamin Wilson, "Cornstalk's Address," Chillicothe, Ohio, November 1774, quoted in Sipe, "Cornstalk," *Indian Chiefs of Pennsylvania*, p. 434.

31. Cornstalk to the Mingo, Kiskapoo, June 21, 1776, Morgan's Journal, pp. 31–32.

32. Ibid., 32.

33. Ibid.

34. Ibid.

35. Ibid.

36. The Mingo to Shawnee, Kiskapoo, June 21, 1776, Morgan's Journal, p. 32.

37. Ibid., 32–33.

38. Cornstalk to Morgan and Congress, Kiskapoo, June 21, 1776, Morgan's Journal, p. 33.

39. Ibid.

40. Ibid.

41. For a map of tribal territories in the Northeast, see *Handbook of North American Indians: Northeast*, p. ix.

42. Cornstalk to Morgan and Congress, Kiskapoo, June 21, 1776, Morgan's Journal, p. 33.

43. Ibid., 33–34.

44. Tooker, "Wyandot," and Conrad E. Heidenreich, "Huron," *Handbook of North American Indians: Northeast*, pp. 368–88, 398–406.

45. Cornstalk to Morgan and Congress, Kiskapoo, June 21, 1776, Morgan's Journal, p. 34.

46. Ibid.

47. George Morgan to Shawnee and the Mingo, Kiskapoo, June 21, 1776, Morgan's Journal, p. 34.

48. Ibid.

49. Ibid.

50. Ibid.

51. Congress, Declaration of Independence, signed by John Hancock et al., Philadelphia, July 4, 1776, Papers of the Continental Congress, National Archives M332, r10, f72; also printed in *Journals of the Continental Congress*, 5:510–15

52. Mrs. Ezekiel January (sister of the McConnell twins), "Personal Account of Kidnapping on June 23, 1776, at Leestown, Kentucky," Draper Manuscript, file 11 CC,

cited in Thwaites and Kellogg, eds., *Revolution on the Upper Ohio,* pp. 175–76, n6.

53. Ibid.

54. George Morgan to the Commissioners for Indian Affairs, Pittsburgh, July 26, 1776, Morgan's Journal, p. 57.

55. Ibid.

56. Ibid.

57. Ibid.

58. "Indian Depredations," *Pennsylvania Packet,* Philadelphia, August 20, 1776, printed August 27, 1776, cited in Thwaites and Kellogg, eds., *Revolution on the Upper Ohio,* p. 188.

59. Ibid.

60. Morgan to the Commissioners for Indian Affairs, Pittsburgh, July 26, 1776, Morgan's Journal, p. 57.

61. "Indian Depredations," *Pennsylvania Packet,* Philadelphia, August 20, 1776, printed August 27, 1776, cited in Thwaites and Kellogg, eds., *Revolution on the Upper Ohio,* p. 188.

62. George Morgan, Travel Log, Mingo Territory, Ohio to Fort Pitt, July 10–17, 1778, Morgan's Journal, p. 40.

Chapter Nine

1. The primary transcripts of the first U.S.–Indian treaty were preserved in Morgan's Journal, Fort Pitt, October–November 1776, pp. 62–73; and Morgan's Journal II, Fort Pitt, September–November 1776, pp. 57–65. Most of these papers were previously unpublished and not analyzed in concert with other available documents. Some related papers, principally from the Draper Manuscript Collection, were edited by Thwaites and Kellogg, *Revolution on the Upper Ohio,* pp. 185–220. A few additional documents were preserved in *American Archives,* ser. 5, v. 3 and indexed in John Butler, comp., *Index: The Papers of the Continental Congress,* v. 2.

Earlier frontier historians lacked access to most of the key documents vital to unraveling the story of the 1776 treaty. Hassler, *Old Westmoreland,* failed to mention this important conference. Sipe, in *Indian Wars of Pennsylvania,* reported only that the militia were raised during this period. Downes, in *Council Fires on the Upper Ohio,* pp. 194–95, described the treaty in one paragraph based on a letter from Morgan and three letters from the U.S. Commissioners. From this limited information, Downes was unable to recognize the significance of the treaty. Weslager, author of an extensive tribal chronicle of the Lenape, *Delaware Indians,* p. 297, noted the conference only briefly, but has expressed to the author great interest in the subject.

The standard source on Indian treaties, Kappler, ed., *Indian Affairs: Laws and Treaties*, v. 2, lists the 1778 treaty with the Delawares as being the first. The present study offers original documentation to revise and illuminate a previously overlooked chapter in the origins of U.S.–Indian relations.

2.   Archivist Lyman Draper collected extensive material on this episode and included it in his "Life of Boone," Boone Papers, 4:77–99, Draper Manuscript Collection, Library, State Historical Society of Wisconsin, Madison. See also Matthew Arbuckle to Colonel William Fleming, Fort Randolph, August 15, 1776, Thwaites and Kellogg, eds., *Revolution on the Upper Ohio*, pp. 185–87.

3.   Commissioners for Indian Affairs, Circular Letter to County Lieutenants, Pittsburgh, August 31, 1776, Morgan's Journal II, p. 57.

4.   Ibid.

5.   Ibid.

6.   Gnadenhutten Diary, September 29, 1776.

7.   Ibid.

8.   Ibid.

9.   Ibid.

10. Ibid.

11. Ibid.

12. Ibid.

13. Captain Andrew Wagoner and the Commissioners for Indian Affairs, Pittsburgh, October 1, 1776, Morgan's Journal II, p. 58.

14. Six Nations, Deed Delineating the Boundary Line with the English, Fort Stanwix, November 4, 1768, Papers of the Continental Congress, National Archives M247, r52, i41, v. 10, pp. 91–99. For an excellent analysis of the Fort Stanwix Treaty and illustrations of related maps, see Jacobs, *Dispossessing the American Indian*, pp. 98–100.

15. Logan to George Morgan, Kiskapoo, June 20, 1776, Morgan's Journal, pp. 29–30.

16. Commissioners for Indian Affairs to William Lochey, Pittsburgh, October 8, 1776, Morgan's Journal, p. 62.

17. Morgan to Kishanatathe, Pittsburgh, October 9, 1776, Morgan's Journal, p. 62.

18. Morgan's Journal, p. 62.

19. John Anderson, Report, Pittsburgh, October 12, 1776, Morgan's Journal II, p. 61.

20. Ibid.

21. "The Cass–Trowbridge Manuscript, " in C. A. Weslager, *The Delaware In-*

dian Westward Migration, with Texts of Two Manuscripts, 1821–22, Responding to General Lewis Cass's Inquiries about Lanape Culture and Language (Wallingford, PA: Middle Atlantic Press, 1978), p. 173.

22. Anderson, Report, Pittsburgh, October 12, 1776, Morgan's Journal II, p. 62.

23. Thwaites and Kellogg, eds., *Revolution on the Upper Ohio*, pp. 205–06, n47; see also Jack M. Sosin, *The Revolutionary Frontier, 1763–1783* (New York: Holt, Rinehart and Winston, 1967), p. 109.

24. Matthew Arbuckle to Captain John Stuart, Fort Randolph, November 2, 1776, Thwaites and Kellogg, eds., *Revolution on the Upper Ohio*, pp. 211–12.

25. Ibid., 212. For a biographical sketch of Matthew Arbuckle, see Thwaites and Kellogg, eds., *Documentary History of Dunmore's War, 1774,* p. 103, n49.

26. George Morgan, Memorandum, Pittsburgh, October 12, 1776, Morgan's Journal, p. 63.

27. Ibid.

28. Ibid.

29. Ibid.

30. Ibid.

31. Colonel Dorsey Pentecost to Governor Patrick Henry, West Augusta, November 5, 1776, Thwaites and Kellogg, eds., *Revolution on the Upper Ohio*, pp. 212–13.

32. *Pennsylvania Gazette*, November 6, 1776, Thwaites and Kellogg, eds., *Revolution on the Upper Ohio*, p. 210, n54.

33. Morgan, Memorandum, Pittsburgh, October 12, 1776, Morgan's Journal, p. 63.

34. Morgan, Memorandum, Pittsburgh, October 13, 1776, Morgan's Journal, p. 63.

35. Ibid.

36. Ibid.

37. William Heath, *Memoirs of Major-General William Heath,* ed. William Abbatt (New York: W. Abbatt, 1901), p. 216.

38. Colonel Dorsey Pentecost to Captain William Harrod, West Augusta, October 16, 1776, Thwaites and Kellogg, eds., *Revolution on the Upper Ohio*, pp. 207–208.

39. White Mingo to the Commissioners for Indian Affairs, Pittsburgh, October 18, 1776, Morgan's Journal II, p. 62.

40. Half King to State of Virginia, Detroit, Summer 1776, in White Mingo to the Commissioners for Indian Affairs, Pittsburgh, October 18, 1776, Morgan's Journal II, p. 62.

41. Ibid., 62–63.

42. Ibid., 63.

43. Old Wyandot Chief to White Mingo, Detroit, Summer 1776, in White Mingo to the Commissioners for Indian Affairs, Pittsburgh, October 18, 1776, Morgan's Journal II, p. 63.

44. For further information see E. S. Rogers, "Southeastern Ojibwa," *Handbook of North American Indians: Northeast,* pp. 760–61

45. Old Wyandot Chief to White Mingo, Detroit, Summer 1776, Morgan's Journal II, p. 63.

46. White Mingo to Wyandots, Detroit, Summer 1776, in White Mingo to the Commissioners for Indian Affairs, Pittsburgh, October 18, 1776, Morgan's Journal II, p. 63.

47. Ibid.

48. Head Wyandot Counsellor to White Mingo, Detroit, Summer 1776, in White Mingo to the Commissioners for Indian Affairs, Pittsburgh, October 18, 1776, Morgan's Journal II, p. 63.

49. White Mingo to Counsellors beyond the Lake, Detroit, Summer 1776, in White Mingo to the Commissioners for Indian Affairs, Pittsburgh, October 18, 1776, Morgan's Journal II, p. 63.

50. White Mingo to the Commissioners for Indian Affairs, Pittsburgh, October 18, 1776, Morgan's Journal II, p. 64.

51. Ibid.

52. Ibid.

53. Ibid.

54. Ibid.

55. John Jacob Schmick, Gnadenhutten Diary, October 19, 1776.

56. John Heckewelder, report recorded by John Jacob Schmick, Gnadenhutten Diary, October 19, 1776.

57. White Eyes to George Morgan, Pittsburgh, October 24, 1776, Morgan's Journal II, p. 65.

58. Ibid.

59. Graymont, *Iroquois in the American Revolution,* pp. 108–109.

60. White Eyes to Morgan, Pittsburgh, October 24, 1776, Morgan's Journal II, p. 65.

61. Information on Pukangehela was provided by one of his direct descendants, Henry Chisholm, who showed the author the peace medal given at the 1795 Treaty of Fort Greenville. In the summer of 1983 at Anadarko, Oklahoma, the author met with Chisholm and a group of Lenape elders for a conference on Lenape history and culture, organized by Linda Poolaw.

62. Captain Pipe to George Morgan, Pittsburgh, October 24, 1776, Morgan's Journal, pp. 65–66.

63. For a biographical sketch of Pipe, see Sipe, *Indian Chiefs of Pennsylvania*, pp. 420–32.

64. Pipe to Morgan, Pittsburgh, October 24, 1776, Morgan's Journal, p. 66.

65. Ibid.

66. Ibid.

67. Ibid., 66–67.

68. Ibid., 67.

69. Chief Jake Swamp to Gregory Schaaf, Mohawk nation, via Rooseveltown, New York, September 8, 1983, personal communication.

70. Pipe to Morgan, Pittsburgh, October 24, 1776, Morgan's Journal, p. 67.

71. Swamp to Schaaf, Mohawk Nation, September 8, 1983.

72. Pipe to Morgan, Pittsburgh, October 24, 1776, Morgan's Journal, p. 67.

73. White Eyes to George Morgan, Pittsburgh, October 24, 1776, Morgan's Journal, p. 67.

74. For biographical sketches of King Beaver and Shingas, see Sipe, *Indian Chiefs of Pennsylvania*, pp. 287–308.

75. White Eyes to Morgan, Pittsburgh, October 24, 1776, Morgan's Journal, p. 67.

76. Ibid., 68.

77. Ibid.

78. Ibid.

79. Ibid.

80. George Morgan to John Hancock, Pittsburgh, November 8, 1776, Morgan's Journal II, p. 13.

81. For a bibliography on Eastern Woodland clothing styles, see Flannery, *An Analysis of Coastal Algonquian Culture*, pp. 40–53. For an example of more recent scholarship on this subject, see James Howard, "Ceremonial Dress of the Delaware Man," *Bulletin of the Archaeological Society of New Jersey* (1976):1–45.

82. George Loskiel, *History of the Mission of the United Brethren among the Indians in North America* (London: The Brethren's Society for the Furtherance of the Gospel, 1794), 1:105. This tradition was confirmed by Chief Jake Swamp of the Mohawk nation, where the "Peace Song" is still sung.

83. Nicholas Cresswell, *The Journal of Nicholas Cresswell, 1774–1777* (London: J. Cape Ltd., 1925), pp. 115–17. Compare with a later account by Hassler, *Old Westmoreland*, pp. 75–79.

84. George Morgan, U.S.–Indian Peace Treaty Transcripts, Pittsburgh, October 26, 1776, Morgan's Journal, p. 68.

85. Cornstalk to the Commissioners for Indian Affairs, Pittsburgh, October 26, 1776, Morgan's Journal, p. 69.

86. William Wilson to the Commissioners for Indian Affairs, Pittsburgh, September 26, 1776, Morgan's Journal II, pp. 48–57.

87. Ibid., 56.

88. Cornstalk to the Commissioners for Indian Affairs, October 26, 1776, Morgan's Journal, p. 69.

89. Wilson to the Commissioners for Indian Affairs, September 26, 1776, Morgan's Journal II, p. 54.

90. Cornstalk to the Commissioners for Indian Affairs, October 26, 1776, Morgan's Journal, p. 69.

91. Ibid.

92. Ibid.

93. Ibid.

94. Ibid.

95. Cornstalk to Morgan, Pittsburgh, October 29, 1776, Morgan's Journal, p. 70.

96. Ibid.

97. Ibid.

98. Ibid.

99. Ibid.

100. Cornstalk to Six Nations, Pittsburgh, October 29, 1776, Morgan's Journal, pp. 70–71.

101. Ibid.

102. Ibid. For an excellent scholarly study of southern Indian affairs, see O'Donnell, *Southern Indians in the American Revolution*, pp. 34–53. For the account of the Cherokee accepting the black war belts, O'Donnell noted Henry Stuart, *Report*, August 20, 1776, British Public Record Office, Colonial Office, ser. 5, 77:168–69.

103. George Morgan, Ohio, July 4–9, 1776, Morgan's Journal, p. 40.

104. Cornstalk to Six Nations, Pittsburgh, October 29, 1776, Morgan's Journal, p. 71.

105. Ibid.

106. Ibid.

107. Ibid.

108. Ibid.

109. Flying Crow to Morgan, Six Nations Camp, November 3, 1776, Morgan's Journal, p. 73.

110. Coitcheleh to Morgan, Pittsburgh, October 30, 1776, Morgan's Journal, p. 72.

111. Ibid.

112. Ibid.

113. Ibid.

114. Ibid.

115. Ibid.

116. Loskiel, *History of the Mission of the United Brethren,* pt. 3, pp. 116–17.

117. *Zeisberger's History,* p. 115.

118. Ibid.

119. Chief Crow to Lenape, Lenape Camp, November 1776, quoted in Heckewelder, *Narrative of the Mission of the United Brethren,* p. 200.

120. Ibid., 200–201.

121. Ibid., 201.

122. Ibid., 201–202.

123. Ibid., 202.

124. Cornstalk to Congress, Pittsburgh, November 7, 1776, Morgan's Journal, p. 73.

125. Ibid.

126. Ibid.

127. Ibid.

Chapter Ten

1.   White Eyes to Lenape Council, Cooshocking, March 1777, quoted in De Schweinitz, *Life and Times of David Zeisberger,* p. 448; Weslager, *Delaware Indians,* p. 296.

2.   Lenape Council to George Morgan, Cooshocking, March 1777, quoted in De Schweinitz, *Life and Times of David Zeisberger,* p. 448.

3.   General Edward Hand to Lenape Nation, Pittsburgh, October 1, 1777, cited in Sipe, *Indian Wars,* pp. 527–28; see also Weslager, *Delaware Indians,* p. 307.

4.   Cornstalk to Elinipsico, Fort Randolph, Kentucky, November 10, 1777, cited in Reuben Gold Thwaites and Louise Phelps Kellogg, eds., *Frontier Defense on the Upper Ohio, 1777–78* (Madison: Wisconsin Historical Society, 1912), pp. 126, 149, 160, 188–89; Downes, *Council Fires on the Upper Ohio,* pp. 206–207.

5.   George Morgan to Lenape Council, Pittsburgh, Winter 1777, Morgan's Journal II.

6.   Masie Shenandoah, Wolf Clan Mother, to Gregory Schaaf, Oneida Nation, New York, December 1987, personal interview; Congress to Oneida and Onondaga, Commendation for Friendly Actions, *Journals of the Continental Congress,* Philadelphia, December 3, 1777, 9:996; George Washington to Indian Commissioners, March 12, 1778: "I am empowered to employ a body of 400 Indians, if they can be

procured upon proper terms.... I think they may be made of excellent use, as scouts and light troops, mixed with our own parties." Papers of the Continental Congress, National Archives M247, r187, i169, v.4, p.205.

7. White Eyes to George Morgan, Cooshocking, Spring 1778, Morgan's Journal II; De Schweinitz, *Life and Times of David Zeisberger*, p. 422; Weslager, *Delaware Indians*, p. 296.

8. Heckewelder, *History, Manners and Customs of the Indian Nations*, pp. 150–53; Weslager, *Delaware Indians*, p. 298.

9. General Edward Hand, Charges Against George Morgan, Pittsburgh, Fall 1777, no. 14, 17, 20–22, 67–68, 125, 141, 151–52, Hand Correspondence, Library of Congress; Savelle, *George Morgan*, pp. 148–51; Downes, *Council Fires on the Upper Ohio*, pp. 205–206.

10. George Morgan to Thomas Mifflin and Congress, Princeton, May 12, 1784, Papers of the Continental Congress, National Archives M247, r180, i163, p. 365; White Eyes and John Killbuck to George Morgan, Cooshocking, March 14, 1778, Papers of the Continental Congress, National Archives M247, r91, i78, v. 2, p. 419; David Zeisberger to George Morgan, Gnaddenhutten, April 6, 1778, and White Eyes to Morgan, Cooshocking, April 25, 1778, both from Morgan's Journal II; Commissioners to Congress, "Proceedings of Council at Pittsburgh," April 26, 1778, Morgan's Journal III, Carnegie Library, analyzed by Savelle, *George Morgan*, p. 155; U.S.–Delaware, "Treaty with the Delaware Nations, 1778," Kappler, ed., *Indian Affairs: Laws and Treaties*, 2:1–3; Downes, *Council Fires on the Upper Ohio*, pp. 216–17.

11. General George Washington to Colonel George Morgan, Princeton, New Jersey, May 11, 1779, Morgan Papers.

12. Chief Killbuck to George Washington, Princeton, May 12, 1779, Papers of the Continental Congress, National Archives, M247, r187, i169, v. 5, p. 294.

13. George Washington to Delaware Chiefs, Princeton, May 12, 1779, *Writings of George Washington*, 15:54–55; see also George Washington to John Jay, Account of the Conference with the Delaware Indians, Princeton, May 14, 1779, Continental Congress, Manuscript 152, 8:345, Library of Congress.

14. Lenape Chiefs to Congress, Appeal for Justice, Philadelphia, May 25, 1779, Morgan's Journal III, p. 170, signed by Chiefs Killbuck, Captain Johnny, Peyheeling, Teytapacheecon, Weyleycapaland, and Quesacothey.

15. Continental Congress, May 1779, Manuscripts, CC–137, 3:155, Library of Congress; Varnum L. Collins, "Indian Wards at Princeton," *Princeton University Bulletin*, 13:101–06; Savelle, *George Morgan*, p. 196.

16. President Joseph Reed, Proclamation, April 7, 1783, p. 1, *Pennsylvania Archives*, ser. 1, 8:167, 176, 283, 369, 393; Sipe, *Indian Wars of Pennsylvania*, pp. 573, 626.

17. Cornplanter to George Washington, Seneca Nation, New York, July 1779, p. 1, typescript copy at Glenn Black Laboratory, Indiana University, Bloomington, notebook labeled "Iroquois"; Sipe, *Indian Wars of Pennsylvania*, p. 626; George Washington to John Sullivan: "The immediate objectives are the total destruction and devastation of their settlements. It will be essential to ruin their crops in the ground and prevent their planting more." July 1779, quoted in Jacobs, *Dispossessing the American Indian*, p. 155, citing Thomas R. Wessel, "Agriculture and Iroquois Hegemony in New York, 1610–1779," *The Maryland Historian* 1 (1970): 100. See also Graymont, *Iroquois in the American Revolution*, pp. 192–222.

18. Chief Leon Shenandoah to Gregory Schaaf, Onondaga Nation, December 1987, personal interview.

19. Daniel Brodhead, Report on Destruction of Delaware Indian Capital, April 1781, *Pennsylvania Archives*, ser. 1, 9:161; Louise Phelps Kellogg, ed., *Frontier Retreat on the Upper Ohio, 1779–1781* (Madison: State Historical Society of Wisconsin, 1917), pp. 376–80, 382; Edward Hand, Report on the Squaw Campaign, January 1778, Hand Correspondence, no. 98, cited in Thwaites and Kellogg, eds., *Frontier Defense on the Upper Ohio*, pp. 193, 215–20; Downes, *Council Fires on the Upper Ohio*, pp. 210–11, 265–66.

20. *Pennsylvania Archives*, ser. 2, 9: 523–41; Consul Butterfield, ed., *Washington-Irvine Correspondence: The Official Letters Which Passed between Washington and Brig.–Gen. William Irvine and between Irvine and Others Concerning Military Affairs in the West from 1781 to 1783* (Madison: D. Atwood, 1882), pp. 94, 113–18; Downes, *Council Fires on the Upper Ohio*, pp. 273–74.

21. Gregory Schaaf, "Personal Account" (Gnadenhutten, Ohio, June 1988).

22. Sauk, Chippewa, Ottawa, Potawatomi, Delaware, and the Wyandot, Treaty of Fort Harmar, *United States Statutes at Large*, 7:31–33; "Citizens of the U.S. within the territory of the Indian nation subject to the laws of the Indian nation," 7 Stat. 28; *American State Papers: Indian Affairs*, 1:197; Roscoe Buley, *The Old Northwest Pioneer Period, 1815–1840*, 2 vols. (Indianapolis: Indiana Historical Society, 1950), v. 1; Henry M. Schoolcraft, *Historical and Statistical Information Respecting the History, Condition and Prospects of the Indian Tribes of the United States*, 6 vols. (Philadelphia: Lippincott, 1851–57), 6:330; William H. Smith, ed., *The St. Clair Papers*, 2 vols. (Cincinnati: R. Clarke and Co., 1882), 2:108–11, 622–30, and especially Governor Arthur St. Clair to Secretary of War Henry Knox, "Beginning of Treaty of Fort Harmar," December 13, 1788, 2:106–7; Clarence Carter, ed., *Papers Relating to the Period of the First Stage of the Government of the Territory Northwest of the River Ohio, 1787–1791*, vol. 2 of *The Territorial Papers of the United States* (Washington, DC: Government Printing Office, 1934), pp. 174–86; Felix S. Cohen, *Handbook of Federal Indian Law*

(Washington, DC: Department of the Interior, 1942; reprint, Albuquerque: American Indian Law Center, in cooperation with the University of New Mexico, 1971), p. 6, n48; Kappler, ed., *Indian Affairs: Laws and Treaties*, 2:15–20; "Abstract of Treaty at Fort Harmar," *Michigan Pioneer and Historical Collections* 24 (1894):41–42; Ebenezer Denny, "Account of the Indian Treaties from the Diary of Major E. Denny" (December 13, 1788–January 28, 1789), copy at Glenn Black Laboratory; and U.S.–Iroquois, "Treaty of Fort Harmar," January 9, 1789, cited in *Pennsylvania Archives*, ser. 1, 11:529–33.

23. Felix Cohen states: "As early as July 22, 1790, Congress used the expression 'Indian country' in the first trade and intercourse act, apparently with the meaning of country belonging to the Indians, occupied by them, and to which the Government recognized them as having some kind of right and title." 1 Stat. 137, cited in Cohen, *Handbook of Federal Indian Law*, p. 6, n49.

24. See the following resolutions: Resolved: "That the sum of twenty thousand dollars in addition to the fourteen thousand dollars already appropriated be appropriated for defraying the expences of the treaties which have been ordered or which may be ordered to be held on the present year with the several Indian tribes in the northern department, and for extinguishing the Indian claims; the whole of the said twenty thousand dollars together with six thousand dollars of the said fourteen thousand dollars to be applied solely to the purpose of extinguishing Indian claims to the lands they have already ceded to the United States by obtaining regular conveyances for the same, and for extending a purchase beyond the limits hitherto fixed by treaty; but that no part of the said sums be applied for any purpose other than those above mentioned." (*Journals of the Continental Congress*, July 2, 1788, 34:285); and Resolved, "That the Superintendent of Indian Affairs for the Northern department and in case he be unable to attend then col Josiah Harmar immediately proceed to post St. Vincents or some other place more convenient in his Opinion for holding a treaty with the Wabash Indians, the Shawanese and other hostile tribes, that he inform those Indians that Congress is sincerely disposed to promote peace and friendship between their citizens and the Indians; that to this end he is sent to invite them in a friendly manner to a treaty with the United States to hear their complaints, to know the truth and the causes of their quarrels with those frontier settlers and having invited those Indians to the treaty he shall make strict enquiry into the causes of their uneasiness and hostile proceedings and form a treaty of peace with them if it can be done on terms consistent with the honor and dignity of the United States."; and Resolved, "That the Executive of Virginia be requested to give orders to the militia in the district of Kentucky to hold themselves in readiness to unite with the federal troops in such operations as the Officer

commanding them may judge necessary for the protection of the frontiers; and that on the application of the commanding Officer of the federal troops, the said executive be requested to give orders that a part of the said militia not exceeding one thousand be embodied and take such positions as the said comanding Officer shall direct for acting in conjunction with the federal troops in protecting and defending the frontier inhabitants and in making such expeditions against the Indians in case they continue hostile as Congress shall hereafter order and direct. And the militia which shall be called into the actual service of the United States for the defence of the said frontier inhabitants or the purposes of such expeditions shall be paid supported and equipped by the state, and the state shall be credited in the requisition of the current year the Amount of their pay and rations only, computed on the federal establishment for similar service; provided that no charges for the said service shall be valid unless supported by actual musters of the said Militia made by the inspector or by a field Officer of the troops of the United States agreeable to the orders of the commanding officer." (*Journals of the Continental Congress*, 33:385–86). The goal of treaty was the "total extinguishment of all Indian claims to the territory."

25. Charles Thomson, Secretary of Congress, to Governor Edmund Randolph of Virginia, "Indian Lands Between Sciota River and Miami River Being Surveyed for Future Bounty Lands for U.S. Soldiers," July 21, 1788, Papers of the Continental Congress, National Archives M247, r25, i18b, p. 158; Charles Thomson, Secretary of Congress, to Arthur St. Clair, Governor of the Old Northwest Territory, "Indian Lands Between Sciota River and Miami River Being Surveyed for Future Bounty Lands for U.S. Soldiers," August 4, 1788, ibid., M247, r25, i18b, p. 159; Report of Committee on Indian Affairs, August 12, 1788, *Journals of the Continental Congress*, 34:410–12.

26. Congressional Committee, Report on War Department and Indian Affairs, July 28, 1788, Papers of the Continental Congress, National Archives, M247, r34, i27, pp. 350–53.

27. Ibid.

28. Report of Committee on Indian Affairs, August 12, 1788, *Journals of the Continental Congress*, 34:410–12; Charles Thomson to Governors of S. Carolina and Georgia, "Congress approves Treaty with Southern Indians," August 15, 1788, Papers of the Continental Congress, National Archives M247, r25, i18b, p. 160; Charles Thomson to Arthur St. Clair, "Instructions from Congress," September 1, 1788, ibid., M247, r25, i18b, p. 162; Charles Thomson, "Northwest Territorial Board Adds Three New Members: William Irvine, John Taylor Gilman and Abraham Baldwin," September 13, 1788, ibid., M247, r25, i18b, pp. 16–17.

29. Congress, "An Act to regulate trade and intercourse with the Indian tribes," July 22, 1790, 1 Stat. 137. For full citations of related laws and cases, see Cohen, *Handbook of Federal Indian Law*, p. 485, n8.

30. ". . . the power to regulate commerce . . . with the Indian tribes . . . ," U.S. Constitution (1787), Art. 1, sec. 8, cl. 3. See also Cohen, *Handbook of Federal Indian Law* , pp. x,10, 69, 91ff, 353ff.

31. ". . . and Indians not taxed," U.S. Constitution (1787), Art. 1, sec. 2; Amendment XIV, sec. 2. For an analysis of the legislative and administrative history of this phrase in a counterargument, see Opinion of the Solicitor, Indian Division, Manuscript 31039, November 7, 1940; 77 *Cong. Rec.* 79 (January 8, 1941). See also Cohen, *Handbook of Federal Indian Law*, pp. 89, 157, 254; and United States v. Kagama, 118 U.S. 375, 378 (1886); Elk v. Wilkins, 112 U.S. 84, 99 (1884); Act of June 16, 1906, sec. 25, 34 Stat. 257, 280. "New Mexico . . . was admitted to statehood under a special compact with the United States exempting Indian lands from taxation; and with a constitution excluding 'Indians not taxed' from the electorate."

32. For an example, see the excellent article by Harvey Arden and Steve Wall, "Living Iroquois Confederacy," *National Geographic* 172 (September 1987):370ff.

33. Congress, Ordinance for the Government of the Northwest Territory, July 13, 1787, Papers of the Continental Congress, National Archives M247, r72, i 59, v. 1, pp. 229–30.

34. Ibid. Plans for Indian trade and purchase of Indian lands were featured. See also "Report of the Secretary of War on Wabash, Shawnee and other so-called hostile tribes, criminal jurisdiction, civil law," July 19, 1787, *Journals of the Continental Congress,* 32:370–75.

35. The Sac and Fox nation of Stroud, Oklahoma, presently is challenging legal interpretation by contending that Indians should not be taxed as long as there is not a constitutional amendment to the contrary. Indians are presently being taxed under the auspices of the 1924 Indian Citizenship Act. However, a review of the act and the congressional debates about it indicates that the original intent of the legislation was to extend First Amendment rights to protect Indians' religious freedom.

36. Select Committee on Indian Affairs, *Iroquois Confederacy of Nations,* 100th Cong., 1st sess., 1987, S. Hearing 100–610, pp. 7–33.

37. Ibid.

38. Savelle, *George Morgan*, pp. 22–228.

39. Ibid.

40. Ibid.

41. Ibid.

Appendix

THE MORGAN PAPERS
Inventory and Background

History of Past Ownership

1. Colonel George Morgan (1741–1810) m. Mary Baynton
2. Thomas Morgan (1784–1855) m. Katherine Duane
3. William Duane Morgan (1817–1887) m. Matilda; m. Nancy
4. Thomas Morgan (dates unknown). He was never married and passed the collection down to his nephew, William Duane Morgan (1884–1934).
5. William Duane Morgan (1884–1934) m. Susannah Barker
6. Susannah Barker Morgan (1892–1988)
7. Colonel George Morgan Document Company (1977–1989)
    8. Sold at Sotheby's (New York, April 25, 1989), Sale #5837 "Tobias," lots 77–83.

Inventory of Morgan Papers

1. Land Indenture for Restitution of the "Sufferers of 1763" Granted by 1768 Fort Stanwix Treaty
Signed and Dated: William Trent, John Hughes; witnessed by John Hughes, Jr., and Isaac Hughes; dated December 13, 1768.
Subject: A grant at the Fort Stanwix Treaty on November 3, 1768, by a group of Iroquois Six Nations to the Suffering Traders for lands on the Ohio River.

2. Sir William Johnson and Minutes of the Indiana Land Company

Signed and Dated: A. Autographed document signed at end of **B.** "A true copy of the Minutes & Proceedings, George Morgan; September 21, 1775; at Pittsburgh to November 15, 1775, at Carlisle." A copy of this document is on file at the Historical Society of Pennsylvania in Ohio Company Manuscripts, 2:9–29.

Subject: Minutes of the Indiana Land Company, a partnership based on the claims of the Suffering Traders of the French and Indian War, which resulted in a grant at the Fort Stanwix Treaty on November 3, 1768, by a group of Iroquois Six Nations for lands on the Ohio River.

3. John Hancock, President of Congress, to George Morgan

Signed and Dated: Letter signed April 19, 1776.

Subject: Hancock directed Morgan to take a Great Peace Belt with thirteen diamonds and twenty-five hundred wampum beads to the warriors and sachems of the western Indian nations. Hancock advised Morgan: "Convince them of the good intensions of Congress . . . cultivate harmony and friendship between them and the white people . . . inspire them with the sentiments of Justice and Humanity . . . introduce the arts of civil and social life."

4. George Morgan Personal Journal and Letterbook

Signed and Dated: Written in two hands; of George Morgan and his secretary; dated April–July and September–November 1776.

Subject: This part of Morgan's journal represents the missing section for the year 1776, which originally fit with the Morgan journal and letterbooks presently preserved in the Andrew Carnegie Library in Pittsburgh. The 1776 journal provides detailed accounts of speeches about war and peace made by the chiefs, medicine people, and women leaders from over thirty Indian nations. Morgan's personal accounts describe secret intelligence, spy missions, frontier conflicts, and the first U.S.–Indian peace treaty in 1776.

5. Major General Benedict Arnold to Continental Board of War, Forwarded to George Morgan for His Advice.

Signed and Dated: Copy signed B. Arnold, dated July 1777. A copy of this document was given to the Washington County Historical Society, Washington, Pennsylvania.

Subject: This letter discusses a secret plan conceived to secure valuable British centers of trade at Mobile and Pensacola. The twenty-five-hundred-mile journey required over one thousand soldiers. General Arnold finally conceded:

"I have not entered into the minutiae of the affair, as I conceive Col. Morgan, from his intimate acquaintance with the country, more capable of doing it. P.S. Make sure every man has a good powder horn." Two months later Arnold became a hero at the Battle of Saratoga when General Burgoyne surrendered. Two years later he became a traitor.

6. General George Washington to Colonel George Morgan
Signed and Dated: Letter signed May 11, 1779, at Princeton.
Subject: Washington invited Morgan to arrange a meeting with the Delaware chiefs who were en route to Philadelphia to express their grievances over the 1778 U.S.–Delaware Treaty. The Indians had been promised that their nation would become a fourteenth state in the union. This meeting represents a significant historical event.

7. U.S.–Indian Treaty at Fort McIntosh
Signed and Dated: Document signed by Charles Thompson (Secretary of the Continental Congress), January 21, 1785.
Subject: A controversial treaty which assigned reserved lands for the Delawares, Wyandots, Ottawas, and Chippewas within the Northwest Territory.

8. Articles of the New Jersey Land Company
Signed and Dated: Document signed by Ernst Van Winckle, William Edgar, Aaron Burr, Alex Macomb, Moore Furman, Henry Van Dike, Oliver Pollock, C. T. S. B. Poelnitz, William Newbold, John Cox, Clayton Newbold, Joseph Newbold, George Morgan, Joseph Bloomfield, Joel Gibbs, Dan Vardon, Jr., Isaac Smith, Sam W. Stockton, David Brearly, Aaron Dunham, Richard Stockton, and Frederick Frelinghuysen; dated May 1, 1788.
Subject: A request for a two-million-acre grant of land from Congress.

9. Robert McClure to John W. Hilliard and Thomas Serngeins
Signed and Dated: Document signed March 8, 1803, Ohio County.
Subject: Related to the whiskey trade and commerce of supplies; financial claim by Jacob Whitoil.

10. Morgan Neville to George Morgan, Jr.
Signed and Dated: Autographed letter signed January 21, 1806.
Subject: Discusses a duel in which Mr. Stewart killed Mr. Bates; Morgan Neville, the son of Revolutionary War veteran John Neville, contemplated fleeing the country.

11. George Morgan to Thomas Morgan
Signed and Dated: Autographed letter signed July 4, ca. 1807.
Subject: George Morgan's philosophical advice to his son after Thomas had
become involved in a duel: "I have seen the Tree [of Liberty] and am not
surprised at the Exultations of the United Parties. . . .To aid you in these
studies [of your moral and social duties] . . . I send you Shaftsbury's
Characteristics and Cicero's *Offices*. . . .True courage consists of in my opinion."

12. Mary Morgan to Thomas Morgan
Signed and Dated: Autographed letter signed July 4, ca. 1807.
Subject: Mary Morgan's philosophical advice to her son after Thomas had become
involved in a duel: "Yes my Dear Son, you have a Roman Mother when
Honour, and your Country's cause, calls you into the Field of Battle. . . .Your
Parents have lived to see, another daring outrageous conduct, committed by
the tyrants of the Ocean. . . .Trust me my son, there is much to be gained from
the conversation of a lovely sensible woman."

13. Power of Attorney by Sir William Munro in Favour of Andrew Munro, Esq. Sworn before Dan Macluggan and Colin MacLarty
Signed and Dated: Document signed December 5, 1807.

14. William Leet, Survey of G. Morgan's Estate, Morganza
Signed and Dated: Document signed May 4, 1821.
Subject: Description and map of Morganza, Pennsylvania, along the forks of
Chartiers Creek. George Morgan spent the last years of his life at Morganza,
studying scientific methods of agriculture.

15. Thomas Jefferson to Katherine Duane Morgan
Signed and Dated: Autographed letter signed Thomas Jefferson; dated January 26,
1822, at Monticello.
Subject: This letter is an affectionate response to George Morgan's daughter-in-law,
Katherine Duane Morgan, who had sent the eighty-year-old statesman a list
of suggestions, compiled by a group of intelligent women of the day, which
outlined how to run the affairs of government more efficiently. Jefferson
commended their "patriotic efforts," but conceded his life was drawing to a
close and the "law of Nature" was warning him to retire and to "leave to the
generation of the day the direction of its own affairs." Jefferson's philosophical
statements reveal his personal reflections four years before he passed away.

16. William Norris to Joseph Henderson
Signed and Dated: Autographed letter signed June 8, 1836.
Subject: The Indiana Land Company, which claimed land in Illinois. Originally
   sent to the Land Office in Harrisburg, Pennsylvania, and forwarded to the
   heirs of George Morgan.

17. Manuscript Seating Chart for the Pennsylvania House of Representatives
Signed: "A copy for Thomas Morgan" (son of George Morgan).
Subject: A diagram of the House chambers, featuring the seats of the following
   congressmen: Philadelphia County, Joel B. Sutherland, I. Tryon, J. Porbury,
   Jacob Holgate, Geo. Morton, Holmes; Washington County, Thomas Morgan,
   J. Hamilton, W. Vance, Stevenson, Darlington . . . and seventy-six others.

BIBLIOGRAPHICAL ESSAY

THE PRIMARY SOURCES of information on the establishment by the Continental Congress of the first U.S. Indian agency in the Middle Department are the records of Agent George Morgan, Personal Journal and Letterbook (Pittsburgh, April–November 1776), Morgan Papers. The Morgan Papers, including the journal and letterbook, were passed down through a branch of the Morgan family that settled on the West Coast. The manuscripts eventually came into the possession of Mrs. Susannah Morgan, the widow of one of Morgan's great-great-grandsons, and were made available to the author in 1976. Thereafter they were preserved initially by the George Morgan Document Company, then sold at Sotheby's in New York on April 25, 1989. Microfilm copies of the Morgan Papers are deposited in the Special Collections, University of California, Santa Barbara; the Special Collections, California State University, Chico; and the Grand Council, Iroquois Confederacy, in the care of Chief Leon Shenandoah, Onondaga Nation, via Nadrow, New York.

Over 350 additional pages of Morgan's journal and letterbook, known as Morgan's Journal I, II, and III, are located in the holdings of the Andrew Carnegie Library, Pittsburgh; the Pennsylvania State Library, Harrisburg, has typescript copies. The author examined both parts of Morgan's journal and found them to be written on the same paper, with an identical watermark. The reason the journal was separated is unknown.

Sections from the Carnegie Library manuscript were edited by Reuben

Gold Thwaites and Louise Phelps Kellogg and published in two volumes: *The Revolution on the Upper Ohio, 1775–1777* (Madison: Wisconsin Historical Society, 1908) and *Frontier Advance on the Upper Ohio, 1778–1779* (Madison: State Historical Society of Wisconsin, 1912). These books contain other related documents on frontier history during the Revolution, largely from the Lyman Draper Manuscript Collection at the University of Wisconsin, the alma mater of prominent frontier historian Frederick Jackson Turner.

Many historians have relied on the Draper Collection to reconstruct U.S.–Indian history during the period 1775–1782. The relationship of this period to the larger historical framework was established by Randolph C. Downes, *Council Fires on the Upper Ohio: A Narrative of Indian Affairs in the Upper Ohio Valley Until 1795* (Pittsburgh: University of Pittsburgh Press, 1940). Downes first recognized Morgan's important role in Indian affairs in an earlier article, "George Morgan, Indian Agent Extraordinary, 1776–1779," *Pennsylvania History* 1 (October 1934): 202–16. Downes expanded a previous sketch of Morgan written by Walter R. Fee, "Colonel George Morgan at Fort Pitt," *Western Pennsylvania Historical Magazine* 11 (October 1928):217–24. Fee did not cite his sources, but both authors clearly based their studies on the documents edited by Thwaites and Kellogg; the Morgan papers in the Library of Congress; the *Journals of the Continental Congress, 1774–1789*, ed. Worthington C. Ford et al., 34 vols. (Washington, DC: Government Printing Office, 1904–37); and the printed sources in the *American Archives*, ed. Peter Force (Washington, DC: M. St. Clair Clarke and Peter Force, 1837–55), ser. 4, 6 vols, ser. 5, 3 vols. The same primary sources were used in a chapter on agent George Morgan by his biographer, Max Savelle, in *George Morgan: Colony Builder* (New York: Columbia University Press, 1932; reprint New York: AMS Press, 1967). Savelle's contribution focused on Morgan's land dealings and his later attempt to establish an interracial colony at New Madrid, Missouri.

Brief secondary references to Morgan's mission to the Indians in 1776 were found in Edgar Hassler, *Old Westmoreland: A History of Western Pennsylvania during the Revolution* (Cleveland: Arthur H. Clark Co., 1900), pp. 20–23; Savelle, *George Morgan*, pp. 136–39; and Downes, *Council Fires on the Upper Ohio*, pp. 189–90. These accounts are based primarily on Morgan's summary report, which was reinterpreted in Indian Commissioners to Congressional Committee on Indian Affairs, July 30, August 2, 1776, Morgan's Journal II, Carnegie Library, pp. 1–4.

The primary transcripts of the first U.S.–Indian Treaty were preserved in Morgan's Journal (Fort Pitt, October–November 1776), pp. 62–73; and Morgan's Journal II (Fort Pitt, September–November 1776), pp. 57–65. Most of these papers previously were unpublished and had never been analyzed in conjunction with other available documents. Some related papers, principally from the Draper Manuscript Collection, were edited by Thwaites and Kellogg, *Revolution on the Upper Ohio*, pp. 185–220. A few additional documents were preserved in *American Archives*, ser. 5, vol. 3, and indexed in John P. Butler, comp., *Index: The Papers of the Continental Congress, 1774–1789*, 5 vols. (Washington, DC: Government Printing Office, 1978).

Earlier historians of the frontier lacked access to most of the key documents vital to unraveling the story of the 1776 treaty. Hassler, in *Old Westmoreland*, did not mention the important conference. Chester Sipe, in *The Indian Wars of Pennsylvania* (Harrisburg, PA: Telegraph Press, 1931) reported only that the militia were raised during this time period. Downes, in *Council Fires on the Upper Ohio*, pp. 194–95, described the treaty in one paragraph based on a letter from Morgan and three letters from the commissioners. Downes failed to recognize the significance of the treaty. C. A. Weslager, author of an extensive tribal chronicle of the Lenape, *The Delaware Indians: A History* (New Brunswick, NJ: Rutgers University Press, 1972), p. 297, noted the conference briefly, but since has expressed to the author great interest in the subject.

The standard source on Indian treaties, Charles Kappler, ed., *Indian Affairs: Laws and Treaties*, 5 vols. (Washington, DC: Government Printing Office, 1904–41; reprint, New York: AMS Press, 1971), vol. 2, lists the 1778 U.S.–Delaware Agreement as the first treaty. The present study offers original documentation to revise and illuminate a previously overlooked chapter on the origins of U.S.–Indian relations.

The history of colonial Indian affairs has been the subject of hundreds of books and articles. Among the earliest studies are Samuel P. Hildreth, *Pioneer History, Being an Account of the First Examinations of the Ohio Valley* (Cincinnati: For the Historical Society of Cincinnati by H. W. Derby and Co., 1848) and the famous narrative by Francis Parkman, *History of the Conspiracy of Pontiac, and the War of the North American Tribes against the English Colonies after the Conquest of Canada* (Boston: Little, Brown and Co., 1851). Popular accounts were dramatized in James Fenimore Cooper's "Leatherstocking Tales."

Frontier research pioneered by Francis Parkman and Frederick Jackson Turner and refined by Savelle and Downes subsequently has been developed by more recent scholars. Historian Jack M. Sosin, in *The Revolutionary Frontier, 1763–1783* (New York: Holt, Rinehart and Winston, 1967), advanced the study of frontier expansion to analyze the process of settlement and "the embryonic economic, social, political, and cultural forms evident . . . during the Revolutionary era."

The interdisciplinary approach to frontier Indian studies is exemplified by the ethnohistorical and cross-cultural analysis of Wilbur R. Jacobs, *Dispossessing the American Indian: Indians and Whites on the Colonial Frontier* (New York: Charles Scribner's Sons, 1972). His first major study analyzed political, social, and trade relations: *Diplomacy and Indian Gifts: Anglo-French Rivalry along the Ohio and Northwest Frontiers, 1748–1763* (Stanford: Stanford University Press, 1950). It was reprinted as *Wilderness Politics and Indian Gifts: The Northern Colonial Frontier, 1748–1763* (Lincoln: University of Nebraska Press, 1966). Jacobs surpassed the earlier efforts of Parkman and Turner by using more sophisticated research techniques and methods of cultural analysis. Furthermore, his work was enhanced by contacts with contemporary American Indian societies, such as the Iroquois Six Nations.

Anthropologist C. A. Weslager also consulted with Indian elders, particularly Delaware herbalist and speaker Nora Thompson Dean, "Touching Leaves." When writing his brief account of the Delawares or Lenni Lenape during the American Revolution, Weslager researched the published letterbooks, characterizing Morgan as "a capable executive, fur trader, and colonizer" in *Delaware Indians*, pp. 295–317.

Historian Barbara Graymont also touched upon Morgan's activities in her study of northern Indian affairs, *The Iroquois in the American Revolution* (Syracuse: Syracuse University Press, 1972). Graymont focused her research farther north than Morgan's general sphere of authority, relying on the Papers of the Continental Congress in the Library of Congress. Like previous scholars, Graymont was hampered by the awesome task of sifting through thousands of congressional documents without benefit of the comprehensive index compiled by Butler. This catalog is an invaluable tool for researchers, providing over ten thousand pages of entries arranged by name, place, subject and chronology.

While Graymont studied northern Indian affairs during the American Revolution, James H. O'Donnell III studied the south in *Southern Indians in the American Revolution* (Knoxville: University of Tennessee Press, 1973), pp. 30–53. O'Donnell's study provided perceptive analysis of original sources, especially in British–Indian and military papers, such as Clarence Carter, ed., *The Correspondence of General Thomas Gage*, 2 vols. (New Haven: Yale University Press, 1931–33), and documents in the British Public Record Office, Colonial Office, Series 5. Both O'Donnell and Graymont have received favorable scholarly reviews for their extensive research of original documents.

For a documentary study of eyewitness accounts of the American Revolution, especially during the tenure of American troops in New York, consult George Scheer and Hugh Rankin, *Rebels and Redcoats* (Cleveland and New York:

World Publishing Co., 1957). Of particular interest are the diaries and letters of Washington's troops.

For a critical analysis of Washington's decision to draft Indians into the war, see Jack M. Sosin, "The Use of Indians in the War of the American Revolution: A Re-Assessment of Responsibility," *Canadian Historical Review* 46 (June 1965):115–25. Sosin's research was carried forward by subsequent scholars.

Among the more recent studies of Indian affairs during the American Revolution, two works figure prominently. Both were published during the Bicentennial. The first is an article by the director of the Newberry Library, Francis Jennings, "The Indians' Revolution," in *The American Revolution: Explorations in the History of American Radicalism*, ed. A. F. Young (DeKalb: Northern Illinois University Press, 1976), pp. 320–48. Jennings presented an excellent summary of the subject, but his overview was too limited in length to allow more in-depth analysis, for which his books are highly noted. The second study, by Edward G. Williams, "Fort Pitt and the Revolution on the Western Frontier," *Western Pennsylvania Historical Magazine* 59 (January 1976):1–38, (April 1976):129–52, (July 1976):251–88, (October 1976):379–40, is a four-part series on Morgan's headquarters, Fort Pitt. Williams linked together a series of unpublished documents that are reprinted verbatim, thus providing a rich source of primary materials interwoven among the standard sources.

Previous authors have been able to provide only a cursory account of Morgan's activities in 1776 without access to the unpublished pages of the agent's Personal Journal and Letterbook. The reason this original manuscript was kept private by the Morgan family for five generations is unclear, but the material represents the key to understanding the significance of a large body of related documents. The present study attempts to unravel the events surrounding Morgan's initial actions in establishing the first U.S. department of Indian affairs on the Ohio frontier. The legacy of over two hundred years of U.S.–Indian relations now may be traced back to these early activities. The official orders of the Continental Congress pertaining to the establishment of the Indian agency at Fort Pitt were written by John Hancock to George Morgan, April 19, 1776, Morgan Papers. For further documentation see *Journals of the Continental Congress*, 4:294–95.

Morgan was chosen Indian agent for the Continental Congress in part because of his knowledge of Indian history and customs. He became so adept at the art of wampum diplomacy that the Lenni Lenape addressed him as Brother Tamanend. The treaty papers of the "Great Peace" between William Penn and Tamanend, along with the original wampum belt, were presented by Penn's great-grandson to the Historical Society of Pennsylvania. See Granville Penn et al., "The Presentation to the Historical Society of Pennsylvania of the Belt of Wampum Delivered by the Indians to William Penn, at the Great Treaty under the Elm Tree, in 1682," *Memoirs of the Historical Society of Pennsylvania* (1858), 6:205–82. For an excellent secondary account see the biography by Harry Emerson Wildes, *William Penn* (New York: Macmillan, 1974).

Although Penn became disillusioned with his "Holy Experiment," Morgan encountered similar efforts being conducted by Moravian missionaries. They served Morgan by keeping him informed of frontier activities, and their papers, along with later analyses, represent a formidable body of data on Indian–white relations.

A daily chronicle of events on the Ohio frontier was preserved in the diaries of German Protestant Moravian missionaries. The original manuscripts are in the Records of the Moravian Mission, Bethlehem, Pennsylvania. For a comprehensive index to the microfilm, see the Reverend Carl Fliegel, comp., *Index to the Records of the Moravian Mission among the Indians of North America* (New Haven, CT: Research Publications, 1970). Part of the manuscripts were translated and analyzed by Edmund De Schweinitz, *The Life and Times of David Zeisberger: The Western Pioneer and Apostle of the Indians* (Philadelphia: J. B. Lippincott, 1870; reprint, New York: Arno Press and the New York Times, 1971). Zeisberger and his assistant, John Heckewelder, were the principal Moravian missionaries during the late eighteenth century in Ohio. The papers of the younger missionary were edited by Paul A. W. Wallace, *Thirty Thousand Miles with John Heckewelder* (Pittsburgh: University of Pittsburgh Press, 1958). Heckewelder also wrote an account of this period of history, *Narrative of the Mission of the United Brethren among the Delaware and Mohegan Indians, from its Commencement in the Year 1740, to the Close in the Year 1808* (Philadelphia: McCarty and Davis, 1820; reprint, New York: Arno Press and the New York Times, 1971).

Although the Moravians recorded the most exhaustive body of eyewitness accounts among the Indians, scholars interpreting this material must consider their cultural and religious world view, which influenced their mission to convert the "heathens" to Christianity. The Moravians were devout pacifists who provided a place of refuge for hundreds of dispossessed Indian people.

The study of the Morgan Papers also required extensive research into the history of the Indian trade and western land business. Most of George Morgan's early records and journals as an Indian trader are available on microfilm: see *Baynton, Wharton and Morgan Papers in the Pennsylvania State Archives*, Donald H.

Kent, project director (Harrisburg: Pennsylvania Historical and Museum Commission, 1975).

In 1775 George Morgan was elected secretary of the land company formed by the "Sufferers of 1763," involving lands granted to traders by the Iroquois signers of the 1768 Fort Stanwix Treaty. For the original transcript of the 1775 meetings in which Morgan became secretary, see George Morgan, Minutes of the Indiana Land Company, Pittsburgh, September 21, 1775, and Carlisle, November 15, 1775, Morgan Papers. A copy of this transcript is in the holdings of the Historical Society of Pennsylvania, in Ohio Company Manuscripts, 2:9–29.

The grant of the "Suffering Traders" was based on an agreement worked out at the 1768 Fort Stanwix Treaty. Therefore, research was conducted into the original documents, such as Six Nations, Deed Delineating the Boundary Line with the English, Fort Stanwix, November 4, 1768, Papers of the Continental Congress, National Archives M247, r52, i41, v. 10, pp. 91–99. For an excellent analysis of the Fort Stanwix Treaty and illustrations of related maps, see Jacobs, *Dispossessing the American Indian*, pp. 98–100.

One of the most in-depth studies of western land speculation by George Washington and others was written by Thomas Perkins Abernethy, *Western Lands and the American Revolution* (New York: Russell and Russell, 1959). His research revealed that many of the founding fathers had invested in western land grants and that the Revolution was deeply involved with economic considerations. For further information on the disposition of Indian lands, see George E. Lewis, *The Indiana Company, 1763–1798: A Study in Eighteenth Century Frontier Land Speculation and Business Venture* (Glendale: Arthur H. Clark Co., 1941) and the letters of Washington edited by John C. Fitzpatrick, *The Writings of George Washington from the Original Manuscript Sources*, 39 vols. (Washington, DC: Government Printing Office, 1931–44); a revised edition of Washington's papers now is being prepared at the University of Virginia.

Part of the study of western lands involved research into place names and Indian trails from historical and archaeological evidence. A history of the Indian place names of the Pittsburgh area, Morgan's headquarters, was written by George Donehoo, *A Story of the Indian Villages and Place Names in Pennsylvania* (Harrisburg, PA: Telegraph Press, 1928). Several well-documented articles on the findings of archaeological studies of the area, written by James A. Tuck, James E. Fitting, and James B. Griffin, were published in Bruce G. Trigger, ed., *Northeast*, vol. 15 of *Handbook of North American Indians* (Washington, DC: Smithsonian Institution, 1978), pp. 28–57, 547–59. A series of eyewitness descriptions of this early frontier settlement were compiled in a book by Leland D. Baldwin, *Pittsburgh: The Story of a City, 1750–1865* (Pittsburgh: University of Pittsburgh Press, 1937). An earlier study was completed by George Thornton Fleming, *History of Pittsburgh and Environs: From Prehistoric Days to the Beginning of the American Revolution*, 2 vols. (New York: American Historical Society, 1922). An interesting cultural history of frontier life in this area was researched by J. E. Wright and Doris S. Corbett, *Pioneer Life in Western Pennsylvania* (Pittsburgh: University of Pittsburgh Press, 1940). A historical description of the "Great Trail" leading from Pittsburgh westward to Indian territory was composed by Frank Wilcox, *Ohio Indian Trails: A Pictorial Survey of the Indian Trails of Ohio*, ed. William A. McGill (1933; reprint, Kent, OH: Kent State University Press, 1970), pp. 43–47. Further information on frontier place names may be found in Thwaites and Kellogg, eds., *Revolution on the Upper Ohio*.

The details of the description of Fort Pitt are the results of a meticulous study by Charles Stotz, "The Fort Pitt Museum," *Western Pennsylvania Historical Magazine* 52 (October 1969):30–35 and 53 (January 1970):36–39. The text was later rearranged and numerous illustrations were added for a special booklet, *Point of Empire: Conflict at the Forks of the Ohio* (Pittsburgh: Historical Society of Western Pennsylvania, 1970). The old blockhouse is still standing, and there is a diorama of the former appearance of the area on display in the Fort Pitt Museum. Life-sized reconstructions of some of the rooms, complete with wax figurines and tape-recorded voices, help to give the visitor a vision of the old frontier fortress.

A vivid, eyewitness account of activities in Pittsburgh during the early stages of the 1775 Indian treaty was recorded by the English diarist Nicholas Cresswell (1750–1804), *The Journal of Nicholas Cresswell, 1774–1777* (London: J. Cape Ltd., 1925). The authenticity of the diary has been established in a well-documented provenance presented by Samuel Thornely, the owner of the diary in 1924, who arranged for the manuscript to be published complete with a brief biographical sketch of the author. Although Cresswell was a British Loyalist and a suspected spy, his personal observations appear credible down to minute details of people, places, and events. He had recently returned from a trading expedition in the Ohio Indian country when he arrived at Pittsburgh two weeks before the start of the treaty.

The Morgan Papers recorded the names of hundreds of people whose biographies needed to be researched. A series of biographies of the men who served at the fortress from the time of its construction to the revolutionary era was written as a joint effort by the Daughters of the American Revolution, Bicentennial Committee, Pittsburgh Chapter, *Pittsburgh Patriots* (Pittsburgh: The Chapter, 1974).

A comprehensive biography of Alexander McKee, the British Indian agent at Pittsburgh, has yet to be written, but an introduction to his extensive career in Indian affairs can be pieced together by comparing three articles: Walter R. Hoberg, "Early History of Colonel Alexander McKee," *Pennsylvania Magazine of History and Biography* 58, No. 1 (1934):26–36; Walter R. Hoberg, "A Tory in the Northwest," *Pennsylvania Magazine of History and Biography* 59 (January 1935): 32–41; and John H. Carter, "Alexander McKee, Our Most Noted Tory," *Northumberland County Historical Society Proceedings* 22 (1958):60–75.

Simon Girty, Morgan's Iroquois translator, was a complex personality in frontier history, and more scholarship and even psychoanalysis would be necessary to unravel his many-sided character. Two early sketches of his life were attempted by John MacLeod, "A Sketch of the Life of Simon Girty," *Amherstburg Echo* (Amherstburg, Ontario, November 21, 1884), later reprinted in *Michigan Pioneer Collections*, 7:123–29; and T. L. Rogers, "Simon Girty and Some of His Contemporaries," *Western Pennsylvania Historical Magazine* 8 (July 1925):148–58. Research also was done on other frontiersmen, such as Daniel Boone. Many of the original documents related to Daniel Boone are offered by Reuben Gold Thwaites, *Daniel Boone* (New York: D. Appleton and Co., 1902).

Finding biographies of American Indians often posed a more perplexing challenge. For original documents and biographical sketches of many of the Indian leaders during this period, refer to Reuben Gold Thwaites and Louise Phelps Kellogg, eds., *Documentary History of Dunmore's War, 1774* (Madison: Wisconsin Historical Society, 1905). For a biographical sketch of Half King, see Frederick Webb Hodge, ed., *Handbook of American Indians North of Mexico*, 2 vols. (Washington, DC: Government Printing Office, 1907–10),1:527. Hodge's *Handbook* is still an invaluable research tool for American Indian studies.

For biographical information on numerous Indian leaders during the late colonial and revolutionary eras, such as the Cayuga Chief Logan, see Chester Sipe, "Logan, Chief of the Mingoes," *The Indian Chiefs of Pennsylvania* (Butler, PA: Ziegler Printing Co., 1927), pp. 437–48; and Paul A. W. Wallace, *Indians in Pennsylvania* (Harrisburg, PA: Pennsylvania Historical and Museum Commission, 1968), pp. 155–58, 175, 178. Logan's famous 1774 speech and a sketch of the chief's life were preserved by Thomas Jefferson, *Notes on the State of Virginia*, ed. William Peden (Chapel Hill: Published for the Institute of Early American History and Culture by the University of North Carolina Press, 1955), p. 63.

Studies in Indian demography also were useful. For example, population estimates for the Mingo were compiled by Erminie Wheeler-Voegelin, *An Ethnohistorical Report on the Indian Use and Occupancy of Royce Area II, Ohio and*

Indiana, in *Indians of Ohio and Indians Prior to 1795,* 2 vols. (New York: Garland, 1974), 1:29–463 and 2:9–468. One of the latest studies on eastern woodland demographics is by Henry F. Dobyns, including an essay with William R. Swagerty as co-author, *Their Number Become Thinned: Native American Population Dynamics in Eastern North America* (Knoxville: Published by the University of Tennessee Press in cooperation with the Newberry Library Center for the History of the American Indian, 1983).

By following the lead of Wilbur R. Jacobs in blending historical and cultural research, the study of the Morgan Papers involved ethnohistorical analysis. One of the most recent sources of cultural information intended to replace Hodge's *Handbook* is the new series by the Smithsonian Institution organized by William Sturtevant, general editor, *Handbook of North American Indians* (Washington, DC: Smithsonian Institution, 1978–), 20 vol. (some in process). The lead article in the most recent volume was written by Jacobs, "British Indian Policies to 1783," *History of Indian-White Relations,* ed. Wilcomb Washburn, 4:5–12. Sturtevant contributed an excellent ethnohistorical summary of the Mingo, "Oklahoma Seneca-Cayuga," *Handbook of North American Indians: Northeast,* pp. 537–43. Morgan met the Mingo chiefs in council to smoke the sacred pipe; see George Morgan to the Mingo, Kiskapoo, June 20, 1776, Morgan's Journal, p. 29. For information on the peace pipe see Hodge, ed., *Handbook of Indians North of Mexico,* 1:442–43; and Wallace, *Indians in Pennsylvania,* pp. 71–72.

Morgan's approach to Indian affairs honored Indian customs of presenting strings and belts of wampum shell beads. An extensive historiography exists for the ritual of wampum diplomacy. An excellent analysis was recorded by Wilbur Jacobs, "Wampum, the Protocol of Indian Diplomacy," *William and Mary Quarterly,* ser. 3, 6 (October 1949):596–604.

Morgan's negotiations in Indian council houses required ethnohistorical research into the structure of Indian villages and ceremonies, such as the Lenni Lenape or Delaware culture. Perhaps the earliest description of the Lenape Big House was preserved by Peter Lindestrom, *Geographia America, with an Account of the Delaware Indians, Based on Surveys and Notes Made in 1654–1656,* trans. and ed. Amandus Johnson (Philadelphia: The Swedish Colonial Society, 1925), p. 211. Later accounts were recorded in William Penn to Free Society of Traders, Philadelphia, August 16, 1683, Shackamaxon, *Narratives of Early Pennsylvania, West New Jersey, and Delaware, 1630–1707,* ed. Albert Cook Meyers (New York: Charles Scribner's Sons, 1912), pp. 230–33; Charles Beatty, *The Journal of a Two Months Tour, with a View of Promoting Religion among the Frontier Inhabitants of Pennsylvania and of Introducing Christianity among the Indians to the Westward of the*

Alegh-geny Mountains (London: Printed for W. Davenhill, 1768), p. 72; David McClure, *Diary of David McClure, Doctor of Divinity, 1748–1820*, with notes by Franklin B. Dexter (New York: Knickerbocker Press, 1899), p. 61; and Mark Harrington, *Religion and Ceremonies of the Lenape* (New York: Museum of the American Indian, Heye Foundation, 1921), pp. 828–83, 119, 148–50, pl. vi, drawing by Ernest Spybuck (December 23, 1912).

For analysis of the Big House symbolism, see Frank Speck, *A Study of the Delaware Indian Big House Ceremony* (Harrisburg, PA: Pennsylvania Historical Commission, 1931), pp. 22–23, 85–87; Jay Miller and Nora Thompson Dean, "A Personal Account of the Unami Delaware Big House Rite," *Pennsylvania Archaeologist* (1977):39–43; and Herbert Kraft, "Model of the Big House by Ruben Wilson," *Bulletin of the Archaeological Society of New Jersey* 35 (1978):40.

An extensive historiography exists for the Ga'muing or Big House Ceremony of Thanksgiving. Most of the early sources were analyzed by Speck, *Study of the Delaware Indian Big House Ceremony*. The last time the ceremony was known to have been performed was during World War II, to pray for the Lenape soldiers. All reportedly returned safely. A brief account subsequently was composed by H. L. McCracken, "The Delaware Big House," *Chronicles of Oklahoma* 34 (Summer 1956): 183–92. The best recent oral history account was narrated by Dean to Miller, "A Personal Account of the Unami Delaware Big House Rite," pp. 39–43. Additional Lenape cultural material was preserved in "The Cass-Trowbridge Manuscript," in C. A. Weslager, *The Delaware Indian Westward Migration, with Texts of Two Manuscripts, 1821–22, Responding to General Lewis Cass's Inquiries about Lanape Culture and Language* (Wallingford, PA: Middle Atlantic Press, 1978).

A reconstruction of Indian social customs also required an analysis of Indian art and dress. For illustrated examples of authentic eighteenth-century clothing and jewelry worn by the Shawnee and other eastern woodland people, refer to an exhibition catalog of two thousand years of North American Indian art, Ralph T. Coe, ed., *Sacred Circles* (Kansas City: Nelson Gallery of Art–Atkins Museum of Fine Arts, 1977), pp. 72–105.

In regard to native systems of justice, Shawnee society was governed by twelve sacred laws, which formed a covenant among all living things. For further information see Charles Ovegelin, John F. Yegerlehner, and Florence M. Robinett, "Shawnee Laws: Perceptual Statements for the Language in and for the Content," in *Language in Culture,* ed. Harry Joijer (Chicago: University of Chicago Press, 1954), pp. 32–46.

This essay represents only a brief summary of some of the sources consulted in researching the Morgan Papers. Ultimate credit for the development of the author's perceptions of Indian history and cultures must be extended to contemporary traditional Indian elders. The chiefs and clan mothers of the Iroquois Six Nations and the elders of the Lenni Lenape, as well as numerous other Indian people, kindly devoted long hours to explaining the intricacies of Indian societies. Without their wise counsel, many misconceptions contained in the literature could not have been clarified.

INDEX

Adams, John, 11, 12, 119
Adams, Samuel, 207, 208
Adena, 129
Adongot, 108
African, 28, 32
Alabama, 130
Algonquian, xx, 6, 14, 117, 156, 174
Allegheny Mountains, 27, 139
Allegheny River, 26, 52
American Philosophical Society, 5, 6, 25, 207
Anderson, "Honest" John, 47, 54, 74–76, 96, 162, 166
Andrew Carnegie Library, xvii, 256, 261
Anglican, 14, 16, 95, 128
Apache, 42
Appalachians, xvii, 4, 23–25
Arapaho, 42
Arbuckle, Matthew, 68, 168, 176, 198
Arnold, Benedict, xvi, xvii, 30, 41, 89, 135, 176, 256
Articles of Confederation, 208
Assunnunk, 76, 130

Baldwin, Loammi, 60
Bawbee, 122
Baynton, John, 4, 93
Bearskin, 147
Benigna, Anna, 82
Big Beaver Creek, 112
Big Cinder, 62
Bill of Rights, 208
Black Hawk, 204

Blain, Alexander, 93
Blaine, Ephraim, 20, 129
Blue Ridge Mountains, 12
Boone, Daniel 29, 38, 95, 161, 167
Boone, Jemima, 161
Boonesborough, 161, 167
Boreman, John, 64, 95, 169
Braddock's Defeat, 26, 52
Brady, Sam, 202
Brant, Joseph, 178
British, 8, 9, 31, 39, 58, 65
British Army, 6, 26, 58
British Crown, 5, 26, 27, 35
British Navy, 39
British treaty conference, 29
Brodhead, Daniel, 200, 202
Buckshenutas, 160
Buckungahelas, 178
Bullock, Joseph, 93
Bunker Hill, 171
Burgoyne, General, xvi, 257
Burr, Aaron, xvii, 257
Bush, George, 202
Bushy Run, 25
Butler, John, 29, 49, 51, 55, 99, 100, 101, 102, 103, 105,
    106, 107, 108, 109, 193
Butler, Richard, 29, 30, 35, 36, 93
Butterfield, Issac, 104, 251

Caldwell, Colonel, 56, 100, 103, 107

Callaway, Fanny, 161
Callaway, Richard, 161
Calotte, 122, 173
Cambridge, 8
Canada, xx, 5, 13, 30, 31, 41, 89, 109, 133, 135
Canhaudenhauden, 160
Canhawa, 68, 165, 169, 177, 186
Cape Fear, 58
Caribbean, 5
Carlisle, 20, 148
Carolinas, 130
Cawcowcaucawketeda, 107
Cayuga (see also Six Nations), 34, 51, 94, 143, 145
Cedar, 104, 135
Checalese, 178
Cherokee, 41, 42, 58, 67, 94, 167, 185, 189, 196, 203
Cherokee River, 173
Cherry Valley, 202
Chestnut Ridge, 25
Cheyenne, 42
Chillicothe, 131
Chilloway, William, 83, 128
Chippewa, 108–109, 118, 155, 161, 167, 174–175, 204
Choctaw, 203
Christianity (see also missionaries), 12, 15
Chumash, xxiii
Claus, William, 51
Clinton, Henry, 58
Cloudy Boy, 131
Cohen, Felix, 204
Coitcheleh, 68, 131, 152, 191–193
Colesquo (see also Cornstalk), 105, 151, 184
Comanche, 42
Concord, 5, 28, 97
Conestoga Road, 18, 148
Conneodico, 122–124, 147, 150, 179
Conneodighes, 179
Connolly, John, 10, 29, 41, 55
Constitution, xx, 139, 204, 205
Continental Army, 7, 9, 22
Continental Congress, xv, xvi, xx, 1–6, 13–14, 20, 39, 50, 57, 72, 81, 89, 100, 119, 120, 135, 153, 161, 207
Coochocking, 115, 132, 166
Cooper, James, 161
Cooshocking, 15, 72, 120
Corn Husk Faces, 144
Cornplanter, 202
Cornstalk (see also Colesquo), 37, 40, 45, 53, 68, 83, 95, 105, 151–156, 163–164, 184, 186–191, 195, 198
Cornwallis, Charles, 58, 171
Cosar, 166
Coshocton, 15, 128, 129, 199, 203
Council House, xx, 101, 114, 116, 133, 135, 143, 151, 153, 159, 184, 191
Crawford, William, 34, 35, 203
Creek, 58, 189, 196

Cresap, 146
Croghan, George, 11, 25, 56, 99
Cumberland Gap, 38
Cumberland Valley, 29
Cuyahoga, 143

Dane, Nathan, 206
Daunghquat (see also Half King), 122, 172
Declaration of Independence, xx, 1, 4, 120, 139, 158
Delamatteno, 84
Delaware Valley, 18
Delaware (see also Lenni Lenape), xx–xxi, 1, 25, 115, 161
Deloria, Vine, 206
Dragging Canoe, 189
Dunmore's War, 34, 94, 128, 145, 151, 190
Dunmore, Lord, 10, 29

East River, 171
Edgar, William, 257
Ellinipsico, 164, 198
Elliott, Matthew, 161, 162, 171
Emistisign, 189
England, 4, 31, 55, 89

Finger Lakes, 122
Fish Creek, 169, 170
Flint Ridge, 129
Flying Crow, 107, 108, 188, 189, 191
Forester, Captain, 104, 135
Fort Albany, 51
Fort Chartres, 98
Fort Detroit, 10, 22, 39, 41, 49, 172–173, 185, 199, 200
Fort Duquesne, 26
Fort Erie, 98
Fort Niagara, 22, 49–51, 99
Fort Pitt (see also Pittsburgh) 7, 15–17, 25–28, 34, 39, 42, 53–55, 58, 64, 88, 160–161, 164, 166, 169
Fort Pitt treaty conference in 1775, 30, 50, 151
Fort Randolph, 249
Fort Stanwix, 255
Fox, 155
France, 31, 52
Franklin, Benjamin, xvii, 5, 6, 11, 13–14, 20, 25, 207
Frederick Ferry, 178
Fredericktown, Maryland, 55
French and Indian War, 38, 111, 130, 172
Frog's Neck, 171
Furman, Moore, 257

Ga'muing, 115
Gage, Thomas, 10, 55, 58
Galloway, John, 68
Gates, 58
Gelelemend (see also John Killbuck), 42, 73, 77, 84, 85, 114, 115, 195
Georgia, 42, 130

German Hessians, 119, 172
Gibson, George, 106
Gibson, John, 32, 34, 111, 149, 169
Gieschenatsi (*see also* Hard Man), 36
Girty, 44
Gist, Christopher, 52
Glickhikan, Issac, 82–83
Gnadenhutten, 73, 113
Goschachgunk, 72, 77, 87, 114, 127
Gratz, Bernard, 90, 93
Gratz, Michael, 90
Grave Creek, 165, 169, 170
Great Britain, 11
Great Buffalo Swamp, 129
Great Lakes, 4, 40, 49, 90, 121, 139, 155, 172, 176
Great Peace Belt (*see also* Wampum), 20, 33, 61, 62, 256
Great Plains, 42
Great Warrior, 189
Greathouse, Jacob, 146–9
Green Corn Ceremony, 143
Gutkigamen (*see also* Thomas Killbuck), 82
Guyashusta (*see also* Kiasola and Keyashuta), 29, 30, 31, 32, 33, 50, 51, 52, 53, 60, 65, 98, 102, 103, 108, 179

Half King (*see also* Daunghquat), 122, 156, 172, 173, 185
Hamilton, Henry, 41, 49, 51, 88–89, 99, 121, 173, 177, 185, 193, 200
Hancock, John (*see also* Karanduawn), xvi, xvii, 4, 7, 10–12, 15, 16, 20, 22, 29, 49, 50, 119, 133, 195, 256
Hand, Edward, 171, 198, 203
Hard Man (*see also* Gieschenatsi), 36, 37, 38, 39, 53, 94, 95, 136, 137, 139, 152
Harris's Ferry, 20
Harrisburg, 20, 148
Harrod, William, 172
Harrodsburgh, 167
Harvard College, 9
Harvie, John, 35, 162
Haudenausaunee (*see also* Six Nations), xx, 51, 202
Hawcawohcheykey, 136, 137
Heath, William, 171
Heckewelder, John, 26, 72, 84, 85, 114, 163, 177
Henry, Patrick, xvii, 6, 151
Heron, James, 98
Hi La Japen, 127
Hockhocking River, 129, 130, 168
Hopewell, 129
Hopi, xxiii, 205
Hopocan (*see also* Pipe, Captain), 75, 114, 197
Howe, William, 171
Hughes, John, 255
Huron, 40, 139, 155
Hutchins, Thomas, 204

llinois, 42, 130
Indian Citizenship Act, 205, 254
Indiana, 54
Indiana Land Company, 6, 256
Inouye, Daniel, 206
Ironcutter, John, 148
Iroquois (*see also* Six Nations), xx, xxiii, 6, 14, 29, 30, 40, 63, 94, 100, 120, 143, 55, 190, 196, 202, 203, 204, 205
   Confederacy, xx, xxiii, 29, 51, 188, 197, 204, 207

Jacob, Wilbur, xxiii
Jake Swamp, 180
Jefferson, Thomas, xvi, xvii, 5, 7, 12, 14, 58, 119, 145, 158, 258
Johnny, Captain, 76, 114, 115, 130, 160, 184
Johnson, Guy, 51, 55, 177, 178
Johnson, William, 51, 82, 127, 152, 256
Justina, 82

Kakowatcheky, 137
Kanaghragait, 172
Kanawha River, 68
Kanhawa, 173
Karanduawn (*see also* John Hancock), 7, 120
Katepacomen, 43
Kentucky, 38, 40, 42, 58, 95
Kentucky River, 158
Keyashuta (*see also* Guyashusta), 65
Kiasola (*see also* Gutkigamen), 29
Kickapoo, 118, 155
Killbuck's Island, 35
Killbuck, John (*see also* Gelelemend), 35, 73, 114, 127, 163, 167, 177, 181, 195–197, 200–201
Killbuck, Thomas (*see also* Gutkigamen), 82, 201, 202
King Beaver (*see also* Tamaque), 182
King George, 71
King Louis XVI, 52, 120
King George, of Great Britain, 119
King's Bridge, 171
King's Store, 100
Kiowa, 42
Kishanatathe, 68, 69, 136
Kiskapoo, 131, 143
Koketha, 184
Konischquanoheel, 178
Kuhn, Abraham, 122

Lake, 49, 183
Lake Erie, 41, 75, 79, 99, 143, 172
Lake Huron, 99
Lake Indians, 118, 140
Lake Michigan, 99
Lake Ontario, 30, 99
Lakota, xxiii, 42
Lancaster, 18, 20, 23, 148

Lee's Town, 158
Lee, Charles, 50
Lee, Richard Henry, 112, 151
Lenape Wolf Clan, 31
Lenni Lenape (*see also* Deleware), xx, xxiii, 1–3, 6, 8, 11, 15, 25, 31, 38, 40, 42, 47, 54, 57–58, 68, 74–76, 79–80, 84, 86–87, 94–95, 105, 111, 114, 117, 118, 123–127, 132, 137, 139, 154, 156, 165, 183, 193, 196, 198, 203–205, 208
Lernoult, Captain, 55
Lexington, 5, 28, 97
Liberty Bell, xvii
Library of Congress, xxiii, 208
Lichtenau ("Pasture of Light"), 72, 76, 84, 85, 87, 127
Licking Creek, 129, 160
Ligonier, 53
Linn, William, 106
Little Beaver, 112
Logan Thachnechdorus, 34, 145–150, 165, 179, 190
Logstown, 111, 112
Long Island, 60, 178
Long, Paul, 50, 53, 60, 98, 99, 100–101, 108–109
Lord, Hugh, 98
Louisiana, 209
Lupwaaeenoawuk, 114
Lyons, Oren, 206

Macomb, Alex, 257
Manhattan Island, 60, 171
Manitou, 114
Maryland, 55, 130
Mascouten, 155
Massachusetts, 12
McClelland's Station, 168
McConnell, Adam, 158, 159
McConnell, Andrew, 158, 159, 190
McConnell, William, 158, 159
McIntosh, Lachlan, 200
McKee, Alexander, 54–57, 88, 99, 111–114, 127
McNutt, Joseph, 168
Menachk-sink, 25, 26
Menominee, 155
Metompsica, 147
Miami, 118
Michilimackinac, 99
Middle Island Creek, 166
Midwinter Ceremony, 144
Mifflin, Thomas, 58
Mingo (*see also* Six Nations), 83, 124, 127, 140–141, 143, 144, 154, 159–161, 167, 170–172, 183, 185
Miro, 209
Misi'ngw, 114
missionaries, 16, 47, 48, 71–87, 113
Mississippi, 4, 6
Mississippi River, xvii, xx, 39, 98, 139, 208
Missouri, 208, 209
Mohawk (*see also* Six Nations), 51, 58, 94, 104, 143

Mohican, 113, 183
Molloy, 11, 55
Monongahela, 26
Montgomery, John, 162, 184
Montgomery, Richard, 41, 89
Montour, Andrew, 45, 184
Montreal, 30, 52
Moravian, 17, 32, 47, 48, 72, 73, 75–76, 81, 83, 85, 127, 128
Morgan, George (*see also* Shanashase, Tamanend, Weepemachukthe, and White Deer), xv, xvi, xx, xxii, xxiii, xxiv, 2, 4, 5, 7, 8, 10, 11, 16, 17, 21, 23, 25, 26–27, 31–32, 42, 44, 47, 48, 50, 53, 58, 60, 61, 63, 65, 66, 87, 88–90, 93–97, 99, 100, 106, 111–118, 120, 121, 123–126, 127, 129, 131, 137, 143, 144, 146, 161, 162, 165, 166, 177, 179, 181, 184, 195, 197, 206, 207, 208, 255
    Lenni Lenape mission, 111–126
    Shawnee mission, 127–142
    Mingo mission, 143–160
Morgan, John, 9
Morgan, Katherine Duane, xvi, 258
Morgan, Mary Baynton, 5, 255, 258
Morgan, Susannah Barker, xv, xxi, xxiii, 255
Morgan, Thomas, xv, 255.
Morgan, William Duane, xv, 255
Morris, Lewis, 66
Moundbuilders, 129
Munsee, 82, 105, 113, 183, 203
Muscouton, 118
Muskingum River, 48, 71, 77, 79, 112, 127, 129
Muskogean, 6, 41, 94

National Archives, xxiii, 208
Native Americans, 1, 9, 12, 14, 152
Netawatwees, 2, 72, 73, 77, 81, 83, 84, 85, 115, 163, 182, 184, 193
Neville, John, 28, 30, 34–35, 64–66, 68, 87, 95, 167, 169, 170
New Jersey, 207
New Madrid, 208, 209
New Orleans, 106
New York, 9, 122, 171
Newport Harbor, 9
Niagara, 29, 30, 179
Niagara Conference, 52–55, 60, 90, 95, 100–101
Niagara Falls, 29
Nicholson, Joseph, 87–88, 127, 157, 159
Nimwha, 68, 131, 132, 184, 187, 190
Nipissing, 155
Non-Intercourse Act, 205
North Carolina, 58
North, Lord, 11
Northwest Ordinance, 205, 206
Northwest Territory, 257
Nova Scotia, 8

Ohio, 15, 26, 130
Ohio River, 34, 35, 87, 95, 111, 139, 158, 172, 198
Ohio River Valley, 4, 6, 29, 30, 33, 38, 39, 75, 100, 115,
    124, 141, 165, 170, 204
Ojibwa, 174
Oklahoma, 203
Old Kiskapoo, 130
Oneida (*see also* Six Nations), 51, 94, 143, 198
Onondaga (*see also* Six Nations), 30, 51, 61, 88, 100,
    119, 143, 147, 150–152
Onondago, 62
Orvachtonese, 167
Ottawa, 112, 108, 118, 155, 161, 170, 204
Oubache, 54, 124
Oubache Confederacy, 67

Paine, Thomas, 10
Pakanke, 82
Pametamah, 179
Parker, Peter, 58
Patterson, Robert, 168
Pawnee, 42
Paxton Boys, 19, 148
Pelaiwa, 187
Penn, William, 2, 17, 18, 25, 126, 134, 193
Pennsylvania, 1, 2, 14, 18, 25, 27, 130, 148, 158
Pentecost, Dorsey, 172
Pethamoh, 37
Philadelphia (*see also* Shackamaxon), xvii, 1–5, 10–
    11, 16–18, 39
Pickaway Plains, 130
Picts, 32, 139, 161
Pipe's War Marks, 129
Pipe, Captain (*see also* Hopocan), 31, 32, 75, 105, 114–
    115, 177–181, 197, 199
Pitt, William, 26
Pittsburgh (*see also* Fort Pitt), xvii, 10, 11, 15, 16, 43,
    50, 170
Pluggy, 159, 168, 173, 179, 193
Pluggy's Gang, 158, 168, 186, 189
Pluggy's Party, 173
Pluggy's Town, 159, 173, 185, 190
Pluk-kemeh-notee, 168
Point Pleasant, 95, 151
Pontiac, 38
Pontiac's War, 19, 52
Potawatomi, 118, 155, 167, 175, 204
Prescott, William, 171
Presque Isle, 79, 177
Princeton, xxii, 200, 207
Providence, 9
Pukangehela, 178, 179, 182, 190
Pumpkin King, 189

Quaker, 2
Quebec, 41, 89

Raven, 189
Red Hawk, 198
Reed, Joseph, 10
Rhode Island, 9
Rounded Side, 131
Rousseau, Jean-Jacques, 7
Rutledge, Edward, 58

Sachem Netawatwees, 35, 73, 77, 78, 114
Salt Licks, 112, 122, 179
Sample, Samuel, 55
Sandusky, 75, 79, 143
Sauk, 155, 204, 205
Savelle, Max, xvii
Schmick, John Jacob, 163, 176
Schonbrunn (*see also* Welhik-Tuppeek), 112, 113
Schuyler, Philip, 7, 59, 60, 65, 94
Schuylkill River, 17, 18
Schwickley Bottom, 111
Scioto River, 130, 143, 173
Seconet Point, 9
Senate Select Committee on Indian Affairs, xxiii, 206
Seneca (*see also* Six Nations), 29, 30, 31, 43, 51, 94,
    109, 188, 199
Seven Nations, 41
Shackamaxon (*see also* Philadelphia), 2, 17, 126
Shanashase, xx, 151
Shawnee, xx, 32, 34, 38–40, 58, 67–69, 87, 94, 95, 105,
    111, 118, 127, 128, 130–132, 143, 145, 151–152,
    154, 163, 165, 166, 171, 183, 185, 188, 190, 196,
    198
Shawnese, 57, 68, 123, 161, 183
Shenandoah, Leon, 261
Shenango, 111
Shickellamy, 145
Shingas, 182
Shirties Island, 111
Silver Heels, 45, 68, 128
Simon Girty, 43, 44, 53, 61, 64
Simons, Joseph, 93
Siouan, 6
Six Nations (*see also* Iroquois, Onondaga, Mohawk,
    Seneca, Oneida, Cayuga, Tuscarora and Mingo),
    xx, 14, 29–30, 33, 40, 43, 51, 59, 65, 68, 80, 88, 94,
    104, 108, 118, 122, 139, 145, 161, 174, 183, 188,
    255
slavery, xx, 14, 32–33
Smallman, Thomas, 56, 57
Smith, Isaac, 257
Smithsonian Institution, xxiii
Snake Egg Camp, 129
Soyouca, 108
St. Lawrence River, 41
St. Louis, 208
Still, Isaac, 20, 53
Stony Creek, 25

Strawberry, 148, 149
Stuart, John, 58
Stump, Frederick, 149
Sullivan, John, 9, 202
Sun Dance, 143
Susquehanna, 20

Tallassee King, 189
Tallega, 129
Tamanend, xx, 2, 17, 125, 126, 134
Tamaque (*see also* King Beaver), 182
Tarhe Crane, 122
Tatodaho, 51, 94
Tawahs, 167, 170
Taxes, 6, 205
Tecumseh, 204
Tegasah, 122
Tennessee River, 196
Thompson, Charles, 257
Thomson, Charles, 8, 16
Thunder Beings, 143
Tippecanoe, 54
Totadaho, 62
Treaties, 2, 7, 136
    American–Indian treaty conference, of 1775,
       54, 116
    Fort Pitt Treaty of 1775, 4, 19, 31, 33, 36, 39, 66,
       71, 75, 97, 102, 107, 132–134, 163
    Fort Stanwix Treaty of 1768, 35, 164, 255
    Treaty of Fort Harmar of 1789, 204
    Treaty of Lancaster in 1744, 18
    Treaty at Niagara, 98
    U.S.–Indian Peace Treaty of 1776, 161–196
    U.S.–Delaware Treaty of 1778, 200, 257
Tree of Peace, xx, 2, 51, 102, 103, 126, 134, 193, 203
Trent, William, 11, 96, 255
Turkey Clan, 76, 114, 115, 130, 182
Turtle Clan, 77, 84, 114, 115, 182
Turtle Island, 152
Tuscarawa, 71, 77
Tuscarora (also *see* Six Nations), 51, 94, 199

Valley Forge, 198
Van Dike, Henry, 257
Van Winckle, Ernst, 257
Vermillion, 54
Virginia, 10, 11

Wabach Confederacy, 41, 118, 139–140, 223
Wabash, 41, 42, 54
Wagoner, Andrew, 45, 164, 169, 173
Waketameki, 128
Walehaketuppan, 160
Walhonding, 77
Walker, John, 7
Walker, Thomas, 162

Wampum (*see also* Great Peace Belt), 6, 20, 29, 30, 53,
    58, 62, 64, 68, 95, 116, 118, 121, 123, 124, 132,
    139, 143, 151, 157, 179
Wandohela, 182
Wandoohala, 178, 179, 182
Warriors' Path, 130
Warriors' Trail, 190
Washington, George, xvi, xvii, 7–9, 11, 22, 26, 49, 52,
    58–60, 89, 96, 98, 100, 104, 118, 132–133, 165,
    171–172, 189, 198, 200, 207
Washington, Martha, 199
Weepemachukthe, xx, 156
Wegh-we-law-mo-end, 8
Welapachtschiechen (*see also* Johhny, Captain), 42,
    76, 114, 130
Welhik-Tuppeek, 112
Weliechsit, 182
Wenthissica, 187
Wernock, James, 168
West Augusta, 57, 64
West Virginia, 27
Westmoreland County, 158, 172
Wethexthuppek, 48
Wharton, 4
White Deer (*see also* Morgan, George), xx, 127, 151,
    156–157, 186
White Eyes, 1–8, 11–17, 23, 25–27, 35, 42, 47, 53, 54,
    71–85, 94, 105, 114–116, 121–123, 127–128,
    160, 163, 177–179, 181–184, 197–200
White Eyes, George Morgan, 200, 201
White Fish, 40
White Mingo, 172–176
White Oak Camp, 112
Wiandot, 32, 79, 121, 124, 155, 161, 166, 167
Williamsburg, 225
Wilson, James, 6, 14, 29–30
Wilson, William, 34, 36–37, 39–45, 87, 113–114, 127,
    157, 184
Winchester, Virginia, 28
Wingenund, 129
Winnebago, 155
Wolf Clan, 75, 114–115, 178–179, 197
Wry Neck, 190
Wyandot (*see also* Wiandot and Huron) 40, 80, 84, 94,
    112, 118, 121–123, 155–156, 172–173, 179, 183,
    196, 204
Wyoming Valley, 137

Xi'ngwikan, 114

Yeates, Jasper, 20, 162, 184

Zeisberger, David, 47–49, 72–78, 81–82, 85, 113